W9-BOY-491

LIST
PRICE

$37.00 02

IIS
PRICE

$27.75 3

JOURNEY INTO SEXUALITY

AN
EXPLORATORY VOYAGE

JOURNEY INTO SEXUALITY

AN EXPLORATORY VOYAGE

IRA L. REISS

University of Minnesota

PRENTICE-HALL, ENGLEWOOD CLIFFS, NEW JERSEY 07632

Library of Congress Cataloging-in-Publication Data

Reiss, Ira L.
  Journey into sexuality.

  Bibliography: p.
  Includes index.
  1. Sex customs—Cross-cultural studies.
  2. Sex role—Cross-cultural studies.   I. Title.
  HQ21.R425   1986   306.7   85-30158
  ISBN 0-13-511478-0

Editorial/production supervision
  and interior design: Kate Kelly
Cover art: "Das Paar" by Sepp Biehler
Used by permission of Ingeborg Biehler.
Cover design: Photo Plus Art
Manufacturing buyer: John B. Hall

© 1986 by Prentice-Hall, Inc.
A Division of Simon & Schuster
Englewood Cliffs, New Jersey 07632

All rights reserved. No part of this book may be
reproduced, in any form or by any means,
without permission in writing from the publisher.

Printed in the United States of America

10   9   8   7   6   5   4   3   2

ISBN 0-13-511478-0   01

Prentice-Hall International (UK) Limited, *London*
Prentice-Hall of Australia Pty. Limited, *Sydney*
Prentice-Hall Canada Inc., *Toronto*
Prentice-Hall Hispanoamericana, S.A., *Mexico*
Prentice-Hall of India Private Limited, *New Delhi*
Prentice-Hall of Japan, Inc., *Tokyo*
Prentice-Hall of Southeast Asia Pte. Ltd., *Singapore*
Editora Prentice-Hall do Brasil, Ltda., *Rio de Janeiro*

TO MY WIFE, HARRIET, AND OUR CHILDREN, DAVID STEPHEN, PAMELA FAYE, AND JOEL ALAN.

With appreciation to the powers that be in the universe which have helped to make all of them possible.

CONTENTS

In our endeavor to understand reality we are somewhat like a man trying to understand the mechanism of a closed watch. He sees the face and the moving hands, even hears its ticking, but he was no way of opening the case. If he is ingenious he may form some picture of a mechanism which could be responsible for all the things he observes, but he may never be quite sure his picture is the only one which could explain his observations. He will never be able to compare his picture with the real mechanism and he cannot even imagine the possibility or the meaning of such a comparison. But he certainly believes that, as his knowledge increases, his picture of reality will become simpler and simpler and will explain a wider and wider range of his sensuous impressions. He may also believe in the existence of the ideal limit of knowledge and that it is approached by the human mind. He may call this ideal limit the objective truth.

Source: Albert Einstein and Leopold Infeld, *The Evolution of Physics: The Growth of Ideas from Early Concepts to Relativity and Quanta,* p. 33 . New York: Simon & Schuster, 1950. With permission of Hebrew University, Jerusalem, Israel.

PREFACE

In my senior year at Syracuse University I took a course in philosophy. The professor asked the class to write a paper about a controversial social issue of our choosing. I chose to write on premarital sexuality. I had always been interested in sexuality on a personal level—which I suppose does not distinguish me from most other humans. But I had other reasons to be interested—I had grown up in a coal-mining town with open prostitution, and that was at least a bit unusual. Because of this background, when I entered the army what surprised me was the tameness regarding sexuality of the men in my outfit compared to the men I knew in my hometown. My curiosity was aroused concerning just how such different sexual customs could be produced within the same gender. That was why, when my philosophy professor asked us to do a paper on a social issue, I thought I would, in that assignment, begin to unravel the sexual enigma. It wasn't quite as simple as I thought, and it began a lifetime devotion toward the scientific understanding of human sexuality.

Surely those events were not the only reasons for my interest in sexuality. Since early childhood I have been fascinated by intellectual puzzles. Sexuality was very much a puzzle to me. Why did people feel so strongly about it? Why did they differ so much, and how do they change? Eventually I chose sociology as a field that would help in the clarification of this and other socially relevant questions. This book is a natural outcome of all the research and theory work I have done since receiving my Ph.D. It surely does not remove all the mystery of sexuality, but this book has shed more light in that direction than anything else I have done.

I am very certain about the value I place on sociology as an explanatory approach. Until now, there has not been any overall explanation of sexuality from a societal perspective. To be sure, there have been a few attempts. Some people, and I am one of them, have developed mini theories explaining this or that aspect of sexuality. But no overarching theoretical explanation from a sociological perspective exists. I wrote this book to fill that gap.

I am not writing this book just for my fellow sociologists. They already are convinced of the value of sociology. I am also writing it for those in other sciences and for those who in their day-to-day professional work deal with problems of human sexuality, and also for the intellectual curious whatever their specialty might be. I think my explanatory schema will be useful to all who have sufficient motivation to consider seriously the reasoning and evidence underlying my approach.

I have written this book with one goal in mind: To develop an overall explanation of human sexuality that will apply cross-culturally and will explain how society organizes and shapes our sexual lives. Whether you agree or not regarding my success in doing this, I hope you will remain among those who seek such an answer.

Ira L. Reiss

Minneapolis
December, 1985

ACKNOWLEDGMENTS

I would like to make my acknowledgments chronologically—the way they occurred over the past five years. In September of 1980 I had been talking informally with one of my doctoral students, G.C. Sponaugle. We had just finished a joint research project on extramarital sexuality in America and had published an article on that work. I mentioned to him that I thought we needed more than just specific theories explaining areas like extramarital sexuality. I felt we needed an overall sociological explanation of sexuality. G.C. shared my view and encouraged me to undertake to develop such a theory. At about that same time a colleague and friend of mine, Joel Nelson, and I also discussed the possibility of my undertaking such a project and he supported my doing it and suggested that I write for a wider audience than just sociologists. I owe a great deal to such encouragement for it was important in motivating me further to undertake such an immense project.

My minor fields in graduate school had been philosophy and anthropology. I had partially kept up with these areas in my teaching and reading, but this book would afford me an excuse to deepen my relationship with those exciting fields. I was enthusiastic about anthropology and philosophy because I believed that I could utilize these disciplines to expand my sociological insights. In that way I would be doing sociological work, yet it would be work deeply aided by increased knowledge of these other disciplines.

The actual writing of the book occurred in one year from the summer of 1984 to the summer of 1985. But in the four years before that writing began, I worked intensely on becoming more familiar with the cross cultural literature that might be relevant to my project. I consulted with many individuals who gave me advice regarding what to read. No one was more helpful than Judy Modell—an anthropologist herself. She put me in touch with the most recent literature on sexuality and gender and she raised the key philosophical issues I would have to face as my project proceeded. There were many others with whom I spoke at some length to gain deeper insight into their work and to obtain additional sources of information in their fields. These include: Larry Baron, Joseph Bohlen, Vern Bullough, Ed Donnerstein, David Goldfoot, Michael Gordon, Sarah Hrdy, Virginia Johnson, David Kopf, Berl Kutchinsky, Andrew Mattison, William Masters, John Modell, Ron Nadler, Len Rosenblum, Murray Straus, Jan Trost, and Dolf Zillman.

In the middle of my writing I decided I needed more than just familiarity with specific ethnographic accounts of how sexuality operated in another society. I wanted a broader overview and I became interested in working with the Standard Sample composed of 186 societies. I discovered that most of the information on sexuality for Standard Sample societies was contained in very recent additions by individual professionals. I contacted and received permission to use the data of five researchers: Gwen Broude, Martin Whyte, Marc Ross, Ralph Hupka and Peggy Sanday. Without their data I could not have analyzed my ideas anywhere near as carefully as I did. I am grateful to them for their willingness to share.

Within my own department I received advice on methodological problems from Professors Robert Leik, Roberta Simmons, and especially Willy Jasso. In the course of the computer work on the Standard Sample, two students assisted me: Gigi Carr, an undergraduate at the University of Minnesota, and G.C. Sponaugle, the doctoral student who had encouraged me to undertake this project. Their technical skills were an important asset. Another of our graduate students, Craig Roberts, taught me to use my newly purchased word processor on which I wrote the book. The student codirector of our data center, Terry Schmidt, was always willing to show me how to access the mainframe computer and precisely what to do to accomplish many complex computer operations. Also of importance, my university not only gave me a sabbatical but a year later gave me a quarter leave to finish writing the manuscript. The executive secretary of the Family Study Center, Mary Ann Beneke, assisted me in many of the tasks connected with the book. All this was essential to the completion of my work.

Finally, after the manuscript was written, it was important to obtain the judgment of other professionals. Three colleagues read the manuscript and gave me the benefit of their comments. One was professor Hyman Rodman, who is a sociologist in the Family Research Center of the University of North Carolina at Greensboro. He is widely known for his cross-cultural work on the family. Professor David Klein, a sociologist at Notre Dame University, was my second reader. I had earlier discussed many of my ideas with him and received excellent suggestions. He specializes in the family area and for many years has taught courses in theory construction. My third reader was Professor Paul Rosenblatt from the Department of Family Social Science of the School of Home Economics at the University of Minnesota. Professor Rosenblatt is trained in psychology but has a long-term interest in anthropology and is the current president of the Society for Cross-Cultural Research. The comments from these three professionals came from a variety of expert perspectives and were immensely helpful to me. I hope I may return the favor to them someday.

As I write this down, I realize even more fully how much in debt I am to a great many people. But there is one debt that I owe more than any other, and that is to my wife, who is really my number one colleague. Despite being busy with her own work as a researcher and interviewer, she discussed with me almost every major idea I had and gave me the benefit of her insights. She also read and edited the manuscript and made me aware of the many places where I had not sufficiently clarified or explained my thinking. Several of my ideas were sharpened and in some cases radically changed by this ongoing process of intellectual exchange. Throughout this project she has been an insightful critic and yet my staunchest supporter. The book would not be what it is without her help.

I owe a very special thanks to Sepp Biehler and to his widow, Ingeborg Biehler. In 1969 Sepp Biehler, a West German artist, created a wood print called "Das Paar" (The Pair). I was given a copy as a present shortly thereafter and was taken by it immediately. Ingeborg Biehler has graciously given me permission to use this print on the cover of the book. As you can see, the print is that of a couple—it is a generic couple whose gender and age are unknown but whose union is overwhelmingly apparent. To me it symbolizes a great deal about human relationships and sexuality, and I am proud to be able to use it as a motif for my book.

Finally, let me express my appreciation to Prentice-Hall. They have been most cooperative and supportive. Not all publishers are that helpful. I give special thanks to College Editor Bill Webber, and also thank his assistant Kathleen Dorman and Kate Kelly who managed the production of the book. They did their work on the book with a great deal of skill and expertise.

JOURNEY INTO SEXUALITY

AN EXPLORATORY VOYAGE

CHAPTER ONE

UNCHARTED WATERS

A NEW PERSPECTIVE

We have lived long enough with only Freudian, Marxist, and sociobiological explanations of human sexuality. Many of us have found these explanations to be limiting, somewhat dogmatic, and uninteresting, but we have done little to offer alternative explanations of human sexuality. This book is an attempt to offer a societal-level interpretation of human sexuality that presents a new vision of human sexuality—one that strives to avoid some of the limitations of older explanations and one that selects and organizes the world of sexuality in a different fashion.

I have written this book with a particular audience in mind. I wish to reach all those who are searching for a scientific explanation of human sexuality that stresses the contribution that the type of society in which we live makes toward the way we think, feel, and behave sexually. The reader does not have to possess a Ph.D. in order to comprehend such ideas. What is needed is simply a strong curiosity about human sexuality and an interest in a societal-level explanation. Unlike some popular books on sexuality, this book is aimed predominantly at the intellectual stimulation of the reader. If you are intellectually curious, I believe, you will find this book fulfilling.

I particularly want to reach those people who have but little background in my discipline of sociology. I surely am not excluding sociologists. I feel assured that they will read this book. I also am certain that those interested in anthropology will be attracted to this book. But I am making a special effort to write in a manner intelligible to others as well. I avoid complex tables and I minimize jargon and thereby seek to make the book readable to a broader audience. I do this because I feel that those with interests in other fields like psychology or biology and those with applied or simply personal interests may thereby become aware of the value of a societal-level approach for increasing our understanding of human sexuality.

Such people may be therapists or educators who regularly deal with sexuality, or they may be people in fields not directly related to sexuality but who desire to know more about how sexuality operates in their society. Many of these people have had their curiosity abused rather than satisfied by journalistic accounts that clarify little and mislead a great deal. Furthermore, even if they were to search for a scholarly, integrated, societal-level explanation of human sexuality, they would find that there is none available at this time. I am striving to fill that gap.[1] This is a book, then, that I believe will throw new light on the social nature of human sexuality.

Over the years I had been critical of most of the common explanations of sexuality. I rejected the emphasis of orthodox Freudianism on fixed stages of psychosexual development aimed at a very narrow turn-of-the-century Viennese conception of *normality*, defined as the preference for heterosexual coitus above all other sexual acts.[2] Accordingly, I found this Freudian formulation to be more a moral position than a scientific explanation of sexual normality.

In terms of Marxism, I had also been critical of what I perceived to be a too heavy emphasis on a one-factor theory where sexuality is viewed as a form of male oppression and exploitation based on male economic power and a property view of women. A very similar version of this theory has been put forth more recently by some feminists.[3] I found this approach too intellectually restrictive. Among other problems, it was unable to explain differences in sexual customs in societies with similar levels of male control over property. Nor did it explain how subordinate females and societal customs could each restrict the sexuality of the economically powerful males. Another bone of contention for me was that to many Marxists, ideologies were simply rationalizations to support those in power. I objected to this limited view of ideologies, for I conceive of ideologies as also playing an innovative role in changing our sexual customs.

In the 1970s the sociobiologists strove to explain current sexual behaviors of males and females as resulting from the seeking of reproductive advantages by males and females many thousands of years ago. Supposedly, it was to the male's reproductive advantage to have many sexual partners and thereby maximize the passing on of his genes to the next generation. On the other hand, it was supposedly to the female's reproductive advantage to behave more restrictively sexually and pick the best genetic inheritance for her offspring. This explanation seemed to me unconvincing and indeed was a point of debate among sociobiological writers like Symons and Hrdy.[4]

I believe the sociobiological explanation projects a conservative Western view of male and female sexuality on evolving humans hundreds of thousands of years ago. How could we ever really know what humans were like hundreds of thousands of years ago? Why should we assume that the male-female differences we find in traditional Western sexual codes are eternal when we know they do not even fit many of our present-day societies?

Of even greater importance is the fact that such a long-term evolutionary perspective is of little help in understanding changes in sexual customs that occurred in the last 20 years in the Western world. Nor does it explain the sharp differences in sexual lifestyles that exist among societies all composed of the same Homo sapien species. We cannot assume that significant changes in our genetic makeup have occurred in that short time, nor can we assume that genetic differences explain why the Russian sexual lifestyle is different from the American sexual lifestyle, or why the rape rate is several times as high in California and Alaska compared to North and South Dakota.[5] In fairness to the sociobiological approach, I should note that the Freudian and Marxist explanatory schemas would also have great difficulty in showing how their theories would account for the recent societal changes in sexual customs in the West.

I will not attempt to analyze in greater detail these older explanations of sexuality. I have briefly set forth my reservations about their utility for explaining many important questions about human sexuality. *My major point is that none of the existing schemas allow for adequate explanation of why people in various societies are so different in their sexual lifestyles.* These approaches do not permit one to scientifically handle questions concerning the full range of societal structures that might account for the differences or similarities that are present in sexual lifestyles. Since these are some of the central questions inherent in a societal-level explanation of sexuality, a new approach is needed if they are to be answered.

Please note that I do not reject all elements of these explanatory schemas. In point of fact, I do end up with some interpretations that would be particularly compatible with parts of the Marxist and feminist approaches. But many other aspects of my final theoretical position are incompatible with all three approaches. My major objection to these older approaches is that they have become stylized and rigidified in order to conform with the views put forth by their founders and their disciples. I prefer a new approach that is restricted only by the scientific principles of sociology. It, too, in time may become less flexible, but at present it is fresh and new.

The task of devising a societal-level approach to sexuality was an enormous one! If I was to explain variation in human societies, then I could not deal with just the United States of America, or even the Western world. Rather, I would have to devise explanations that would be applicable to all types of societies. Also, I did not want just to compile a list of hundreds of different premarital, marital, or extramarital customs. I desired to create an integrated, overarching set of explanations, not an inventory of sexual customs.

I spent the better part of four years researching for this book. Among other things, this involved reading scores of books and hundreds of articles. My aim was to broaden my cross-cultural understanding of human sexuality. I had spent most of my career up to that time doing empirical research, writing explanatory books and articles, and reading extensively in the field of sexuality. I had developed explanations of selected aspects of sexuality such as American premarital and extramarital customs.[6] But what I needed now was a broader cross-cultural orientation and one that would apply to all the many varieties of human sexuality. I had some training in anthropology and had taught the subject for four years, but that was not enough.

In addition to the extensive reading, I called and spoke to people in anthropology to find out what they considered to be the key studies of human sexuality. I also purchased the existing computer data files covering almost 1200 cultures. These files consisted of the Ethnographic Atlas and a subset of that file composed of some 186 cultures known as the Standard Cross-Cultural Sample (hereafter referred to as the Standard Sample). These 186 cultures are a representative sample of the world's best-described nonindustrialized cultures, and it was this sample that I used in many places in this book. I also examined a considerable amount of new information relevant to sexuality that individual researchers had recently added to the files on these 186 cultures. Of course, I also examined the literature available on industrialized societies.

On a smaller scale I did a search of the literature in psychology, primatology, endocrinology, and history. Here, too, I spoke to professionals at the top of these fields to gain further understanding of their specialties. However, I must emphasize that the work I did in these other fields was predominantly for supplementary reasons. The anthropological resources were much more central to my goals.

I hoped in these other fields to find information that would better define what that discipline could or could not explain about human sexuality. This might be useful in setting the parameters for what needed to be explained by my approach. For example, it is helpful to learn from primatology that most primate females have a period known as estrus (or "heat") during which they are ovulating and are sexually interested.[7] The evidence on human females indicates no clear increase in sexual interest during ovulation. Thus, one cannot logically deduce from how primate females act during ovulation, how human females will act during ovulation. This knowledge is important if one wants to examine the degree to which human sexuality is free from reproductive consequences. Without such knowledge of human and nonhuman primates one might assume similarities or differences that do not exist and thereby distort one's explanation of human sexuality.

We also know from endocrinologists' research on levels of androgen in human males that it is difficult to predict male sexual activity levels from knowledge of hormonal levels except in quite extreme cases. Knowing this, we will be aware that our theory will have to explain differences in sexual activity levels, for we cannot assume that hormonal factors are a sufficient explanation for a group's behavior.

In other instances biologists might offer competitive theories claiming to explain group variations in sexual lifestyles by reference to their major causal variables. For example, some biologically oriented scientists would argue for the power of hormones in explaining sexual behavior differences between men and women. Any societal-level explanation would have to take account of such a claim. But a societal explanation would still have to account for the fact that male-female differences in sexual behaviors are not identical in all societies. Even if hormones explain why the range in sexual behavior for each genetic sex is different, societal conditions can still explain how much of that potential is actualized in any one society.

In all these cases it is important to know the thinking in other fields, at least rudimentally, so as to better define precisely what areas of human sexual life are *not* predominantly explained by these other fields. In that way one can delimit more clearly that which may be explained by sociology. Most everyone today accepts the notion that our sexual relationships are caused by forces studied by a variety of scientific fields. Nevertheless, as a sociologist my goal is to cover all that sociology can explain while still striving to be aware of the obvious causal overlap within those areas that are also covered by other fields.

I hope it is clear that I am *not* seeking to create a total explanation that will cover evolutionary, psychological, and physiological factors of sexuality as well as sociological aspects. In fact, I firmly believe that it is the nature of science to abstract and select a particular perspective. We must, in our role as scientists, leave the search for ultimate reality to religion and to those philosophies of life that strive to present the total "truth" about any subject. What I am seeking in this book is a much more modest goal, and that is to explain the ways in which our membership in society shapes our sexuality. Other scientific disciplines will inform and aid in this specialized goal, but I will not venture to develop a theory that explains sexuality from the perspective of all these other disciplines. Instead, my quest is to develop a sociological explanation.

WHY A SEARCH FOR UNIVERSALS?

As my work progressed over that four-year period, I had to decide about the societal scope of the explanation that I would seek to develop. Would I seek to develop a special explanatory theory for industrial societies and a different one for agricultural societies and another one for hunting societies, and so forth? Or would I seek to find what commonalities existed and what sort of general set of explanations would apply to all societies, regardless of their specific type? My final choice combined these two strategies. Although I place major emphasis on the search for common explanations, I also spend considerable time explaining the variation that occurs among societies.

Let me specify my approach a bit more. When I speak of searching for commonalities I am talking about finding those basic features of human society that everywhere have a significant impact on human sexuality. One can be glib and say everything relates to sexuality, but such vagueness is hardly helpful. Therefore, my first task is to find those fundamental features of all societies that relate to the sexual lifestyle in any society. So, it is not enough that in some societies religion is related to attitudes toward sexuality. I want to know whether religion in all societies has some type of predictable relationship to sexuality. If in many nonliterate societies religious orientation does not distinguish people's sexual attitudes, then religion would not be a societal feature that is *universally* related to sexuality.

Now some readers may wonder if this search for universal "societal linkages" to sexuality will stop us from understanding differences among societies. After all, if the basic societal linkages are *common* to all cultures, then how do we explain *differences* in sexuality? This is a legitmate question. Let me respond by noting that the stress on the importance of universals increases our motivation to explain why we have differences within those crucial universal linkages in various societies. The very search for these common, universal causes of sexual lifestyles necessitates a search of the full range of variations that exists. Only in that way can one be confident that one has found a universal linkage.

Let me illustrate this briefly. One of the universal societal linkages that I shall point out in this book is the power structure in a society. Clearly, power structures can be highly rigid or flexible and may contain many levels or a few. Power structures may also differ from each other in many other specific ways. It follows, then, that although all shared sexual lifestyles will be influenced by the particular power structure in that society, it still is true that the specific way a power structure relates to a sexual lifestyle may vary considerably by society.

One example of such differences in the way power structures relate to sexual customs will be discussed in Chapter 4, where I point out that the more stratified the social class system in a society, the more likely the sexual customs of that society will reflect male dominance. Relatedly, I note that agricultural societies compared to other nonindustrial societies generally have greater class stratification. In this way I assert that power links to sexuality in all societies but in agricultural societies, that linkage will express more male dominance due to the type of class stratification agriculture promotes. So the search for universal areas of linkage with sexuality will afford us the knowledge needed to explain such variations that occur. *My conclusion is that the very search for universal societal linkages forces us to face a broader range of differences than would be the case if we were trying to generalize about only one type of society.*

The reason I do not seek only to explain variation or differences in the way sexuality is integrated into societies is that I feel we first need to know what differences are most worth explaining. If a particular custom in one society affects sexuality in that society but that sort of custom does not have this impact in any other society, why should we spend our time explaining it when that will not help us understand sexuality in any other society? If we are dealing with universal relationships between the major features of human society and our sexual customs, then our explanations will be relevant to understanding sexuality in all societies.

Thus, the universal search will perhaps lead us to the primary storehouses of societal influence on sexuality. We will be dealing with societal features like jealousy, gender role, and concepts of normality. My strategy is first to discover and analyze universal influences on sexuality and then to strive to explain differences related to these few universal societal linkages. To be sure, explaining unique ways in which some societal feature influences sexual customs is of value for those with explanatory goals different than mine. But my objective is to develop a societal-level explanation of sexuality that will be applicable to the full range of human societies, and so I choose to emphasize those universal societal features that are linked to sexual customs.

The reader should know that some people feel that cross-cultural comparisons are not possible. Such people—and some anthropologists are among them—feel that each culture is unique and cannot be compared to another. These people contend that although two cultures may both have a norm instructing mothers to take care of newborn children, the meaning of this custom may well be quite different in each culture, and so one cannot generalize and say that "maternal care" is present in both cases.

Surely we would all agree that no two cultures are identical. The disagreement centers on whether differences that exist make intercultural comparability impossible or meaningless. Frankly, I believe a good part of the reason for the relativistic viewpoint derives from the large amount of time and energy that anthropologists spend in the field studying a society. That investment means that they will likely identify personally with that culture and will have learned a great deal about that culture that distinguishes it from their own native culture. Accordingly, I believe that some anthropologists choose to focus on the distinctiveness of the culture they have studied rather than make comparisons with other cultures.

This same position is held by some people who study individuals closely. They, too, may well stress the difficulties in comparing two human beings and point out how similar things have different meanings to each person. There are also historians who hesitate to compare historical events, for they prefer to see each historical event as unique and as never occurring in exactly the same way ever again. This position, of course, increases the importance of studying such a unique event.

The position I adopt in this book acknowledges that there surely are differences in every culture and that we must understand such differences. But I do not start with the assumption that meaningful comparison is not possible. *Instead I start with the opposite assumption to that of the relativists, and I assume that, with careful attention to the social context, intercultural comparisons can be made.* I hold to this position unless there is clear evidence to the contrary.

Still the relativists would assert that comparing societies is like comparing apples and oranges. In response I would note that apples and oranges are both fruits, and so we can locate a common trait that does allow comparison and yet does not deny that there are differences in these two types of fruits. Science abstracts from total reality and need not deal with all differences that exist in a comparison. To accept a "subjectivistic" view of the world is to deny the possibility of comparing or analyzing conflicting perceptions. In addition, if we cannot compare, then we cannot generalize. Once we accept such a position, we deny the possibility of science because science aims at developing generalizations that explain the phenomena under scrutiny, and this cannot be done if everything is unique.

Some of this disagreement may dissolve if we agree, as I have emphasized earlier, that science does not take into account the total reality of anything it studies. Science is an abstraction from reality.[8] Science affords only a specialized level of understanding. It is not the role of science to explain "ultimate reality"— that is more the role of religious or individual philosophies. The common role of science is to generalize, but from a singular perspective. In the examples above, to generalize and call both apples and oranges fruits does lose some of the distinctive nature of apples and oranges per se, but it allows us to develop explanations that will apply to all such fruits. Przeworski and Teune have said it plainly in their classic book on comparative cultural research:[9]

> General theoretical statements, valid regardless of the social systems involved, should be sought. . . . It would be nonsensical to believe that no other person behaved like Catherine II or Napoleon, or that there was only one cosmopolitan elite. Unique events manifest properties of general classes and can be explained by general statements, even if incompletely. (Przeworski and Teune, 1970: pp. 74, 87)

Therefore, I will start with the assumption that societies can be compared despite the great variation that exists among them. We will surely deal in depth with differences among cultures, but I believe that those differences largely occur within a framework of a few common societal structures that shape the sexual lifestyle of all societies. I will analyze those common societal elements in detail in the chapters that follow.

PROBLEMS IN THE DATA

Having set forth this very ambitious task of seeking to explain universal societal linkages to sexuality and the variation that occurs in such linkages in different societies, it is necessary to say a few words about the quality of the data available for this project. Only a few anthropologists have set out with the primary goal of studying the sexual customs of a particular culture. This means that much of the information we have on sexual customs comes from passing comments made as part of the study of other societal aspects. In connection with describing a marital system, for example, the anthropologist may comment on the fact that sexual jealousy was rather common. But there was no planned, careful study of sexual jealousy. Thus, much of the information on sexuality is not as carefully and deliberately gathered as we would like. Nevertheless, let me add that there have been several fine studies of societies where one of the primary goals *was* the description of sexual customs. I shall refer to these accounts often in this book. Unfortunately for my project, such studies are not too common, and so it is important to have broader sources of information such as that contained in the Standard Sample.

Despite the lack of complete data on sexuality some professionals have ventured to analyze what is available and thereby to develop additional codes to classify many of the 186 nonindustrialized societies in the Standard Sample in terms of various sexual lifestyle characteristics. One such code system of 20 sexual variables was developed by Broude as part of her dissertation work at Harvard.[10] I soon discovered, partly from the warnings that Broude herself put forth, that there were problems concerning just how reliable and valid these data are, that is, just how much confidence one could have in this information.[11] Although Broude and the other coders are quite aware of such problems, the researcher who would use these data must still somehow cope with this problem.

As an indication of some of the problems in coding, let us examine the two different codes for rape incidence devised by Gwen Broude and Peggy Sanday.[12] Peggy Sanday and Gwen Broude both sought to code rape for any of the 186 societies in the Standard Sample, which had what they felt to be sufficient information to permit such coding. Broude coded 31 of the 186 societies as having sufficient information and Sanday coded 95 of the 186 societies as having sufficient information to permit giving a rape incidence code. When you examine the 25 societies they both coded, although they agree on most cases, there are a number of instances of disagreement. Furthermore, Broude compared to Sanday coded a higher proportion of her societies as "rape prone" (41% versus 18%) and a lower proportion as "rape free" (24% to 47%).

Rather than throw up my hands in despair when confronted with such reliability and validity problems, I devised several ways of choosing among the codes available. One way was to take what I thought were known relationships and check which codes would produce that known relationship. If one takes as given that the acceptance of machismo correlates with the acceptance of rape in a society, for example, then one can select whichever measure of rape best displays such a relationship with machismo attitudes. Alternatively, if the variable in question is not crucial to one's research, and the differences cannot be resolved in this fashion, then one can simply drop the variable.[13]

Other bases for choosing between conflicting codes exist. One can utilize the codes of the anthropologist with the best scientific reputation; or lacking this knowledge, with the largest number of societies coded. Another procedure is to judge the reliability and validity of several codes by whether the analysis of the data using these codes reveals a clear pattern of relationship among the variables examined. If variables are coded in a meaningless fashion, there is no reason to expect any clear pattern of relationship among them. The reader shall see in Chapters 3 to 6 that I did indeed find a clear set of relationships among many of the variables I chose to utilize.[14]

Much of the coded data on the 186 societies in the Standard Sample avoid these problems of reliability and validity. There are, for example, codes concerning a society's emphasis on male descent, common residence, the extent of class stratification, and the role of agriculture. The dependability of this information is much more established, and these codes do measure societal aspects that are important to the understanding of sexual customs. I do not want to overstress the problems in coding that occur for some variables and thereby deemphasize the dependability of many other coded variables. The reader needs to be aware of such limitations, but he or she should also know that even these problems have been resolved in as careful a manner as possible.[15]

In addition to some elaborate analysis of the Standard Sample, this book relies heavily on my reading of those cultures whose sexuality has been studied in depth. These additional sources are essential, for many aspects of sexuality have not been coded by anyone for the Standard Sample. Thus, to obtain information on these areas I had to do my own investigation into the available ethnographic literature.

Finally, I am familiar with the information on industrial societies like our own, and throughout the book I will comment on our society and other Western societies, even though they are not included in the Standard Sample. We do need to step back and gain perspective on America by looking not only at other industrial societies but at those societies that are quite distinct.

Given my discussion of some of the limitations of the information that is available on sexuality, the reader should bear in mind that much of what I conclude will have some speculative element in it and will require additional research and corroboration by others. But the choice is to proceed this way or not to proceed at all. I feel it is far better to put forth a logically coherent and as carefully empirically based explanation as possible, rather than to do nothing or to focus on a much narrower explanation applying to only a very few societies.

WHOSE VALUES?

To orient the reader to this book, one final question remains. How shall I deal with the controversial moral issues that inevitably come up in discussions of sexual customs?[16] No researchers can claim that they will achieve perfect value objectivity in their scientific work. But we have in social science the practice of reviewing each others' published work, and since we do not all have identical values, there is therein the potential of a colleague challenging one's fairness. This potential challenge is one major factor that pressures toward impartiality and fairness in social scientific research and theory.

There are a minority of social scientists who would assert that we all have a bias and that we should not try to hide it beneath the guise of striving for objectivity. Such people would say that if you take research money from the government for your study, then you will be pressured to support the established government power groups. Others may operate from a Marxist or a religious philosophy, and that can bias their presentations. So, the "subjectivists" say you might as well choose your value system and accept your biases.

Most social scientists reject such an approach for several reasons. First, if there is not even a way of approximating objectivity or fairness in the examination of a controversial area, then we are in effect eliminating the possibility of science from such areas. We would then be saying that these are fully polemical arenas and the more powerful group will have its way, and so there is no such thing as an unbiased perspective. Now, it is surely true that value conflict abounds on many issues and the more powerful group often does decide how the controversy shall be resolved. Scientific understanding does not guarantee a different resolution of the conflict. But the fact that powerful groups win in conflicts does not deny the possibility of a fair and objective analysis of the conflict situation.

I remember a few decades ago when Medicare was being debated. A study, financed by those who opposed Medicare, was undertaken about the living standards of elderly people. The study reported that most elderly people were well off financially and that Medicare was not needed. However, an examination of the study indicated that predominantly those elderly who lived in the wealthy suburbs had been interviewed.

If one accepts the inevitability of bias and the unachievability of objectivity, then that study is just one more bit of support for that perspective. According to that perspective, those favoring Medicare may best be advised just to interview the elderly in low-income areas so as to present as strong a biased case as they can. Yet if we all really believed that research was incapable of giving unbiased information, why would we undertake any studies of this sort? So, the fact that we do research indicates our belief in the possibility of a fair outcome. When we all stop believing this, the research process will also cease.

Further, the fact that the Medicare study was severely criticized by social scientists shows that those adherents to the fairness or objectivity doctrine are very much present in the social sciences. Eventually, we did get studies that were less biased in their sample selection. That would not have occurred had we abandoned our belief in the possibility of approximating objectivity and fairness in our research on humans.

Let us be explicit, though that science itself has its own value system to which scientists are committed *for the time they are in the role of scientist.* The approach I am following in this book is based upon acceptance of the values of science. However, no one is a scientist all the moments of his or her life—people have values other than those that are part of the scientific enterprise. But one of the key values of science directs the scientist to avoid personal values in research work and to seek to describe and explain rather than to judge morally. This is the value we have called fairness or objectivity. The acceptance of the value of publication and the acceptance of criticism from one's peers are other values of science. In addition, scientific values direct one to use measurements that can be repeated by others with the same results (reliability) and that actually measure what one wishes to measure (validity).

So, during those times when we are in our scientific roles, we are not free of all values. Rather, we are temporarily setting aside the personal moral values we hold and striving to abide by the scientific values. There is nothing in science that favors or opposes any form of sexuality. Science can afford us explanations and understanding of the outcomes of various types of sexual behaviors. The final judgment of the worth of the various sexual customs we are studying is based on a personal set of values that is outside the realm of science.

In conclusion, I feel that the scientific enterprise offers us a way of understanding the world that is different from the perspective promoted by political, religious, and private values. I will not argue here the vast payoffs that have come from accepting the scientific approach as *one* of our ways of viewing the world. Rather, I will simply assert that this is the perspective I take in this book. I strive, and the reader can judge with how much success, to present a view of human sexuality that does not seek to support any personal value system—mine or others. My purpose in this book is, not to moralize, but to gain understanding of the social nature of human sexuality.[17] I leave it to each individual to seek, for his or her own personal values, the possible usefulness of what is being explained and described here.

SELECTED REFERENCES AND COMMENTS

1. In this book I emphasize a "macro"-level sociological approach. This is a level of analysis that stresses the broad, overall societal characteristics such as institutions and shared customs. Some sociologists focus more on a "micro" level of analysis and therefore focus more on specific groups and interaction patterns between individuals. Both approaches are surely legitimate parts of sociology. I use both in this book but emphasize much more the macro level of analysis. Since I compare various societies my approach would also be called "comparative sociology." For a discussion of macro/micro approaches see Bruce H. Mayhew, "Structuralism Versus Individualism. Part One: Shadow Boxing in the Dark," *Social Forces*, vol. 59, no. 2 (December 1980), pp. 335–375.

2. For the uninitiated I would suggest a very simple book on Freudian ideas by Appignanesi, which I feel is a good place to begin to understand Freud. I also list three other important sources.

Appignanesi, Richard, *Freud for Beginners*. New York: Pantheon Books, 1979.

Halberstadt-Freud, Hendrika C., "Freud's Libido Theory," Chapter 5 in John Money and Herman Musaph (eds.), *Handbook of Sexology*. New York: Elsevier North-Holland, 1977.

Freud, Sigmund, *Three Contributions to the Theory of Sex*. New York: Dutton, 1962. (Originally published in 1905.)

Freud, Sigmund, *Civilization and Its Discontents*. London: Hogarth Press, 1930.

3. There is an immense literature on Marxism. As a start, I suggest the following.:

Bottomore, Tom, *Marxist Sociology*. New York: Holmes & Meier, 1975.

Burawoy, Michael, "The Resurgence of Marxism in American Sociology," Introduction in *Marxist Inquires: Studies of Labor, Class and States.* Chicago: Univesity of Chicago Press, 1982.

Engels, Friedrich, *The Origin of the Family, Private Property, and the State.* Chicago: Charles H. Kerr, 1902. (Originally published in 1884.)

Engels, Friedrich, *Socialism: Utopian and Scientific.* New York: International, 1935.

On the question of overlap between Marxism and present-day feminism, I suggest reading some of the far-ranging selections from the following two anthologies:

Eisenstein, Zillah R. (ed.), *Capitalist Patriarchy and the Case for Socialist Feminism.* New York: Monthly Review Press, 1979.

Sargent, Lydia (ed.), *Women and Revolution: A Discussion of the Unhappy Marriage of Marxism and Feminism.* Boston: South End Press, 1981.

4. For a presentation of the sociobiological view I suggest examining first the original statement by Edward Wilson. The authors of the other two books listed here present different sociobiological views on human sexuality.

Wilson, Edward O., *Sociobiology: The New Synthesis.* Cambridge, Mass.: Harvard University Press, 1975.

Symons, Donald. *The Evolution of Human Sexuality.* New York: Oxford University Press, 1979.

Hrdy, Sarah Blaffer, *The Woman That Never Evolved.* Cambridge, Mass.: Harvard University Press, 1981.

5. For general statistical information on the United States, I list here some publications with which to start. Note that sophisticated understanding of statistics requires more than just these sources. A myriad of other government publications as well as private sources can be consulted. See

U.S. Department of Commerce, Bureau of the Census. *Statistical Abstract of the United States.* Washington, D.C. (Published annually.)

For statistics specifically on crime in the United States, some of which is clearly related to sexuality, see

U.S. Department of Justice. *Uniform Crime Reports for the United States.* Washington, D.C. (Published annually.)

U.S. Department of Justice, Bureau of Justice Statistics. *Criminal Victimization in the U.S., 1981: A National Crime Survey Report,* NCJ–90208. Washington, D.C., November 1983.

6. For a brief statement of these explanations of premarital and extramarital sexuality, see

Reiss, Ira L., and Brent Miller, "Heterosexual Permissiveness: A Theoretical Analysis,"Chapter 4 in W. Burr, R. Hill, I. Nye, and I. Reiss (eds.), *Contemporary Theories about the Family.* (vol. 1): Free Press, 1979.

Reiss, Ira L., Ronald E. Anderson, and G.C. Sponaugle, "A Multivariate Model of the Determinants of Extramarital Sexual Permissiveness," *Journal of Marriage and the Family,* vol. 42 (May 1980), pp. 271–283.

I have not attempted to systematically interrelate my specific propositions from these works with those in this book, However, I do make specific observations on this in footnote 48 of Chapter Four and footnote 13 in Chapter Eight.

7. For an introduction to information on primates relevant to genetic sex and sexuality differences between human males and females and among primates see

Mitchell, Gary, *Behavioral Sex Differences in Non Human Primates.* New York: Van Nostrand Reinhold, 1979.

For further biological information with some comparisons with environmental theories see

Beach, Frank A. (ed.), *Human Sexuality in Four Perspectives.* Baltimore: John Hopkins University Press, 1977.

Singer, Barry, "A Comparison of Evolutionary and Environmental Theories of Erotic Response," *Journal of Sex Research,* vol. 21, no. 3 (August 1985), pp. 229-257.

8. For a discussion of the nature of science, I suggest reading the several articles on science in the encyclopedia noted here and also recommend reading the short and nontechnical book by Conant. In addition, I suggest the more technical account given in the Przeworski and Teune book listed under note 9.

Edwards, P. (ed.), *The Encyclopedia of Philosophy* (8 vol.). New York: Macmillan, 1967. (See especially articles in Volume 7.)

Conant, James B., *On Understanding Science.* New Haven, Conn.: Yale University Press, 1951.

9. Przeworski, Adam, and Henry Teune, *The Logic of Comparative Social Inquiry.* New York: Wiley Interscience Books, 1970.

10. Broude, Gwen J., and Sarah J. Greene, "Cross-cultural Codes on Twenty Sexual Attitudes and Practices," *Ethnology,* vol. 15, (October 1976), pp. 409-429.

11. Reliability refers to the ability to repeat the measurement and obtain the same results. Validity refers to whether you are really measuring what you want to measure. Both are key scientific concepts, for surely you want stable measures and you want measures that get at what you intend them to measure. In this sense these concepts are indexes of the quality of the measure you are using. See the Glossary for definitions of these and many other key concepts used in this book.

12. Sanday, Peggy Reeves, "The Socio-cultural Context of Rape: A Cross-cultural Study," *Journal of Social Issues,* vol. 37, no. 4 (1981), pp. 5-27.
I should note here that the correlation of the Broude and Sanday rape incidence measures is .43. This is significant but clearly indicates that there is disagreement on how to code the 25 societies they both coded.

13. One code that I did drop dealt with whether the society in question considered sexuality to be dangerous. On this code, Broude and Green said 62% of the 37 societies in the Standard Sample they were able to code viewed sexuality as dangerous at least under some specific circumstances (pp. 413-414). But Martin Whyte said that he found only 22% of the 68 societies he was able to code that viewed sexuality as dangerous (pp. 73-74). Part of the difficulty is that Whyte used only a yes or no code and coded more societies than Broude and Green. Even examining only those societies they both coded shows there are significant differences. Since I did not find this variable essential to my analysis, I simply discarded it.

Broude, Gwen J., and Sarah J. Greene, "Cross-cultural Codes on Twenty Sexual Attitudes and Practices," *Ethnology,* vol. 15 (October 1976), pp. 409-429.

Whyte, Martin King, *The Status of Women in Preindustrial Societies.* Princeton, N.J.: Princeton University Press, 1978.

14. In addition to sexual codes devised by Broude and Sanday (cited in notes 10 and 12), I also used new codes on sexuality from the following:

Hupka, Ralph B., "Cultural Determinants of Jealousy," *Alternative Life-*

styles, vol. 4, no. 3 (August 1981), pp. 310-356.

Ross, Marc Howard, "Political Decision Making and Conflict: Additional Cross-cultural Codes and Scales," *Ethnology,* vol. 22 (April 1983), pp. 169-192.

Whyte, Martin King, *The Status of Women in Preindustrial Societies.* Princeton, N.J.: Princeton University Press, 1978.

15. The reader interested in a more technical description of the Standard Sample and my analysis of it should refer to Appendix A in this book.

16. For a brief summary of the relation of value judgments and science see

Reiss, Ira L., "Value Judgments and Science," Appendix 1 in Ira L. Reiss, *Family Systems in America* (3rd ed.). New York: Holt, Rinehart & Winston, 1980.

17. To aid in understanding I have striven to avoid jargon and I have included a glossary of key terms used at the end of the text.

CHAPTER TWO

THE SOCIAL NATURE OF HUMAN SEXUALITY

A UNIVERSAL CONCEPTION OF HUMAN SEXUALITY

Our first task is a difficult one. Since my purpose is to examine the way human sexuality integrates into societies around the world, I must settle upon a definition that is suitable for that goal. I require a definition that is universally applicable. It cannot be an arbitrary definition, chosen for its utility or convenience. Rather, since my definition must have universal applicability, it will be possible to test it empirically. This is so because if we find one culture lacking in what this definition claims is the unique and essential quality of human sexuality, then at least the universal aspect of the definition must be rejected, for in such a case what I define as sexuality will not have been present in every society.

I want to develop a definition that eliminates the incidental aspects and focuses upon what appears to be the essential aspects of human sexuality. To illustrate, in some groups the norms stipulate that affection should always be part of a sexual relationship. But since we seek a universally applicable definition and we know that for many groups and in many societies affection is not a required aspect, then we must discard affection as part of the essence of sexuality. After our discussion of personal value judgments in the last chapter, it should be clear that we are not talking of what sexuality universally *should* be like (the moral essence) but what sexuality universally actually *is* like (the empirical essence).

We are searching for a societal-level definition, and thus we need to seek the essential nature of sexuality in the shared conceptions that societies put forth. We are not interested in what one individual may conceive of as the essence of sexuality. The essence we are searching for consists of *the qualities that when present all societies would label as sexual.* In short, we are looking for that without which the sexual would not exist. That is what I mean by the essence of sexuality. Affection does not fit that requirement. The question remains—what does?

In 1983 I examined the index in 20 colleges textbooks in human sexuality to search for a definition. I found that there was no index reference to a definition of human sexuality in 15 of the 20 textbooks. I list here the definitions in the remaining 5 textbooks:[1]

Sexuality means a dimension of personality instead of referring to a person's capacity for erotic response. (Masters, Johnson, and Kolodny, 1982: p. 2)

Sex means all the physical, emotional and social implications of being male and female. (Diamond and Karlin, 1980: p. 3)

[Sexuality] refers to the awareness of a reaction to the biological characterizations of male and female. In essence, sexuality is our reactions to sex. (Luria and Rose, 1979: p. 6)

The term sex will be used in this book to refer specifically to sexual anatomy and sexual behavior. (Hyde, 1979: p. 3)

There is no single unidimensional definition of sexuality. (Sandler, Meyerson, and Kinder, 1980: p. 216)

I will add here part of the definition of sexuality which the Sex Information and Education Council of the U.S. (SIECUS) put forth after an international conference in 1980 that sought to develop an internationally acceptable definition of sexuality:[2]

The Siecus concept of sexuality refers to the totality of being a person. It includes all of those aspects of the human being that relate specifically to being boy or girl, woman or man, and is an entity subject to life-long dynamic change. (*SIECUS Report*, January 1980: pp. 1–2)

These definitions make it obvious that much of the confusion in our discussions of sexuality can be traced to the fact that we use vague and unclear concepts when we speak of sexuality, and thus very often we really do not know precisely what we are discussing. This lack of conceptual clarity is apparent in the preceding list of attempts at defining human sexuality.

Let me detail the evidence of some conceptual confusion. The first definition cited hardly gives much insight by asserting that sexuality is a dimension of personality. Temperament, intelligence, empathy, and many other characteristics may also be conceived of as "a dimension of personality." So we are not brought very close to the special and unique characteristics of sexuality by such a definition. The same is even more apparent with the second definition, which involves "all the physical, emotional and social implications of being male and female." That would involve all aspects of gender roles such as the greater likelihood of one gender holding top occupational positions, or being a minister, or majoring in engineering. On the physical level it would involve the ability to become pregnant, the relative life expectancy, or the amount of body hair. Reflection makes it clear that this definition does not bring into sharp focus the unique or distinctive characteristics of human sexuality.

The other definitions suffer from the same overinclusiveness and vagueness of the first few. In fact, the third and fourth definitions actually use the term they are trying to define in the definition. That makes the definition circular and of little value, for it hardly illuminates to say that sexuality is sexuality. The SIECUS definition is perhaps the broadest and includes "the totality of being a person," which is about as far from specificity as one can move. Such definitions may be good politics because their vagueness permits each person to assume that his or her personal meaning is included. However, such definitions contribute little to a clear comprehension of sexuality.

Part of the reason for this vagueness and confusion can be found in our everyday use of the term *sex*. We have three distinct meanings that one word can express. To illustrate consider the following three sentences:

1. Her sex is female.
2. Her sex role is that of a woman.
3. She had sex with her partner.

In the first sentence the word *sex* is used to mean genetic sex, that is, chromosomal sex or whether one is an XX or an XY. The reference here, then, is to a biological fact. In the second sentence the word *sex* is intended to mean gender role or the set of rights and duties a culture assigns to someone classified as a man or a woman. In the third sentence reference is made to an act such as heterosexual or homosexual intercourse.

We must have some agreement regarding separate and distinctive terms for these three potential meanings of the word sex, or we will not be able to clearly write or talk about sexuality. I suggest that we use the term *sex* to refer to genetic sex or what is called the chromosomal makeup of the individual (XX or XY). Further, that we use the term *gender* role to refer to the set of rights and duties that societies usually apply to those segments they call women and men. Some people prefer to use the term *sex role* over *gender role*, but since *sex role* uses the word *sex* in a second way, for clarity's sake it is preferable here to use the term *gender role.*[3]

Finally, we are left with the remaining use of the term *sex*—something to do with activities like heterosexual or homosexual intercourse. For this meaning I suggest that we use the term *sexuality* instead of the short form *(sex)* in order to avoid any confusion with genetic sex.[4] Of course, we will not change the everyday usage of people, but we can change our scientific concepts to gain greater clarity than everyday usage affords. Such reconceptualization is an essential part of the scientist's attempt to use concepts in ways that are clear and precise as to meaning.[5]

But we are still left with the need for a clear definition of sexuality that stresses the distinctive nature of that which we call sexual. We cannot exclusively base our definition on behavior, like genital contact, for at times genital contact is not what we would conceptualize as sexual and the sexual can occur without genital contact. We may respond sexually just to the sight of an attractive person. Further, a visit to a gynecologist may well involve contact with genitalia, but our cultural definition would stress that such touching is nonsexual. In fact, if the gynecological exam led to sexual excitation, our norms would say that was inappropriate and subject to criticism. So, as in all sociological concepts, it is the common meaning of the act that must be tended to and not simply the physical behavior. The behavior is surely not irrelevant, but it is insufficient by itself to define what is sexual.

Ask yourself this queston: What is present in one's thoughts and feelings when there is genital contact with a lover that is not there in a medical exam of one's genitalia? I would submit that the missing element is erotic response or the feeling of being excited or "turned on." To be fully sexual in a societal sense, the action not only must involve what the culture considers the proper forms of sexual behavior but it must occur in a context that is *supposed* to produce an erotic response, that is, a feeling of excitation that makes one want to continue the activity.[6]

The gynecological exam lacks the erotic response just as would a kiss to our parents. The point here is that a society makes explicit which types of interaction are supposed to lead to erotic responses and which are not. The gynecological exam is not one of our "interaction models" or "cultural scripts" for producing a sexual response; whereas, dancing close with a lover is one of our cultural scripts for producing a sexual response. It is the excitement that accompanies a cultural script aimed at erotic response that we then label to ourselves as erotic.[7]

I use the term *cultural script* to mean a shared, group definition of the type of situation, type of people, and type of behavior appropriate in a particular social context. There are cultural scripts aimed at producing an erotic response in the participants, and I shall call these sexual scripts. Used this way the broad concept of cultural script is quite close in meaning to an "interaction model" or a social role, but since the term *script* is more informal and has been popularized by sociologists like Gagnon and Simon, I will also use it here. The sexual scripts derive from the shared, consensual beliefs people have about what is good and bad sexuality in their society. These sexual scripts act as guides regarding what that society believes is the proper circumstances for experiencing an erotic response. When we are dealing with a complex society such as our own, the sexual scripts will vary somewhat by ethnic groups, social classes, and age groups. But there will be much similarity, and within each social group there will typically be a dominant script shared by the majority of people in that group.

One other element besides culturally shared scripts and erotic arousal is a second essential part of what all societies call sexuality. That other element is genital response. It is true that some minor erotic arousals may not lead to any obvious genital response. We may respond erotically to a smile or a touch of the hand of another person, and yet it may be so mild that it would be difficult to measure any genital response like penile erection or vaginal lubrication. Yet I am assuming that those mild erotic acts in our society are in the direction of producing a genital response; that is, if they were continued, they would move toward acts like hugging and kissing, which would be much more likely to produce a genital response. Further, if the hugging and kissing were to continue, they would produce even higher likelihood of genital responses. Our culture teaches us these scripts and the expected genital outcomes, and if for some reason the genital responses do not occur, we usually ask ourselves what is wrong.

Clearly, then, I am not talking only of acts that involve touching the genitalia. Of course, particular acts of genital touching when part of our society's sexual scripts are one way to promote genital response. But I am also speaking of less direct actions that are on the path toward genital response and that produce genital responses without actual contact with the genitalia. As noted, visual displays and kissing and fondling can, when in accord with our sexual scripts, produce pronounced genital reactions.

In addition to learning the sequence of acts that our society asserts should produce genital responses, we also have been taught norms (standards for behavior) informing us when and with whom such acts should occur. This entire "package" is what I mean by a sexual script.

Although our norms regarding sexuality promote specific types of sexual responses, they may at times interfere with our genital responses by making us feel that the situation is not one that permits a desired sexual activity. Our group norms may teach us that oral sexuality is an acceptable erotically arousing act but one that we should not engage in on the first date. Then even though we desire to speed up the sexual script and engage in oral sexuality with a new partner, we may hold back. Such normative controls *implicitly* assert the power of certain sexual acts to evoke genital responses when performed in a particular setting. Nevertheless, such norms also *explicitly* assert that specific scripts must be followed if we are to achieve our sexual pleasures in socially sanctioned fashions. In this sense the same norms that instruct us about what is erotic also seek to control our performance of those erotic actions when we are not acting in accord with the shared sexual script.

Now I would like to offer my definition of the universal, shared meaning of human sexuality. *Human sexuality in all societies consists of those scripts shared by a group that are supposed to lead to erotic arousal and in turn to produce genital response.*

The definition is illustrated in Diagram 2.1

I assume that there is a feedback relationship between erotic arousal and genital response. By this I mean that erotic arousal and genital response mutually

Cultural Scripts ─────────▶ Erotic Arousal ─────────▶ Genital Response

DIAGRAM 2.1   Definition of Sexuality.

reinforce each other. The stronger either one of them is, the more likely the other will be strengthened. They are separable, though, for erotic arousal is the state of feeling turned on and genital response is a physiological response such as penile erection or vaginal lubrication. Certainly in the case of a paraplegic the erotic arousal may be in various degrees disconnected from any genital response. Also, a genital response may occur from nonerotic sources. There are research reports of strong emotions such as fear producing erection or lubrication. But in a social system one would expect that most of the time it would be erotic arousal that would lead to genital response. In addition, my assumption is that the erotic arousal occurs in most instances because of the congruence of the behavior with the sexual scripts present in that group. Thus, what arouses us is not a given, biologically fixed set of stimuli but rather a set of stimuli that a particular group decrees to be erotic.

If one is not socially trained regarding which cultural scripts are supposed to be sexually arousing, one can experience considerable difficulty in sexual inter-actions. One person may, for example, be turned on by his or her script, which might seem strange to the other person. When Westerners introduced our type of lip kissing to Polynesia, it was not immediately welcomed. At first it was thought to be a rather unpleasant way to exchange saliva. Polynesians had kissed by touching their noses to the side of the other person's face and smelling their skin; that is called an "Oceanic" kiss. An American doing the Polynesian "Oceanic" kiss in this country might well be thought of as unusual. So, learning the culture's sexual scripts makes compatible sexual interactions more easily achievable.

It also happens, in complex societies, that some people, compared to others, are raised in groups that are relatively very sexually restrictive. In such cases these young people may well not respond to what are considered erotic interactions by people raised in more sexually permissive groups. In this sense, if young people are taught that premarital sexual intercourse is unacceptable and they are dating others who believe that premarital sexual intercourse is a desirable part of a love relationship, then conflict will ensue because of these incongruent conceptions of sexual scripts.

In other instances low-permissive people who do become erotically aroused in situations that are taboo to them may fail to label their erotic arousal as sexual because they find that arousal unacceptable. In this connection we know from research by Gunter Schmidt on genital reactions to erotic slides that similar per-centages of females and males do exhibit genital responses.[8] Despite the genital responses, in their verbal reports females were more likely to assert that they found the films disgusting and unpleasant. The sexual scripts presented in the erotic slides did not fit with these females' sense of proper sexual stimuli, and thus they likely allowed their feelings of disgust to overwhelm any awareness of erotic feelings. They could not legitimate their feelings by calling them sexual.

In an analogous vein, those who are raised in high-permissive groups that label a great many interaction models as erotically arousing may well contain people who "fake" their response. Some people may not be erotically aroused but may feel pressure from their group's norms to act aroused. One way to handle that situation is to pretend to be aroused so as not to be viewed as unable to perform. Thus, both blocking of erotic feelings and pretending to have erotic feelings may be occasional consequences of being socially trained into specific sexual scripts. In most instances, I assume, there is reasonable congruency between one's erotic arousal and the accepted script; but that is surely not always the case.

Each society promotes compatibility among individuals in sexual experience to the degree that they train people to react in compatible ways to specific sexual scripts. In this sense having shared scripts is important. Nevertheless, it is not just to avoid conflict that agreed-upon scripts are required but because sexuality is learned predominantly by interacting with other people. Without reasonably compatible sexual scripts in a society, there would be a block to initial social interaction and future learning of the basic aspects of sexual interaction might not take place. Thus, even though a wide variety of different social groups exist in America, we can still arrive at an overall description of our sexual customs. We can fairly state, for example, that most American young people support the right of the unmarried to have premarital intercourse.[9] This does not contradict the fact that there are sizable minorities who would strongly reject such a position. It surely is a legitimate sociological investigation to study these diverse groups and their different shared sexual customs as much as it is to study the overall consensus on sexual customs.

I should note here that we are focusing on the major heterosexual patterns in human societies, but the reader should be aware that a sociological approach must also be able to explain homosexuality. Whether homosexuality can be attributed to a failure of the existing heterosexual scripts or to other factors is a much-debated question. Regardless of what one decides on that question, there surely are informal, covert sexual scripts that exist to direct sexual interactions for homosexuals. The key difference is that sexual scripts promoting heterosexuality are given priority, and therefore one typically does not come in contact with homosexual scripts until after joining the homosexual community in some fashion. The details of gay and lesbian sexual interaction models are not widely known. Thus, the question remains as to how the initial movement toward homosexuality occurs in societies like ours that do not promote homosexual scripts. We shall deal with this and other related questions at several places in this book and at length in Chapter 6.

The work of Harry Harlow with rhesus monkeys supports the conclusion that we learn our sexuality by interacting with other individuals.[10] Harlow found that infant monkeys who were raised in isolation from the playful interaction of peers and the nurturance of their mothers were unable to perform sexually when they matured. The monkeys seemed to require experience in grooming and touching each other in order to learn the interaction skills and motives needed for sexual intercourse.

In our own society we complicate sexual interaction by teaching men and women different beliefs about what are the preferable sexual interaction models. We train females to place great importance on the presence of stable affection, and we train males to place great importance on physical pleasure. In this sense we eroticize the romantic component for females and we eroticize the pleasure component for males. It is no wonder, then, that such differently socialized genders have difficulties living up to the expectations of each other's sexual scripts. Surely this may interfere with the achievement of sexual satisfaction. Later in the book we will explore the kinship, power, and ideological elements that support such conflicting gender-role training, but it is instructive here to point to the different sexual scripts passed down to each gender in most Western countries.

Some sexual scripts stress that only one partner will obtain erotic arousal and genital response from the encounter. We can see this, for example, in prostitution. In most cases, the prostitute does not become erotically aroused by her sexual activity—but the customer is expected to be aroused. Some readers may wonder if prostitution, since it is illegal in all states but one (Nevada), is part of our culture, that is, part of our shared ways of thinking, feeling, and believing that are the basis for the norms in our society. In a formal, overt view of our norms, prostitution would not be an institution with social guidelines about how to behave. However, certainly there are informal, covert norms that support prostitution and that set up interaction models for both the prostitute and the customer. In this informal and covert sense the sexual scripts related to heterosexual prostitution are part of our cultural heritage and are known and shared by large numbers of people.

On the other hand, there are sexual acts that do not fit even informal cultural patterns. In most but not all cases, rape would be an action much like murder and would not be directly supported by cultural norms, formal or informal. (I deal here only with heterosexual rape of females.) Nevertheless, one might contend that the conflict built into our gender roles, our male-dominant traditions, our acceptance of violence, and the view that sexuality is degrading may all indirectly pressure toward rape. There is some truth in that perspective, but these factors are unintentional supports of rape. We do have some direct normative support in views that assert if a female acts in particular ways, then she "deserves to be raped." But I do believe that the support for such views is far less than the support for other covertly approved acts such as visiting prostitutes or having an extramarital relationship.

Now, there are instances when Western culture has normatively supported rape as proper. Wartime is one such instance.[11] It is not uncommon during wartime for soldiers to believe they have the right to rape enemy women. But here I am not referring to such structured and "institutionalized" rape but rather to individual rape in a peacetime Western society.

To be sure—as I shall discuss in Chapter 7—rape is predominantly an act that expresses anger and power motives. However, it is not unusual for sexual acts to express motives other than physical pleasure. In many primate sexual acts it is difficult to discern the difference between an attempt to dominate and a sexual act. One sign of deference of a male primate to a more powerful male is to assume the female lordotic position (bent over with the rear up in the air) in front of the more powerful male. This seems to imply that the female sexual position has a submissive meaning, and thus primate sexuality may well have at least a partial power component.

All this aside, research indicates that there is also in most rapes an element of erotic arousal on the part of the rapist. To the rapist the sexual act symbolizes both his arousal and the degradation of the female.[12] It is this view of sexuality as a way to degrade a woman that facilitates the combination of eroticism with anger and power.

According to our definition of sexuality, rape in American society would be predominantly an individual act even though it may, as noted, unintentionally result from shared views concerning sexuality and gender. But a common sexual act like rape becomes a challenge to any sociological explanation of sexuality. If sexuality is heavily determined by cultural scripts, then why do we have such a large number of so-called individual rapes in our country? For now it will have to suffice to say that a culture may produce forces that promote outcomes that are not desired.[13]

There are other sexual acts that are only partially in line with sexual scripts. One common source of such acts is rapid social change. An act that was once not acceptable can become acceptable, and an act that was once thought of as not part of our sexual customs can become sexual. The increase in anal intercourse reported among married couples in the last 20 years, for example, may be one such change. Also, the increasing popularity over the past 20 years of oral sexuality would be another example.[14]

So, any sociological explanation of sexuality requires that we regularly monitor the shared ways of thinking, feeling, and believing that prevail in a society. In this fashion we become aware when changes occur due to new conceptions of sexuality becoming more acceptable. Some degree of change is inevitable, for the shared sexual scripts cannot possibly spell out every action, thought, and feeling that should occur. In this sense the individual is constantly "editing" the sexual scripts of his or her society. That process individualizes the script to better fit the person, and it also opens up the possibility of social change when a number of people, due to common social pressures, alter their scripts in the same fashion. The mechanism of the rapid changes in premarital sexuality in the 1965-1975 decade in America consisted of just such common individual script alteration in the face of common societal pressures.[15]

But other individual acts that lead to erotic arousal may be largely individual "discoveries" that do not become part of any social change. One may find that riding a horse, for example, affords erotic arousal. Surely this would be personal erotic arousal, for it would not be based upon a shared sexual script concerning this possible source of arousal and it is not a reaction to any common societal pressure. There are many such acts, and often individuals feel guilty about them because they haven't been given group support for these types of individualized sexual behaviors.

My point here is that these acts are "outside" the social system. They are not fully sexual in the social sense of being based upon shared scripts, nor are they the result of common societal pressures such as we discussed in the case of rape. As noted, a private discovery may grow into a shared custom, but until it does, it is outside the sociological explanatory schema. It may be valuable for sociologists to study such individual behavior in order to understand the potential sources of new sexual customs, but it would be a psychologist or perhaps a biologist who might be intrinsically interested in explaining many such types of private sexual acts.[16]

Even if not fully social, such private sexual acts are certainly sexual in a psychological sense in that they entail erotic arousal and genital response even if the source of the arousal does not come from a shared cultural script. If, as I contend, interaction models are the primary cause of erotic and genital reactions in the world, then such individualized sexual acts should be the source of only a minority of the total number of erotic and genital reactions that occur in any society. This should be even more the case for the adult, more socialized population in a society. The explanatory power of a sociological explanation can be tested by ascertaining how much of the genital response in a society is due to sources outside the shared sexual scripts.

In looking at other societies we must be careful that we do not impose our sexual scripts on them and label their different sexual behaviors as idiosyncratic and not shared just because they violate *our* sexual scripts. Indeed, when we examine cultures around the world, it is obvious that the sexual scripts of different cultures vary greatly. The reader may think, for example, that there is a "natural" progression of sexual acts from kissing to petting and finally to coitus that would be found in all societies. This is not so, for in other societies, as I have pointed out earlier, one would not even kiss as we do. Further, in some societies couples get down to the business of copulating with hardly any preliminary sexual activities and may fondle each other mostly after, and not before coitus. This is particularly true for adolescent sexuality. For example, Robert Suggs reports on the Marquesan sexual customs as follows:[17]

The typical sex act in adolescence and early adulthood begins with practically no foreplay. . . . The sex act seldom takes more than five minutes, most often two to three minutes. (Suggs, 1966: pp. 71–73)

Donald Marshall describes coitus on Mangaia in the South Pacific:

There is seldom any kissing or affectionate foreplay and demonstration prior to coitus. . . . Sexual intimacy is not achieved by first demonstrating personal affection; the reverse is true. (Marshall and Suggs, 1971: p. 118)

Finally, let me quote from Verrier Elwin's description of a youth commune in central India:

> This belief in sex as something good and normal gives the Muria a light touch . . . the penis and the vagina are in a "joking relationship" to each other. . . . Sex is great fun; it is the best of the ghotul [youth commune] games; it is the dance of the genitals. (Elwin, 1947: p. 419)

This cross-cultural perspective helps to afford us an awareness that in each society we are indeed acting on specific cultural scripts that are a very narrow selection of all possible models. The specific reasons why one society selects a particular set of sexual scripts different from another is a major concern of this book and will be examined in depth in the chapters that follow.

My definition of the universal essence of human sexuality can easily be scientifically tested. One can search for a society that does not have shared sexual scripts to serve as models for erotic and genital responses. If a society were found without such scripts, then erotic arousal and genital response would be viewed as resulting from nonsocietal causes. Further, if a society is found in which there are sexual scripts but most of the erotic arousal and genital response can be explained biologically, then my definition is in error. Many people do seem to believe that sexuality is "natural" or biological and that we do not need to be trained how to behave sexually. If this is true, my conception of sexuality would not explain very much of the sexual behavior that occurs. But note that if one accepts this natural, biological view of sexuality, then societies should not differ very much in their sexual patterns, for they all contain "natural" individuals. The evidence from Harry Harlow's work with monkeys questions such a natural view, for it documents that monkeys brought up in isolation for the first six months of their life are unable to perform sexually.[18]

Another explanation that contradicts mine is one that views sexuality as completely individualized and due to the distinct learning experiences of different people. If this perspective were valid, then an immense number of patterns of sexual interaction would characterize each society. Sexual activity would depend on the varied and unique experiences of each person. If this were so, my views about sexuality would surely be shown to be in error.

In contrast to the alternative views just presented, my perspective asserts that sexual customs are established by the group or society to which we belong and that they vary by the social nature of that group. Surely, biological factors are essential as a general basis but, I presume that biological factors are relatively equally distributed across cultures. It follows, then, that such biological similarities cannot account for the vast differences in sexual lifestyles that prevail in different social settings.

I am saying that rather than looking to biology or individual experience, we must search for the sources of our sexual lifestyles by looking at our basic social system. Somewhere in that social system lies the answers to the reason for the particular sexual scripts that exist in that group. Where direct sexual scripts do not explain sexual patterns, as in rape, I shall argue that indirect societal forces contain the explanation more fully than any biological trait. We shall systematically pursue this search for societal explanations at length in the chapters that follow, but first we must pursue our conception of sexuality a bit further.

REPRODUCTION: JUST HOW RELEVANT IS IT?

Now that we have formulated a universal conception of human sexuality, we must examine what it is about the social nature of human sexuality that ensures that all societies will have sexual scripts. Why would societies not just leave sexual interaction to chance and individual learning? This question concerns the assumptions underlying my conception of sexuality, which asserts that all societies will have sexual scripts. As the reader will soon see, some of the answers are not so obvious.

My cross-cultural examination of human sexuality leads me to conclude that *the most distinctive social characteristic of sexuality is the high importance in which it is held in virtually all societies.* This is so regardless of the degree of sexual permissiveness in a society. There are those societies like the Inis Baeg near Ireland or the East Bay in Melanesia that would argue that we Americans overvalue heterosexuality and stress it too much.[19] Yet even those cultures assert the importance of sexuality by their stress on the need to control it.

There are other cultures that are very accepting of sexuality. Some were mentioned earlier, but there are additional ones that have been carefully studied, such as the Lepcha of Sikkim in the Himalayan Mountains, the Baiga in Central India, or the Tiwi off the coast of North Australia. People in these cultures may place less importance on any one act of intercourse but would stress the pleasure value of sexuality in general.[20] Accordingly, these societies would place great importance on sexuality as a high-priority life activity even though any one sexual act may be seen as a simple pleasure.

If we agree that no society takes a stance of indifference to human sexuality and that all societies accept this high evaluation of the importance of human sexuality, then we can expect that all societies will strive to organize this important element of our life into sexual scripts. Thus, these scripts will be universally present and they will be designed to integrate with other important aspects of a society. These other aspects we will deal with in the next chapters, but first we need to answer the question of why sexuality is everywhere thought of as important.

Many people believe that the importance of sexuality in all societies is based predominantly upon its relationship to pregnancy and childbirth. Of course, this empirical connection is in most societies today one basis for viewing sexuality as important. However, the meaning of the connection of sexuality to reproduction is not that of a direct causal relationship. Reproduction has meaning predominantly in connection to the mediating variables of kinship and marriage. By this I mean that it is not the biological connection of sexuality to pregnancy that is most important in many non-Western societies. In such societies a large number of kin, other than the biological parents, participate in actions that promote the birth of a child and also participate in future actions involving care for the offspring. It is the set of meanings placed upon sexuality by such kin that is important, and the reproductive outcome is but one of those meanings. Let me elaborate on this thought.

In cultures like those in Polynesia the social connection of parents, relatives, and siblings to the newborn is what is crucial and not the biological fact of who supplied the sperm and egg for that child.[21] Adoption is widespread, and a shared form of upbringing by siblings and other adults is common. Robert Levy estimates that 25% of the Tahitian children were not living with either biological parent because of this common system of adoption and group upbringing.[22] This is about ten times as high a proportion as in the United States.

The point here is that although reproduction is important in all societies, it is important not just to the biological parents but to all the kin who may be involved in actions related to that reproduction. This is so because the "production" of children in many societies is viewed as a group activity, not as a straightforward biological activity. Reproduction is not simply conceived of as a consequence of a sexual act. Rather, reproduction is seen as a consequence of agreements made by various families regarding marriage and understandings that exist among many kin about caring for that child. The child is in that sense produced by the actions of all these kin and is born into a network of kinspeople. This approach is quite different from our own. We emphasize the individual bride and groom who make their own marriage decision and whose plans determine the birth of "their" child. In this fashion, we in the West do tie reproduction more closely to the actions of just the married couple.

This ability to at least partially separate sexuality from reproduction is further illuminated by those cultures in which the biological connections are not fully known, as among the Trobrianders in Melanesia.[23] There and in many other cultures it is believed that sexual acts alone will not produce pregnancy. Pregnancy is produced by a spirit entering an opening in the body of the woman, perhaps while she is bathing. It is as a consequence of being married that pregnancy and childbirth occur and not simply because of the sexual relations of a particular couple.

Among the natives in and around Northern Australia, for example, it is the husband who offers the spiritual element needed for the woman to become pregnant. Among the Tiwi the husband must first dream of the child before it can be born. In Western Arnhem Land on Goulbourn Island, the husband must complete the pregnancy by bringing the spirit of the child to the wife.[24] Sexuality alone is not seen as producing pregnancy. Such views surely weaken the argument that sexuality gains its importance by its tie to reproduction, for once again that tie in this and many other societies is seen as conditional, indirect, and partial.

To elaborate upon my thinking here, let me comment briefly about some popular beliefs that illustrate the nonscientific nature of the reasoning in many societies concerning sexuality and pregnancy. This is conspicuous in beliefs about the consequences of sexual intercourse. Consider, for example, the belief in some nonliterate societies that a woman is not likely to become pregnant if she has intercourse with many different men. Conversely, it is believed that the focusing of sexual relations upon one male produces pregnancy. Elwin comments on the trends among Muria youth in India toward having many sexual partners and states that this custom was encouraged by the belief that having a variety of partners restricts pregnancy. In connection with another central India society, the Baiga, he quotes an informant on this same point:[25]

> When a girl is going always to everyone, the mouth of her bag or womb never shuts, and so the man's seed runs in and out. That is why a loose girl never has a child. (Elwin, 1939: p. 220)

Many Polynesians, such as the Mangaians near Cook Island, also believe that having a variety of partners will prevent pregnancy. Also the Berndts' report that the Australian aborigines they studied believed that focusing intercourse on one man was what produced pregnancy. They also note that the aborgines believed that, in addition, a spiritual element is involved in producing pregnancy:[26]

> To impregnate a woman five to six ejaculations on successive days are required. During that period the woman must not have coitus with any man but her own husband, nor herself eject the semen by bodily exertion, abdominal pressure, etc. This accumulated substance serves as a basis for the foetus, which is termed an "egg". . . . At the stoppage of the menstrual flow, the blood which would normally be ejected goes now to help in the formation of the "egg". . . . About this time the father "brings the spirit child" to his camp; this spirit child resides in the father from the time of its finding. He does not give the "spirit child" directly to his wife, but awaits his opportunity. He first finds out if his wife has been constant in her affection for him and whether her menstrual flow has stopped. (Berndt and Berndt, 1951: p. 81)

My explanation for such beliefs would be that they constitute logical, though imperfect, reasoning based upon the fact that these people see a young woman marry and focus her sexuality on her husband and then they see her become pregnant. In these societies, prior to marriage women had many partners and did not usually become pregnant. Thus, pregnancy to them seems to result from the focus on one man—the husband. What they overlook is that prior to marriage, females may well have been too young to become pregnant easily, for it is not uncommon to start coitus by age ten and to marry young.

Notice also that the belief about the pregnancy potential of focused sexuality acts as a control on the wife's extramarital relationships, for if she wants to bear a child she must focus her sexuality on her husband. In the quote on the Australian aborigines in Arnhem Land, it is apparent that the husband will not add the "spirit child" element needed for pregnancy unless his wife has been attentive to him. In sum, these beliefs further document the lack of any belief in a simple connection of intercourse to pregnancy and show how embroidered that causal connection is with other beliefs and qualifications in the minds of these peoples.

On this same point, if the tie to reproduction is the reason for sexuality being considered important, then a different set of sexual norms might be expected to apply to menopausal women. Their sexuality should not be viewed as necessitating the same cultural restrictions as apply to fertile individuals. Furthermore, if reproduction were the key reason for the importance of sexuality, then prepubertal children would be allowed widespread sexual freedom, for they cannot become pregnant. In Western societies it is surely well known that 10-year-olds cannot become pregnant, and yet the opposition to sexual relations among 10-year-olds is surely stronger than it would be for 20-year-olds, who could become pregnant. It appears that other meanings of sexuality besides the reproductive are dominant in our sexual norms.

In one sense we in the West, like many nonindustrial cultures, have separated reproduction from sexuality. We have done this by using contraception and abortion to modify the causal connection of reproduction to sexuality just as other societies do this by involving the wider kin network in the production and care of infants or by bringing in magical and spiritual elements in their explanations of reproduction. It is relevant to note that as we in the West have separated sexuality from reproduction, the importance our culture has placed on sexuality has not decreased. If anything, some people have said we have today placed a higher value on the importance of achieving a satisfying sexual life for both genders than ever before. *Clearly, then, if we separate reproduction from sexuality, and the value of sexuality increases, then something other than reproduction must be supporting the view that sexuality is important.*

This illustration and our previous discussion concerning non-Western societies' ways of separating sexuality from reproduction point out that reproduction is not the everpresent reason for people judging sexuality to be important. Reproduction can be controlled, and it can be believed to be inoperative. What is much more essential to the meaning of sexuality are the physical and psychological aspects of sexuality. Accordingly, I shall argue in the next section that they and not reproduction are the key to the universal importance of sexuality.

Permit me one final and speculative thought on this question of the role of reproduction in the importance given to sexuality. As I conceptualize the lifestyle of our earliest ancestors I would reverse the common way of thinking and picture sexuality as leading to the importance placed on reproduction rather than reproduction leading to the importance placed on sexuality. Allow me to briefly speculate on our ancestors of hundreds of thousands of years ago and I will try to explain my thinking here.

There is no reason to expect our earliest ancestors to know the connection of sexuality to reproduction. Many of our high school students today do not know it! I believe that one of the earliest social bonds would have been the sexual linkage to another human being. The physical and psychological pleasures of sexuality would in my judgment have served as an initial bonding element for the couple involved.

We see this in other primate species today. Later as offspring were born, rudimentary ties to these children would over time tend to further unite the members of these primitive families. Such ties to descendants would be the stimulus to the development of kinship systems, but it would take considerable time for such kinship systems to formalize and conceptualize the role of sexuality in the production of future kin members.

These early beliefs relating sexuality to reproduction would surely not match those described in a modern biology course. As I have noted, even today in many societies these ties are partial and interwoven with many other societal elements. At some point, though, reproduction would become one *additional* basis for the importance placed upon sexuality. In sum, then, in my speculative vision of the past, sexuality creates the importance of reproduction because of the bonding power of sexuality, which in turn promotes the growth of kinship notions. Only after the development of rudimentary kinship relationship would the concept of reproduction contribute somewhat to the importance of sexuality.

Reproduction for its own sake is not important in almost any society—it is only reproduction that integrates into an existing kinship system that is conceived of as important. For that to occur, we must first have a kinship system in place. Sexual bonding promotes the development of kinship systems. It is for these reasons that I would play down the role of reproduction in the importance placed upon sexuality today and I further believe that historically the causal relationship was the reverse of the common view today.

THE TWO KEY CHARACTERISTICS OF SEXUALITY

The preceding discussion suggests that sexuality would be universally viewed as important even if storks brought babies. If we accept this position, then what is the basis of the universal feeling that sexuality is important? I think at the most fundamental level the importance of sexuality is based upon the two most common characteristics that everywhere accompany sexual behavior. Relevant to our discussion of the role of reproduction is the fact that these two characteristics are much more likely to accompany sexuality than is pregnancy. These characteristics are *physical pleasure* and *self-disclosure*. Neither of these characteristics is guaranteed to accompany every sexual act, nor will the presence of either always be maximal. They are nonetheless the most common characteristics of human sexuality. I am proposing that they are the reason that sexuality is viewed as important in all human societies.

Physical pleasure as an accompaniment of human sexual activity is only in part related to human physiology. Surely the abundant nerve endings in the genital area aid in any societal attempt to eroticize the genitalia. But more than nerve endings are needed to create an erotic zone. We need only look at the last 20 years to become aware of the vast increase in oral and anal sexuality in America. Nerve endings always existed in the oral and anal body parts, but our culture in the past had not encouraged their use as an erotic zone. It is the cultural labeling of a body part as an erotic zone that greatly enhances the liklihood of that body part being utilized in sexual encounters.

Research on genital responses to erotic stimuli show the power of cultural training. The Kinsey report on female responses to erotica indicated vast male and female differences in erotic responses to such stimuli as nude bodies and viewing genitalia.[27] However, in terms of erotic response to romantic movies, females responded more than males, and both genders were about equal on responses to literary materials. Our sexual scripts for females stress romance and for males stress genital pleasure, and thus such gender differences in response to erotica are not surprising. As our culture has become more equalitarian, these differences have accordingly been muted.[28]

Breasts in some cultures are eroticized and in others they are not. Some cultures stress slimness; some value the rotund body. However, there are a few similarities among cultures in erotic responses; for example, females with wide hips and males with wide shoulders are admired sexually in most all cultures.[29] This reflects the fundamental body silhouette difference between genetic males and females, and thus its centrality in heterosexuality would be expected.

I would speculate that the same societal standards of sexual attraction apply in homosexuality as in heterosexuality. A lesbian would find the hips and breasts of her partner sexually attractive just as a man would in that society. I assume this because homosexuals are socialized into the same standards of sexual attraction as are heterosexuals. The difference is simply that they are attracted to the appeals of the same gender rather than the opposite gender.

The penis and clitoris are also accepted as eroticized in most all cultures. There are exceptions, though. Some cultures attempt to restrict female sexuality in an extreme fashion by performing clitoridectomies, that is, removing the clitoris surgically. This is done today in some African countries.[30] In the nineteenth century and part of the twentieth in the Western world clitoridectomies were at times recommended by medical doctors to control what they felt was the "unnatural" sexual interest of some females.[31] The reader should notice that in these instances, the very fact that such surgery is undertaken indicates a belief in the physical pleasure derivable from the clitoris.

In the Sudan and elsewhere infibulation is practiced today.[32] Not only is part of the clitoris and the labia cut off but the remaining labia are then sewn together to almost completely block access to the vagina. Intercourse becomes very difficult and childbirth requires the opening of these stiches. After delivery the area may be resewn. This is the physiological equivalent of the chastity belt of the European Middle Ages. No clearer indication is needed of the desire to control female sexuality. Related to this is the common belief in such cultures that females are sexually insatiable and infibulation is therefore necessary to control their lust. Thus, these practices distinctly show a belief in the high pleasure value of sexuality.

In America, also, we have evidence of the common awareness of the pleasurable aspects of sexuality even during the Victorian era. Historical studies of the

Victorian era in the United States by Carl Degler indicate much higher female orgasmic rates and pleasure orientations than was formerly believed.[33] Western cultures generally believe that it is the male who is more physically insatiable. Outside the Western World, about 75% of the societies believe that sexual "drives or urges" are equal.[34] Regardless of such differences the awareness that physical pleasure is part of human sexuality is universal even though, as we have seen, some cultures use radical methods to control the pursuit of such pleasure.

Note that I refer to physical pleasure and not necessarily orgasm. The occurrence of orgasm is one type of physical pleasure. The pursuit of orgasm is encouraged in some societies, while in some others (ancient India and China) the delay of orgasm was taught.[35] In summary, although the physiology of the body is essential for pleasure to occur, the way in which the body is utilized is variable and dependent upon the particular society's values. But all societies in their customs, either by direct praise or radical attempts to control, pay homage to the physical pleasure potential in sexual relationships.

The second common characteristic of sexuality is much more overlooked by observers than is physical pleasure. I refer to this characteristics as self-disclosure. This may not strike the reader as an obvious characteristic of sexuality. Nevertheless, upon reflection, I believe most of you will agree that self-disclosure is an essential part of human sexuality. We need first to pay attention to the meaning of the word *disclosure*. It refers to making known to another some previously unknown aspect of oneself. Self-disclosure affords the other person a deeper understanding of what one is like. The more complete the disclosure, the more intimate and private are the things being shown. To disclose, then, means to show the less obvious and apparent aspects of the self and thereby display our inner thoughts and feelings.[36]

In no culture that I know of do people routinely experience the heights of sexual pleasure in public. To be sure, there are ceremonial occasions where such public sexuality occurs. In Polynesia there used to be a traveling group of entertainers, called the Aroia Society, who would put on public sexual displays.[37] But the vast majority of sexual behavior is private even in the most sexually permissive cultures. In fact, I would suggest that one of the appeals of erotic films is that they show in public what most of us keep private. If sexuality were not private, such films would have much less appeal.

As a way of becoming aware of the private nature of sexuality, the reader may be interested in composing his or her own "orgasm-disclosure ratio." I devised this measure as a way of illustrating the private aspect of sexuality. For one time period in your life estimate the number of people who have seen you have an orgasm and divide that by the total number of people you were socially interacting with at that time. To have a ratio of 1.0 a person would have to have had an orgasm in the presence of both genders and all age groups among their friends, acquaintances, and family members. I doubt if there are any such people. Most people would have a very small ratio score, indicating that orgasm is a private act that they do not easily display even to close friends.

Another indicator of the disclosure aspect of sexuality can be seen in the "altered state" quality of human sexuality. Murray Davis has perhaps best developed this sexual concept.[38] From the subjective point of view, the key indicator of sexual arousal is precisely this altered state quality. One way of seeing that is to realize that sexual excitation produces physiological and psychological effects that reduce one's awareness of what is going on outside of the sexual encounter. A hooker who wishes to lift the wallet of a John knows that when he is most excited, he will be least aware of what is going on. We also subjectively know the difference when we move from what Davis called "everyday reality" to the altered state of "erotic reality" which Davis also calls embodiment.

In Western societies, males are expected to move quickly into the zone of erotic reality and become sexually excited. Males are also often expected to move out of that erotic reality shortly after their orgasm. Females, on the other hand, are viewed as being slower to enter the altered state of erotic reality and also to be slower in leaving it. Some of this difference may be physiologically based. Research by Masters and Johnson indicates that after orgasm the male's physiological signs drop sharply from their levels of arousal, whereas the female's physiological signs drop much slower. It is this difference that is one important basis for the female's greater ability to achieve multiple orgasms, for she remains longer at a level close to orgasm.[39] The work of Goldfoot, Hrdy, and Mitchell on nonhuman primates yields similar male-female differences.[40]

Some of this gender difference in humans is due to cultural training that inhibits women from being more assertive sexually at the start of a sexual encounter and encourages men to feel that achieving their orgasm is the primary goal of the sexual encounter. Still, part of this male-female difference does seem to be due to the physiological factors mentioned. Allow me to add here, however, that such biological differences will not be part of sexual disclosure scripts unless the culture of the group encourages that outcome. Reflect on how recent it is in America that we have been aware of the widespread ability of females to achieve multiple orgasms.[41] This is so despite the fact that the ability of females to achieve multiple orgasm is part of female physiology.[42]

In all societies sexuality alters our state of mind. This is a common element in sexuality, regardless of what the sexual scripts are like. It is this altered state that promotes self-disclosure. The altered state means that what was important in everyday life may become unimportant in erotic reality. In erotic reality, the focus is upon the erotic, not upon one's workmates, religious duties, intellectual curiosities, or such. The physical pleasures become primary as one moves more into erotic reality. There is, in this sense, a loss of freedom and flexibility once one is in the altered state of erotic reality. In the physical exchange of a sexual encounter we are altered in ways that lead people to disclose their desires quite differently than they would in a nonsexual interaction involving the very same people. Fundamentally, sexual disclosure consists of showing another your enjoyment of physical pleasure. That very act may well encourage other, even more revealing, forms of disclosure. Thus, some disclosure is almost inevitable—how much occurs depends on a variety of factors.

There is also in sexuality a vulnerability produced in part by the altered state and the disclosures of these private aspects of the self. Some people, in our culture females in particular, often feel the need to have tenderness and affection in order to be willing to enter the altered state of sexuality. Fear of pregnancy may be involved, but it does not seem to be the paramount reason because this difference is present even when women are contraceptively protected. Perhaps the greater social power of males makes them feel less vulnerable and encourages them to feel less of a need for an affectionate setting for their sexuality. Whatever the reasons, the movement from everyday to erotic reality is taken with various degrees of ease in different cultures and by different groups in any one culture. The reasons for this will become more apparent in future chapters.

The key point here is, if one does not take this journey into an altered state, then one has probably not been erotically stimulated and sexual satisfaction is not likely. Although we surely vary by how quickly and how deeply we enter this altered state, it seems clear that it is the doorway to sexuality. If one is thinking of his or her job or children or how to pay the bills, the likelihood of sexual satisfaction is small, for one will still be in everyday reality. The importance of this altered state to one's partner is evidenced by the commonness with which people fake orgasms in order to convince their partner that they are in such an altered state. Note that the best way to fake an orgasm is to act as if one is in an altered state. In all forms of sexuality I believe a good lover is probably defined the same way by most people: A good lover is someone who has learned to take pleasure in the partner's pleasure and thereby aids both himself or herself and the partner in achieving an altered state.

Finally, since that altered state implies displaying actions and feelings that are generally kept private, we do indeed have an act of disclosure that is a basic part of the sexual experience. However, it is important to be clear about the distinction between disclosure and affection. One can be sexually disclosing to someone without being affectionate to that person. Analagously, one can be affectionate to a partner without being sexually disclosing. Casual sexual relations are a prime example of sexual disclosure without deep affection.

This distinction of sexual disclosure and affection is an important one to make. Having made it, though, I must qualify by asserting that one reason that the private-disclosing aspect of sexuality is valued is that it is seen as a catalyst for promoting intimacy and nonsexual self-disclosures. The elemental physical and emotional disclosures of sexuality can promote further and deeper psychic disclosures. This is an outcome of the built-in pleasure and disclosure aspects of sexuality. This potential can be encouraged or discouraged by the people involved and by the society in which they live.

In short, when we assert that sexuality usually contains pleasure and disclosure characteristics, it becomes apparent why sexuality is everywhere viewed as important. This plainly follows if you assume as I do that almost all humans value physical pleasure and the psychic release and intimacy potential of self-disclosure. How many parts of our life can easily produce pleasure and disclosure possibilities? In a few areas like friendship and kinship relationships this may occur. There is a nonsexual but yet physical pleasure aspect to friendship and kinship—hugging and kissing are often involved. There is surely a self-disclosure aspect as well, and this is most often stressed as an essential quality of friendship and kinship.

Sexual relationships like friendship may also be characterized by emotional involvement with the other person, but this is not as central a requirement in sexuality. One can have intercourse with a partner and think only of one's own pleasure—as with a prostitute or a casual partner. Further, one can masturbate and need not have any partner. In this sense sexuality is more of a self-oriented pleasure than is friendship.

This is not to say that friendship does not involve self-orientation but to assert that friendship demands, in virtually all instances, that concern for the other person be shown. No one argues for the superiority of friendship that does not involve serious caring. However, some have argued for the superiority of sexuality without affection because there is then no interference with the pleasure involved by any sense of duty felt toward the other person.[43] So, the mixture of self- and other-focused pleasures is different in friendship and sexuality.

I am not pointing out these difference to label sexuality as selfish and of less value than friendship. The meaning of such a difference depends on one's philosophical assumptions. My philosophical assumption is that all actions are self-oriented, but that some are aimed at gratifications that accrue only to oneself while others are aimed at gratifications that accrue, in addition to oneself, to others. We tend to call the latter actions altruistic and the former selfish, but in my view they both are clearly self-oriented. The difference is that the altruistic person has learned to take pleasure from other people's pleasures, not just from his or her private pleasures.

I believe it is important in a scientific work to make explicit the philosophical assumptions that underly one's positions. My assumptions regarding human behavior are a modified version of hedonism as originally put forth by Jeremy Bentham and elaborated upon by other, more recent philosophers.[44] Basically, this position asserts that all humans seek to avoid pain and to pursue pleasure. This hedonistic philosophical position is quite relevant to my view on the importance of sexuality: It is this self-orientation of human beings that makes physical pleasure and self-disclosure the universal basis for judging sexuality to be important. If we were other-oriented creatures, why would we value such self-oriented pleasures?

Surely we humans are still very much distinguishable from each other, for it makes a great deal of difference as to the specific sources of our pains and pleasures. One way of seeing this point is to classify yourself and others you know on the degree to which each of you has incorporated the pleasures of other people as part of your own pleasures. There are sharp differences in such a comparison, and generally the more altruistic person is more highly valued in a society. But according to this philosophical position, all of us are in one way or another self-oriented despite our differences regarding how we obtain our pleasures. To be sure, this difference is an important one on most people's value hierarchies. But if we fail to see the similarity in self and other orientations that we all share, we may well exaggerate the differences that exist among us.

Certainly sexuality is not alone among life's valuables in its potential rewards, but equally apparent is its special nature and thus its potential influence over our lives. It is the realization of the importance and power of sexuality that induces some societies that value self-oriented pleasures to promote sexuality and some societies that are more fearful of loss of control and less openly hedonistic to seek to restrict sexuality. Nevertheless, both types of societies assert by their actions the importance of human sexuality and their recognition of the pleasure and disclosure aspects of sexual relationships. At the most elementary level, pleasure and disclosure are the building blocks of social relationships. Whether those relationships be kinship, friendship, or sexual—pleasure and disclosure are involved. So, the importance of sexuality rests upon its partial possession of the key ingredients upon which the social relationships in society are founded.

SUMMARY AND CONCLUSIONS

The stage is now set for a sociological analysis of human sexuality. I have defined sexuality as erotic and genital responses produced by the cultural scripts of a society. Furthermore, I have suggested that such cultural scripts are universal because sexuality is everywhere viewed as important and therefore in need of societal regulation of some sort. The basic reason for this importance is that sexuality typically encompasses the elements of physical pleasure and self-disclosure, at least in some rudimentary form. From a societal perspective, pleasure and disclosure are the crucial elements in forming the key relationships in a society, whether they be sexual or otherwise. The precise way that sexuality is expressed will reflect the social system in question. It is apparent that the possibilities are vast and, as we shall see, they include both heterosexual and homosexual forms.

It is important that the reader is aware that I have developed a sociological definition and not a physiological or psychological definition. I am interested in tying sexuality in with human society and not with the human body nor with the human unconscious. Of course, there are connections to physiology and psychology that we must be aware of, and we have already spoken of some of them. But I intend to focus in this book upon societal linkages and leave to others the task of developing connections to these other areas.

There is one exercise in imagination that I believe will give the reader more of a feeling for the important linkages of society to sexuality and set the stage for the chapters that follow. Try to imagine a world without sexuality. Suppose that children were bred in laboratories by scientific means and humans had no erotic feelings. The genital area was to be used only for elimination. How would that alter our world? I think the answer is—immensely! We would, for example, have no more political scandals concerning homosexual or heterosexual liaisons of politicians. We would have no such thing as sexual jealousy, and people living together would not be concerned that an outside friendship might develop into a sexual relationship. One's physical appearance could not be used as a lure or as a means of materially advancing oneself. In these and many other ways much of our political, economic, and intimate life would be radically altered.

I do not think an increase in gender equality would be a necessary outcome of a world without sexuality. By removing sexuality from marriage, one may remove some of the special ties of females to males, and this may remove one of the factors that restrains the exploitation of one gender by the other. The very tie of men and women with the physical and psychic rewards of sexuality may be a major impediment to more abusive male dominance. Thus, sexuality may well, in part, operate as a force for equality. We all know that sexuality can be used to promote inequality, but its equalitarian possibilities must also be kept in mind. In this same vein it would be worth thinking about the contribution to same-gender welfare that homosexual relationships make. Homosexual ties also promote a sense of shared welfare that may mute conflict.

Once we accept the societal importance of sexuality, the question that is primary in a sociological approach is, what are the specific ways in which sexuality links to other parts of human society? I believe there are three major areas of social life wherein sexuality is closely intertwined in every human society. These three parts of human society determine the ways in which sexuality will be integrated in that society and the particular sexual attitudes and behaviors that will be accepted. In formal terms, these three areas are the kinship system, the power structure, and the ideology of that society.[45]

It is not the entirety of each of these three areas that is centrally linked to sexuality. Rather, it is a specific aspect of each of these three institutionalized areas that is central. Thus in terms of kinship, I will, in the next chapter, examine marital sexual jealousy. Marriage is, of course, a part of our kinship system and where it joins sexual jealousy is a most revealing point of entry for our purposes. In terms of power, the most intimate linkage is with gender roles. Gender roles will reflect the power differentials of males and females that exist in a society and thereby afford us a direct path potentially connecting sexuality with power. Finally, ideologies put forth the group's conception of what is normal human behavior. Since sexuality is an important part of all societies, ideologies will define normality partially in sexual terms. We will explore how such conceptions of sexual normality shape our notions concerning homosexuality and erotica. Thus, when I say the key linkages of sexuality are to kinship, power, and ideology, what I specifically mean is that sexuality is linked to marital jealousy, gender roles, and notions of normality. These linkages overlap with each other in many places. These overlapping areas, too, will be brought out in the chapters that follow. I stress the broader areas from whence these more specific foci derive because near these central sources may well be additional linkages that others may wish to explore. But now it is time for our exploration to begin!

SELECTED REFERENCES AND COMMENTS

1. The five textbooks that did have a definition of sexuality noted in the index were

Masters, William, Virginia Johnson, and Robert Kolodny, *Human Sexuality*. Boston: Little, Brown, 1982.

Diamond, Milton, and Arno Karlin, *Sexual Decisions*. Boston: Little, Brown, 1980.

Luria, Zella, and Mitchel Rose, *Psychology of Human Sexuality*. New York: John Wiley, 1979.

Hyde, Janet, *Understanding Human Sexuality*. New York: McGraw-Hill, 1979.

Sandler, Jack, Marilyn Meyerson, and Bill N. Kinder, *Human Sexuality: Current Perspectives*. Tampa, Fla.: Mariner, 1980.

2. *SIECUS Report*, vol. 8, no. 3, January 1980. Human Sciences Press, New York.

3. To young people today it may seem that the· concept of gender has always existed. In reality it is a very new concept that John Money states he introduced in 1955. However, Money's current usage combines gender identity and gender role into one concept, and that is not my usage. For the sake of conceptual clarity, I would separate these concepts. The widespread use of gender role as a definition of the roles culture creates for males and females is really confined to the last 15 or 20 years. For Money's perspective see

Money, John, "The Conceptual Neutering of Genders and the Criminalization of Sex," *Archives of Sexual Behavior*, vol. 14, no. 3 (June 1985), pp. 279-290.

4. The term *sexual* is an adjective that indicates that something possesses the characteristics of sexuality, for example, a particular act, a particular object, or a particular story.

5. Hempel, Carl G., "Fundamental of Concept Formation in Empirical Sciences," pp. 1-93 in *International Encyclopedia of Unified Science* (vol. 2). Chicago: University of Chicago Press, 1952.

6. The term *sensual* is often used in connection with sexuality. I conceive of the sensual as including all responses of the senses. In this broad sense it would include the appreciation of a sunset as well as an orgasm. In the interests of clarity we must be aware that not all sensual responses are sexual, but all sexual responses are sensual, for they do involve the senses. Sensual, then, is a such broader concept. Like love, the sensual may be emphasized in sexuality by massage and in other ways, but the essence of sexuality is not the sensual nor the possible connection with love. The core of sexuality in my conceptualization is the societal scripting of the pleasure and disclosure aspects of human interactions involving erotic and genital responses. Keep reading this chapter for the full details!

7. The concept of scripts derives from the work of William Simon and John Gagnon. Their most recent statement of their position is contained in

Simon, William, and John Gagnon, "Sexual Scripts: Permanence and Change," *Society*, vol. 22, no. 1 (November/December 1984), pp. 53-60.

Their concept of script is somewhat complex. In this most recent piece they distinguish between cultural scenarios, interpersonal scripts, and intrapsychic scripts. I do not wish to get involved in the intricacies of these fine distinctions, for they are still in the process of being developed by these authors. Suffice it to say that I use the term *cultural scripts* basically to mean those ideas shared by most members of a group concerning how people should behave and think and feel in any area of social life. *Sexual scripts* are those cultural scripts relating to our erotic and genital responses.

Alternatively, I believe the older concepts of interaction models or social roles are a close equivalent to the concept of cultural scripts. An adherent of "script theory" might want to become more involved in the fine distinctions that can be made, but I leave that to others. I use the term *script* primarily because it has a face validity, a clarity of meaning that is useful. Basically, the term *script* implies that we are taught a way to behave and think and feel, and that is the essence of all cultural training. It is because it fits so well with clear sociological thinking that I utilize it here. Gagnon and Simon's approach is not a macrosociological one but rather a micro level approach stressing social psychological factors relevant more to the individual than to large social structures. For an early statement of their concept of scripts, see

Gagnon, John, and William Simon, *Sexual Conduct.* Chicago: Aldine, 1973.

8. Schmidt, Gunter, "Male-Female Differences in Sexual Arousal and Behavior during and after Exposure to Sexually Explicit Stimuli," *Archives of Sexual Behavior,* 4 (July 1975), pp. 353-365.

There are many other articles on this topic. For sexuality research on this topic and others, I recommend two journals: *Journal of Sex Research* and *Archives of Sexual Behavior.*

9. The National Opinion Research Center's polls indicate that since 1975 about 70% of the adult population in the United States feels that there are conditions under which premarital intercourse is acceptable. The National Survey of Family Growth (NSFG), Cycle 111, entailed interviews with a representative sample of almost 8,000 women aged 15-44 and found that 21% of the brides marrying in the late 1970s delayed first intercourse until marriage. In the early 1960s the comparable figure was 48%. See

U.S. Department of Health and Human Services, National Center for Health Statistics, C.A. Bachrach and M.C. Horn, "Marriage and First Intercourse, Marital Dissolution, and Remarriage, U.S., 1982," *Advance Data from Vital and Health Statistics,* no. 107. Hyattsville, Md.: Public Health Service, April 1985.

10. Harlow, Harry F., "The Heterosexual Affection System in Monkeys," *American Psychologist,* vol. 17 (January 1962), pp. 1-9.

Harlow published a large number of articles on his classic research on this topic. Several are in the American *Psychologist* and others are in more popular form in the *Scientific American.*

11. Schwendinger, Julia R., and Herman Schwendinger, *Rape and Inequality.* Beverly Hills, Calif.: Sage Publications, 1983.

12. Groth, A. Nicholas, *Men Who Rape: The Psychology of the Offender.* New York: Plenum Press, 1979.

13. Another example of unintended and unwanted outcomes occurs when parents who are afraid that their daughters will engage in coitus restrict contraceptive information. This behavior increases the chance that if the daughter engages in coitus, she will become pregnant. For discussion of this point see

Rodman, Hyman, Susan H. Lewis, and Saralyn B. Griffith, *The Sexual Rights of Adolescents: Competence, Vulnerability, and Parental Control.* New York: Columbia University Press, 1984.

14. I have discussed this trend in Chapter 11 of

Reiss, Ira L., *Family Systems in America* (3rd ed.). New York: Holt, Rinehart & Winston, 1980.

15. For a brief overview of trends in premarital and other areas of sexuality in America, see

Reiss, Ira L., "Human Sexuality in Sociological Perspective," pp. 39-50 in K.K. Holmes et al. (eds.), *Sexually Transmitted Diseases.* New York: McGraw-Hill, 1984.

16. Although there can be a theoretical bridge between a psychological and a sociological approach to sexuality, so far no one has constructed such an edifice in a lasting fashion. Some writings that bear upon such a project are listed here:

Abramson, P.R., *The Sexual System: A Theory of Human Sexual Beahvior.* Orlando: Academic Press, 1982.

Mosher, D.L., "Three Dimensions of Depth and Involvement in Human Sexual Response," *The Journal of Sex Research,* vol. 16 (February 1980), pp. 1-42.

Storms, M.D., "Theories of Sexual Orientation," *Journal of Personality and Social Psychology,* vol. 38, (1980), pp. 783-792.

17. Suggs, Robert C., *Marquesan Sexual Behavior.* San Diego: Harcourt Brace Jovanovich, 1966.

Marshall, Donald, and Robert C. Suggs, *Human Sexual Behavior.* New York: Basic Books, 1971.

Elwin Verrier, *The Muria and Their Ghotul.* New York: Oxford University Press, 1947.

18. Harlow, Harry F., "The Heterosexual Affection System in Monkeys," *American Psychologist,* vol. 17, (January 1962), pp. 1-9.

Harlow's work with monkeys illustrates the point that our physiological equipment, while essential, needs to be programmed by the society in which we live.

19. Messenger, John C., "Sex and Repression in an Irish Folk Community," Chapter 1 in Donald S. Marshall and Robert C. Suggs (eds.), *Human Sexual Behavior.* New York: Basic Books, 1971.

Davenport, William, "Sexual Patterns and Their Regulation in a Society of the SW Pacific," Chapter 8 in Frank A. Beach (ed.), *Sex and Behavior.* New York: John Wiley, 1965.
Although both Inis Baeg and East Bay are low on sexual permissiveness, they are radically different in that East Bay allows older males to have anal intercourse with teenage males and allows homosexual masturbation among young males as a means of restricting heterosexual coitus. The very thought of that would send shock waves through Inis Baeg and perhaps other places too!

20. Gorer, Geoffrey, *Himalayan Village: An Account of the Lepchas of Sikkim* (2nd ed.). New York: Basic Books, 1967.

Elwin, Verrier, *The Baiga.* London: John Murray, 1939.

Goodale, Jane, *Tiwi Wives.* Seattle: University of Washington Press, 1971.
I choose these three accounts because they concern distinct societies and they are, relatively speaking, complete.

21. There are several books that are useful to examine for an understanding of child rearing in Polynesia. For an in-depth account read

Levy, Robert, *Tahitians.* Chicago: University of Chicago Press, 1973.
For a less scholarly account that covers all of Polynesia see

Danielsson, Bengt, *Love in the South Seas.* New York: Reynal, 1956.

Ritchie, Jane, and James Ritchie, "Polynesian Child Rearing: An Alternative Model," *Alternative Lifestyles,* vol. 5, no. 3, (Spring 1983), pp. 126-141.

The group nature of reproduction is brought out by Paige and Paige. They point out how reproductive rituals related to menarche, male puberty, childbirth, and menstruation are intended to persuade others as to the value of what is exchanged at marriage.

Paige, K.E,, and J.M. Paige, *The Politics of Reproductive Ritual.* Berkeley: University of California Press, 1981.

22. Levy, Robert, *Tahitians.* Chicago: University of Chicago Press, 1973, pp. 474–483.

23. Two books are worth examining on the Trobriand view of sexuality and pregnancy. The classic work was done by Malinowski almost 70 years ago. The more recent examination was done by Weiner some 15 years ago. Weiner qualifies Malinowski's views somewhat, but not in any way that affects my presentation on this point.

Malinowski, Bronislaw, *The Sexual Life of Savage in North-western Melanesia.* New York: Harvest Books, 1929.

Weiner, Annette, *Women of Value: Men of Renown.* Austin: University of Texas Press, 1976.

24. Goodale, Jane, *Tiwi Wives.* Seattle: University of Washington Press, 1971.

Berndt, Ronad M., and Catherine H. Berndt, *Sexual Behavior in Western Arnhem Land.* New York: Viking Fund, 1951.

25. Elwin is one of those rare anthropologists who have written extensively and carefully on sexual customs. He lived for many years among the Baiga, an aboriginal tribe in central India.

Elwin, Verrier, *The Baiga.* London: John Murray, 1939.

Berndt, Ronald M., and Catherine H. Berndt, *Sexual Behavior in Western Arnhem Land.* New York: Viking Fund, 1951.

27. Kinsey, Alfred C., Wardell Pomeroy, Clyde Martin, and Paul Gebhard, *Sexual Behavior in the Human Female,* pp. 651-678. Philadelphia: Saunders, 1953.

28. I have already mentioned the work of Gunter Schmidt in West Germany concerning gender similarities in responses to erotica (see note 8). In a recent article he and his colleagues compare the 1966 student sample with a 1981 West German student sample and report much greater gender similarity. One area where large male-female differences remained is rates of masturbation. Interestingly, in almost all primates males masturbate more than females.

Clement, Ulrich, Gunter Schmidt, and Margret Kruse, "Changes in Sex Differences in Sexual Behavior: A Replication of a Study on West German Students (1966-1981)." *Archives of Sexual Behavior,* vol. 13, no. 2, (March 1984), pp. 99-120.

29. Ford, C.S., and F.A. Beach, *Patterns of Sexual Behavior.* New York: Harper & Row, 1951.

30. For a brief account of one African group that practices clitoridectomy see

Schneider, Harold K., "Romantic Love among the Turu," Chapter 3 in Donald S. Marshall and Robert C. Suggs, (eds.), *Human Sexual Behavior.* New York: Basic Books, 1971.
For an interesting analysis of this custom see
Lyons, Harriet, "Anthropologists, Moralities, and Relativities: The Problem of Genital Mutilations," *The Canadian Review of Sociology and Anthropology,* vol. 18, (November 1981), pp. 499-518.

31. Comfort, Alex, *The Anxiety Makers: Some Curious Preoccupations of the Medical Profession.* London: Thomas Nelson, 1967.

32. A book on this topic was recently finished by H. Lightfoot Klein based

on her studies in the Sudan. She presented a paper on this topic at the 1984 meetings of the International Academy of Sex Research in Cambridge, England.

33. For a full account of a remarkable study of nineteenth-century women carried out by a woman physician (Dr. Mosher), see the book by Degler and also the book by Dr. Mosher:

Mosher, Clelia, *The Mosher Survey.* New York:Arno Press, 1980.

Degler, Carl, *At Odds: Women and the Family in America from the Revolution to the Present.* Oxford: Oxford University Press, 1980.

34. Whyte, Martin K., *The Status of Women in Preindustrial Societies.* Princeton, N.J.: Princeton University Press, 1978. (See p. 72.)

35. For a brief scholarly historical account see the book by Bullough listed here. For a popular account but with good references and glossary see the Douglas and Slinger book:

Bullough, Vern L., *Sexual Variance in Society and History.* New York: John Wiley, 1976.

Douglas, Nik, and Penny Slinger, *Sexual Secrets: The Alchemy of Ecstasy.* New York: Destiny Books, 1979.

36. The concept of self-disclosure is used widely in the social sciences. I used it as part of my "wheel theory" explaining how love develops. Sidney Jourard used it later in a very influential book. See

Reiss, Ira L., "Toward a Sociology of the Heterosexual Love Relationship," *Marriage and Family Living,* vol. 22 (May 1960), pp. 139-145.

Jourard, Sidney M., *Self Disclosure: An Experimental Analysis of the Transparent Self.* New York: John Wiley, 1968.

37. Danielsson, Bengt, *Love in the South Seas.* New York: Reynal, 1956.

38. Davis, Murray, *Smut: Erotic Reality/Obscene Ideology.* Chicago: University of Chicago Press, 1983.

39. Masters, William H., and Virginia F. Johnson, *Human Sexual Response.* Boston: Little, Brown, 1966.

40. Goldfoot, David, H. Westerborg-Van-Loon, W. Groeneveld, and A. Koos Slob, "Behavioral and Physiological Evidence of Sexual Climax in the Female Stump-Tailed Macawue (Macaca Arctoides)," *Science,* vol. 208 (June 27, 1980), pp. 1477-1479.

Hrdy, Sarah Blaffer, *The Woman that Never Evolved.* Cambridge, Mass.: Harvard University Press, 1981. (See especially Chapter 8.)

Mitchell, G., *Behavioral Sex Differences in Non Human Primates.* New York: Van Nostrand Reinhold, 1979.

41. The public awareness of multiple orgasm by females followed the publication of Masters and Johnson's 1966 book (see note 39). It is significant that Kinsey's mention of this was largely overlooked. It may be that the social climate was not ready for such a revised view of female sexuality until the 1960s.

42. Multiple orgasm has been recognized in much of the world outside the West for a long time. In parts of Polynesia the male and female are both trained at about the time of puberty in techniques that will encourage female multiple orgasm. See

Marshall, Donald S., "Sexual Behavior on Mangaia," Chapter 5 in Donald S. Marshall and Robert C. Suggs (eds.), *Human Sexual Behavior: Variations in the Ethnographic Spectrum.* New York: Basic Books, 1971.

43. Vannoy, Russell, *Sex without Love.* Buffalo: Prometheus Books, 1980. On this same topic see also

Schofield, Michael, *Promiscuity.* London: Victor Gollancz, 1976.

44. For articles on hedonism as put forth by Jeremy Bentham in the eighteenth century and by other philosophers, I recommend several of the articles in

Edward, Paul (ed.), *The Encyclopedia of Philosophy.* New York: Macmillan, 1967.

45. The process by which I arrived at kinship, power, and ideology as the three areas of major linkage with sexuality was a lengthy one. I took extensive notes on all the readings I did and then integrated my notes into propositions aimed at explaining how sexuality operated in various societies. I composed over 60 such propositions and then examined them to see what common societal structures were involved in those propositions. The three areas of kinship, power, and ideology were by far the most common linkages in my propositions, and that is why they were chosen.

CHAPTER THREE

THE DELICATE BOUNDARY

Sexual Jealousy

POPULAR EXPLANATIONS OF SEXUAL JEALOUSY

Probably the most popular view today about sexual jealousy pictures jealousy as due to personal feelings of insecurity as reflected in lack of trust, low ego strength, and excessive dependency. This is a psychological view, and it implies that one can overcome jealousy by altering those feelings of insecurity that lead one to feel threatened by an "outsider."

In line with this approach, Larry Constantine has proposed that one effective way to manage jealousy is to realize how unique and irreplaceable we each are.[1] No one in the world is identical to any one of us (even identical twins have differences). Therefore, we need not be so concerned that our mates or partners will find someone who will replace us, for no one can really do that. This perspective, I contend, would satisfy only those who are desperately searching for reasons to feel more secure. Although it is true that we cannot be precisely replaced, it is equally true that we can be *improved* upon. To be sure, we may be unique, but not necessarily in the most admirable fashion. This orientation is thus hardly a consolation to those realistically searching for reasons to feel secure.

Still, there is evidence that would support the connection of personal insecurity to feelings of jealousy.[2] Insecure individuals may generally be near the top of the level of jealousy that is customary in a particular society, but my point here is that the insecurity level in a society does not establish the customary level of jealousy in that society. Accordingly, the limit of such a psychological perspective is that it does little to explain why societies relatively equal on level of personal insecurity can differ so much on jealousy expectations. To illustrate, my impression is that Spain endorses the expression of jealousy more than does Sweden. Can we simply say that this is due to a higher proportion of insecure people in Spain? I think not. Rather, the level of jealousy can be understood by reference to the norms of that society and to the ways in which important relationships are structured into the basic societal institutions. Psychological explanations would be valuable mainly for comparing individuals within one society or group. I believe a societal-level explanation, not a psychological explanation, is needed for understanding the variation in jealousy that exists *among* different groups of people.

Before putting forth my own view, let me deal with a competitive societal-level view. A traditional Marxist conception is that jealousy results from the capitalistic tendency to treat the person with less power as a piece of property that we possess and therefore have the right to control. This perspective emphasizes that husbands feel they own their wives' bodies, and this belief leads to strong jealousy reactions by husbands. I would not deny that there is an element of truth in such a Marxist perspective, but I would contend that it explains only a limited amount of societal differences in jealousy. I would prefer to accept the linkage of male power with male jealousy as the general proposition and not bind myself to the proposition that such male power expresses itself in a property view of women. That is but one way that male power may express itself. Such power may also express itself in the general attempt to achieve whatever one desires, and such desires may well include maintaining the emotional commitment of one's wife. Viewing women as property is not necessary as a means of exercising power. One can view women as subject to male control but as valuable creatures in their own right, with their own powers, who should be treated quite differently than one's property. Some Western societies have conceptualized women very much this way.

Let me elaborate. How do we explain jealousy in communal societies like the Israeli kibbutzim? They are not taught to conceive of people as property, for they are not capitalistic and they are communal. In fact, many of these kibbutzim are Marxist and would explicitly oppose such a property view of people.[3] Further, the property explanation would not account for jealousy in the many hunting and gathering societies that lack private property. Finally, in capitalistic societies property is controlled predominantly by males, and so even there how do we explain jealousy by females regarding their husband?

We in America surely live in a capitalistic society, and yet it would be a caricature of reality to state that married couples think of each other as property. Do we also think of parents and friends as property? We can become jealous about the actions of these people also. There was more truth to the "property" notion in the middle ages, when the doctrine of coverture demanded that upon marriage the wife turn over all her property to her husband. But that doctrine has little meaning in Western societies today. There surely are possessive attitudes and attempts to control a mate's sexual behavior, but I do not believe this is because we view our mates as our property. This is not to deny the importance of male power in the explanation of jealousy, but to assert that male power affects jealousy in more ways than the property view of women permits us to envision. Thus, it seems that the narrow property explanation of jealousy distorts reality to fit the procrustean bed of orthodox Marxist ideology. I will expand upon my own views and findings concerning how power affects jealousy later in this chapter.

THE SOCIAL NATURE OF JEALOUSY

In the interest of clarity it is always well to begin with a definition. *From a sociological or group perspective, jealousy is a boundary-setting mechanism for what the group feels are important relationships.* That is, jealousy functions in the social system as a force aimed at defining the legitimate boundaries of important relationships such as marriage. When those normative boundaries are violated, jealousy occurs and indexes the anger and hurt that are expected to be activated by a violation of an important norm.

Dovetailing with the societal-level definition, we can define jealousy from an interpersonal or social psychological perspective as a response to a socially defined threat by an outside person to an important relationship.[4] The knowledge that jealousy can occur is by itself a factor that other individuals have to reckon with if they seek to disturb the legitimate socially defined boundaries of an established relationship. Of course, there is no guarantee that because there are jealousy reactions, violations will not occur. Rather, jealousy norms are indicative of the existence of strong beliefs about the legitimate boundaries of a particular relationship.[5]

Finally, we can look at jealousy from a personal, that is, subjective, emotional perspective and define jealousy as a *secondary* emotion.[6] That is, it consists of a situational labeling of one of the more primary emotions such as anger or fear. When one interviews people and asks them what they are feeling when they say they are jealous, they most often respond by saying they feel angry or fearful. It seems that when a felt threat to a marital sexual relationship is interpreted as jealousy, it is because that society teaches one to label as jealousy angry and fearful feelings that occur in such situations.

It is informative to note that in many societies around the world women are more likely to react to jealousy with depression and men more likely to react with anger. Several anthropologists have noted this gender difference. This is not surprising in a male-dominant culture, where one would expect women to turn anger toward themselves and thereby produce depression. However, even in more equalitarian societies it seems that the cultural emphasis on women not expressing aggression may prevail even if less common. Alice Schlegel, for example, in discussing the relatively equalitarian Hopi Indians in Arizona says:[7]

> Sexual infidelity is also regarded as a violation of trust, and the typical response to it, particularly among women, is despondency and depression. (Schlegel, 1979: pp. 132–133)

In a recent study of seven European countries Bram Buunk found analogous differences between men and women.[8] He reports that men were given more autonomy in all seven societies and thus were allowed to be more independent of the constraints of any relationship. Buunk reports that in the more democratic societies in his sample (the United States, the Netherlands, Ireland, and Mexico), women were given more autonomy than they were in the less democratic nations (the Soviet Union, Hungary, and Yugoslavia). Nonethless, men were granted higher levels of free choice even in democratic societies. In part, the difference between the democratic and other nations was due to the greater affluence in the democracies, which produced an overall higher general belief in autonomy. These findings would lead one to believe that, in general, females would be less permitted to provoke male jealousy and also less able to restrain their men from actions that make women jealous. The feelings of powerlessness that this situation produces in women is likely a major reason for depression as a common female response to jealousy.[9]

I believe that boundary limitations on relationships apply to all relationships that are thought to be important in a culture, whether they are sexual or not. Close friendships are defined in terms of what interactions with others are acceptable.[10] Kinship relationships, other than with mates, such as with parents and siblings are also defined in ways that indicate when each of those relationships is to have priority over other relationships. An illustration of how some relationships are given priority over others can be seen in cultures that have patrilocal residence in which the husband brings his bride to live in or near his parents' home. The husband's mother most often demands that the groom give first allegiance to her and not to the new bride. In our culture the marital pair would live alone and would generally give their relationship priority over relationships with parents. In both situations, any violation of those priority boundaries could lead to feelings of jealousy.

Our interest here, though, is not in all types of jealousy. Instead, we shall focus upon sexual jealousy in marriage. Nevertheless, what we say may well have applicability to nonsexual forms of jealousy as well as to sexual jealousy in homosexual and heterosexual nonmarital situations. I choose to focus upon marital relationships because I believe that sexual jealousy is universally present there. An even more important reason is that the marital focus reveals much about the nature of the close tie of sexuality to kinship in cultures around the world. Thus, by this exploration we gain further insight into one way that sexuality is linked to kinship structures in all societies.

The proposition I am asserting here is that all human societies are aware of sexual jealousy in marriage and have cultural ways of dealing with it. Furthermore, although some cultures have surely learned how to cope effectively with sexual jealousy more than others, no culture has learned how to eliminate sexual jealousy. It follows, then, that the societal linkage of jealousy to marital sexuality would not be an unknown connection in any culture, though the strength of jealousy and the value placed upon it do vary considerably for reasons we shall soon explore.

Why should there be a universal connection of jealousy to marital sexuality? One key reason is that, as discussed in Chapter 2, all societies place high importance on human sexual relationships. Now not all specific sexual relationships need be highly valued, but the high value of sexuality in general is supported everywhere. Given this fact, when we link sexuality with a kinship institution like marriage, which is also viewed as an important part of society, we make it inevitable that norms concerning marital sexual jealousy will evolve and will set limits on sexual relationships with outsiders.

Let me emphasize that a society can, and many do, define *some* nonmarital sexual relationships as unimportant and that in such relationships boundary limits are very vague and jealousy is unlikely to develop. The classic example would be prostitution. A man would not likely feel jealous if he saw a friend with the same prostitute that he had just left. Yet if a man saw his friend enter his house to have sexual relations with his wife, this surely would be evaluated differently. So it is predominantly those sexual relationships that are considered important that are ringed with the alarm system of jealousy.

The essential point underlying my thinking here is that since marriage and sexuality are nowhere matters of indifference, marital sexuality will be "protected" by boundaries "armed" with jealousy norm sensors. As the reader will soon discover, some of these boundaries include the acceptance of other sexual partners besides the mate; yet the priority of marriage is still promoted by these broader, but still clearly defined, boundaries.

Ralph Hupka's research on marital sexual jealousy in 92 cultures (80 of which are part of the Standard Sample) is the only extensive cross-cultural source of such data of which I am aware.[11] One of the most powerful predictors of jealousy in his research was the emphasis placed on the importance of marriage. The greater that emphasis, the greater the jealousy response. In all 92 cultures, he found evidence of sexual jealousy in marriage. He reports that in all his cultures, the husband was permitted to attack his wife physically if he found her in the act of intercourse with an unsanctioned male. These findings support my assertions concerning the universal presence of marital sexual jealousy and its roots in the importance placed upon marriage and sexuality. We will, later in this chapter, use more of Hupka's data to try to account for differences in the extent of marital sexual jealousy in various societies, but for now let's examine the evidence supporting the universality of marital sexual jealousy.

In addition to Hupka's data, we can at this time further consider the universality of marital sexual jealousy by examining a few very distinctive cultures and some relevant marital systems to see if marital sexual jealousy fits into these societies. These societies are unusual enough to act as good test cases for the universality notion of marital sexual jealousy.

One such unusual Western culture is that of Inis Baeg, off the coast of Ireland, where Messenger informs us that sexuality is treated as extremely dangerous and as something to be discouraged and not openly discussed.[12] Messenger believes that women in this society are generally not even aware of their potential for orgasm. In less extreme form this negative cultural approach to sexuality was widespread elsewhere in the Western world until a generation ago.

Remember that even in such a restrictive society sexuality is felt to be important; that is, it is a matter of some concern to the society even though that concern focuses on ways of controlling and restricting sexuality. In addition, that society, like all societies, values a marital union; and when its restrictive views of sexuality are linked with the importance the society places on marriage, we have the makings of a very strong jealousy boundary surrounding marital sexuality.

At the opposite end of the permissiveness continuum are the many societies all over the non-Western world where sexuality is highly valued and encouraged. In such cases, we may well ask why any single sexual relationship would be valued by an individual in such highly permissive cultures. But we must not forget that in such societies, one's overall sexual life is considered very important—even though any one partner may not be thought of as essential. Because of the value placed upon sexuality any action that interfers with sexual activity by luring away a current, even though casual, partner might well arouse jealousy, for although the partner or partners may not be highly valued, the activity is. Such cultures also value marital relationships, and thus sexual relations in marriage would be given boundaries even though in sexually permissive societies those boundaries might be somewhat more fluid and allow for other sexual partners under more conditions.

In order to examine the evidence further, let us look at one of the most sexually permissive cultures, the Marquesas on the eastern edge of Polynesia. We find Suggs reporting thus:[13]

> Extramarital exploits are most carefully concealed in most cases, but news generally leaks out. . . . Extramarital relations, if discovered, usually arouse extreme manifestations of sexual jealousy (Tomakou) in the injured party. Wives who are known or suspected to have had extramarital relations are generally beaten by their husbands. . . . Women who suspect husbands of being unfaithful respond by adopting a behavior pattern in which they display moods of depression and/or shrewish irritability. . . . [One informant's wife] spent a day sobbing intermittently, saying that he no longer loved her. . . . Since then [ordered him] . . . to leave the house . . . and go to the other woman. (Suggs, 1971: pp. 119–120)

Similarly, in northern Australia in the highly sexually permissive Goulbourn Island area studied by the Berndts, we find reports of how a husband reacted when he discovered his wife having coitus with another man:[14]

> The husband suspecting that his wife was having a liaison, had followed her tracks and eventually, hidden behind a clump of bushes, observed the two of them copulating. And he said to himself, "This woman doesn't like me; she likes him better than me." (Berndt and Berndt, 1951: p. 202)

Thus, it seems certain that there are in these highly sexually permissive cultures marital sexual relationships that are felt to be important and inviolate. This is so even though the emphasis and meaning of love in these societies varies a great deal from that of the Western world.

Another interesting area to examine is polygamy, that is, kinship systems wherein there are multiple mates of at least one gender. Here, one might reason that since it is acceptable to have multiple mates, then sexual jealousy must have been eliminated within the marriage. To check this expectation let us examine the operation of polygyny, by far the most common form of polygamy.[15] Polygyny is the marriage of one man with more than one woman.

The usual way of avoiding overall jealousy among multiple wives of the man is to invoke some clear distinction among the several wives. This can be done by making the first wife dominant over the others and by giving her veto power in the choice of additional wives. Furthermore, new wives, especially if they are not sisters, are most often housed in separate huts with their respective children. In addition, the rules of polygyny usually set down routinization of sequential visits to the various wives so that an unaccepted sexual focus on one wife will be avoided. To illustrate, in many such polygynous systems, if a husband slept two nights in a row with one wife, he would have seriously breached the norms of marital sexuality.

So, even in societies with legitimate multiple mates, there is awareness of the difficulty of avoiding sexual jealousy and fixed sexual sequences are often normative. Even in imperial China the emperor was restricted to a fixed order of sexual relations with his various wives.[16] In the Near East, the historical accounts regarding the wives of Muhammad indicate the clear presence of jealousy. A search through Greek, Roman, and other civilizations reveals the same full awareness of marital sexual jealousy and the presence of a set of customs dealing with its management. The power of sexuality to evoke jealousy is easy to demonstrate historically as well as cross-culturally in polygynous as well as monogamous marriages.

The connection of jealousy to polygyny is made more apparent by the fact that in Africa and elsewhere the word for polygyny and jealousy is often the same. Schapera mentions this in his book on the Kgatla section of the Tswana tribe among the Bantu in Africa:[17]

> The word lefufa, whose primary meaning is "jealousy", is also used for "polygamy", an extension that Kgatla explain by pointing out how seldom it is that co-wives can live together amicably! (Schapera, 1941: pp. 279–280)

Our examination of polygyny reveals that jealousy customs operate in ways that may minimize negative emotions among the kin and friends of married people. The married individuals are intimately related to other marital units through various kinship ties (parents, children, clan members, and so forth), and these relations can easily be disturbed by unsanctioned sexual relationships. This does not mean that jealousy is used as a reason to stop all such extramarital relationships; rather, it tends to restrict those additional relationships that are thought to be disruptive of kinship and friendship ties.

My assertion of the universality of marital sexual jealousy contradicts the popular relativistic view of all customs which usually contends that "it all depends on the society." Such a perspective implies the existence of cultures where marital sexual jealousy does not occur. If this were so, then my notion of the universal linkage of sexual jealousy to marriage would be in error. Thus, it is strategic to examine now two cultures where it has been claimed jealousy does not exist.

One of the cultures that some have claimed lacks jealousy is the Lepcha in the Himalayan Mountains, studied by Geoffrey Gorer. Gorer reported that the Lepcha language has no specific word for jealousy. Some observers took the lack of a word for jealousy as evidence that marital sexual jealousy does not exist. But I believe the account by Gorer indicates that jealousy situations are recognized and are emotionally disturbing, although seemingly less so than in the majority of cultures. To examine this point, let me quote Gorer:[18]

> When I presented hypothetical jealous situations to Lepchas and asked them what their feelings would be, the greater number say they would be angry; but this word, sak-lyak, does not carry very strong emotional connotations; it is the word used by parents if their children are naughty, or by workmen if they come across an unexpected difficulty in their work. . . . [Nevertheless,] married women who show marked preference even for perfectly hereditable spouses, and married men who show preference for women other than their wives produce and have produced many disquieting situations, sometimes leading to open disputes and even suicide. (Gorer, 1967: pp. 162–163)

So, even in this very unusual culture with its high degree of sharing and its strong norms against aggression and its direct teachings against jealous reactions, we still find that the jealous reaction makes sense to them, although it is controlled and in part minimized. One control on the emotion of jealousy is the Lepcha norm that extramarital affairs should be kept casual and emotionally unimportant to the person involved. In effect, this norm defines one aspect of the protective boundary this culture places around marital sexuality. This restriction reflects the desire that marriage have first priority, and this is so despite the fact that the Lepchas do not have a very romantic view of marriage.

In addition, in the Lepcha marriage ceremony the woman is told, "If you had any other lovers you must leave them" (p. 336). When you interpret this demand together with the Lepchas' admission of reacting negatively when their mate gets involved sexually with others, and their norms regarding a low priority for extramarital partners, then it does seem that we have additional evidence for the existence of normative sexual jealousy boundaries in Lepcha marriage.

But what about the fact that the Lepcha lack a word for jealousy? That lack does not necessarily mean they are unaware of that emotion or have no norms concerning jealousy, but rather it may indicate that culturally they are trying to contain jealousy. A comparable situation prevails in Tahiti.[19] There is no Tahitian word for deep feelings or emotions. The Tahitians know about such emotions but they want very much to control them, and so their language reflects this desire in its avoidance of that concept.

On this point, I should mention that the Lepcha have no word for puberty, either. They surely recognize the growth of breasts, pubic hair, and musculature but do not stress this period, and so they have no separate term for the entire complex of changes associated with puberty. They view puberty as a natural consequence of having intercourse as a child and do not give puberty any separate existence.

Lack of a term, then, does not mean lack of recognition; it may simply mean a lack of stress on what that term represents. In fact, in some cases, the lack of a term implies that the custom is so obvious, no special word is needed. What is essential is the search for whether the behavior and belief pattern that a word represents is present. Then one may search also for the presence of special words to represent that pattern. As one interesting illustration, I would cite the fact that the San Blas culture in Spain has no word comparable to our term *macho*.[20] Yet the San Blas culture is often cited as an ideal example of a culture with macho male beliefs and behavior patterns.

Finally, I should mention our own hesitancy when we speak to small children to use explicit words for genitalia or for sexual acts. American parents often say "Don't touch *it*" or "Don't do *that*" when referring to sexuality. This is another example of how a lack of explicit terms does not mean that a group has no customs concerning that area of behavior. Rather, the very hesitancy to be explicit in an area may be an obvious expression of strong normative beliefs concerning the desire to control that aspect of behavior.

Some of the Eskimo groups comprise a second type of society that has been cited as lacking marital sexual jealousy. Traditionally some Eskimo societies have had the custom of sharing mates with others such as guests or friends. To conclude from this that marital sexual jealousy is absent, however, confuses the act of accepting one type of extramarital arrangement with the act of accepting all types of extramarital arrangements. O'Kelly makes this point in a review of Eskimo sexuality:[21]

> Extramarital sexuality is a source of great jealousy among the Eskimo and both wives and husbands are quick to suspect their spouses. However, this jealousy exists alongside the practice of sharing or swapping spouses which requires the mutual approval of all participating parties and serves to establish close kinshiplike ties among the non-kin involved. (O'Kelly, 1980: p. 97)

After examining these and other societies, I would contend that no culture is indifferent to sexual jealousy in marriage—not even a culture with a very high degree of sexual freedom such as the Lepcha or some of the Eskimo societies. Of course, this conclusion is subject to further empirical testing, but for the theoretical reasons I have already stated, I doubt if any society will be found totally lacking in marital sexual jealousy.

IS MARITAL SEXUALITY SPECIAL?

In order to further explain my perspective on marital sexual jealousy I will have to speak a bit about the institutions of marriage and the family. These are our basic kinship institutions. It is the linkage with these institutions that joins sexuality with kinship. I developed some of my thinking here in the preceding chapter. There I emphasized the power of sexuality with its physical pleasure and self disclosure characteristics to bond people together into stable relationships and I stressed this as the basis for the importance given to sexuality. Many of these stable relationships will be heterosexual and the female will become pregnant. This leads to kinship systems composed of marriage and family relationships and as a *result* reproduction then takes on importance.

All peoples regardless of their biological knowledge of reproduction are aware that the birth canal of the infant is the same area used in sexual intercourse. Even if a society does not believe that intercourse is the main cause of pregnancy, it will usually assert that males have a role in pregnancy. So there is an *association* of sexuality with pregnancy *but* this is not the same as saying that all peoples see a biological causal connection of sexuality to pregnancy, such as we do. In the preceding chapter we discussed some non-biological ways that in which the male role in reproduction is perceived, and therefore I will not repeat them here.

The female contribution to reproduction is considered obvious in all societies. However, there are great differences as to what the female contributes to the offspring besides her womb. In Western history it was the Greek philosopher Aristotle whose beliefs were the most influential. He viewed the male as supplying the semen and the female as providing the material for the semen to work upon:[22]

> If, then, the male stands for the effective and active, and the female, considered as female, for the passive, it follows that what the female would contribute to the semen of the male would not be semen but material for the semen to work upon. (McKeon, 1941: p. 676)

Aristotle's views were widely accepted until recent centuries. It was only at the end of the nineteenth century that we scientifically understood the operation of fertilization. Understanding the recency of our scientific knowledge should make it easier to grasp the widespread prevalence outside the west of unscientific views of fertilization.

Regardless of how people related sexuality to reproduction, peoples everywhere desired to set up some expected ways that their daughters and sons would become involved in the bearing and rearing of children. The resultant kinship structures comprise the marital and family institutions found in all societies.[23] The key point here is that the linkage of sexual jealousy is more with the bonds related to the marital and family institutions than with the possible reproduction of children. Hupka's data on marital sexual jealousy shows no relationship between the emphasis a culture places on offspring and the occurrence of marital sexual jealousy.[24] Any sexual act which threatens the marital bond will evoke jealousy. It is not essential that illegitimate pregnancy be involved for marital sexual jealousy to occur.

Exactly how much responsibility each parent will have for the ensuing children is more variable for the father. In matrilineal societies such as the Hopi Indian society in Arizona, or the Trobrianders near New Guinea, the man will spend much of his time with his sister's children. This is so because in such societies one traces their descent through the female line and therefore a man belongs to his mother's and sister's descent group while his wife and all their children belong to her mother's descent group. It is the man's duty to tend to the children in his lineage and that means his sister's children. Of course, this means that the man's wife will analogously have the assistance of her brother in the care and instruction of her children.

Regardless of the ways men and women are attached to children, in all these cases, specific arrangements are societally put forth as the expected way in which a woman will be attached to a man at the period of her life when she bears children. Sexuality symbolizes the bond between the man and woman more than it symbolizes fertilization. In this sense the ties of sexuality is to marital and family relationships more than to reproduction. It is this type of linkage of sexuality with kinship which produces the unversal presence of marital sexual jealousy.

The specific types of unions which are the social context into which children are expected to be born spell out the precise nature of marriage and the family in that society.[25] Note that there is no requirement for any legal marital ceremony. Most of the nonindustrialized societies do not have formal legal systems in any case. The transition to marriage may be marked by the simple eating of a meal together by the woman and man or it may be an elaborate ritual with a celebration lasting over a period of days. In some cases the couple do not even live together. This is the case for the matrilineal Nayar in India where the husband visits his wife in the evening but both mates live separately in their own mother's dwelling.[26] Nevertheless, the obligations and bonds of marriage and the concomitant feelings of jealousy exist even in this type of kinship structure. But jealousy here is not tied to reproduction for in the traditional Nayar society the woman would have "secondary" husbands and lovers and most of her children would be fathered by such men. Nevertheless, it is not such reproduction by other men that produces jealousy but rather it is both sexual and non-sexual actions which display a lack of concern which are more likely to produce jealousy.

Beliefs that symbolize the association of marriage to reproduction are apparent in patrilineal societies, wherein descent is traced through the male line. Jack Goody and others have pointed out that marriage in a patrilineal society symbolizes that all the infants born from that woman's womb belong to the husband's descent line.[27] In matrilineal descent systems, the mother's relatives are also interested in all the products of her womb, for children belong to the mother's descent group.[28] Our society is bilateral and therefore traces descent through both the mother's and father's line and thus all the close relatives from both parental lines are concerned about the offspring produced by a marital couple.

The reader should note that it is marriage which is tied to reproduction here. The shared desire is to have children born into a marriage between two individuals who are socially tied to each other. Sexuality is involved only as it is conceptualized to have a role in this process and its key role is more as a sign of the couple's bond than a cause of pregnancy. In many societies extramarital relationships of some sort are allowed and all children born to the woman are legitimate. Relatedly, an unsanctioned extramarital lover would be seen as a threat to the marital bond and would produce jealousy regardless of whether or not pregnancy occurred. I want to emphasize that the association of sexuality and reproduction *follows* from the bonding power of sexuality. It is that bonding power which is one major foundation of the marital relationship into which children will be born. The jealousy norms of a society protects the bonding potential of marital sexuality more than it does the risk of unwanted pregnancy. Such a pregnancy is but one of many potential threats to a marital relationship.

I fully believe that societies would strongly associate sexuality with marriage even if all reproduction were occurring in scientific laboratories with artificial wombs. Ask yourself: Would not husbands and wives still be jealous even in such a situation? Are not sterile mates as jealous as fertile mates? Can you explain wive's sexual jealousy as due to fear of their husbands impregnating other women? Is there not jealousy in homosexual relationships? Is not the heart of jealousy in the bonds of the relationship and their meaning, more than in any reproductive outcome?

I began this section with the question is marital sexuality thought to be special? The answer is yes! Marriage is the most valued home of the sexual relationship. Sexuality has its importance due to its pleasure and disclosure characteristics and marriage has its importance due to its tie to reproduction and the related kinship system. The importance placed on marriage demands that rights in the key areas of sexuality be present in marriage. This union of sexuality and marriage is what marital-sexual jealousy is protecting. Sexuality is felt to belong naturally in a valued relationship like marriage. This reasoning is universally present and universally understood. In this sense, the association of sexuality with reproduction is a result of the societal joining of two areas of importance. More significant than any biological connection to reproduction is the fact that sexuality in marriage takes on associations with other interpersonal qualities of that marital relationship. This is another quite important dimension in any explanation of marital sexual jealousy. I will elaborate upon this point in the next two sections.

LOVE IS NOT ENOUGH

In the Western world we think that the basis for the jealous response is the affectionate quality of the marital relationship. Many people still feel that the self disclosure involved in sexuality symbolizes the love relationship and therefore sexuality should not be shared with extramarital partners. However, romantic and affectionate marital sexual relationships are not the only "triggers" that set off the sexual jealousy responses around the world. Any act that symbolizes a "betrayal" of the marital relationship, that is, a lowering of marital priority, can evoke jealousy.

In many cultures power and prestige related to duty-based marriages underlie marital sexual jealousy even more so than affectionate ties. Outside the Western world and even in parts of Eastern Europe, the choice of a mate is more heavily determined by economic or kinship ties. Affectionate compatibility, though almost always considered a positive characteristics, is not of first importance. In such a "pragmatic" marriage a male may, despite his lack of love for his wife as a person, believe that his wife has flagrantly violated his legitimate power over her by having an extramarital sexual relationship. Though the wife in such a society has less power, she may feel that her husband owes her the respect and honor of abiding by whatever the norms are concerning extramarital relationships. In this sense she has a belief that she is entitled to control her husband's sexuality within the limits set by the society. Underlying this belief in the legitimacy of controlling a mate's sexuality is an affirmation of the power of the cultural norms that regulate marital sexuality. Each partner feels justified in requiring that his or her mate abide by the shared cultural norms concerning marital sexuality. Let me reiterate that such a mutually binding agreement does not necessarily imply that one is treating people as property, as the Marxist position asserts. Agreeing to abide by any set of societal norms entails having rights to control other people's behavior without any necessary implication about property rights in the other people involved.

In addition to norms that stress affection or obedience to power rules (duty) as the bases for feeling a "violation of boundaries," males and females may feel jealous because of a third reason, the pleasure value of sexuality. Sharing with someone else the sexual pleasure that one's mate desires for himself or herself is thus another basis for feeling the boundaries of that relationship have been violated. In some Polynesian societies, the pleasure value of sexuality is highly valued, and accordingly there are restrictions upon married people sharing that valued good with others.

In sum, the norms of all societies usually stress affection, duty, and pleasure as the three key reasons for marital sexual boundaries, but societies do differ considerably on the relative emphasis they place on these three factors. We stress the importance of love in marriage, but even in a loveless marriage, contracted for reasons of duty or pleasure, many Americans would want their mate to avoid extramarital partners. The importance of these three factors for the marital sexual jealousy norms of a society is good evidence for my assertion that the tie to reproduction is not the sole, or even the most important, reason for sexual jealousy in marriage. Rather, the particular value of sexual relationships in marriage is due heavily to the specific linkages in a society to the love, duty, and pleasure aspects of marriage.

INTRUSION AND EXCLUSION:
THE STRUCTURE OF JEALOUSY

In all societies, whether marriage is based on love, duty, or pleasure, there occurs a similar individual assessment of extramarital relationships. This assessment involves the relationship concepts of intrusion and exclusion. Awareness of this will highlight the boundary-marking nature of marital sexual jealousy. It is therefore worthwhile here to take a social psychological perspective concerning the participants' feelings about extramarital sexuality.

When I have discussed the experience of sexual jealousy with friends, one response has stood out above all others. The response entails the feeling of being excluded by the mate from an important personal aspect of the relationship.[29] If one's mate flirts with another person, that action exludes the uninvolved person from this part of the mate's life and leads to the feeling of being neglected in favor of some new attraction. That feeling of exclusion also leads to the judgment that the established relationship has been devalued by the person flirting with a new partner.

The other side of *exclusion* by one's mate is the *intrusion* into the original relationship by the new sexual partner. This reduces the privacy feeling of the original relationship and, like exclusion, also leads to the feeling that the priority of the marital relationship has been thereby reduced.

The mate who is sexually involved with an unauthorized new person is making an implicit statement about the marital relationship. Such persons are asserting by their action that the existing martial relationship is not important enough for them to forego going off with an unauthorized lover. Now, it should be clear that we are speaking here only of culturally unallowed actions. As mentioned earlier, if in most cultures with the levirate a younger brother has an affair with his older brother's wife, that would not have the jealousy-provoking potential of an older brother having an affair with his younger brother's wife. The former affair is authorized; the latter is not.

It is important to note here that in most of the cultures about which I have been able to obtain information, even when there is acceptance of outside relationships, those relationships are pursued with delicacy and with concern for the feelings of the partners who are not involved. Accordingly, a younger brother will usually wait for his older brother to leave his home for a period of time before seeking a sexual encounter with his brother's wife. It is clear to the people involved that this is a more thoughtful and more caring way to carry on an extramarital relationship.

The potential exclusion and intrusion feelings are something that is taken into account by most of the norms that regulate extrarelationship actions. A comment by the Berndts in their study of Australian aborigines indicates the importance of discretion in this highly permissive society:[30]

> Jealousy is a big factor in pre and extramarital relations; . . . This is why most extramarital . . . affairs are carried out surreptitiously, so that the

husband or wife, as the case may be, does not lose face. (Berndt and Berndt, 1951: p. 51)

Of course, in love-based marriages, the precise meaning of the exclusion when a mate adds a new, unauthorized sexual partner is different than in a duty-based or pleasure-based marriage. But, as I shall soon illustrate, the same general principle of seeking to avoid an exclusionary and intrusive action that violates the boundaries of the relationship is present in all three types of marriages.

The sexual relationship with a new partner is often seen as a potential rival to the time and energy devoted to the uninvolved person or persons. There is widespread awareness that both the pleasure and self-disclosing aspects of sexuality can draw one away from an original relationship. Having disclosed oneself in a sexual context may encourage one to disclose more in other contexts. The awareness of this possibility is present even in cultures where the love aspects of sexuality are not stressed and serves to support my assertion of the universal recognition of the disclosure potentials of sexuality.

Perhaps of even more importance for understanding the feelings of exclusion and intrusion involved in sexual jealousy is that marital sexuality over time becomes associated with a network of nonsexual self-disclosing acts. Sexuality in a stable relationship can come to be associated with declarations of love, with affectionate touching, with revelations of need, with sharing of stressful experiences, with public approval, and with much more. Sexuality is a repetitive aspect of a marital relationship, and thus it can easily take on special symbolic meanings concerning that relationship. For this reason, the extramarital sexual act is usually not seen as an isolated action by a marriage partner. Rather, since the sexual act symbolizes a great deal of the emotional and intimate aspects of the marital relationship, when that sexual act is done with a new partner, it is often perceived as threatening the total meaning of the existing relationship.

In cultures where love in marriage is not encouraged, the sexual act can still have much significance beyond the physical act. First, it is possible for affection to develop even when it is not culturally demanded. More importantly, in such cultures the act may well symbolize loyalty to the partner or obedience to the partner; or it may be a sign of the honor of their relationship, or even a symbol of reproduction connected to their children.

So, the Western romantic model is not the only one that leads to the association of marital sexuality with other important marital relationship aspects. The very importance of the sexual act in all societies guarantees that sexuality will integrate with other key relationship values—whatever they might be. This can be seen in our own society in the repeated findings affirming the close integration of sexual satisfaction with general marital satisfaction.[31]

In many different cultures the sharing of the sexual act by a married person with someone not culturally sanctioned is analogous to the revelation of a shared confidence to an outsider. No doubt this is part of the intrusive feelings about extramarital relationships. As we have discussed, sexuality has a private meaning to the couple; it is a meaning composed of a mixture of affection, duty, and pleasure.

A married couple's sexual act takes on the overall meaning of the relationship and becomes a personal act symbolizing the nature of that relationship. To share that symbolic sexual act with an unauthorized outsider is often felt to devalue the special quality of the marital relationship. In this sense, the sharing of sexuality is similar to the sharing of a confidence that was given by one's partner with the expectation that it was something special belonging only to their relationship.

Schapera, in his study of the Bantu in Southern Africa, affords us some of this confidential aspect of marital sexuality:[32]

> When our men keep going out at night we feel very jealous, because they make these other women know the insides of our homes and all the secrets of our lives. (Schapera, 1941: p. 207)

Many societies that accept extramarital partners recognize what we have discussed here and make a special effort to encourage people to compartmentalize or separate marital sexuality from the permitted extramarital sexuality. In that way the extramarital sexuality is kept from being intrusive upon the marital relationship. That such intrusiveness is so commonly felt in cultures around the world is evidence in support of the boundary mechanism view of jealousy. Only if one accepts a boundary about a marital relationship can another relationship intrude, for to intrude means to violate an existing boundary.

THE ACCEPTANCE OF EXTRAMARITAL PARTNERS

Regardless of the importance of dyadic boundaries it is crucial that we be aware that such extra partners can be legitimized. This point appears to have been overlooked by Pines and Aronson in their study of jealousy in a small California commune.[33] They argue that Kerista Village in California has eliminated jealousy by its communal style of living involving 17 people. They stress that the 15 adults do not get jealous when sexual partners are rotated. However, they do report jealousy reactions if any of the members have sexual interests in "outsiders." This situation simply represents a change in boundaries from a dyad—normal for the West—to a somewhat larger group. Clearly, boundaries are still there, for sexual jealousy does occur when outsiders are involved.

Cross-culturally we can observe in polygyny a similar type of acceptable boundary that exceeds the dyad. In polygyny the husband and his wives comprise the group boundary that sexual jealousy norms surround. Surely, as we have discussed, even jealousy among cowives is quite common. In a sense the husband's relationship with each wife is a "separate" marriage, and thus some tendency toward jealousy would be expected. But as we noted earlier, this jealous reaction is considered inappropriate in polygyny and is blocked by various structural arrangements that attempt to order the interactions among the various wives with the husband. However, if a polygynist husband has sexual intercourse with a woman to whom he is not married and who is not approved of by the society, then the sexual jealousy response by his wives and their families would be much stronger.

I have mentioned that it is common in Polynesia and most of the nonindustrialized world to allow extramarital coitus for a younger brother with an older brother's wife. In a culture with this levirate custom, the younger brother will marry his older brother's wife if his older brother dies. The levirate tradition existed among the ancient Hebrews also. The sin of Onan mentioned in the Old Testament was that he did not impregnate his deceased older brother's wife.[34] Instead, Onan "spilt his seed upon the ground." The offense to Hebrew society was not as many have supposed, that Onan masturbated or practiced coitus interruptus; it was, rather, that he did not fulfill his duty to his deceased older brother to produce children for his brother's line of descent.

In most levirate systems the legitimate sexual boundary extends beyond the simple dyad. Therefore, the older brother will strive to avoid feeling jealous if his younger brother exercises his levirate rights. The reader knows that the older brother has no sexual rights in his younger brother's wife. Such older brother and younger brother's wife relationships are often viewed like parent-child relationships. This restriction on the older brother may be part of a system of avoiding conflict that could result from the older brother using his greater power to gain sexual access to his younger brother's wife. Once again, we have a limit placed on power by other values in the society. This realization will qualify the position on power that I propose later in this chapter.

Thus, we have many instances of societies wherein extradyadic and extramarital partners are accepted. But we are also made aware that such arrangements are delicately balanced. The question arises, just how might we classify the strategies societies have utilized to deal with the potentially conflicting desires for extramarital relations and for maintaining the priority of a particular marital relationship?[35] I would classify the societies that have been studied regarding such extra-partner sexual customs as presenting three basic ways of handling the potential clash of a new sexual partner with an existing stable relationship. These alternative approaches can be called (1) avoidance, (2) segregation, and (3) integration. I will briefly discuss these in turn.

The first normative approach to extra partners is to instruct people to strive to avoid any new sexual relationships. This is the way the Western world has formally chosen for dealing with extramarital relationships. Formally, the West has proposed that people should avoid such relationships entirely. In actuality, the female has been the one restricted by our Western customs much more so than the male, for society's punishment for transgression of "avoidance" norms has been harsher on the female than the male. To illustrate, the Napoleonic Code allowed a husband to kill his wife and her lover if they were found together in bed by the husband. The wife in the reverse situation had no such right.

Outside the Western world in the Trobriand Islands, with its society's very open premarital sexual norms, the double standard still prevailed in extramarital sexuality. The offended Trobriand husband did at times physically attack his wife, while the wife did not take comparable actions against her husband.[36] Clearly, then, the avoidance approach has been applied more to the woman than to the man both in and out of the Western world.[37]

Outside the Western world there are some interesting variations. Davenport's study of East Bay in Melanesia offers a rather interesting case dealing with premarital sexuality.[38] In this society the premarital sexual avoidance strategy for males is to permit homosexual relationships for adolescent males but to avoid all premarital heterosexual relationships. Such a strategy could work in extramarital relationships if a society accepted the promotion of homosexual relationships as a way of avoiding such heterosexual relationships. There is a connection between premarital and extramarital avoidance, for many avoidance cultures believe in the potential disruptiveness of both premarital and extramarital sexual relationships upon a marriage. Such ideological tenets help support many types of restrictive sexual approaches in a society.

The second general approach to extramarital sexual partners is to segregate the extramarital relationship from the marital relationship. This tactic places the other relationship outside the life space of the uninvolved partner. One version of this has been the common way that Western males have been engaged in extramarital sexual relations. They have had prostitutes or mistresses or lovers who were not known to their mates. This segregation of the "extra" person is intended to make conflict less likely by lowering the social visibility of the other relationship.

A more modern and equalitarian version of the segregation approach occurs when both mates agree that an outside seuxal relationship can occur *for either of them* but that it must be kept separate from the life space of both partners.[39] Extramarital agreements usually include restrictions so that the marital relationship receives priority and the competitiveness of the outside relationship is kept within bounds.[40]

One of the most common segregated extramarital arrangements is found among those non-Western societies that have the levirate customs.[41] In most but not all of those arrangements a married person can have sexual intercourse with a sister-in-law or brother-in-law in part because they are potential future mates. But, as I have emphasized, even these outside relations are expected to be conducted with concern for the priority of the spouse and with the proper amount of low social visibility.

The third societal approach is to integrate the extramarital sexual relationship into the existing marital relationship. In modern America this would be exemplified by a sexually open marriage agreement that specifies that each mate should know the new partner and be free to veto choices he or she did not like. Furthermore, the uninvolved mate might wish to be kept informed as to how the new relationship is progressing and to be able to interact with the new outside partner.

There are cultures, such as the Turu in Tanzania, the Bantu in South Africa, and the Marquesans in Polynesia, where such outside arrangements are not uncommon and where the outside male may have to pay the husband for the privilege of such an agreement.[42] In the Marquesans males or females are sometimes added to the household for economic reasons and given limited sexual rights. Among the Turu the integration of the lover is sometimes quite explicit:[43]

> During the period that an affair continues, the lovers give each other gifts and meet secretly when they can. The husband and his wife's lover become friendly to the extent of exchanging invitations to beer feasts and helping each other with housebuilding, cultivation and other cooperative labors. They may even lend livestock to each other. The mistress becomes friendly with her lover's wife, helps her to grind grain, and makes beer for her and the husband. (Schneider, 1971: p. 66)

Sometimes among the Turu the husband will not go along with the love affair of his wife. Such a wife has pressure she can exert:

> A wife will throw her husband's double standard in his face by pointing out that he has a mistress though he forbids a lover to her. (Schneider, 1971: p. 66)

Even in such open cultures the emphasis on avoiding public displays of the outside relation is stressed and the priority of the marriage prevails. In that sense, some of these affairs might be better classified as halfway between the segregated and integrated approaches.

Each of the three basic alternative strategies to handle the additional person has its own costs and rewards. The avoidance approach involves a great deal of constraint, especially in a society where extramarital opportunity is common. Violation of the norms in an avoidance culture can lead to strong emotional reactions involving guilt, violence, and divorce as well as, of course, sexual jealousy. But there is in such a system the security of believing you are promoting a stable marriage by the attempt at self-control, and the complexities of extramarital arrangements are avoided.

Segregated agreements by American couples have been reported in many studies in recent years. Here, too, violations of whatever the agreed-upon standards are may occur, and that would be a serious strain on the marital relationship. Also, the very presence of an extramarital agreement adds complexity to the relationship, for time and commitment must be divided in ways that do not disturb the priority of the marriage. But this system has one advantage in that there will be discussion of what type of extramarital relationship is or is not acceptable to each mate. In this sense they have more awareness of what risks and rewards such affairs involve for their relationship. This may enable such couples to make more informed choices regarding extramarital behavior and thereby be less likely to offend their mate.

In America, the integrative alternative involving a fully sexually open marriage has very high failure rates.[44] The ability to accept emotionally the specific knowledge of and acquaintance with the extramarital partner is not widespread here. One way this can be handled is if the original relationship is not very highly valued. This, in fact, is part of the Polynesian cultural approach. Levy talks of the Tahitians' attempt to control the degree to which they become emotionally dependent upon their mates.[45] In part, this aids the carrying out of extramarital relationships. But it is equally true that if the original marriage does not involve very high mutual dependency, then the outside relation may more easily replace it. However, this may not occur if the people involved are not seeking highly dependent relationships in the first place.

What about trends in the Western world among the three basic cultural strategies for handling marital sexual jealousy? These three modes (avoidance, segregation, and integration) are closely related to the three major aspects of marriage that trigger sexual jealousy (love, duty, and pleasure). It seems to me that if we stress the love aspect of marriage, then we make the integration approach very difficult and encourage the avoidance or the segregation approach to extramarital relationships. This is so because love does encourage a focus upon one mate and that leads to the desire for sexual exclusivity. On the contrary, if we stress pleasure in marriage, then we make the avoidance approach less likely and the segregation and integration approaches more likely. The pursuit of pleasure, when not combined with love, does encourage seeking other partners in a more open fashion. Given these likely interrelations of extramarital strategies and marriage structures, toward what directions are we heading?

I would contend that we in the Western world have been moving toward an era of greater choice in sexual relations and relatedly a lower value on sexual exclusivity. There are many reasons for this, including the far greater sexual experience of our young people today and their higher education, which tends to make them more willing to entertain new alternatives.[46] Another reason for less sexual exclusivity today concerns the more diffuse nurturance of youngsters today. Due to high divorce rates we have large proportions of our population who have more than two parents with whom they may identify. This can reduce the focus of attention on any single parent, and that, in turn, may reduce the focus of attention on any single adult love relationship.

On this very point, recall that there is in Polynesia a diffuse nurturing of children.[47] Adoption is quite common, and being raised by more than just one's biological parents is the norm in much of Polynesia. Thus, perhaps the Polynesian reluctance to seek exclusive love relationships is integrated with that diffuse upbringing. The Polynesians speak of "sympathy" and "empathy" and "concern" for each other and avoid the more demanding meanings of "the one and only" romantic love notions. Relatedly, Polynesians have a strong sense of autonomy that is antithetical to the high dependency implied by romantic love. A few in the West have also argued for the advantages of "pure" sexuality, unfettered by the demands of love, but they are clearly in the minority.[48]

Most importantly, we should not forget that diffusing affection will not necessarily reduce jealousy unless the duty and pleasure aspects of marital relationships are also controlled. This is so because duty and pleasure may also serve as a reason for jealousy norms. In this regard, I know of no marital relationship system in any society that has eliminated from marriage all three of the key characteristics of affection, duty, and pleasure. Upon reflection it seems that it would be a strange sexual relationship indeed, in or out of marriage, that would eliminate duty, pleasure, and affection! Why would one bother with such a relationship? It follows, then, that while there is ample room for change in the structure of marriage and sexual jealousy, there are also severe limits to the reduction of marital sexual jealousy.

I think that for reasons of stability and security most people in the West will continue to elect avoidance of extramarital affairs of any kind, although even they will perhaps discuss this choice more thoroughly than has been the case in the past. I do think the integrative approach is too difficult for most people to cope with—it involves too many constant decisions and adjustments to the changing partners and to the number of people involved. In a real sense, the integrative approach gives new meaning to Jefferson's famous quote, "Eternal vigilance is the price of liberty." The unpredictability of negative outcomes and the constancy of the awareness of the extra partner will discourage all but a small number from the integrative approach.

In social life, everything else being equal, the more complex the custom, the less likely it will be adopted. One interesting evidence of this is that no culture has group marriage (multiple mates of both genders) as a preferred form of marriage, and only a very few cultures even have it as a rare option. The reason is the complexity of relating several husbands and wives to each other in one marriage. If monogamy, polygyny, and polyandry have problems with jealousy, imagine what the problems would be in group marriage! The rarity of group marriage, then, does support my point concerning the appeal of the less complex lifestyle of avoidance.

The approach most likely to grow is the segregation approach, where couples may inform each other that an affair might occur, but it will be kept separate from day-to-day life and will not become competitive with the existing stable relationship. In a large volunteer sample analyzed by Blumstein and Schwartz, 15% of the married couples stated they had such an agreement. This percentage is likely higher than what a representative sample would show for America today, but the point is that such marriages are not extremely rare events. Blumstein and Schwartz also studied extradyadic agreements among cohabiting and homosexual couples as well as married couples. Here is how they sum up all those agreements:[49]

> An open relationship does not mean that anything goes. . . . We never interviewed a couple who did not describe some definite boundaries. . . . The most important rules provide emotional safeguards—for example, never seeing the same person twice, never giving out a phone number, never having sex in the couple's bed, or never with a mutual friend. . . . These rules remind the partners that their relationship comes first and anything else must take second place. (Blumstein and Schwartz, 1983: p. 289)

The segregation approach, like all approaches, still has to deal with sexual jealousy, but I believe there are more people who can handle jealousy in this less intrusive form of extramarital sexuality than could handle the demands of the integrative approach.

Nevertheless, the segregated approach is likely to remain for some time considerably less popular than the avoidance approach. Most people probably enjoy the security of the avoidance approach, despite its restrictions. Changes in important boundary protection customs take considerable time to develop on the individual or the cultural level. Premarital sexuality changes much more easily, for it does not involve risk to an established relationship but rather can be the basis for establishing a marital relationship. Changes in extramarital sexuality involve important marital and family boundaries in a more direct, confronting fashion, and thus change occurs much more slowly. Nonetheless, our boundaries are changing.

SEXUAL JEALOUSY OUTSIDE MARRIAGE
AND HETEROSEXUALITY

I have focused upon sexual jealousy in marriage, but I do believe that other forms of sexual relationships will also display the boundary mechanism of jealousy. In addition, I have focused here on heterosexual relationships in marriage and I realize this ignores the homosexual world, but for establishing universal linkages to kinship this was necessary. Nevertheless, the intergration of sexual jealousy with important relationships is assumed to hold for homosexual as well as heterosexual relationships.

The recent work of Blumstein and Schwartz indicates that male homosexual relationships are the most likely to have extradyadic agreements, usually of the segregated type.[50] Lesbian relationships are less likely to have such arrangements. However, both groups of homosexual couples were found to be more acceptant of agreements regarding outside sexuality than were married heterosexual couples. Cohabiting couples were also more acceptant of such relationships with others than were married couples. So, the strongest restrictions on sexual affairs outside the primary relationship does seem to occur among married couples. I would suggest that this is so because of the conjuncture of marital sexuality with complex kinship relationships that themselves promote stronger jealousy boundaries.

The abundant evidence of sexual jealousy in gay and particularly lesbian relationships supports my position that the reproduction connection of marital sexuality is *not* a necessary element in the producton of marital sexual jealousy. The greater emphasis on sexual exclusivity by lesbians as compared to gays is best explained by gender-role training. Both gays and lesbians indicate, though, that the sexual relationship tends to symbolize the nature of the bond in the couple, and it takes conscious effort to modify that association. The gays' weaker emphasis on sexual exclusivity aspect of stable relationships is congruent with the much higher change of partners in gay as compared to lesbian relationships. Such higher break-age fits with the notion of sexual jealousy as a protective boundary. In many cases gays resolve the question of sexual jealousy by removing sexuality from a long-term relationship.[51] The need to eliminate sexuality in order to stabilize a relationship speaks to the importance of sexuality. Nevertheless, in such desexualized relationships jealousy in other areas is quite possible if the relationship is considered important. The same desexualization solution occurs in some heterosexual marriages, although it appears to be much more common in stable gay relationships than anywhere else.

MALE DOMINANCE AND JEALOUSY: CROSS-CULTURAL EVIDENCE

Before leaving this chapter I want to use the Hupka data on 80 cultures in the Standard Sample to test one major explanation of cultural differences in marital sexual jealousy. This explanation asserts that the marital sexual jealousy of husbands will be greater in societies where males have more power. Marital sexual jealousy by wives will be greater in societies that are more equalitarian. The logic behind this is that sexuality is a valued element of society and thus the more powerful will have greater access and fewer restrictions concerning their sexuality. Consequently, the more powerful will also expect to be able to exercise their power to restrict the sexuality of others and will be jealous when that fails.

We briefly discussed the place of male power in jealousy earlier in this chapter. What I am proposing here is a modification of the orthodox Marxist view. I accept the importance of social power in sexual jealousy norms, but I conceptualize somewhat differently the way power operates. The Standard Sample and Hupka's data will help in testing out these explanations. Since the next chapter deals with the general issue of gender power and sexuality, this specific examination is preparatory for that exploration.

In order to check my proposed explanations, I used a technique of data analysis called path analysis. This book is not the place for a technical discussion of this approach, but I must briefly explain the process so the reader can understand the diagrams that are presented.[52] Basically, this type of analysis allows one not only to examine which variables are related to which other variables but to further specify the order in which these variables interrelate. For example, I could have simply utilized multiple-regression techniques to observe the net effect of each of the several variables on jealousy. In that way I could tell whether these measures of male power were each independently correlated to jealousy. That surely is worthwhile. But I wanted to go one step further, and so I also sought to find out how these various predictors of jealousy related to each other. The resultant diagram is a causal diagram in that, going from left to right, it hypothesizes the earliest causes in the specific relationships and moves to the right to hypothesized later results. I believe these procedures will become quite clear as we examine the outcome of my analysis of predictors of sexual jealousy in husbands.

I present the basic causes of differences in husband's sexual jealousy in 80 societies of the Standard Sample in Diagram 3.1.

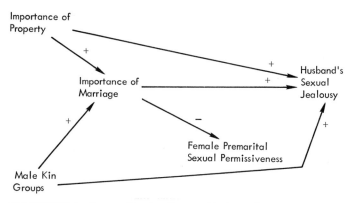

DIAGRAM 3.1   Causes of husband's sexual jealousy.*

*A negative relation is symbolized by a − sign and indicates that as one of the two connected variables increases, the other decreases. A positive relation is symbolized by a + sign and indicates that as one of the two connected variables increases or decreases, the other does the same.

First, here is a brief explanation of each of the five variables in Diagram 3.1. The "importance of property" variable is a measure devised by Hupka. He measured the importance each culture placed on private ownership of property and the severity of punishment for theft of property. Hupka took this as a measure of how likely people would be to generalize to their mates their protective sentiments toward property and therefore more easily become jealous. I interpret this variable somewhat differently. I believe it is better used as a measure of male power. We know that males virtually everywhere control private property; thus, the greater the importance of property, the greater will be male power. It would therefore be the sense of power, not the particular source of power in property, that led to jealous reactions. This perspective better accounts for the jealousy of the majority of males who have very little property.

The "male kin groups" variable was one I composed using two measures from the Standard Sample. Basically, it is a measure of whether a society traces descent through the male line (patrilineal) and whether males live together (patrilocal). My reasoning is that the more these customs are present, the greater the male ties to each other, and therefore males will be more powerful in that society.

The "importance of marriage" variable comes from Hupka and measures how much a culture's marital conceptions stresses marriage as necesary for survival and for being accepted as an adult. Hupka took this variable to predict jealousy because if marriage was important, then a mate would be more desirous of protecting the marriage against intruders. I use this as an indirect measure of male power. My reasoning is that if males are in power and wish to pass on their property and their group power to their offspring, they will stress the importance of marriage because that is the vehicle by which they can perpetuate their power in a society.

"Female premarital sexual permissiveness" is a variable contained in the

Standard Sample. Hupka had used a general measure of sexual restrictiveness because he felt that there would be more jealousy if sexuality were restricted outside of marriage.[53] I use this female measure for another reason: to see if greater male power produces restrictions on female premarital sexuality that might affect male jealousy.

The dependent or *effect* variable, that which we are trying to explain, is "husband's sexual jealousy." Hupka measured this by indexes of the severity of the response to an extramarital affair. This could range from a mild reaction to a requirement to kill the offenders.

Now let us examine the paths or lines connecting the variables in Diagram 3.1. First, the reader must be aware that the causal path lines that are drawn in the diagram are only those paths, of all possible paths, that came out statistically significant.[54] In short, only the lines that an examination of the 80 cultures showed to be statistically important are included.

Starting with the variables that are the earliest in time, namely, those at the left of the diagram, we see that both the importance of property and male kin groups variables relate to the importance of marriage. The plus sign on each line indicates that the relation is positive or direct. Thus, as one variable increases, so does the other. In these specific cases it means that as the importance of property increases, so does the importance of marriage. Further, as the presence of male kin groups increases, so does the importance of marriage. Note that these two correlations support my idea that the importance of marriage is a reflection of male power as measured by these two other variables.

One might expect the importance of property and male kin groups measures to relate to each other, since they are both assumed to be measures of male power, but they are not significantly correlated to each other. This is indicated by the lack of a path (line) connecting them. Also, they are in the same column, which indicates that I am hypothesizing that they occur at the same point in time and therefore cannot cause each other. Many explanations may be tentatively put forth. First, it may well be that more than the importance placed on property promotes male kin groups. This makes sense when we realize that many hunting and gathering societies have very little in the way of property but are organized around male kin groups. This fact also qualifies the Marxist view of property notions being related to jealousy. We find jealousy in hunting and gathering societies, but we do not find much in the way of property.

Marxist writers and others have emphasized the role of agriculture in the development of male power. Were agricultural an important variable then it could be placed into the diagram as an early cause of both the importance of property and the presence of male kin groups. To examine this I introduced into the causal equation of Diagram 3.1 a variable measuring the degree to which agriculture was present in the society. I found that agriculture was not related to the importance of property, but it did modestly relate in a positive direction to the presence of male kin groups. This means that agriculture does promote patrilineal and patrilocal customs. Yet it does not directly relate to jealousy or any other variable. Thus, other factors, not detected by my search, must produce change in the importance of property in a society.

Let us follow the diagram further. The first three variables at the left of the diagram, just discussed, have a direct, positive relationship with husband's sexual jealousy. This is congruent with my expectations that the stronger these indexes of male power, the stronger would be husband's sexual jealousy.

Finally, the last causal path goes from the importance of marriage to female premarital sexual permissiveness. The relationship there is negative, meaning that as marriage becomes more important, female premarital sexual permissiveness becomes less acceptable. This is congruent with my expectation that male power would restrict female premarital sexuality as part of the effort to control sexual outcomes.

Now look at the total diagram: Clearly, the findings imply that as the importance of property and male kin groups increase in a society, the importance of marriage increases also. In turn, increases in the importance of marriage lead to restrictions upon female premarital sexuality. In addition, the importance of property, male kin groups, and importance of marriage variables each directly affects the occurrence of husband's sexual jealousy. There are a few more such diagrams in this book, and I hope that spending this time on the first one will make the others easier to comprehend.

Our examination of this diagram has brought to our attention what I consider one of the most important aspects of scientific explanations. This crucial point is that the same research results can at times be used by different people to support alternative explanations. I, of course, used the results we just went over to show how they are congruent with my theory of male power being a primary cause of increased husband's sexual jealousy. Nevertheless, one could find in these same results support for a property explanation of husband's sexual jealousy. One could show how the importance of property promotes the importance of marriage and how both relate to husband's sexual jealousy. I interpreted those same relationships of property and marriage to jealousy to be a measure of how male power influences jealousy. My explanation allows for nonproperty sources of jealousy such as are seen in Diagram 3.1. I prefer my explanation because it can be generalized more broadly. Others may argue their own case, however. The important lesson here is how difficult it is to find research results that support just one interpretation. I will further defend my interpretation by showing how the next diagram, on wife's sexual jealousy, fits my ideas. Furthermore, in the next chapter we will see how power is intimately related to sexuality. The point remains that although I promote my explanatory schema, there is room for alternative explanations.

Now let us look at the findings for factors that influence wife's sexual jealousy. I examined the exact same possible causes, the only difference being that the outcome variable in this case is wife's, not husband's, sexual jealousy. The result is interesting and is presented in Diagram 3.2.

The causal connections of the importance of property and male kin groups variables to the importance of marriage variable is the same in both the husband

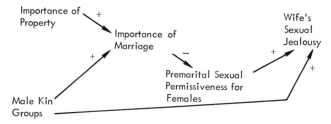

DIAGRAM 3.2   Causes of wife's sexual jealousy.

and wife diagrams. Also, the connection of the importance of marriage variable to the female premarital sexual permissiveness variable is the same. The connection of the male kin groups variable to jealousy is also the same for wife's as for husband's jealousy.

In terms of the two remaining paths present in the husband's diagram, there are dramatic differences. There are no direct causal connections of the importance of property and the importance of marriage variables to wife's sexual jealousy as there was to husband's sexual jealousy (see Diagram 3.1). Allow me to offer some possible explanations for these important differences. Although the importance of marriage varies in different societies, the impact of such a norm is different for women than for men. Since females are generally raised in all cultures to give priority to marriage, in each culture the female gender would always be high on this normative belief. Therefore there is little room for variation in the belief systems of females concerning the importance of marriage, and so it does not affect jealousy.

In terms of the importance of property affecting jealousy, another common gender difference may play a role. A change in the importance of property will have its greatest impact on the gender in power. Since males are virtually everywhere in power, a change in the importance of property is significant to them and may signal a change in the amount of wealth in a society. But to those not in control, such changes do not bring their gender into greater or lesser control over property and thus are of less import in their lives.

Why does a change in presence of male kin groups have importance for wife's sexual jealousy? This is the most difficult path for me to explain. The logic of my explanation of why the importance of property variable had no relation to wife's jealousy should apply to the male kin groups variable as well. Changes in such a variable affect males more than females. First let me say that the statistical support for the connection of male kin groups to jealousy in wives is the weakest. I refer the reader to Appendix A, Table A-2, for more detailed information, but I must add here that we need to further check this relationship in other samples. If this relationship does hold, then we will have to reason it out further. At this point, all I can put forth is the possibility that the male kin groups variable reflects the proportion of polygyny in a society, that is, the more emphasis on male groups, the more polygyny. If so, it may be the polygyny, not the grouping of males together, that increases the sexual jealousy of wives.

There is one new causal path that adds considerable theoretical insight. Wife's sexual jealousy varies directly with female premarital sexual permissiveness. This is indicated by the positive relation between the two. High premarital female sexual permissiveness would be a sign of a more equalitarian society.[55] It takes power to be able to respond to a wound by attacking. Thus, in a more gender-equal society, not only would female premarital sexuality be higher but, as the causal line between it and female jealousy indicates, so would the expression of sexual jealousy by wives.

The interesting differences between the causal diagrams for husband's and wife's sexual jealousy fits very neatly into our suggestion of the importance of power for sexual behavior. Surely there are many other factors that influence sexual jealousy that are not in these diagrams. I could examine only those factors that were measured by researchers. Also, the variables are crudely measured; more precise and refined measures would be invaluable in helping to interpret the meaning of these findings. These diagrams present what I would call a plausible theory, not a final explanation; but they do paint the beginning strokes of a theory explaining the variation in jealousy, and this theory is well worth further exploration.[56]

SUMMARY AND CONCLUSIONS

In sum, then, each society sets boundaries for important relationships, particularly marital relationships, in which people are expected to invest themselves deeply in terms of duty, pleasure, or affection. The culture defines what ought to be considered a threat to that relationship. The range is quite broad, but there is always a boundary-setting structure. The basic function of such boundaries is to minimize conflict, particularly among those who will likely have high investment of self in each other, for example, kin, friends, and the intimates themselves.

Basically, then, I am taking issue with those who, like Havelock Ellis in the past, say we can eliminate jealousy or even have it fully under control.[57] We have also noted that others assert that sexual jealousy is simply due to capitalistic notions of possessiveness of one person over another. My position asserts that jealousy is basically a statement of the value of a particular relationship to a group. That value may have a property dimension to it, but marital relationships have value in cultures completely devoid of private-property notions.

As I see it, the essence of sexual jealousy is not a sense of property nor a dispensible emotion; rather, it is a statement concerning the importance placed on a particular sexual relationship. To be sure, the power dimension is a most important one. But power does not create sexual jealousy. Power enhances and elaborates upon the basic feeling of sexual jealousy that derives from the importance of sexuality to even those who are totally devoid of social power.

The question of whether the human sensitivity to jealousy is shared with other primates is an interesting one. The research on some nonhuman primates shows evidence of rudimentary forms of sexual jealousy when extra partners are added. About 80% of the primates species are polygynous. This is very close to the percentage of nonindustrialized human societies that prefer polygyny over monogamy.[58] Despite this preference, because of the common equality in numbers of males and females and the lack of wealth, most individuals in all societies have but one mate.

In nonhuman primates like gibbons and other simians, females help maintain monogamy by chasing away other females who approach their mates. In the titi monkey the male is monogamous and is hostile to other males who show sexual interest in his mate. Mitchell describes this scene as follows:[59]

> There is a strong and enduring emotional bond between individual males and females in titi monkeys. Titi monkeys show clear evidence of "jealousy" including marked enhancement of attraction by the male to his mate as a function of increasing proximity between that mate and a strong male. Female titi monkeys, on the other hand, are more attracted to their mates when other females are not around. (Mitchell, 1979: p. 130)

What are the roots of such primate reactions? One can only speculate that it is to preserve their own sources of physical pleasure and perhaps also to achieve emotional or dominance needs that are fulfilled by their partner. These nonhuman primates lack the complex social ties to kinship systems and to normative expectations, but the seeds of human sexual jealousy seem to be there. In human societies, sexual jealousy may have psychological roots in our egos, our sense of self, our desire to be treated as important, or even our wish to restore some of the secure feelings we may have had as a child. Surely human sexuality has a self-affirming quality. Regardless of what psychological forces or primate roots may be operative, however, I stress the importance of various sociological forces that produce jealousy. The human situation, then, is far different than that involving the display of primitive forms of jealousy by other primates.

Despite my assertion that marital sexual jealousy is universal, there are means of eliminating sexual jealousy that logically follow from my theoretical position. One solution would be to stop placing high importance on sexual relationships of any kind. However, due to the connection of sexuality to the valued components of psychic and physical pleasure, this is quite unlikely to occur. Further, since sexuality is connected to marriage, a society would have to devalue that institution as well—another unlikely occurrence. However, a society could disassociate sexuality from marriage and devalue all sexuality. Individuals have tried this, as I mentioned earlier, but no society has. Thus, the Gordian knot of universal sexual jealousy consists of its intertwining with physical and psychic pleasures and with marriage. I doubt if any society will ever sever those ties.

Of course, we can learn to reduce our sexual jealousy responses. Some cultures do stress friendship or parental kin ties and minimize marital relationships.[60] Even in those cultures, sexual activity has important meanings that can arouse strong emotional reactions like jealousy. So, we will have to learn how to live with sexual jealousy, for it is simply our human testimony to the significance of sexuality in our lives. To be sure, there are individuals who can learn virtually to eliminate sexual jealousy from their lives. It is up to the psychologists to sort out the ways in which this is accomplished. I am dealing with societal structures— not of what a few people are capable but of what a social system is capable. On this societal level I am proposing that we shall always find sexual jealousy tied in with our marital relationships as well as with most other important sexual relationships.

In this chapter I have striven to elaborate upon the ways in which sexuality relates to our basic kinship ties in the marital and family institutions. I have pointed to its basic importance in all societies but stressed how social power enhances the meaning of sexuality. In the next chapter, I will develop that theme and show how the relative power of each gender affects our sexual lives.

SELECTED REFERENCES AND COMMENTS

1. Constantine, Larry, "Jealousy: Techniques for Intervention," Chapter 18 in Gordon Clanton and Lynn G. Smith (eds.), *Jealousy.* Englewood Cliffs, N.J.: Prentice-Hall, 1977.
See also the following for other suggestions for dealing with jealousy:
Constantine, Larry, and Joan Constantine, *Group Marriage.* New York: Macmillan, 1973.
Im, Won-Gi, R. Stefanie Wilner, and Miranda Breit, "Jealousy: Interventions in Couples Therapy," *Family Process,* vol. 22 (June 1983), pp. 211-219.
2. For reports on empirical work on jealousy, start with a perusal of the articles in the August 1981 issues of the journal *Alternative Lifestyles,* which are entirely devoted to the topic of jealousy.
3. For a classic account of a Marxist kibbutz see Melford E. Spiro, *Kibbutz: Venture in Utopia.* Cambridge, Mass.: Harvard University Press, 1956.
4. It is necessary to distinguish envy from jealousy. Jealousy refers to a felt threat from an outsider. Envy refers to the feeling that you would like to be in someone else's situation; it does not imply that you are threatening any relationship. You are jealous of your mate's lover, but you are envious of Rockefeller's money.
5. As a sociologist my main interest is in the norms regarding jealousy and the patterns of jealous behavior. The question of whether people who act jealous feel jealous is more of a psychological question. It is surely true that some people act jealous mainly because they feel they are supposed to do that.
6. The question of whether jealousy is a secondary emotion has been dealt with by Hupka. See
Hupka, Ralph B., "Jealousy: Compound Emotion or Label for a Particular Situation?" *Motivation and Emotion,* vol. 8, no. 2 (1984), pp. 141-155.
7. The quotation is from one of the many pieces Schlegel has written about the Hopi Indians:
Schlegel, Alice, "Sexual Antagonism among the Sexually Egalitarian Hopi," *Ethos,* vol. 7, no. 2 (Summer 1979), pp. 124-141.
8. Buunk, Bram, and Ralph B. Hupka, "Autonomy and Togetherness in Close Relationships: A Study of Seven Nations." Paper presented at the meeting of the National Council on Family Relations, St. Paul, Minnesota, October 1983.

Buunk, Bram, and Ralph B. Hupka, "Cross-cultural Differences in the Elicitation of Sexual Jealousy," *Journal of Sex Research,* vol. 21 (in press).

9. Hupka was able to code 80 of the cultures in the Standard Sample on husband's sexual jealousy but only 39 cultures on wife's sexual jealousy. I believe one of the reasons is that the expression of female sexual jealousy is often in terms of depression and thus is not very visible to a visiting anthropologist.

Another line of reasoning would assert that there are stronger norms against female extramarital sexuality and therefore it is easier to become aware of them. As an example see

Rodman, Hyman, *Lower-class Families: The Culture of Poverty in Negro Trinidad.* New York: Oxford University Press, 1971.

10. For an excellent cross-cultural account of friendship see

Brain, Robert, *Friends and Lovers.* New York: Basic Books, 1976.

11. The reader should know that Hupka found that three variables were his best predictors of husband's sexual jealousy. They were the importance of marriage, the importance of personal property, and the restrictiveness of sexuality. I analyzed the 80 of his 92 cultures that were included in the Standard Sample and found somewhat different results than he did. I report on this further in this chapter and in note 53. Hupka measured jealousy itself by the consequences of the extramarital affair for the marriage in terms of fines, physical abuse, divorce, and so forth.

Hupka, Ralph B., "Cultural Determinants of Jealousy," *Alternative Lifestyles,* vol. 4, no. 3 (August 1981), pp. 310-356.

Hupka, Ralph B., and James M. Ryan, "The Cultural Contribution to Emotions: Cross-cultural Aggression in Romantic Jealousy Situations." Paper presented at the meeting of the Western Psychological Association, Los Angeles, 1981.

12. For a lengthy account of Inis Baeg see

Messenger, John C., *Inis Baeg: Isle of Ireland.* New York: Holt, Rinehart & Winston, 1969.

13. The quotation is from Robert Suggs, an anthropologist who knew the local language and spent considerable time in the Marquesan Islands. This is the best account of this island that I have been able to find.

Suggs, Robert C., *Marquesan Sexual Behavior.* New York: Harcourt Brace & Jovanovich, 1966.

14. The quotation comes from the first anthropological study made of the Australian aborigines' sexual behavior:

Berndt, Ronald M., and Catherine H. Berndt, *Sexual Behavior in Western Arnhem Land.* New York: Viking Fund, 1951.

15. There are three forms of polygamy or multiple-mate marriages: (1) polygyny (many wives and one husband) (2) polyandry (many husbands and one wife), and (3) group marriage (many husbands married to many wives). Only a handful of cultures have polyandry as a common mode, and no cultures stress group marriage, and so almost all polygamous marriages are polygynous.

16. A good general source for non-Western historical information on sexuality is

Bullough, Vern, *Sexual Variance in Society and History.* New York: John Wiley, 1976. (See Chapter 11 for a discussion of sexuality in China.)

17. Schapera is an anthropologist who devoted much of his work to the study of sexuality as related to changes in the marriage and family institutions:

Schapera, I., *Married Life in an African Tribe.* New York: Sheridan House, 1941.

18. The quote is from a most interesting account of the Lepchas first published in 1938. Gorer was specially trained by three well-known anthropologists: Margaret Mead, Ruth Benedict, and John Dollard. He spent three months in the spring of 1937 living with the Lepchas in the small village of Lingthem.

Gorer, Geoffrey, *Himalayan Village: An Account of the Lepchas of Sikkim* (2nd ed.). New York Basic Books, 1967.

19. Levy, Robert, *Tahitians.* Chicago: University of Chicago Press, 1973. (See especially Chapter 9.)

20. For a brief account of the San Blass culture see

Brandes, Stanley, "Like Wounded Stages: Male Sexual Ideology in an Andalusian Town," Chapter 6 in Sherry B. Ortner and Harriet Whitehead (eds.), *Sexual Meanings: The Cultural Construction of Gender and Sexuality.* Cambridge: Cambridge University Press, 1981.

21. The quote is from

O'Kelly, Charlotte G., *Women and Men in Society.* New York: D. Van Nostrand, 1980.

For an overview of the range of social life in Eskimo society, I would recommend starting with the following:

Sanders, Irwin T. (ed.), *Societies Around the World.* New York Dryden Press, 1956. (See especially pp. 34-335 in Volume 1.)

22. McKeon, Richard (ed.), "Generation of Animals," pp. 665-680. *The Basic Works of Aristotle.* New York: Random House, 1941.

23. Reiss, Ira L., *Family Systems in America* (3rd ed.). New York: Holt, Rinehart & Winston, 1980. (See especially Chapter 2.)

24. Hupka, Ralph B., "Cultural Determinants of Jealousy," *Alternative Lifestyles,* vol. 4, no. 3 (August 1984), pp. 310–356.

For a view stressing the relation of male paternity to jealousy see:

Daly, Martin, Mango Wilson and Suzann J. Weghorst, "Male Sexual Jealousy," *Ethnology and Sociobiology,* vol. 3 (1982), pp. 11–27.

25. I have developed universal definitions for the family, marital and courtship institutions. Consult the Glossary for these definitions. For a full discussion with references see

Reiss, Ira L., *Family Systems in America* (3rd ed.). New York: Holt, Rinehart & Winston, 1980. (See Chapter 2.)

26. For a general account of matrilineal societies as well as a specific account of the Nayars see:

Schneider, David M., and Kathleen Gough (eds.), *Matrilineal Kinship.* Berkeley: University of California Press, 1961.

27. Two books in this area by Jack Goody are worth examining. They are complex, but I believe interested lay people can follow his logic and evidence:

Goody, Jack, *Production and Reproduction.* Cambridge: Cambridge University Press, 1976.

Goody, Jack, and S.J. Tambiah, *Bridewealth and Dowry.* Cambridge: Cambridge University Press, 1973.

28. One of the most insightful, careful thought out, and investigated explanations of key aspects of matrilineal societies can be found in the work of Alice Schlegel. I suggest reading

Schlegel, Alice, *Male Dominance and Female Autonomy.* New Haven, Conn.: HRAF Press, 1972.

29. Buunk reports similar exclusionary feelings from his respondents. Buunk, Bram, "Jealousy in Sexually Open Marriages," *Alternative Lifestyles,* vol. 4, no. 3 (August 1981); pp. 357–372.

30. Berndt, Ronald M., and Catherine H. Berndt, *Sexual Behavior in Western Arnhem Land*. New York: Viking Fund, 1951.

31. For a summary of this research see
Reiss, Ira L., *Family Systems in America* (3rd ed.). New York: Holt, Rinehart & Winston, 1980. (See Chapter 11.)
For a recent study bear on this point see
Blumstein, Philip, and Pepper Schwartz, *American Couples*. New York Morrow, 1983. (See especially pp. 191-267.)

32. Schapera, I., *Married Life in an African Tribe*. New York: Sheridan House, 1941.

33. Pines, Ayala, and Elliot Aronson, "Polyfidelity: An Alternative Lifestyle without Jealousy?" *Alternative Lifestyles*, vol. 4, no. 3 (August 1981), pp. 373-392.

34. Old Testament, Genesis 38: 7-10.

35. Havelock Ellis posed the basic sexual dilemma facing human beings as the clash between the desire for variety and the desire for stability. He never quite resolved it during his own lifetime. For an interesting account of his views see
Robinson, Paul A., *The Modernization of Sex*. New York: Harper & Row, Pub., 1976.
For a revealing account of his private life see: Grosskurth, Phyllis, *Havelock Ellis: A Biography*. New York: Alfred A. Kropf, 1980.

36. For the classic account on the Trobrianders see the Malinowski reference that follows; for a more recent and somewhat different interpretation see the Weiner reference that follows:
Malinowski, Bronislaw, *The Sexual Life of Savages in North-Western Melanesia*. New York: Harvest Books, 1929.
Weiner, Annette, *Women of Value: Men of Renown*. Austin: University of Texas Press, 1976.

37. For an analysis of extramarital sexual norms using the Standard Sample, see
Broude, Gwen J., "Extramarital Sex Norms in Cross-cultural Perspective," *Behavior Science Research*, vol. 15, no. 3 (1980), pp. 181-218.

38. Davenport, William, "Sexual Patterns and Their Regulation in a Society of the SW Pacific," Chapter Eight in F.A. Beach (ed.), *Sex and Behavior*. New York: John Wiley, 1965.

39. For recent research relevant to this point see
Reiss, Ira L., Ronald E. Anderson, and G.C. Sponaugle, "A Multivariate Model of the Determinants of Extramarital Sexual Permissiveness," *Journal of Marriage and the Family*, vol. 42 (May 1980), pp. 395-411.
Buunk, Bram, "Jealousy in Sexually Open Marriages," *Alternative Lifestyles*, vol. 4, no. 3, (August 1981), pp. 357-372.
Blumstein, Philip, and Pepper Schwartz, *American Couples*. New York. Morrow, 1983.

40. For popularly written books on sexually open lifestyles see
Ramey, James, *Intimate Friendships*. Englewood Cliffs, N.J.: Prentice-Hall, 1976.
Nass, Gilbert D., Roger W. Libby, and Mary Pat Fisher, *Sexual Choices* (2nd ed.). Monterey, Calif.: Wadsworth Health Sciences Division, 1984.
Ziskin, J., and M. Ziskin, *The Extramarital Sex Contract*. Los Angeles: Nash Publications, 1973.

41. Analogous to the levirate is a custom known as the sororate. In the sororate, when an older sister dies, her younger sister marries her older sister's

husband. The sororate is not as widespread as the levirate. The levirate occurs in over two thirds of the nonindustrialized cultures.

Whyte, Martin K., *The Status of Women in Preindustrial Societies.* Princeton, N.J.: Princeton University Press, 1978. (See especially pp. 76-77.)

42. Good sources to begin with for these cultures are

Schneider, Harold K., "Romantic Lover among the Turu," Chapter Three in Donald S. Marshall and Robert C. Suggs (eds.), *Human Sexual Behavior: Variations in the Ethnographic Spectrum.* New York: Basic Books, 1971.

I. Schapera, *Married Life in an African Tribe.* New York: Sheridan House, 1941.

Suggs, Robert C., *Marquesan Sexual Behavior.* New York: Harcourt Brace Jovanovich, 1976.

43. Schneider, Harold K., "Romantic Love among the Turu," Chapter Three in Donald S. Marshall and Robert C. Suggs (eds.), *Human Sexual Behavior: Variations in the Ethnographic Spectrum.* New York: Basic Books, 1971.

44. One interesting bit of evidence on failure rates of integrative approaches comes from a study of group marriage in America that indicated that the life of group marriages is usually measured in months. See

Constantine, Larry, and Joan Constantine, *Group Marriage.* New York: Macmillan, 1973.

45. Levy, Robert I., *Tahitians.* Chicago: University of Chicago Press, 1973. (See especially Chapters 6 and 9.)

46. A research project that I undertook with two colleagues examined the evidence on the relationship of educational background to extramarital sexual attitudes:

Reiss, Ira L., Ronald E. Anderson, and G.C. Sponaugle, "A Multivariate Model of the Determinants of Extramarital Sexual Permissiveness," *Journal of Marriage and the Family,* vol. 42 (May 1980), pp. 395-411.

47. For a recent article with some good references on this point, see

Ritchie, Jan, and James Ritchie, "Polynesian Child Rearing: An Alternative Model," *Alternative Lifestyles,* vol. 5 no. 3 (Spring 1983), pp. 126-141.

48. Two recent books have interesting accounts of the nature of sexuality without affection:

Vannoy, Russell, *Sex without Love: A Philosophical Exploration.* Buffalo: Prometheus Books, 1980.

Schofield, Michael, *Promiscuity.* London: Victor Gollancz, 1976.

49. This study is based on about 6,000 volunteer couples from Seattle, San Francisco, and New York City. There were about 3,600 married couples, about 650 cohabiting couples, almost 1,000 gay male couples, and almost 800 lesbian couples. The percentage of married couples and of other couples with an agreement is cited on page 585 in footnote 27 of their book:

Blumstein, Philip, and Pepper Schwartz, *American Couples.* New York: Morrow, 1983.

50. Blumstein, Philip, and Pepper Swartz, *American Couples.* New York: Morrow, 1983. (See especially pp. 267-306.)

51. McWhirter, David P., and Andrew M. Mattison, *The Male Couple: How Relationships Develop.* Englewood Cliffs, N.J.: Prentice-Hall, 1984.

52. For reading on path analysis see

Heise, David R., *Causal Analysis.* New York: John Wiley, 1973. (See Chapter 4.)

Blalock, H.M., Jr. (ed.), *Causal Models in the Social Sciences.* Chicago: Aldine, 1971. (See Part 2.)

Asher, Herbert B., *Causal Modeling.* Beverly Hills, Calif.: Sage Publications, 1976. (This is a small book that summarizes causal modeling rather well.)

53. I did find some different relationships than Hupka reported for his sample. This may have been so partly because I used only 80 of his 92 cultures, since the other 12 were not in the Standard Sample, which was the set of societies I used for all my statistical analyses.

One key difference concerned his sexual restrictiveness variable. I did analyze the correlation of his general measure of sexual restrictiveness with other measures that I had on premarital and extramartial sexual permissiveness. His variable was purported to measure males and females on both premarital and extramarital sexuality. That immediately caught my eye, for by lumping all this together he was ignoring the double-standard influence and assuming a very high correlation of pre-marital and extramarital sexuality. I correlated his sexual restrictiveness measure with Broude's measure of male and female extramarital sexuality and found very close to a zero correlation for each gender. It seemed that Hupka was not measuring extramarital sexuality—at least not the way Broude was. Then I correlated Hupka's sexual restrictiveness measure with Broude's premarital measures for males and females and with the Standard Sample's measure of female premarital sexuality and found correlation of about .5. These results indicated to me that what Hupka was measuring in his sexual restrictiveness variable was predominantly premarital sexual permissiveness.

I found male premarital sexuality not to relate to any of the other variables in Diagram 3.1, and so I decided to drop it and focus upon female premarital sexual permissiveness and its role in marital sexual jealousy. I used the Standard Sample measure for this because Broude's measure of female premarital sexuality was coded only for 114 of the 186 societies while the Standard Sample code was for all 186 societies. This variable did relate to some of the other variables in Diagrams 3.1 and 3.2, and so it was included in my analysis.

Hupka had stated that sexual restrictiveness did relate to husband's sexual jealousy but not at all to wife's sexual jealousy. I believe these results were spurious and were due to his measure combining male and female sexual restrictiveness. Since male and female premarital sexuality do not relate in the same way to husband and wife jealousy, the use of them in combined form can be misleading. Thus, I believe my use of only female premarital sexuality is a clearer and more easily interpretable measure.

I have given considerable detail here concerning the analysis of this one variable, for this illustrates the type of validity checks I have done throughout on all the variables I use in my diagrams. For more specific details on all the diagrams in the book and on my research using the Standard Sample, the reader should consult Appendix 1.

54. The entire question of statistical significance is discussed in simplified form in Appendix 2, "An Elementary Approach to Probability Statistics," in

Reiss, Ira L., *Family Systems in America* (3rd ed.). New York: Holt, Rinehart & Winston, 1980.

55. Analysis of the Standard Sample indicates that matrilocal and matrilineal societies do permit women greater sexual rights. Such societies also have somewhat greater gender equality than patrilineal and patrilocal societies. Other researchers in the past have reported similar findings. This is congruent with my conception of the role of male power in female sexual rights.

56. Additional support for the key role of male power in terms of female sexuality comes from my analysis of the determinants in the Standard Sample of the frequency with which wives engage in extramarital relationships. I found that the two best determinants of wives' extramarital frequency was the husband's

extramarital frequency and whether the society believed that females were inferior to males. In short, if husbands were low on extramarital relations, that tended to decrease wives' participation in extramarital sexuality. Also, if females were believed to be inferior to males, that also lowered female extramarital experiences. One could interpret these regulations to show how males in their sexual behavior and in their beliefs determine their wife's sexuality. Admittedly this is only suggestive, but it is another finding compatible with the view that male power is a key determinant of female sexuality.

57. For a good overview of Havelock Ellis's position on jealousy and also of his other contributions, see

Ellis, Havelock, *Psychology of Sex: A Manual for Students.* New York: Emerson Books, 1964. (Originally published in 1933.)

Grosskurth, Phyllis, *Havelock Ellis: A Biography.* New York: Knopf, 1980.

58. Murdock, George P., "Ethnographic Atlas: A Summary," *Ethnology,* vol. 6 (April 1967), pp. 109-236.

59. A good overall summary of sexuality and genetic sex differences in non-human primates can be found in

Mitchell, G., *Behavioral Sex Differences in Non Human Primates.* New York: Van Nostrand Reinhold, 1979.

60. Brain reports that the Bangwa tribe that he studied ranks friendship ties as more important than kinship ties. See

Brain, Robert, *Friends and Lovers.* New York: Basic Books, 1976.

CHAPTER FOUR

THE POWER FILTERS

Gender Roles

THE SOCIAL NATURE OF GENDER

There are those who feel that what men and women do in a society is what is "natural" for them in accord with their biological makeup. Thus, women care for children because, by their nature, they bear them and enjoy nurturing them; men tend to warfare because they are, by their nature, aggressive. This perspective is similar to what we encountered in our discussion of sexuality in Chapter 2. We noted there that many people felt sexuality was just "doing what comes naturally" and was explainable by its tie to reproduction. The reader is aware that we rejected much of that position. Here, analogously, I will qualify biological determinism by evidencing the societal impact on gender roles. Even though most of you may reject such determinism, it is well to spell out the boundary limitations of a biological and a sociological explanation of gender.

To be sure, female wombs and male hormones cannot be denied. What can be disclaimed is that they explain the bulk of gender-role behavior. Surely, biological explanations are almost totally inadequate when our questions concern differences in gender roles among cultures, for if a common genetic base accounts for male-female differences in gender roles, then that *similar* base cannot account for *differences* among cultures. If that common genetic base was the full explanation, there would be zero variation in gender roles around the world. I certainly do not deny that biology has some influence on gender roles, but biology is not helpful in explaining why gender roles are not the same in various societies.

One other qualification of the common biological deterministic view of gender roles needs to be put forth. There is no necessity that females take the lion's share of childrearing just because they have a womb in which that child was created. Societies do modify the role of mothers in accord with pressures from the economic system and elsewhere. If female labor is needed outside the family role, then males, children, and the elders will share in childrearing so as to free women for outside work. We can see this in some matrilineal societies where women work together and play the important economic roles. In such a setting the woman's brothers and her mother and older children will make it possible for the woman to work cooperatively with other women, and people will not expect mothers to be the predominant source of childcare.

In the Standard Sample, 8% of the cultures have other people who do more than mothers in caring for infants, and another 39% have others who have important roles in infant caretaking.[1] In the remaining 53% of the societies the mother is the predominant caretaker of the infant, while others have very minor roles. Low involvement in infant care is much more common for fathers; in 23% of the societies fathers have almost no caretaking roles with infants, and in 47% they have only occasional roles. In only 30% of the cultures do fathers have frequent or regular companionship with their infants.

This still means that there are societies where childrearing is considered equally a father's and a mother's task. Margaret Mead described the Manus society off the coast of New Guinea as one such society. Males are considered more nurturant than females, and Mead reported that when she introduced dolls to the people, it was the boys, not the girls, who treated the dolls like babies.[2]

Thus, while a clear cross-cultural male-female difference in care of infants is evident, it is equally apparent that there is considerable variation in the role of mothers and fathers in infant care. Much of this variation is due to societal pressures and norms that affect the relative involvement of mothers and fathers in infant care. Surely the fact that the mother has carried the child during pregnancy is a powerful force toward future infant care, but societal pressures always organize the ways in which that care will be carried out. So, culture has the power to program any biological capacities that we may possess. In fact, since we are all raised within some type of social structure, we will never really experience our "biological nature" in any pure sense.

The importance of knowing more about societal sculpturing of biological differences between males and females lies in the implications of this knowledge for social change. If biology were fully determinant of gender roles, then little could be done to alter them. But if biology only establishes tendencies and if society always organizes and structures these tendencies, then regardless of what biological differences there are between men and women, we can, through our socialization process, achieve the types of gender roles we desire.

True, it may be difficult to alter dramatically the female tie to infants because females carry the fetus during pregnancy and because hormones like oxytocin reinforce the female-infant tie. The cry of the infant releases oxytocin in the mother, which aids in the flow of her breast milk.[3] Such outcomes may well encourage mothers to nurse infants; but before you are seduced by biological determinism, think about the fact that most American women do not nurse their infants although they have oxytocin in their bloodstreams. Clearly, then, the shaping of these flexible biological tendencies by societal demands is possible and inevitable. It may well be wise to be aware of what biological tendencies exist so that we know what dispositions we are working with in human societies. It would be foolish, however, not to realize the plasticity of these biological propensities. I believe that most biologists today would agree with this point.

Looking at the genetic male for possible biological determinants of his gender role, I would agree with Maccoby and Jacklin's conclusions concerning the higher levels of aggressiveness in males that prevail in almost all primates.[4] Evidence from human and nonhuman primates indicates that male aggressiveness is likely tied in some ways to the presence in males of much higher levels of the androgen hormone. Evidence suggests that among other male primates physical combat increases androgen levels in the victor and decreases them in the vanquished. Administration of androgen to male primates, especially dominant males, does increase their levels of aggressivity.[5] Finally, in virtually all cultures the act of warfare or of organized killing is done by males. Without belaboring the point, it seems that males have a biological tendency for higher physical aggression than do females. Maccoby and Jacklin define such physical aggression, as most scientists do, as an attempt to hurt someone.

That the average male may be more aggressive than the average female may mislead the reader into ignoring the considerable overlap between the sexes. It is likely that a large proportion of males and a large proportion of females are very similar in aggressive potential, but the remaining proportion of males move toward the higher levels and the remaining group of females move toward the lower levels of aggression. Thus, the averages do come out significantly different. This point is important to grasp, for it makes it easier to appreciate that if large proportions of males and females are already similar on aggression, then male-female differences can certainly be muted by social training.

To illustrate the role of learning in aggressiveness, one need only note that in our society males and females under five years of age are quite different in physical aggression despite the fact that at that early age they are rather similar in androgen levels. It is after age nine or ten that the large male-female differences in androgen appear.

Apparently, then, social factors train very young male and female children into their gender roles without much support from androgen levels. The ease of modification can be seen by comparing violent-crime rates in different Western societies. We are the leader in this measure, but I doubt if our males have any more androgen than the Scandinavian males who have relatively low rates of violent crime.

If you accept my position—that although there are biological differences between males and females, such tendencies are molded and modified by societal conditions—then it follows that we can alter gender roles in accord with our values if we are willing to put forth the effort required. Relatedly, if we grant this flexible view of biological tendencies, it then becomes pointless to argue over the reality of male-female biological differences.

Such arguments over how much is biologically determined are often undertaken in order to support one's ideological position regarding gender-role equality. Accordingly, those who reject gender-role equality seek to establish male dominance by stressing biological differences, while those who defend gender-role equality seek to establish the validity of their views by denying male-female differences. Once we grant that whatever biological tendencies exist are constantly being socially modified, then we need no longer debate such issues.

Aggression hardly establishes dominance by itself. One needs social skills and group alliances to obtain political power, and aggression alone is insufficient. Were it otherwise, professional football players would be our leaders, for they are probably very high on physical aggression. We have had more professional movie actors in Washington than professional football players. This should tell us something about what it takes to gain power.

My conception also implies that having more oxytocin or possessing a womb does not guarantee devotion to infant care. Those women with the highest oxytocin levels are not necessarily the leaders in childcare, for that form of leadership also takes social skills and knowledge of how to nurture children for the specific type of society in which they must live. Furthermore, we have seen that in almost half the societies there are other important nurturers of infants besides the mother, and in three out of ten societies, fathers are heavily involved in infant care. Once more the flexibility of our biological inheritance is demonstrated. There are biological tendencies, but they are demonstrably malleable if we are willing to pay the cost of shaping them in the directions we prefer.

In sum, since we are all born into existing social systems, biological tendencies will be unable to express themselves without being shaped by the social environment. Most biologists today would accept this position even if they do focus upon the biological tendencies and not the societal sculpturing of these potentials. Biologists know now that the hypothalamus affects the pituitary gland and through it the workings of the endocrine system, which regulate our hormonal syntheses. The hypothalamus is part of the brain and as such is affected by our brain processes. Thus, biological research itself has revealed that our societal training, which also affects our brain processes, has a direct pathway toward shaping the biological potentials of our bodies.

The relationship between the biological and social is clearly an interactive process. But having said that does not specify the precise ways in which each factor operates nor how both factors interact. Some scientists may choose to deal with the interactive process and specify how these two types of causes affect each other. I prefer to specialize on the power of the societal. This does not deny the importance of biological potentials or tendencies; rather, it takes biology as a constant and then looks to explain the variation in male-female roles by examining the variety of societal systems involved in shaping such roles.

One final little-known illustration should convince the reader that societal gender roles have a high degree of freedom from biological determination. Although this sounds impossible to many Westerners, there are cultures that have more than two genders.[6] One of the best-known examples occurs among the Navajo Indians in North America. They have a third gender known as the nadle. The entry into this gender is by two pathways: (1) if an infant is born with ambiguous genitalia that makes it difficult to know if the child is a male or female and (b) if a person feels very unhappy in the male or female gender role and wishes to change to another gender. The nadle gender can combine the rights and duties of the male and female genders with the exception that they cannot hunt and cannot participate in warfare. They may marry and dress in any way they wish and perform a wide variety of tasks.

Other societies recognize more than two genders; some, four or five. Usually the reasons given are the same as with the Navajo: either the presence of ambiguous genitalia at birth or the unhappiness of being assigned to the male or female gender. Although such instances are not common, their very presence supports the separation of biology and gender. Clearly, genetic makeup of individuals, though obviously important, is only partially the basis for being classified into a gender. Each society not only shapes the content of a gender but, in some cases, also decides how many genders will exist.[7] Thus, one may conclude that while there are obvious conjunctures of biology and gender, there are equally obvious disjunctures, and the role of culture in structuring gender looms large in any explanation.

POWER AND GENDER

It is the seemingly universal difference in societal power of the genders that sparks one's intellectual curiosity to ask why. As I have discussed, the biological determinist's answer is unsatisfactory and incomplete. Even if we were to examine only one society, we know that the power differentials of the genders may vary in each generation whereas biological differences between males and females changes only over the eons. We therefore must search for societal-level explanations whether we deal with one or a thousand societies.

First, let us define *power* as the ability to influence others and achieve one's objectives despite the opposition of the other person.[8] Thus, power is a measure of interpersonal influence. I mention the opposition of the other person, for it is not a test of power to persuade someone who is indifferent on the issue or who already agrees. It is a test of power when someone puts up resistance, for then we have a measure of the force one can exert.

In society there are two basic types of power. The first we can call *authorized* or legitimate power, and it is based upon the norms of a group or society. Such legitimate power is thus authorized by the role one plays or the social position one occupies. A teacher, for example, has an element of legitimate, normatively assigned power over the students in his or her class. Also, in many traditional Western countries, a husband still has authorized or legitimate power over his wife, as the phrase "to honor and obey" implies. A second type of power is *unauthorized* power, which is a measure of the degree of influence one person has over another that goes beyond what the norms dictate. Thus, a student who persuades a professor to change a grade because he or she is the son or daughter of a close friend, has unauthorized power. Likewise, if a wife in a traditional Western society dominated her husband, that would be a sign of her power, but it would be normatively unauthorized power.

Sociologists generally agree that the positions a group holds in the basic institutions in a society are the key sources of what power any group possesses. These basic institutions are familial, political, economic, and religious.[9] To understand the level of authorized power of males, females, or any group, one needs to examine authorized and unauthorized influence of that group in these major institutions. Consider for a moment the place of the female gender in American society in terms of our basic institutions.

In the family institution the female, even today, is viewed as the homemaker.[10] Traditionally, the male who is her husband has been assigned authority over her. This is changing, but even at present a husband who has the predominant share of influence in a marriage raises fewer eyebrows than does a wife who has the predominant share of power in a marriage. Although equalitarian marriages have become acceptable in America, female-dominant marriages are still far from widely accepted. This perspective points out just how much and how little has changed.

Examine the political institution. Women in America occupy about 10% of the elective offices in the country. They control only about 4% of the seats in Congress, though they represent over 50% of the population of the country. The percentage of women in political office increases as the prestige of the position decreases.[11] There is today one female governor but quite a few female mayors. It is not difficult to discern the lack of female political power in our society, and this is rather typical for a Western society.

In the economic institution, full-time employed women earn about 60% of what full-time employed men earn. Further, about half the employed women work part time, whereas only about 20% of the men employed work part time. Small segments of women in the professions such as law, medicine, and dentistry have made economic gains, but about 75% of women are still employed in jobs stereotyped as women's work and ranked low in the prestige values of our culture.

How many women are rabbis, priests, or ministers? Some religions like the Catholic Church, many Protestant sects, and Orthodox Judaism forbid women to occupy the leadership role men have held for centuries. Even in those religions that have recently accepted the presence of a female religious leader, very few women are in the pulpit.

Finally, in education we still find female college students electing those fields that pay the least in future jobs. More women elect majors in home economics, the humanities, and primary school teaching than do men. Even in Scandinavia, one of the most gender-equal of the Western countries, we find a similar difference in choice of fields in the universities, although not as one-sided as in America. In fact, an overview of Scandinavia reveals that although we would find more gender equality in all the major institutions, it is obvious that the Scandinavian countries have not achieved anything near full gender equality in any of these institutional areas.[12]

The place of women in these basic institutions in the West is not a mere chance occurrence. The traditional definition of the female gender role promotes precisely such an unequal integration of women in the societal institutional structure. Even at the present time, many Americans probably expect a woman to give priority to her family and not to pursue a career with the vigor that a male does. That expectation is part of the consensual gender role of women, and it acts as a block to any change in gender power. When women's priority is in the home, women will have a most difficult time achieving equality outside that home. The inequality in outside roles will inhibit equality even in the home. The woman may gain some unauthorized power by her special talents or by her behind-the-scenes maneuvers, but the very dependence upon such unauthorized power evidences the lack of authorized power.

What our brief institutional analysis indicates is that women are low in power in all major institutions in the West. This structural basis of low power is reinforced by the day-to-day interactions with women who devote themselves to the home, who do not seek careers, and who pursue positions traditionally occupied by women, like secretary, nurse, or public school teacher. One should not lose sight of the fact that men pick up these gender perceptions via social interactions with traditional women as well as by traditional views being passed down to them in the male culture.

Many employers still view women as earning "extra spending money" and lose sight of the millions of women who are the sole support of their families. This is a sort of Catch-22 situation wherein if women strive to break into high-status professions, they are blocked by the traditional expectations; and if they do break into such professions, they are not afforded fully equal status and are often relegated to the lower echelons of that profession. It seems that women must first be viewed as equal before they can gain equality.

One illustration of the Catch-22 status of women in the Western world can be seen in the status of female medical doctors in the Soviet Union. In part due to the great loss of males during the Second World War, the Soviets encouraged women to enter the medical profession and become general practitioners. Women did enter and now comprise about 80% of the general practitioners. One might surmise that this would raise the status of women, but what happened was otherwise: The status of general practitioner went down as the percentage of women in that role increased. Today, the general practitioner in the Soviet Union earns less than an industrial worker. Yet in accord with their broad institutional power, males are still the surgeons and hospital administrators and earn much more income.

What appears to have happened in the preceding instance is that since women were viewed as unequal to men, when they entered the profession of medicine, instead of raising the female status, the worth of their part of that profession declined. My conclusion from this is that a group that wants to increase its power must somehow first convince those in power that it deserved more than it has. This is not an insurmountable obstacle, but it clearly complicates the movement toward female equality in the Western world. This is not the place for discussing educational and other strategies for equalizing gender roles. For our purposes it is sufficient to make the point that in the Western world the female gender role has less authorized power than the male gender role in all the major institutions.

A TEST OF A THEORY OF GENDER INEQUALITY

Now let us develop a macro or overall view and see how the power of each gender reflects the general type of society. Most of the anthropologists who have written on gender power have noted that there are significant changes when one moves from hunting and gathering societies to agricultural societies.[13] Following up that lead, I examined the data available on the 186 nonindustrialized societies in the Standard Sample. My basic assumption was that the greater the male power and status in a society, the more likely female status and power would be low. This assumption states that whoever is in power will rule both genders due to their integrated roles in that society. By status I mean prestige or honor.[14] Status and power can vary somewhat independently of each other. Think of college professors: They have high status but only modest power in our society. Nevertheless, generally status and power levels are closely related.

As a background for discussing my findings I want to mention the extensive study of the general status of women in nonindustrial societies done by Martin King Whyte.[15] He examined 52 measures of female status in 93 of the societies in the Standard Sample. Given the lack of cross-cultural studies of gender power, this study of status is a strategic one for our purposes.

Whyte's results were in many ways inconclusive. He found that the 52 measures of female status fit into ten different scales, and these ten scales of female status did not relate to each other. One conclusion, then, would be that female status was a broad, multidimensional concept and no single way of measuring it would suffice.[16] Remembering our earlier discussion about the vagueness of much of the data in the Standard Sample, one might also conclude that Whyte's findings were inconclusive because the data were not precise enough to reveal what interrelations did exist among these ten scales measuring female status. In any case, for my purposes I needed a simple measure that would at least get at one of the important aspects of female status. I could not get involved in the intricacies of precisely how to measure all the key aspects of female status.

I chose one of Whyte's female status questions: "Is there a clearly stated belief that women are generally inferior to men?" Out of the 93 societies he studied, 27 held such a belief and 66 did not.[17] These 27 societies probably represent those societies with the very lowest female status, for we know that male status is higher in virtually all societies; and so those with this public belief probably represent those "lowest" on female status. This should highlight what differences exist and set the stage for others to specify further whatever relationships were found. I searched for what other societal characteristics went with the inferiority beliefs and in that way sought a better understanding of how those inferiority beliefs develop.

Diagram 4.1 presents the six societal features that comprise my explanation of how such beliefs in female inferiority develop and are supported.

The reader should be aware that the terms *positive* and *negative* refer to the direction of the relationship and not the strength of it. A negative relationship can be just as strong as a positive one. This causal diagram, like the ones in Chapter 3, presents changes through time going from the earliest events at the left to the most recent one, which is being explained, at the right of the diagram. It is really very easy to read—just don't let yourself get scared off by the initial complexity.

Now, a few words about the theory underlying this explanation. As noted earlier, almost all the writers on female power and status posit that the development of agricultural societies led to a significant drop in female power and status. The reasoning is that agriculture leads to a greater dependence on cooperative male labor and that is one factor promoting male power. The dependence on male labor results, in part, from the physical effort needed in agricultural societies that use the plow. Relatedly, agriculture emphasizes the value of male children and pressures the female to produce such valued agriculture workers.

In addition, agriculture leads to the development of more complex societies. The basic reason for this is that agriculturally based societies are capable of

DIAGRAM 4.1   Causes of female gender inequality.

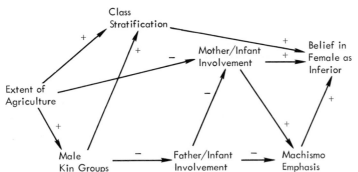

producing surpluses in food supplies; that means much larger and more stable populations can be supported, and that increase in numbers adds complexity to the social organization. As a consequence there is a development of sharper social class distinctions in agricultural societies. In good part this is due to the development of more specialized political systems, as well as to the opportunity for accumulating wealth because of agricultural surpluses that can be bartered to others.

As these changes occur, women are increasingly excluded from leadership positions in these complex political and economic structures and are instead segregated into the domestic sphere or into subordinate farm labor. The end result of this less central societal role of females is a decline in the status of females from what it was in hunting, gathering, and horticultural societies.

I tested part of these ideas by using measures of the presence of agriculture, the event of male kin groups practicing patrilineal descent and patrilocal residence, and the development of highly stratified societies. These forces were measured by the first three variables to the left in the diagram. I also wanted some measure of gender roles that would indicate the extent to which women and men were involved in caretaking and companionship with infants. I felt this would indicate whether women were segregated from the center of power by their family commitments. I found two such variables in the Standard Sample (they are next in the diagram). Finally, I felt that a machismo[18] attitude stressing male physical aggressiveness would also be a likely predictor of a belief in female inferiority.[19]

When I looked at the results of my causal analysis, I was truly surprised that the data so clearly were congruent with my expectations. The results did add specificity regarding how these six causal variables interrelate with each other as well as how they produce the belief in female inferiority. Given the limitations of the cross-cultural data, I did not expect to find any such clear pattern emerging. A sharp causal pattern usually does not emerge from vague codes because such codes may not clearly represent what they are purported to measure. Only very powerfully related variables would show through the fog of such imperfect codes, and so I was not optimistic. Yet the causal analysis revealed a pattern of relationships among the seven variables that was indeed impressive!

The lines in this diagram represent all the significant correlations among variables found in the statistical analysis of the data. Note that many possible lines relating these variables are not present. There are 21 possible interrelations of these seven variables as they are presented here. Of those 21 possible relationships, 11 showed themselves to be statistically significant. Most importantly, almost all of the 11 relationships that did meet the statistical standards and are in the diagram strongly supported my expectations.[20]

The order of the variables represents what I felt to be a time sequence of events starting with the advent of agriculture and ending with a belief in female inferiority. To my knowledge this is the first time such an extensive test of cross-cultural data has been used to examine in a causal analysis this entire set of widespread beliefs about social changes in female status.

The results in Diagram 4.1 do show that, as expected, the advent of agriculture increases class stratification and male kin groups. In turn, male kin groups seemed to encourage greater class stratification, as can also be seen in the diagram. In addition, these male groups lower the likelihood that fathers will be involved in the care of their newborn, and that in turn increases the likelihood that mothers will be involved in the care of the newborn. Finally, one can see by the lines connecting mother- and father-infant involvements to machismo that the less fathers are involved in infant care and the more mothers are, the greater the level of machismo in a society.

One causal line may surprise the reader—that is the negative relationship of the advent of agriculture with mother-infant involvement. I had not expected this relationship, but I believe it may reflect the fact that in agricultural, as compared to, say, hunting societies, the greater food supply supports higher population densities. This means that women in agricultural societies are encouraged to have more children. Relatedly, the greater number of children may necessitate that others such as older children and grandmothers take on a share of the caretaking and nurturing of infants. Thus, even though mothers are still heavily involved with infants, a higher share of the total nurturance of these large families will be done by others. Finally, it may well be that in agricultural societies women are assigned additional minor economic tasks by males. This, too, would lead to mothers seeking help in infant care from others.

The diagram presents a way of understanding the societal factors that promote male power and status over female power and status. There are surely other factors, but they are not represented in this diagram because I had to restrict myself to what variables were measured and were useable. Despite this restriction there are in the diagram many places for intervention should one wish to change attitudes toward females. Consider the impact of changing the emphasis upon male groups (in work, in descent, in residence) or the impact of increasing the female's chance to enter more fully the economic and political systems. In fact, these changes are precisely the sort of alteration that have occurred in the Western world in the twentieth century. They have been accompanied by a rise in female status and power, which further supports our theory of the societal causes of female status.

I must qualify any bald economic deterministic interpretation of these findings. Diagram 4.1 does not indicate that the economic change—in this case to agriculture—is the only factor that will bring about the outcomes in other variables. The findings do not preclude changes due to warfare, new value systems, or new political systems from also producing similar changes even if the economic system were unaltered. In my discussion of Diagram 3.1, I noted that agriculture was not a powerful determinant of changes in the importance of property nor in changes in the presence of male groups.

The key point here is that anything that increases class stratification and male groups will likely have similar outcomes in the other variables. Further, agricultural systems are varied, and not all changes toward an agricultural system will produce the same outcomes. It depends on, among other things, the amount of geographic and social mobility involved in that particular type of agriculture.[21] Agriculture that involves geographic mobility would not encourage the formation of stable social classes.

The economic system is a pragmatic system, easily changed in most societies compared to religious, political, or family systems. Thus, it is often the economic system that initiates change. The role of the economic system is nevertheless a matter to be investigated rather than a foregone conclusion. Today many Marxists would also agree to that caution.

One other important theoretical implication of this diagram requires some comment. Examine the relationship of mother-infant nurturance to the emphasis on machismo and to the belief in female inferiority. The diagram indicates that the more the mother nurtures infants, the stronger the emphasis on machismo and the stronger the belief in female inferiority. Start at the left of the diagram and trace the lines leading into mother-infant nurturance. You will find that as agricultural tendencies increase, so do the strength of male kin groups; and as that increases, the father-infant involvement decreases; and that, in turn, increases the mother-infant involvement.

Now return to the connection of mother-infant involvement to machismo and the belief in female inferiority. It seems apparent that, given the pathway leading to mother-infant involvement, the reason for this variable relating to machismo and to the belief in female inferiority is that this measure of mother-infant nurturance is in part an indirect index of a male-dominated society. In such a society the mother will nurture the infant and will likely socialize the child in values and behaviors that will maintain the dominance of males. In this sense the mother-infant nurturance will emphasize machismo attitudes and promote a belief in female inferiority. Of course, not all societies that stress mother-infant nurturance are high on male dominance. Here, as elsewhere, the parts of a society can be put together in many ways. However, on the average, our statistical results indicate that such a custom of mother-infant involvement reflects male dominance in a society.

Some psychologists might examine the relationships of the mother-infant nurturance variable and develop psychoanalytic reasons why mother-infant involvement leads to an emphasis on machismo and a belief in female inferiority. Science generally operates on the principle of parsimony sometimes known as Ockham's razor, which favors the simpler explanation where there are several explanations put forth.[22] I believe the simpler explanation is that such relationships are part of the overall pattern that makes up a male-dominated society. I do not believe that the involvement of the mother in infant care, per se, is what is causally important. The key is that mother-infant involvement is one way of freeing males for more powerful and prestigious positions in society. Therefore, in male-dominated societies that type of female gender role will be encouraged.[23] At the same time that type of society will encourage the mother to pass along that society's male-dominant values even if they deprecate the female gender role. In this fashion, the tie of mothers to infants promotes a belief in female inferiority in particular types of social systems.

THE LINKAGES OF POWER, KINSHIP, AND GENDER

We have presented a general theory purporting to explain partially the relative power and prestige of males and females in different types of societies, but gender roles are themselves in large part a reflection of the kinship system in a society. Diagram 4.1 shows kinship linkages in part through the male kin groups variable, which measures patrilocal residence and patrilineal descent. Such measures inform us of the important consequences of strong male kinship ties measured by descent and by where one lives after marriage. Still, more intimate knowledge of kinship will assist us in understanding how the influence of the broader societal structure makes its way into gender roles. In all these linkages involving kinship and gender, the power dimension is significantly engaged. Follow along with my illustrations, starting with one very interesting culture, and I will try to clarify my meaning.

The Tiwi are a fascinating culture existing in Melville Island, North Australia. They will help us illustrate the ways in which kinship organizes our gender roles in a moderately male-dominant hunting society. The kinship system in this society has been extensively studied, most recently by Jane Goodale.[24] The entry point for our purposes is the custom for the maternal grandfather in this society to arrange for the marriage of his granddaughter before she is ever born.

Female children are married from the moment they are born. When a female child reaches puberty and has her first menstrual period, her father will pick a *son-in-law* for her. One unusual feature of his choice is that the man he picks as his daughter's son-in-law will often be ten or twenty years *older* than the daughter who will be that man's mother-in-law. The father promises that all the female children his daughter bears will be given to the son-in-law as wives (Polygyny is accepted in this society and in about 75% of all the societies in the nonindustrialized world.) In return the son-in-law promises to help supply food for his mother-in-law and from then on will live in her camp.

Let us follow through the events after the birth of a female child to this man's mother-in-law. At age 7 the child is sent to live with her husband (the son-in-law) as his wife. The husband is often 30 or more years older than his 7 year-old bride, but both he and the child bride are prepared for sexual relations to occur usually within a year. Like the Lepcha, whom we discussed in previous chapters, the Tiwi believe that having intercourse at these early ages encourages female puberty. Without such intercourse young girls are believed incapable of developing breasts, pubic hair, hips, and menstruation. Thus, sexuality between an adult husband and a child bride is an accepted custom in this society.

When this child bride begins to menstruate, her father will pick a son-in-law for her, and this man will marry her female children and reside near her and help her. The process continues generation to generation. Note that under this system all girls are married before they are born, and so premarital sexuality is impossible for females in this type of society.

Interestingly, due to changes in husbands, the wife will eventually end up being older than her final husband. This is so because the Tiwi, like most non-industrialized cultures, have the levirate custom, which means that when the husband dies, his younger brother becomes her husband. Since her first husband is much older than she, he will likely die first. After two or three such brothers die, she may end up with a husband who is younger than she is.

Marriage for a male is an achievement—the more wives, the more power. For a woman it is a fact of life—she can have only one husband at a time, and her power comes not from many mates but from residing near her mother, to whom her husband is indebted. The descent group for the Tiwi is thus matrilineal, and the residence group will consist of females related through their mother's line plus their husbands, who as sons-in-law are also living there. (This is matrilocal residence.) However, the Tiwi also belong to a patrilineage through which all their land is inherited. In this way there is a relatively close balance of power between the genders. A female has the support of her husband and her son-in-law and lives in her home village. A male through his male kin controls ownership of the land and arranges the marriage of his granddaughters to his advantage by often linking them to his nephews.

Note how the nature of the kinship system defines certain key aspects of gender roles. Kinship determines who arranges the marriage and what the rights and duties of those involved will be. Those involved are males and females; thus, by defining marriage roles gender roles are also defined.[25] Further, the specific ways the kinship system is structured determine the balance of power between males and females. If the descent were patrilineal and no labor was owed to mothers-in-law and land was fully controlled by males, then the gender differences in power would be much greater than they are among the Tiwi.

To recapitulate, kinship systems must define how males and females interrelate, and the particular design chosen reflects the power of each gender. This power differential can be causally traced, particularly to key features of the economic and political systems. To illustrate, if males work the land together, then it is highly likely that descent will be traced through their line and they will reside together after marriage.[26] If females work together, then it is more likely that descent and residence will be centered around females. Political influence from outside the society can also affect gender power. Etienne and Leacock assert that European colonists strengthened male power in the colonized societies by projecting their own notions of male dominance and dealing mainly with the males in the conquered societies.[27]

One additional way to illustrate how kinship, gender, and power are linked together is to examine further matrilineally organized societies. I will do this in general, rather than looking in depth at any one society. Matrilineal societies are organized around descent through one's mother's line and usually are more gender-equal than patrilineal societies.

First, we should here be sure the reader is aware that matrilineal societies are not matriarchies. That is, they are not societies in which women have the dominant power. In fact, one of the intriguing power findings is the lack of any society in which women have more normative power than men.[28] There is also no evidence that there ever was such a society.

The Amazon society is a mythological society of women who supposedly removed one breast in order to permit them to shoot their bow and arrows with less obstruction—hence the name *a*(without) *mazon*(breast). Lest I be thought of as imposing this view, let me quote some of the main researchers on this point.[29]

> It is true that we know of no society in which women have been dominant over men in political life generally, i.e., there have been never any true matriarchies. (Whyte, 1978: p. 6).

> Although matrilineality has important consequences for women and can afford them greater power, influence and personal autonomy than patrilineality, it has not given rise in any known societies to matriarchy. Patrilineality is, however, sometimes associated with patriarchy. (O'Kelly, 1980: pp. 113-114).

> A survey of human societies shows that positions of authority are almost always occupied by males. Technically speaking, there is no evidence for matriarchy, or rule by women, Amazonian or otherwise. (Martin and Voorhies, 1975: p. 10).

> Women either delegate leadership positions to the men they select or such positions are assigned by men alone. . . . Since women are the potential bearers of new additions to the population, it would scarcely be expedient to place them on the front line at the hunt and in warfare. (Sanday, 1981: p. 115).

I stress the consensus on this point predominantly because there are those who believe they must support matriarchy as real in order to argue that women are the equal of men. As I have argued earlier regarding the flexibility of biological differences, there is no empirically based logic that forces this conclusion. The reality of gender equality on our planet seems to be that societies range from strong male dominance to close to gender equality. The female-dominant end of the continuum is literally unoccupied. Many explanations have been offered: greater male strength, female restrictions due to childbirth, lesser aggressiveness of females, and greater hunting ability of males. Note that whatever legitimacy these explanations may have had in our distant past, none of them seems very convincing in modern industrial society. In my judgment a matriarchal society has its greatest possibility in the modern world. The talents we stress today in the West are equally achievable by males and females, and so in some societies females may well gain greater power than males.

Now, let us examine matrilineal societies in general. Many of these societies are horticultural and involve women working together in important economic undertakings. One of the first things that puzzled anthropologists was how male dominance was achieved in societies where descent was traced through females. In such a society children belong to the wife. This has been called the matrilineal puzzle. The best answer to this puzzle has, in my opinion, been put forward by Alice Schlegel.[30] She points out that matrilineal societies do generally afford women higher status than patrilineal societies; but, she adds, there are two types of male roles that prevent full equality or female dominance from occurring: husband roles and brother roles. Her thesis is that in matrilineal societies female power is compromised by the husband and brother controlling the women who are wife and/or sister to them.

A brother belongs to the same descent group as his sister, for they descend from the same mother's line. Thus, he will usually have an important role in his sister's life. In the Trobrianders near New Guinea, whom we have discussed before, the brother supplies half the food his sister needs, and he socializes her children into the customs of their lineage.

The brother and the husband will further control the wives in a matrilineal society by picking the mate their children will marry. We saw in our discussion of the Tiwi one unusual way that male control operates via a grandfather picking a mate for his unborn granddaughter. Schlegel examined 66 matrilineal societies to see exactly how mate choice worked. In general, where husbands have the dominant power over their wives, this shows itself in the marital union of the daughters from that marriage to the husband's sisters' sons (matrilateral cross-cousin marriage). In societies where the brother dominates his married sister, the brother marries the sons from his marriage to his sister's daughters (patrilateral cross-cousin marriage).[31]

In both cases the male (husband or brother) is combining the domestic group he controls (wife or sister) with a group in which he has a strong interest (his sister's sons or his sister's daughters). The marriage of this second generation combines his descent group (via his sister's children) and his ties to his wife (via her children) and thereby integrates the male's power in that matrilineal society. By such marriages the male overcomes his not belonging to his wife's children's lineage and asserts his authority about whom the children of his wife shall marry. This is one way that males in a matrilineage compromise the female power that comes from having a female descent system. The interrelationship of kinship, gender, and power is highlighted by Schlegel in this analysis of matrilineages. Her analysis points out how the type of kinship tie that goes with matrilineal descent can be used to pressure toward specific roles of males and females in marriage. These resultant types of marriages shape the relative power of each gender.

The partial economic bases of kinship and gender are equally obvious in Schlegel's account. It is the type of economic system that helps structure the specific type of kinship system. Matrilineages are common where women work together or where women's work is important, as in horticulture. Two thirds of the 66 matrilineal cultures examined by Schlegel were horticultural. The centrality of male groups even in matrilineal societies is evidenced by the fact that when women in these societies bring husbands to live with them, the distance from the husband's home is most often slight. This makes it easy for the husband to continue to work and interact with his sister in his own lineage. This custom indicates that male relationships are viewed as important even in matrilineal systems. In contrast, in patrilineal systems, where men bring wives to their parent's area, the distances are often great. This illustrates a discounting in those societies of the economic importance of female labor and of their continued interaction with their kin.

An illustration from the People's Republic of China (PRC) may even more clearly drive home the power of the economic system in structuring kinship relatonships. The PRC is a patrilineal society, but it clearly illustrates my point regarding matrilineal societies. During the Great Leap Forward (1958-61) the communist government in the PRC sought to create greater gender equality by breaking up the patrilineages that used to work the farm lands.[32] They felt that as long as these male groups existed, females would not gain equal economic power. But the outcome was disastrous to productivity, and the communist leaders reestablished the patrilineal work groups in order to maximize output. The members of a lineage knew and trusted each other and worked well with each other. This occurrence further supports the power of the economic system to organize the kinship system and also highlights the importance of kinship organization for the economic system. These interrelationships are further documented in Diagram 4.1 in the relationships that were found between agriculture and male kin groups. For simplicity's sake I have made all these causal relationships one way. Reality, in most cases, will involve two-way causal relationships. I have chosen to highlight the dominant direction only.

POWER AND SEXUALITY

We have linked power to gender and kinship, but there remains the clarification of the linkage of power directly to sexuality. To accomplish this I will start by asserting the proposition that *powerful people seek to maximize their control over the valuable elements in their society.* If this is so, then it follows that since sexuality is universally considered important, it will be one of the life values over which people in power will seek to gain control. Further, it follows that if males have more power than females, they will seek to gain a larger share of whatever is sexually valued in that society.

This relationship of power and sexuality can be seen in comparing sexual permissiveness for females in matrilineal with patrilineal societies. We saw the integration of power and sexuality in the last chapter in Diagram 3.2, which showed that as female premarital sexual rights rose, so did female willingness to express marital sexual jealousy. In general, matrilineal societies allow greater premarital and extramarital sexual freedom for women than do patrilineal societies. Relatedly, it is also the case that matrilineal societies lean more toward the gender-equal end of the continuum than do patrilineal societies. So, it does appear that, everything else being equal, the greater the power of a gender, the greater the sexual permissiveness allowed that gender.

This relationship is relatively easy to demonstrate in nonindustrialized societies of just a few hundred people. When you examine societies of a few hundred million people—like our own—many other factors complicate the relationship. Not the least of these other factors is the different values that may prevail in various segments of a complex society. In such a complex society, "everything else" would not be equal, and one would have to compare people with the same set of values and then see if the more powerful were also the ones permitted the greatest sexual rights. I assume that within a group of Americans with similar ethical values, those with the most power will have greater ability to obtain what they wish. Even if in a particular group sexuality is circumscribed by all kinds of restrictions, those who are most powerful in that group will be most likely to be able to obtain whatever the acceptable level is—and perhaps a bit more.

Probably the clearest support for this general proposition concerning the relation of power to sexuality comes from a comparison of male and female sexual rights in cultures around the world. The double standard that affords males greater sexual rights than females is widespread. Males are more socially powerful than females in almost all societies, and they do indeed have greater sexual rights than females. More than that, the greater power of males seems to lead to attempts by them to control the sexuality of their wives and other women (see Diagram 3.1).

In part this is so because of the importance of sexuality and the consequent tendency of sexuality to link with jealousy.[33] Powerful males, as well as others, will seek not only to obtain sexual satisfaction but to control the sexual access by others to those who are important to them, such as wives, daughters, and sisters.[34] Being powerful, they have the greatest ability to exercise such control. At the same time, these males seek sexual satisfactions for themselves, which means possibly violating the sexual boundaries set up by other males around their wives, daughters, and sisters.

There is present here what I call the double-standard dilemma of desiring to protect one's sexual partners from others but also wanting to have additional sexual partners for oneself. Societies have tried different solutions—none of them fully resolving this dilemma. Some societies set up a different class of female partners, such as occurs in prostitution or the use of slaves or lower-class female partners, but the availability of female sexual partners in one's own social class is usually too convenient to be ignored.

This situation then leads to a cloak of secrecy about sexual affairs and to guilt feelings if one violates the protective norms. It puts males in potential conflict with each other as they seek partners willing to violate the jealousy boundaries. Men are at the same time striving to enforce their own jealousy boundaries around their women. Clearly, the fact that it is males who are seeking to control female sexuality is itself a statement of a significant power differential.

One of the best-known anthropological theories concerning female sexual rights stresses the role of marriage gifts. The theory has been proposed by Jack Goody. He proposes that a more open acceptance of female premarital sexuality goes with bridewealth marriage systems. In bridewealth exchange systems there is a modest wedding gift, often in the form of cattle, given to the bride's family upon marriage. This custom is common in Africa. The wealth gained is soon transferred when a brother must use it to give as a present to his bride's family. Such exchanges consist of modest amounts of wealth and do not upset the division of wealth in a society. As noted, what you receive for a daughter must generally be used to obtain a wife for your son.

The ultimate bridewealth exchange is *wife exchange*, wherein you send your daughters to marry into another group and another group's parents will send their daughters to marry into your group. Here, too, Goody would claim there is no major economic alteration. Rather, as Claude Levi-Strauss has pointed out, such wife exchange serves as a method for linking two groups together who may be useful to each other in times of stress.[35]

Goody feels that cultures that engage in bridewealth exchanges of any kind are relatively sexually permissive because the daughter's value in such exchanges does not need to be enhanced by her virginity, for there is little of economic value at stake. Once again, the reader should be aware that the very fact that daughters and not sons are exchanged in marriage is testimony to the relative power and importance of females and males in those societies.

There is a second form of marriage gift that Goody stresses as the key basis for restriction of female premarital sexuality. That is a dowry system that consists of linking the woman's wealth to her husband's wealth. In such a system the daughter is in reality receiving her inheritance prior to the death of her parents. A great deal of wealth can be exchanged by this custom, which can lead to a consolidation of wealth in a few families. The dowry system does go with a monogamous marriage system, for few parents would want to be just one of several bride-parents—all of whom are giving wealth to one man. They would not wish to share their wealth with the children of other parents. Dowry is also more likely to be found in a stratified agricultural society where wealth can be accumulated. We already know (see Diagram 4.1) that such stratified societies are generally higher on male dominance than are simple, unstratified societies. The dowry custom is familiar to Westerners because it is part of our European heritage.

Goody argues that the presence of a dowry system means that the value of the female is being stressed. She is inheriting a large amount of wealth, and she can add considerably to the power and influence of her husband. In such circumstances the husband is going to want to be certain of the loyalty (perhaps *controllability* is a better word) of any future wife. Goody describes the situation as follows:[36]

> If one is attempting to control marriage, it is important to control courtship too, . . . in upper status groups where property is more significant . . . restrictions are likely to be placed upon contact between persons of opposite sex before marriage. . . there will be a tendency to taboo sexual intercourse between them . . . [but] there appears little reluctance for men to engage in sexual unions, as distinct from marriage, with women of the lower orders. It is the sexuality of their own sisters they are concerned to protect, and the notions regarding the purity of women that attach to caste systems and the concern with their honour that marks the Mediterranean world cannot be divorced from the position of women as carriers of property. (Goody, 1976: pp. 13–15)

Goody presents data indicating that premarital intercourse of women is restricted in 64% of the dowry societies but only in 40% of the bridewealth societies. Thus, evidence of a sort supports his view. However, in those societies that do not have any fixed rules of dowry or bridewealth, 59% restrict premarital intercourse, which is close to the dowry society's level of restriction.[37] Another point to remember is that the majority of people even in dowry societies are poor and disenfranchised and are thus not involved in a dowry system.

In sum, then, I would accept the marriage-gift custom as one factor in the production of premarital norms, but I see it as more a reflection of a type of society than an important cause of our premarital sexual norms. I view such customs as outgrowths of a previously established gender-power structure rather than as a major cause in the establishment of a specific gender power distribution. By itself Goody's marriage-gift explanation is insufficient to satisfy our need for a theoretical explanation of gender power.

Regardless of how little explanatory weight we give to bridewealth and dowry systems, Goody does explicate the ways in which power relates to sexual customs. Goody spells out how the greater power of males operates to control the sexuality of females while still permitting sexual freedom to males. That situation of unequal sexual rights is, of course, the essence of the double standard. It exists in many cultures without the dowry system, and thus one should not conclude that the double standard is due to a fear of an illegitimate heir who may claim the family's wealth. We must remember that most people have very little wealth about which to be concerned. More importantly, the concern with out-of-wedlock births need not produce a double standard of sexuality. If gender power were equal to begin with, the effort to control pregnancy would not be imposed solely on the female.

One other area relating power to sexuality should be discussed. This area concerns sexual "abuse" by those in power. Even the powerful are restricted by norms concerning how they may exercise this power in relation to other people. In this sense, negotiation is at the heart of all sexual relationships. All societies place some limits on the use of force and fraud in sexual relationships.[38] In sexuality we see such limitations, I believe, in some of our incest taboos. One consequence of a parent-child incest taboo is to prevent the sexual abuse of the child by the parent, who clearly has the ability to force sexuality upon the child.[39]

Schlegel presents an illustration of this in her analysis of matrilineal societies. She found that in societies where the brother had greater power over his sister, there was a stronger incest taboo on brother-sister sexual relationships. Whereas in societies where the husband had greater power over his wife and children, there was a stronger incest taboo on father-daughter incest. This difference in strength of taboo by the power that brothers have over sisters versus the power that fathers have over daughters is instructive. In both instances, it indicates a protection of the weakest from the sexual abuse of power. The specific norms cover those situations with the highest risk that power will be used to force sexual compliance.

One way to make this point relevant to America today is to consider the new legal rulings on sexual harassment. Basically, what these rulings have done is to assert that a person may not abuse his or her power as a superior in a job situation by using that position to coerce sexual acquiesence. Once again, we see a situation in which limits are placed on how the powerful utilize their power in sexual situations. The attempt in all these cases seems to be to promote autonomy and prevent threat or force from being the pathway to sexuality. To be sure, the powerful still possess an advantage in obtaining what the sexual values allow in a society. But it does appear that the use of power is limited by the norms that function to restrain the exercise of power within the bounds of that culture's beliefs.

We must know the basic values and ideology of a society if we are to predict just what greater sexual rights power will bestow upon a person. No society permits even the powerful to do whatever they wish in sexual matters. This means that individuals need to learn to negotiate about sexuality just as they need to learn to negotiate in regard to other important areas of life such as seeking a job or a mate. In fact, some treatment programs for rapists and other sex offenders stress just such a development of a broader range of sexual negotiation skills.[40]

Each society sets up its sexual scripts regarding sexuality, but not all people internalize this in ways that are appropriate for their social setting. In addition, changes in personal sexual ideologies require changes in sexual scripts. When two lovers shift toward different concepts of the limits of force and fraud, for example, conflict is inevitable. In this sense there is a need for constant individual reappraisal of one's sexual scripts and the related negotiating skills one possesses. This is particularly so in a complex society such as ours, where our sexual scripts may differ considerably from those of others.

SUMMARY AND CONCLUSIONS

Many writers on gender-role power have stressed that women exist in the domestic sphere and men exist in the public sphere.[41] There is, of course, truth in this assertion. I have not explicitly developed that distinction because it would not add much to what I have already said and if stressed, can be misleading. The domestic-public distinction is often used to explain why males are more powerful—they operate in the public sphere. The problem with that perspective is that there are many male-dominant societies in which females do spend much of their time in the public sphere and do even produce most of the subsistence the society requires. Participation in the public sphere does not ensure gender equality. Surely this is the case in most Western societies. In the determination of power what is important is the control you have over what you are doing, not your productivity or the area in which it is occurring.

Power, as defined earlier in this chapter, is the ability to influence others. If women produce most of the subsistence but the control of what they produce is in the hands of men, who is the most influential? Slaves produced most of what Athens needed in the fifth century B.C., but they hardly were in control. In short, the domestic role of women is but one indicator of a lack of power. The generic index of power is, as noted, not only the sphere in which you operate but also the control you have over what you are doing. The powerful have the choice to do many things in many places, whereas the powerless must do the specific things they are assigned, whatever and wherever that may be.

Peggy Sanday has a somewhat different position on male and female power, one that expresses an interesting viewpoint.[42] Sanday stresses that societies value the power to give life as well as the power to take it away, and thus women as well as men are highly valued. Power, she believes, goes to the gender that embodies the forces upon which people depend for their needs.[43] People may take what she calls "an inner orientation," which relates nature to being female, or "an outer orientation," which focuses on the outer world where hunting, killing, and the pursuit of power occur and is associated with males. She contends that when cultural change requires aggressiveness and competition, the outer orientation is encouraged and males will dominate a society. When there is easy access to life requirements, then the giving of life and the inner orientation will assume a higher position and there will be more equality of the genders.

I have a mixed reaction to this not uncommon thesis. On the one hand, it sounds reasonable, for we do recognize males to be more aggressive and centered on the outside world, whereas females appear to be more nurturant and child centered. Yet, on the other hand, Sanday's thesis depends on accepting such gender differences as fixed—otherwise her theory cannot predict who will be more powerful. I do not accept such a fixed view of gender differences. As I discussed at the start of this chapter, training shapes whatever basic genetic potentials we have, and aggression and nurturance are always culturally designed.

I would add that were some environmental stress to occur in a society that was already gender-equal, I doubt if her theory would hold up. That is, I doubt if males would take over such a society and become dominant. I believe it is the prior presence of such male dominance that makes it likely that competition will increase that dominance. In most instances males are already in the position of power brokers before the crisis starts. In addition, even peaceful, noncompetitive societies often exhibit male dominance of some degree, and that is difficult to explain with her orientation.

Overall, I believe that many of the positions such as Sanday's "inner-outer" and the "domestic versus public" approach unintentionally accept too much of a fundamental male-female difference. I cannot deny the biological factors are involved in human behavior, but I believe the cross-cultural variation we see shows that such differences are malleable.[44] My position asserts that a biological potential never expresses itself without being shaped by the lifestyle of a particular culture. Therefore, genetic potential is quite flexible and should not be viewed as necessitating sharp gender differences, as implied by Sanday's inner- and outer-orientation notions. What gender differences exist are there because of the cultural shaping of our human potential, not because of any fixed male and female "traits." I suspect that Sanday, too, would accept such flexibility, although her explanation, perhaps inadvertently, assumes inherent male-female differences.

It is puzzling that even some feminists seem not to question so much of the immutability of gender behavior. In this regard the position of Frederich Engels is close to mine. Engels asserted that the cause of male dominance would be found in the change in society toward exploitive productive systems and not in the genetic makeup of males.[45] On this same point, the primatologists tell us about the common presence of competition and assertiveness in female primates.[46] They further point out how female primates are the stable core of a primate group and how they often appear to be influencing the behavior of males. If we believe our human biological heritage has any similarities to our primate cousins, then such reports should give us pause and raise questions about our views concerning the immutability of aggressive-nurturant differences between males and females.

In conclusion, Whyte's research on 93 Standard Sample societies did not find a significant correlation between male dominance and the frequency of warfare that Sanday's thesis assumes to be present. In addition, hunting societies stress the male's aggressiveness in the hunt and his competitiveness, and yet they are generally the most gender-equal of all human societies.[47] All these findings make me feel that we should not endorse any stereotypes, new or old, concerning inherent male-female differences and the necessary consequences of them.

I see the human condition as presenting us with choices far beyond those we have already taken. Therefore, I see gender roles as limited by the interdependencies of a social system more than by any biological forces. By that I mean that if we want to explain gender inequality, we should not refer to innate differences, but attend to the degree of male control of key societal institutions. To illustrate, male control of the political and economic institutions makes the occurrence of a gender-equal marital relationship problematic. Examining these limitations of one systemic structure on another are where we should be placing our research efforts if we are to learn what produces the basic differences in gender roles in human societies. Whyte's research on sources of female status informs us that these causes are far more complex than we may think. That is what we must pursue if we are to find the answers to societal causes of differential gender power and prestige.

My basic purpose in this chapter has been to show how our gender roles reflect the power system in the broad society and in the relevant kinship groups that exist. From there it is but a short step to discern how such power can affect our sexual behaviors and afford us differential access to the sexuality available in a particular society. Finally, we need be aware of the way basic values structure the legitimate areas of sexual rights, even for the powerful. In terms of our basic theory concerning universal societal linkages, the power structure as reflected in gender roles is everywhere a determinant of the sexual customs of males and females and thus is the second of three vital linkage areas.[48] We have already discussed kinship as a linkage to sexuality both in terms of jealousy and now in connection with gender. Ideology is the third societal linkage, and we will begin our discussion of that crucial aspect of our social lives in the next chapter.

SELECTED REFERENCES AND COMMENTS

1. I computed these percentages using the codes in the original data from the 186 cultures in the Standard Sample. See Appendix A for a list of the exact questions used. For an overview of these codes and this sample see

Murdock, George P., and Douglas R. White, "Standard Cross Cultural Sample," *Ethnology,* vol. 8 (1969), pp. 329–369.

For some interesting cross-cultural work on gender roles see

Aronoff, Joel, and William D. Crano, "A Re-examination of the Cross-cultural Principles of Task Segregation and Sex Role Differentiation in the Family," *American Sociological Review,* vo. 40 (February 1975), pp. 12–20.

Crano, William D., and Joel Aronoff, "A Cross-cultural Study of Expressive and Instrumental Role Complementarity in the Family," *American Sociological Review,* vol. 43 (August 1978), pp. 463–471.

2. Mead, Margaret, *Growing Up in New Guinea.* New York: Morrow, 1930.

3. Of all sociologists Alice Rossi has written the most about the biological factors that contribute to gender differences. She argues for more of an integrative approach between sociology and biology. She spoke of this in her 1983 presidential address to the American Sociological Association. I do believe that she overemphasizes the power of the biological and neglects the explanatory power of the sociological. Surely the phenomena of sociology and biology are intermeshed, but the task of every science is to specialize in a particular abstraction of reality rather than trying to present total reality, whatever that may be. My own belief is that we do the best for science when we develop our own field and use other fields only to the extent that they clarify the development of our own specific level of explanation. Nevertheless, I do value her writings and list some here. I also include an article I wrote developing my point about the value of specialization inherent in each scientific discipline. I do believe, however, that applied disciplines, unlike basic science disciplines should be multidisciplinary. I develop this thinking in Chapter Eight.

Rossi, Alice, "A Biosocial Perspective on Parenting," *Daedalus,* vol. 105 (Spring 1977), pp. 1–31.

Rossi, Alice, "Gender and Parenthood," *American Sociological Review,* vol. 49 (February 1984), pp. 1–19.

Reiss, Ira L., "Trouble in Paradise: The Current Status of Sexual Science," *Journal of Sex Research,* vol. 18 (May 1982), pp. 97–113.

4. In 1974 Maccoby and Jacklin published a book surveying the scientific literature for any possible biologically based gender differences. One of their findings asserted the greater physical aggressiveness of males both cross-culturally and cross-species. They also found females better on verbal ability and males better on mathematical and spatial abilities. The evidence they present on differences in aggression is the strongest. A similar position on aggression is taken in the highly acclaimed cross-cultural study of gender by Martin and Voorhies. Many additional sources can be found in these two books.

Maccoby, Eleanor E., and Carol Jacklin, *The Psychology of Sex Differences.* Stanford, Calif.: Stanford University Press, 1974.

Martin, M. Kay, and Barbara Voorhies, *Female of the Species.* New York: Columbia University Press, 1975.

5. For comparisons of males and females with some attention to the role of hormones such as androgen, see

Beach, Frank A. (ed.), *Human Sexuality in Four Perspectives.* Baltimore, MD: Johns Hopkins University Press, 1977.

Hrdy, Sarah Blaffer, *The Woman that Never Evolved.* Cambridge, Mass.: Harvard University Press, 1981.

Mitchell, Gary, *Behavioral Sex Differences in Nonhuman Primates.* New York: Van Nostrand Reinhold, 1979.

Symons, Donald, *The Evolution of Human Sexuality.* New York: Oxford University Press, 1979.

Zillman, Dolf, *Connections Between Sex and Aggression.* Hillsdale, N.J.: Erlbaum, 1984.

Bandura, Albert, *Aggression: A Social Learning Analysis.* Englewood Cliffs, N.J.: Prentice-Hall, 1973.

6. For a fascinating account of "extra" genders in cultures around the world, see "Supernumerary Sexes," Chapter 4 in

Martin, M. Kay, and Barbara Voorhies, *Female of the Species.* New York: Columbia University Press, 1975.

7. There is also the case of transsexuals. A transsexual is a person of one genetic sex who adopts the gender usually associated with the other genetic sex. The occurrence of such people throughout history indicates the disjuncture of genetic sex and gender. Recall our distinction of the terms *sex* and *gender*, which we discussed in Chapter 2. Without that terminological clarity we would have difficulty discussing the transsexual or "extra" gender phenomenon. For an early statement on transsexualism see:

Benjamin, Harry, *The Transsexual Phenomenon.* New York: Julian, 1966.

8. The question of interpersonal power is a complex one. The definition I use is the one generally accepted by sociologists. For an introdcution to the study of male-female power, see

Cromwell, Ronald E, and David H. Olson (eds.), *Power in Families.* New York: Halsted Press, 1975.

9. I am presenting the basic approach of sociologists to the study of stratification and power. In addition to the four institutions I listed in the text of this chapter, other sociologists include the education institution as a universal institution. Most introductory sociology texts cover this area. For a more advanced illustration and analysis of inequality in America see

Nelson, Joel I., *Economic Inequality: Conflict without Change.* New York: Columbia University Press, 1982.

10. One of the most incisive commentators on the family institution from the point of view of the law is Lenore Weitzman. She points out the assumptions made in the law about the rights and duties of husbands and wives. I recommend the following:

Weitzman, Lenore J., *The Marriage Contract.* Englewood Cliffs, N.J.: Prentice-Hall, 1978.

Weitzman, Lenore J., *The Divorce Revolution.* New York: The Free Press, 1985.

11. For statistical information on the political and economic place of women in American society, I suggest examining the Government Series P23, P60, and P70. One additional general source would be

U.S. Bureau of the Census, *Statistical Abstract of the U.S.: 1984*. Washington, D.C., 1984.

For a general *theoretical* overview of women's place in the workforce or in any of the major institutions in America, see

Reiss, Ira L., and Gary Lee, *Family Systems in America* (4th ed.). New York: Holt, Rinehard & Winston, (in press).

12. Skard, Torild, and Elina Haavio-Mannila, "Equality between the Sexes—Myth or Reality in Norden," *Daedalus*, vol. 113, no. 1 (Winter 1984), pp. 141–167.

For an analysis of twelve industrial societies in terms of gender and work see:

Roos, Patricia, A., *Gender and Work: A Comparative Analysis of Industrial Societies*. Albany: SUNY Press, 1985.

13. Virtually no one denies the lowered female status in agricultural societies that use the plow (intensive agriculture), and most authors assume that female status is highest in hunting societies. See

Martin, M. Kay, and Barbara Voorhies, *Female of the Species*. New York: Columbia University Press, 1975.

O'Kelly, Charlotte G., *Women and Men in Society*. New York: D. Van Nostrand, 1980.

14. I use the terms *class, status,* and *power* much the same way as most sociologists do. The tradition was begun by Max Weber, an early twentieth-century sociologist. Class is a group of people with common life chances and a feeling of belonging together; status is the prestige or honor afforded to a particular position or group in a society; and power is the ability to influence others in a group.

15. Whyte, Martin King, *The Status of Women in Preindustrial Societies*. Princeton, N.J.: Princeton University Press, 1978.

16. Whyte takes issue with Sanday's unidimensional measure of female status because he concluded that female status was a multidimensional characteristic. See page 147 in Whyte's book, mentioned in note 15.

17. For the more technically minded reader, I should mention here that there were limitations in my analysis due to the nature of the variables involved. To illustrate, the dependent variable—that which I was trying to explain—was a belief in female inferiority. That variable was a dichotomy and thus not fully suitable to a path analysis approach. However, given the number of missing cases and the resultant small numbers and the difficulty of finding suitable measures, there were few alternative methods. Nevertheless, to the extent I could, I did use alternative analyses more suitable to dichotomous dependent variables and found quite similar results.

18. For a discussion of a new measure of machismo, see

Mosher, Donald L., and Mark Sikin, "Measuring a Macho Personality Constellation," *Journal of Research in Personality,* vol. 18 (1984), pp. 150–163.

19. Of the seven variables in Diagram 4.1, five come from the Standard Sample and two were derived from Whyte's study. The two from Whyte are machismo and the belief in female inferiority. For the more methodologically minded reader I should mention that in my causal analysis I used both listwise and pairwise deletion approaches to help in dealing with the problem of missing data. These two approaches yielded the same results in 46 of 53 relationships. My final diagrams are based on pairwise deletions.

20. The actual number of possible relationships among the 7 variables in Diagram 4.1 is far more than 21. It is 21 only if we assume the exact same ordering

of the 6 independent variables. If we move the causal order of these 6 variables, we create a very large number of other possible relationships. Finally, there is also the matter of whether one expects a positive or a negative relationship, which adds further alternatives. The 21 relationships I mentioned were figured by taking all the variables to the left of a variable as possibly related to that variable, for example, there are 6 such variables for "belief in female inferiority," 5 for "machismo," and so forth.

21. In his comparative book on families Gary Lee points out how the "conditions of life" intervene between any direct impact of the type of subsistence on the type of family. He includes in such conditions, geographic and social mobility, stress on autonomy or on family labor, and many other relevant variables. See

Lee, Gary, *Family Structure and Interaction: A Comparative Analysis.* Minneapolis: University of Minnesota Press, 1982.

22. William of Ockham was a British Franciscan of the early fourteenth century who spoke out against dogmatic Aristotleianism. Ockham stressed an empirical approach. Among other positions, he wanted the simpler explanations to prevail over the complex, and this viewpoint was called Ockham's razor. In many ways he was a forerunner of early modern science. See

Edwards, Paul (ed.), *The Encyclopedia of Philosophy.* New York: Macmillan, 1967. (See especially pp. 306–317 in Volume 8.)

23. I did a further check on the relationship of mother-infant involvement to belief in female inferiority. I examined whether that relationship changed by the degree to which male kin groups were present. I found that the relationship of mother-infant involvement to the belief in female inferiority was more powerful in societies where male kin groups are less common. In societies where male kin groups are common, the belief in female inferiority and the involvement of mothers in infant care is already established, and thus the relationship between those two variables is weak. In societies with weak male groups there is more room for change in both mother-infant involvement and belief in female inferiority, and so the relationship of those two variables is stronger. This specification of the conditions under which that relationship best holds is something I hope others will pursue further.

24. Goodale, Jane C., *Tiwi Wives: A Study of the Women of Melville Island, North Australia.* Seattle: University of Washington Press, 1971.

25. There are rare instances where people of the same genetic sex and same gender are allowed to marry. In such cases one of the people will be permitted to change gender to enable the person to fit into the traditional marriage patterns. As an example, consider the Nuer in Africa. If a woman reaches her late 20s and has not become pregnant, she knows that she cannot conceive. In such a case that woman can choose a younger woman as her bride and marry her. The older woman will become the "father-husband" and the younger woman will be the "mother-wife." A lover of the younger woman will impregnate her, and the child will call the older woman "father" and the younger woman "mother." Once again the lack of isomorphism between genetic sex and gender *in the mind of the people* in many cultures is demonstrated here. It is also worth mentioning that the "husband" in female-female Nuer marriage can restrict his wives from extramarital affairs just as any Nuer husband in a male-female marriage can. This supports my point in Chapters 2 and 3 that it is not reproductive capacity but the sexual relationship that underlies our sexual attitudes. For further details on this Nuer marriage form see

Evans-Pritchard, E.E., *Kinship and Marriage among the Nuer*. London: Oxford University Press, 1951. (See especially pp. 108–109.)
26. There is a classic explanation of the relationships among variables such as the subsistence economy, descent, residence, and polity in Murdock's 1949 book. For a more recent source with a somewhat different approach see Gary Lee.

Murdock, George Peter, *Social Structure*. New York: Macmillan, 1949.

Lee, Gary, *Family Structure and Interaction: A Comparative Analysis*. Minneapolis: The University of Minnesota Press, 1982.

27. Etienne, Mona, and Eleanor Leacock (eds.), *Women and Colonization: Anthropological Perspectives*. New York: Praeger, 1980.

28. At least two anthropological sources discuss the possible existence of societies with females having the power—*in some sense of that word*. First, there is Peggy Sanday's view that some societies have "mythical male dominance," a term borrowed from Susan Rogers. By this she means they have a formal belief that men are dominant over women, but in reality women are the key influence in almost all the major institutional settings and thus have structural or institutional power. However, this structural power is unauthorized by the norms of the group. Societies that seem to fit the view of mythical male dominance would be some of the non-Hispanic Caribbean societies with very high unemployment rates for men. Although Sanday does not deal with it, there is also the possibility of "female mythical power" in societies. This would occur where the behavioral power of females was below their authorized power.

A second recent source discussing female power is found in Guttentag and Secord, who claim that the Bakweri in Cameroon, West Africa, is a society where women have structural power in all the institutions. A book with information on that society was written by Ardener and his colleagues. Upon examination of that book and Guttentag and Secords account, however, that claim does not hold up. Guttentag and Secord take the existence of a bridewealth system as an indication of female power (p. 26). Such a system prevails in almost all of Africa and is simply an exchange of wealth that is lost when the bride's brother marries. Also, they mention that women earn money from casual sexual relations and sometimes become independent of males in that fashion. To accept this as a mark of dominance would make prostitutes dominant in our society. Further, infibulation is reportedly practiced in the Cameroons and that is a sign of male dominance. The very fact such unclear cases are used in the search for a female-dominant society indicates the rarity of such a society.

Sanday, Peggy Reeves, *Female Power and Male Dominance: On The Origins of Sexual Inequality*. New York: Cambridge University Press, 1981.

Rogers, Susan Carol, "Female Forms of Power and the Myth of Male Dominance: A Model of Female/Male Interaction in Peasant Society," *American Ethnologist*, vol. 2 (1975), pp. 727–756.

Guttentag, Marcia, and Paul F. Secord, *Too Many Women? The Sex Ratio Question*. Beverly Hills, Calif.: Sage Publications, 1983.

Ardner, E., S. Ardener, and W.A. Warmington, *Plantation and Village in the Cameroons: Some Economic and Social Studies*. London: Oxford University Press, 1960.

29. The four quotes come, respectively, from

Whyte, Martin King, *The Status of Women in Preindustrial Societies*. Princeton, N.J.: Princeton University Press, 1978.

O'Kelly, Charlotte G., *Women and Men in Society*. New York: D. Van Nostrand, 1980.

Martin, M. Kay, and Barbara Voorhies, *Female of the Species*. New York: Columbia University Press, 1975.

Sanday, Peggy Reeves, *Female Power and Male Dominance: On the Origins of Sexual Inequality*. New York: Cambridge University Press, 1981.

30. For those readers who have been longing for a very carefully executed cross-cultural study, Schlegel's book is the answer to your desire. This book is one of the finest examples of cross-cultural research I have come across.

Schlegel, Alice, *Male Dominance and Female Autonomy*. New Haven, Conn.: HRAF Press, 1972.

31. A brief definition of some terms may be helpful. Cross-cousins are cousins descended from siblings of the opposite sex. Parallel cousins are cousins descended from siblings of the same sex. Patrilateral cross-cousin marriage occurs when a male child marries his father's sister's daughter or when a female marries her mother's brother's son. Matrilateral cross-cousin marriage occurs when a male child marries his mother's brother's daughter or when a female child marries her father's sister's son. If this sounds complicated, try drawing it in a diagram and you will find it less formidable.

32. For those interested in knowing more about the PRC, I recommend starting with the following two books:

Parish, William L., Jr., and Martin K. Whyte, *Village and Family in Contemporary China*. Chicago: University of Chicago Press, 1978.

Stacey, Judith, *Patriarchy and Socialist Revolution in China*. Berkeley: University of California Press, 1983.

33. The reader may recall that in Chapter 3 we spoke of the connection of wife's sexual jealousy to the level of female premarital sexuality in a society. The relationship I found and presented in Diagram 3.2 showed that as premarital sexuality for females increased, so did wife's sexual jealousy. This is congruent with the view that power and sexuality are related, for an increase in female premarital sexuality is more likely in cultures with greater gender equality.

The relationship of power to the expression of jealousy is also revealed in a test I ran to see if husband's or wife's jealousy would correlate with violence in a society (as measured by Sanday). I found no correlation of wife's sexual jealousy to the level of violence in a society, indicating that wives generally are not likely to express violence when jealous. On the other hand there was a positive correlation between husband's sexual jealousy and the expression of violence in a society, indicating that husbands have the power to express their jealousy, particularly in a society that supports violence.

34. The control of females is a significant part of Islamic cultures. For an examination and explanation see

Mernissi, Fatima, *Beyond the Veil: Male-Female Dynamics in a Modern Muslim Society*. Cambridge, Mass.: Schenkman Books, 1975.

35. The developer of the theory of wife exchange is Claude Levi-Strauss. I suggest starting an examination of his work with the following book:

Levi-Strauss, Claude, *The Elementary Structure of Kinship*. Boston: Beacon Press, 1969.

36. Goody expresses his thinking in two small books listed here. These books are tightly reasoned and well thought out but a bit complex to follow. Still, if you make the effort, by the end you will better understand his position. The quotation I use is from the 1976 book.

Goody, Jack, *Production and Reproduction: A Comparative Study of the Domestic Domain*. Cambridge: Cambridge University Press, 1976.

Goody, Jack, and S.J. Tambiah, *Bridewealth and Dowry.* Cambridge: University of Cambridge Press, 1973.

37. Goody presents a table from which one may calculate these percentages. See page 121 of

Goody, Jack, *Production and Reproduction: A Comparative Study of the Domestic Domain.* Cambridge: University of Cambridge Press, 1976.

38. Judgments about "improper" use of force do change. Recall that it is only since 1977 that marital rape has been illegal in any state. Russell reports that 14% of her ever-married women said they experienced marital rape (p. 57). This comprised 87 of 644 women, but only 6 of the 87 called it rape. Russell called the other 81 cases rape because they fit her definition, which was "use of force or threat to obtain coitus, oral sex, anal sex, or digital sex" (p. 43). See

Russell, Diana E.H., *Rape in Marriage.* New York: Collier Books, 1982.

39. Masturbation of infants to placate them is not uncommon by mothers in many cultures. I do not consider this a sexual practice on the part of mothers, for there is no indication that it is conceived as a source of sexual satisfaction to them or the child. It is a practice aimed at relaxing a child. For the infant it is a genital pleasure; but infants are too young to have cultural scripts for sexuality, and thus it is not sexual in terms of my societal definition of sexuality. For an overview of child sexuality in America see

Constantine, Larry L., and Floyd M. Martinson (eds.), *Children and Sex: New Findings, New Perspectives.* Boston: Little, Brown, 1981.

Finkelhor, David, *Sexually Victimized Children.* New York: Free Press, 1979.

Gagnon, John H., "Female Child Victims of Sex Offenses," *Social Problems,* vol. 13 (Fall 1965), pp. 176–192.

40. Groth, Nicholas A., *Men Who Rape: The Psychology of the Offender.* New York: Plenum Press, 1975.

Minnesota's Sex Offender Program in St. Peter is based upon the ideas of Groth.

41. The use of the concepts of public versus domestic domain is common. For an interesting discussion of these terms by those who use them, see

Ortner, Sherry B., and Harriet Whitehead (eds.), *Sexual Meanings: The Cultural Construction of Gender and Sexuality.* Cambridge: University of Cambridge, 1981.

42. Sanday, Peggy Reeves, *Female Power and Male Dominance on the Origins of Sexual Inequality.* New York: Cambridge University Press, 1981.

43. In connection with this broad issue of public versus private societal roles is the question of just how segregated are female and male roles in a society. Sanday (see note 42 for source) stated, "whether or not men and women mingle or are largely separated in everyday affairs plays a crucial role in the rise of male dominance" (p. 7). Interestingly, if you take her research data and correlate her measure of segregation of female activities in a society with her measure of female status in a society, you find no significant relationship. So, her own data belie her assertion. I think this relationship fails to appear because it is the social importance of what you do that matters, not simply whether what you do is done alone.

44. Guttentag and Secord have argued that the scarcer the women, the greater their power in a society. Martin Whyte tested that idea on the Standard Sample and found it did not hold up. Nonetheless, the question remains an intriguing one. How would it fit with America today? Not too well. We have a low sex ratio (excess of females), and yet the status of females has increased.

Guttentag, Marcia, and Paul F. Secord, *Too Many Women? The Sex Ratio Question.* Beverly Hills, Calif.: Sage Publications, 1983.

Whyte, Martin King, *The Status of Women in Preindustrial Societies.* Princeton, N.J.: Princeton University Press, 1978. (See especially pp. 142-144.)

45. Engels, Frederich, *The Origin of the Family, Private Property, and the State.* Chicago: Charles H. Kerr, 1902. (Originally published in 1884.)

46. Hrdy, Sarah Blaffer, *The Woman that Never Evolved.* Cambridge, Mass.: Harvard University Press, 1981.

47. For a discussion of these points and a presentation of his data on 93 societies, see page 129 of

Whyte, Martin King, *The Status of Women in Preindustrial Societies.* Princeton, N.J.: Princeton University Press, 1978.

Janet Chafetz argues for the basis of male power to be rooted in control over the production of valued goods. This view would generally fit with my own concepts. See:

Chafetz, Janet S. *Sex and Advantage: A Comparative Macro-Structural Theory of Sex Stratifications.* Totowa, N.J.: Rowman & Allanheld, 1984.

48. My earlier theoretical writings on premarital and extramarital sexuality had stressed the role of group autonomy in predicting level of sexual permissiveness. The greater the autonomy of a group from other social structures, the higher the level of acceptable sexual permissiveness. How does that tie in with my discussion of the importance of power in this chapter? I think one connection that can be made is that there is a positive relationship between the power of a group and its autonomy. Males, for example, have greater power than females in our society and they also have greater autonomy or freedom from restrictions imposed by other groups such as the family or religion. My autonomy factor is also a measure of group power and therefore can be theoretically integrated with the ideas put forth in this chapter.

Some of the other explanatory factors in my earlier work also relate to the three areas of kinship, power and ideology which I am stressing in this book. The interested reader can examine the 7 propositions in my 1967 book and the 36 propositions in the 1979 chapter and the predictor variables in the 1980 article. In these propositions there are tieups to all of the three major areas which I relate to sexuality in this book but I have not taken the time to carefully search out the precise overlap and to fit my older propositions into the newer explanatory schema of this book. I may do this at some future date but I urge others to also undertake this task now if they are so motivated. The major sources would be:

Reiss, Ira L., *The Social Context of Premarital Sexual Permissiveness.* New York: Holt, Rinehart and Winston, 1967. (See especially Chapter 10.)

Reiss, Ira L., and Brent C. Miller, "Heterosexual Permissiveness: A Theoretical Analysis," Chapter 4 in W. Burr, R. Hill, I. Nye and I.L. Reiss (eds.), *Contemporary Theories About the Family.* (Vol. 1) New York: The Free Press, 1979.

Reiss, Ira L., Ron Anderson and G.C. Sponaugle, "A Multivariate Model of the Determinants of Extramarital Sexual Permissiveness," *Journal of Marriage and the Family,* vol. 42 (May 1980), pp. 395-411.

CHAPTER FIVE

IDEOLOGIES

The Range of Normality

HUMAN BEINGS: COGNITIVE OR EMOTIVE?

The ability to think abstractly is our only area of significant superiority above our fellow animals. By abstract thinking I mean the ability to contemplate what is not directly confronting the senses. This ability allows us to muse about the past and plan for the future. We can analyze and explain what the senses reveal to us to an extent far beyond the abilities of other creatures. Aristotle was correct when he said that humans can be defined as the rational animal.[1] In virtually all other respects we are inferior to other animals. There are other animals who are superior in strength, size, sight, hearing, smell, speed, longevity, and virtually any other characteristic one chooses to examine. Our crown rests, however shakily, upon our ability to think abstractly.

Our sexuality is critically affected by this unique ability. For one thing, abstract thought makes it possible for us to develop a wider range and more elaborate set of sexual stimuli. This, in turn, is probably the key reason that we are the species who spends the most time in sexual interaction. We also use our abstract abilities to create a realm of values defining what we believe is the preferred way to think, feel, and behave sexually. So, our sexual imagination and our moral judgments regarding sexuality are expanded far in excess of that of other living creatures.

The importance of sexuality in our social lives makes it certain that not only will we develop value judgments about it but those judgments will be buttressed by very strong emotions. Accordingly, if we violate a sexual custom, the reaction is likely to be as strong as, if not stronger than, that for violating almost any other social custom. In sexuality our abstract thinking becomes linked with our ability to emote, and these factors reinforce each other.

As societies evolve, they tie together sets of their value judgments into strongly held value systems. These value systems are logically based upon the assumptions a society makes about the nature of human beings. Such fundamental assumptions are what we call ideologies. Ideologies are at the heart of our societal approach to living. They develop in all important areas of our life in every society. Our basic values are logically linked to our ideological positions. We will attend to these ideologies and their relation to sexuality in this chapter.

Marxists would contend that ideologies are derived from our mode of economic production and the social class structure that controls that production. In that sense ideologies simply rationalize the legitimacy of the powers that be. Feminists often have viewed males as the major source of such powers. Surely my own analysis in the last two chapters evidences the power of males and the importance of the economic way of life of a society in promoting such a distribution of power. Nevertheless, we have also discussed other causes. Knowing that we have not been able to analyze carefully much of the potential causal network, I would hesitate to pick male economic power as the only important cause of our fundamental ideological beliefs about sexuality. We must keep in mind the range of sexual lifestyles that exists in societies with the same mode of production and the same degree of male power. Think about the variety that exists in industrialized capitalistic countries, and you will become aware of the complexity of causal analysis and the reasons for avoiding any single-cause explanatory theory.

More important than arguing over specific causes is my desire to challenge the view that ideology is simply a rationalization for maintaining a particular group in power. To be sure, it is beyond dispute that the ideologies in a society will reflect the interest of the group in power. We saw precisely that in the last chapter, wherein the ideological belief in female inferiority appeared to be in good part a reflection of male power in a society. However, particularly in large complex societies, it is equally obvious that conflicting ideologies exist, and thus not all ideologies can directly support the group in power.

Furthermore, some aspects of ideologies have an existence that extends beyond one specific type of society. Some of the present freedom and equalitarian ideologies in America are present outside America and even outside Western Europe. So, some ideologies are apparently not culture bound to just one particular type of economic system.

Finally, some ideologies outlast the power groups they seem to support. One interesting illustration is how the belief in the power of the English king outlasted by over a century the actual power of the Crown. That belief continued to exist long after the prime minister had become the central power figure in England. In sum, then, I am arguing for the independent power of ideologies, not as their only characteristic, but as a key attribute that requires scrutiny. Ideologies do more than reflect the groups in power; they also can alter that power structure by the belief systems toward which they pressure.[2]

Ideologies, then, can retard change or enhance it. They can exist as a latent opposition force for long periods of time and then blossom when other societal aspects change in compatible ways. Our equalitarian ideological beliefs in civil rights for minorities was one such long-standing precept that blossomed in the 1960s and significantly aided the equal rights movement in the United States. That credo had previously had a long history during which in mostly minor ways it affected our society. My point, then, is that we recognize the latent power, independent of economic systems, stored in our ideological beliefs. In this I am departing from any orthodox Marxist interpretation of ideology.

One can classify in various ways the basic types of ideologies that prevail in cultures around the world. Yet there are some common ideological premises. Almost all peoples seem to have ideological beliefs related to the fact that humans are moved both by reason and by emotions. These beliefs divide into two ideological perspectives, which I will call the *cognitive* and the *emotive*. Accordingly, I have found it particularly useful to dichotomize ideologies into these two very general categories: those that stress humans as motivated to act by reason and those that stress humans as motivated to act by emotion. Societies combine elements of both these perspectives, but most often they stress one at the expense of the other.

Ideologies assert what a people believe to be the most fundamental "nature" of human beings. Ideologies thereby reveal our communal assumptions about human beings. We are not always fully conscious of making such assumptions, for often we think of these beliefs as simply stating the way people "really" are. This semiconscious, deeply rooted nature of ideologies implies that ideologies can blind us to other possible ways of viewing humans. By definition ideologies are supported by strong emotions; thus, their ability to bias our thinking is surely present. Although the two ideologies I have selected here are present in various degrees in all societies, we can distinguish societies on the basis of the relative degree of support a society renders to each of these ideologies.

The cognitive ideology views human beings as capable of understanding the choices that confront them. It assumes that most of the time human beings are able to base their choice on a thoughtful analysis of the likely alternative outcomes of different choices. This view does not deny emotional adherence to particular values but rather asserts that individuals develop ranked hierarchies of values and thereby have conceptions concerning which values are the most important. In this view individuals then rationally analyze the situations with which they are faced and create solutions most in accord with the value weights in their hierarchy of values.[3] In the cognitive ideology, the individual would take responsibility for any "mistakes" involved in such choices. It is also assumed that individuals would learn from the process and thereby improve their ability to choose what best fits with their value hierarchies. Over time individuals may alter their values but they will continue to analyze, evaluate, and choose.

The cognitive ideology is probably the most popular basic ideology in America today—particularly among college-educated people. It stresses the rational abilities of humans, that is, the abilities to think abstractly and judge the intricate outcomes of our social behavior. Thus, this ideology plays down the emotional side of our beliefs and behaviors and stresses our ability to control and manage our emotions.

Part of our philosophical tradition has professed views of human nature very much in accord with the cognitive ideology. Consider this quotation:[4]

> Nature has produced him—body and soul, a man who seeks for reason in things in order that he may lead a rational life. . . . He does that picking and putting in order that he may have another universe built upon that which he analyzes. He knows for a purpose. And were his knowledge complete, that purpose would still control his living. He would still go on building out of what he knew a different world to live in. This he does even with his little knowledge and this reveals his essential nature. (Woodbridge, 1926: pp. 136, 138–9)

Because of the popularity of the cognitive ideology many of you will feel that this ideology is not assuming anything about human beings but just stating reality. However, in fairness one would have to admit that many people do not seem to benefit from being given choices. Some people become habitual criminals, and others become uncaring and hostile. By stressing reasoned choices, this ideology minimizes the place of emotions in choice—and that may overstate the rational element in some choices we make. Many choices made by people are not in accord with what a rational analysis of their value system would decree.[5] Choices may be based upon well-ingrained habitual reactions or upon overpowering emotional commitments. Such actions must be viewed as being unusual or as alterable in order to believe that humans are basically rational creatures. However, the acceptance of any ideology is not based upon a scientific analysis of how frequently people behave in certain ways. Rather, ideological acceptance is simply based upon strong value commitments to the beliefs and value judgments underlying that ideology.

Note that the range of human choice in each society is limited to those choices compatible with the basic values of that particular society. We are all surely aware that our society does not offer us a full range of acceptable choices in the sexual sphere or any other. Many sexual, religious, political, and economic acts are categorically forbidden by our shared values. So even those societies that profess a view of human nature in accord with the cognitive ideology are not offering their citizens a full range of choices covering all logically possible alternatives. In our society, normative beliefs concerning acts like stealing or lying or disloyalty, for example, restrain our range of permissible action. Some such limitations are built into all social groups, and this further qualifies the arena within which choice can occur. I mention these qualifications to increase your level of awareness that the cognitive ideology, like all ideologies, selects a view of humanity from the total range of possible conceptions. Each ideology may claim to be in touch with the total reality of the universe, but as scientists we see ideologies as selective perceptions of the world that justify a particular way of structuring social life.[6]

The second basic ideology that is present to some degree in all societies is the one I call the emotive ideology. The assumption in this ideology is that people cannot easily make rational choices because they are emotional creatures controlled by feelings such as anger, lust, fear, and pleasure. Therefore, people often do not appraise the possible outcomes but just follow the dictates of their emotions. Because of this, society must impose its will on its citizens and not permit them too many choices. Rather, society must protect its citizens from being tempted and penalize them when they step out of bounds in order to produce a socially acceptable human being.[7]

Philosophers like Thomas Hobbes were concerned with the social control of a basically brutish human nature. As such they were in this respect quite in agreement with the emotive ideology:[8]

> This alternate succession of appetites, aversions, hopes and fears, is no less in other living creatures than in man: and therefore beasts also deliberate. . . . It cannot be denied but that the natural state of men, before they entered into society, was a mere war, and that not simply, but a war of all men against all men. (Hobbes, 1651: pp. 200, 266)

The assumptions underlying this ideology can also be brought into the question. Recall that it was this perspective regarding human nature that we used to qualify the cognitive ideology. Accordingly, it is fair to use the perspective of the cognitive ideology to qualify the assumptions of the emotive ideology.

First, we do know that many people at times can control their emotions and do analyze problems and seek the "best" solution within a particular value system. There is a self-fulfilling prophecy in the emotive view. Goethe said that if we want people to behave in a certain way, we should start treating them as if they have already achieved that status.[9] In that way we encourage people to become what we want them to become. If we treat people as if we think they cannot control their emotions and constrain and punish them, they may well become as emotional as we expect them to be. Finally, if the distinctive human characteristic is our ability to think, then this approach does little to develop that but instead treats us much the same as any other animal. Here, too, I stress that I am not trying to discredit this ideology but merely to make you aware of what is being assumed. Rarely do we examine what is implied by our ideologies for they are so strong and compelling, that they are most often accepted without question.

The reader may feel that a "reasonable" person would accept a position halfway between the cognitive and the emotive ideologies.[10] Remember, though, that we are seeking to describe the basic ideological beliefs that are present in all cultures. We are not here seeking to develop a new, more "balanced" ideology of our own. In most societies historical and current societal pressures promote a leaning toward one or the other of these dominant ideologies. Therefore, I do believe that most small nonindustrialized societies can be classified as being more acceptant of one or the other of these two ideologies. This does not deny that some societies cannot be so easily classified. Particularly in complex societies like our own, we will find somewhat different ideological positions depending on the major institutional area we examine and the particular subgroup we investigate.

To illustrate this point think about America today and you will see the presence of both ideologies in varying degree in different basic institutions. The cognitive ideology appears present in our supposedly laissez-faire economic system. We are taught that if we allow "free" competition, then the proper rational choices will be made and the businesses that can build the best mousetrap will survive while the inefficient ones will decline. In reality, of course, much of our economy is controlled by a few giant corporations that do not fully economically compete with one another. But when the lack of freedom becomes too obvious, we do have court cases and we do break up some of these giants on grounds of restraint of competition, as we did with our telephone system. Or we deregulate, as we did with our airline system. Thus, our cognitive ideology does have influence, even if it is heavily muted by the power accumulations that have occurred.

Our political system is supposedly premised on the rational ability of the voter to choose. But this too needs to be qualified. It was George Bernard Shaw who put forth the cynics view of democracy and said, "Democracy substitutes election by the incompetent many for appointment by the corrupt few." Our history is filled with limitations on the right to vote. The founding fathers allowed only white males over the age of 25 who owned property to vote. Until 1913 the U.S. Senate was not elected, and until 1920 women did not have the vote. Only after the civil rights legislation of the 1960s were blacks in the South able to register and vote with relative freedom.

The direction has been toward increased trust in the ability of the voter to make a rational choice. Here, too, there are limits. Our election campaigns indicate that politicians are well aware that they can obtain a vote more by an emotional appeal to a shared value like patriotism than by a rational analysis of issues. Were our view of the voter fully in accord with the emotive ideology, we would not enfranchise as many people to vote as we do. So, here, too, although our political activities in part support the position of the emotive ideology, there also are strong elements of action based on the cognitive ideological view of people.

The place of both these ideologies in our thinking about sexuality is even more obvious. The most popular view today is to permit adults to choose many elements of their sexual lifestyles.[11] The range of premarital heterosexuality permitted by our norms has expanded greatly in the last 20 years. In the early 1960s only about 20% of the adult population would accept premarital intercourse under any condition.[12] By 1970 this percentage rose to 50%; by 1975 it was over 70% and it has stayed at that level. Analagous to political and economic rights, sexual rights have expanded—first for males and later for females.

Yet the value limitations in our choice notions are obvious in the sexual area. National Opinion Research Center surveys still indicate that about two thirds of adult Americans believe homosexuality is always wrong—even if it involves two adults who are in love and in a stable relationship. To many of these respondents homosexuality is too "dangerous" to allow it to be a choice.

On extramarital sexuality there are also strong value limitations on choice, with about two thirds of the adult population feeling that any extramarital relationship is wrong.[13] Note that the very fact that extramarital sexuality and homosexuality can be debated is a sign that a choice in these areas is in some sense still a possibility. The attitude toward incest or bestiality is even more restrictive, and very few discuss the advisability of these customs. This sort of comparison allows us a basis for assessing the degree of moral flexibility and the degree of control we exercise over various possible sexual choices.

In general, I believe that the narrower the range of choices permitted by a group, the more likely we have a group that endorses the emotive ideology. Belief in that ideology would tend to make one want to restrict the choices that people can make in order to stop people from emotionally moving toward what the group considers "harmful choices." Another way to discern which ideology is accepted is to explore the reward and punishment customs that act as responses to individual choices in a society. In the emotive ideology people not only are limited as to the range of choices permitted but if they make a "bad" choice, they are supposed to be severely punished. This is so because the emotive perspective asserts that such punishment will establish the necessary emotional fear and stop repetition of the behavior. Adherents of the cognitive ideology permit a wider range of choices and feel that learning is possible by becoming intellectually aware of better ways to achieve the group's values rather than via harsh punishments.

Many Americans choose to emphasize one or the other of these two ideologies in different ways in the various sectors of their lives. To illustrate, many people who strongly believe in economic freedom do not believe in sexual freedom to the same degree. The same people who believe that freedom to act in the economic sphere benefits our nation may believe that freedom to act in the sexual sphere threatens our nation. The assumptions we make about how people will act will vary by the institutional setting we are considering. We thus have difficulty generalizing from one area of life to the other.

It would be a mistake to conclude that we take a predominantly cognitive ideological approach to sexuality.[14] Despite the so-called sexual revolution of the late 1960s we have many people who feel that teenagers should not be allowed to choose to have abortions or to obtain contraception even though they are known to be sexually active. More to the point, we have many people who see sexuality as a very powerful emotional force and one that we must protect ourselves against. To such people, one must not be exposed to the opportunity of sexuality unless it is in marriage. Others may extend the permissable boundaries to include any love relationship. But many hesitate to accept sexuality just for mutual physical pleasure.

It is often stated that young people "cannot handle a sexual relationship at their age" or that one could become "addicted" to sexuality for pleasure, or that teenagers would "abuse" the right to have abortions or use contraception. So, the view that people need to be protected against their own emotions is alive in the land, and with it comes the support for the emotive ideology in the area of sexuality. The stronger the negative evaluation of sexuality, the narrower the range of permissible choice. We have in our historical background a good deal of negative evaluation of sexuality, and so we have the clear presence of the emotive ideology.

Thus, I believe strong elements of both the cognitive and the emotive ideologies operate today in American sexual lifestyles. As would be expected, the cognitive ideology is stronger in the less controversial areas such as premarital intercourse while the emotive ideology is stronger in the more controversial areas like homosexuality.

SEXUAL IDEOLOGIES AT THE END
OF THE TWENTIETH CENTURY

We have analyzed broad societal ideologies such as the cognitive and the emotive, which are applicable to all areas of life, but there are more specific ideologies applicable to the area of sexuality. Our sexual ideologies do logically relate to the more general ideologies, and this will be discussed after we depict more about these specific sexual ideologies.

It is difficult to select which dimensions of sexual ideology to highlight, but I do feel that in the light of the evidence we have gone over and in terms of our theoretical explanations, one division of sexual ideologies stands out as most relevant. I believe we can, in virtually all societies, divide our sexual ideologies in terms of the degree of gender equality encompassed by the sexual ideology. Thus, on the simplest level, I would classify sexual ideologies as equalitarian or nonequalitarian.[15]

The degree of equality can be measured in terms of the power of each gender in the major social institutions and also in terms of gender equality in the specific beliefs about sexual rights and duties. In short, then, the basic assumptions about human nature relevant to sexual ideologies center upon how equal males and females are in general and what implications this judgment has for specific sexual attitudes and behaviors. Since the nonequalitarian view of the genders places more restrictions on females than does the equalitarian view, we may conclude that it is more in accord with the emotive ideology, whereas the rational ideology would be more congruent with the equalitarian sexual ideology.

I will spell out four basic perspectives that distinguish the equalitarian from the nonequalitarian sexual ideology. Although I am speaking mainly of heterosexual ideologies, I shall make some reference to the meaning of these same ideologies for homosexual behaviors. We surely do need to explore the extent to which these heterosexual ideologies are appropriate for homosexual relationships and also to search for any distinctive ideologies that exist for homosexual relationships.[16] We do more of that in the next chapter.

The first tenet that is part of both sexual ideologies concerns the endorsement of gender equality in the key institutional areas of a society. The equalitarian sexual ideology accepts the premise that males and females are of relatively equal worth. This view does not depend on both genders doing the exact same set of tasks in the society.[17] Rather, it depends on their respective tasks being evaluated as of the same worth. The presence of such gender equality would be judged by examining the equality of gender roles in each of the major institutional areas of a society (politics, economics, religion, and family). This point was discussed in depth in Chapter 4.

The nonequalitarian sexual ideology is premised on the position that females are "by nature" of less significance than are males. Females may be valued for what they do contribute, but their general value to the society is considered to be less than that of males. This nonequalitarian evaluation would also be reflected in each of the major institutional areas of a society. As noted, in the nonequalitarian sexual ideology females in particular would be treated in accord with the emotive ideology. The degree of equality underlying the general evaluation of males and females logically implies certain beliefs concerning several areas directly related to sexuality.[18] These sexual beliefs comprise tenets 2, 3, and 4.

The second tenet of these sexual ideologies concerns body-centered sexuality. This is an area that has strong emotions connected with it, particularly in the Western world but also elsewhere. In the nonequalitarian ideology such body-centered sexuality is forbidden predominantly to females. This tenet reflects the control of males over female sexuality. In male-dominant societies, males want females to be loyal to their men, and thus they are likely to restrict females from casual, pleasure-centered sexual relations such as are involved in body-centered sexuality. Males in such societies have greater sexual rights and can participate in body-centered sexuality if they so desire. Of course, this tenet is the heart of a double standard of sexuality and involves male condemnation of the very females who are their partners in body-centered sexual relationships. According to this perspective, such relationships are considered wrong for females but acceptable for males.

We can see censure of body-centered sexuality even today in the Western world. The most popular premarital sexual standard—bar none—for Western women today is "permissiveness with affection." This standard allows for female sexuality, but only when there is a stable affectionate relationship. Males are much more likely to accept a "permissiveness with or without affection" standard.[19] There is an implication here—that at least for women sexuality for its own sake is felt to be wrong. In many cultures, sexuality is legitimated for women only when it is mixed with a stable relationship.

Obviously, then, to be acceptable for women, sexuality needs the purification of stability and/or affection.[20] Underlying this view is an implicit negative evaluation of sexuality for its own sake. If sexuality were good per se, it would not need such strong additional ingredients to make it acceptable. But if we view sexuality as a contaminated drink then some sort of purifying elixir is necessary. Once again, males are afforded greater sexual access and have less need for citing any special justification for the pursuit of sexuality.

By definition, the equalitarian ideology would not restrict any form of sexuality for only one gender. The reader will recall that our examination of the Standard Sample indicated that as female status increased, so did the acceptance of female sexuality both premaritally and extramaritally (see Chapter Three). It follows that in more equalitarian societies, body-centered sexuality is more likely to be acceptable for both genders. However, even for men, body-centered sexuality, although acceptable, is most often judged to be less worthy than person-centered sexuality.

Two quick clarifications of our ideologies are in order here. There are some equalitarian cultures that would be restrictive of both body-centered and person-centered sexuality for both males and females outside of marriage, but such abstinent equalitarian cultures are rather rare. The equalitarian ideology refers not to abstinent cultures but to cultures that accept coitus to the same degree for both males and females. (I do not ignore abstinent equalitarian cultures but treat them as a separate type later in this chapter.) A second qualification: in the nonequalitarian sexual ideology there is the logical possibility of a culture being double standard but restricting males from body-centered sexuality more than females. I know of no such cultures, and so the nonequalitarianism I speak of is the male-dominant variety.

The third tenet of our sexual ideologies concerns the degree of addiction and fear associated with sexuality. Our Western history has stressed the addictive power and fear of sexuality, but much more so for women than for men. It was women who were to be fearful of the power sexuality had to lead them astray. Men, too, could be led astray, but that was not such a tragedy; and even when it occurred, it often was the woman who was blamed for not controlling the situation. Women were the gatekeepers for sexuality, and fear was one way of strengthening their resolve. In true double-standard fashion men would still seek women as sexual partners but would condemn those who acceded to their wishes.

The greater control over female sexuality through fear and other beliefs is familiar in cultures around the world. Recall that in some African cultures today, like the Sudan, infibulation and clitoridectomies are performed on women to prevent their sexual urges from overcoming them. More generally, one of the major findings in Chapter 4 was the greater legitimate sexual rights that power bestows. To the degree that men have more power than women, such differential legitimation of sexuality will show itself in one way or another.

Equalitarian sexual ideologies present a view of sexuality that is less fraught with images of fear and addiction. Both genders are equally legitimated to participate in sexuality, and there is more support for the view that although sexual emotions may be strong, they are manageable much like other emotions. No distinction is made regarding any one gender having more difficulty in managing sexual emotions. The sexual attitudes developed over the last 20 years in America are in accord with the equalitarian version of this tenet. Indeed, a less fearful orientation, especially to premarital sexuality, has developed in most of the Western world.

The fourth tenet of the nonequalitarian sexual ideology asserts that the major goal of sexuality is heterosexual coitus. This tenet centers one's thinking on heterosexuality and on reproduction. There is a gender inequality here, too, for the reproductive focus of this tenet applies most heavily to women. Males are often permitted to engage in body-centered sexuality with women with no goal of reproduction.

One aspect of this effort to concentrate on heterosexual coitus affords us one of the few examples in the Western world of greater sexual restrictions being placed on males as compared to females. This occurs in the greater societal resistance to male as compared to female homosexuality. Perhaps it is because the male gender role is considered more important that we find in many societies more concern with keeping males free from homosexuality. We discussed in Chapter 4 cultures like the Navajo and other American Indian groups that permit the selection of gender roles in addition to the traditional male and female role. But in all those cultures on which I have been able to gather information, a genetic male who selects a different gender, such as the Nadle gender in the Navajo, is valued less than a genetic male who adheres to the male role. The situation with women does not seem to involve a loss of status if they move out of the traditional female role. So, there is also some broader cross-cultural evidence for a stricter imposition of traditional heterosexual gender roles on males than on females.

As shown in the next chapter, many societies that accept male homosexual behaviors do so in ways that conceptualize the homosexuality as aiding or at least being compatible with heterosexuality. Even in these societies, homosexuality that is not socially legitimized is most feared by males.[21] Nevertheless, when it comes to nonreproductive heterosexual behaviors, males are less constrained to avoid manual, oral, or anal sexuality in their heterosexual lifestyles. Of course, placing the focus on coitus more for women is what one would expect in a nonequalitarian sexual ideology.

In the equalitarian sexual ideology this fourth tenet would contain less of an emphasis on coitus as the supreme heterosexual act, and, of course, whatever pressure there was would be placed more equally upon males and females. In general, I would expect that the equalitarian ideology would accept a wider range of behavior beyond heterosexual coitus in part because the stress on producing more children who can be future warriors and workers is less present in societies with weaker male dominance. Sexual pleasures consisting of heterosexual oral, anal, and manual sexual acts would therefore gain higher priorities. In addition, homosexuality would be more accepted because it would be less at odds with equalitarian kinship norms for they do not stress reproduction.

Surely, the equalitarian version of this tenet is congruent with what has been happening in the West. We have had indication of vast increases in oral and anal sexuality reported in studies of marital sexuality.[22] Also, our norms have shifted toward zero population growth, and our marriage and parenthood pressures have decreased. The emphasis, then, has shifted from heterosexual coitus to the two dominant characteristics of sexual interaction: physical pleasure and psychological disclosure, which can be obtained in a variety of sexual acts.

I could extend the list of tenets, but I think these four are sufficient as an outline of the equalitarian and nonequalitarian ideologies. These two sexual ideologies are what one would expect to find today, given the way kinship and power are structured in modern societies. In Chapter 6, on homosexuality, we further analyze the relevance, particularly of tenet 4, for explaining our attitudes toward homosexuality. Awareness of these tenets will be useful in Chapter 7, on erotica, because much of the female opposition to body-centered hard-core erotica may derive from acceptance of tenets 2 and 3, which stress the power of such sexuality and its degrading quality for women.

The first tenet concerning overall gender equality seems everywhere to be a major component of sexual codes.[23] I stress that tenet because so much of my cross-cultural examination of sexuality supported the importance of power differences between the genders for determining sexual customs. The other three tenets are logically related to the degree of endorsement of tenet 1. All three express a judgment relevant to how equal the genders should be treated in terms of sexuality. Table 5.1 summarizes the meaning of these four tenets.

I cannot speak of trends in sexual ideology in the non-Western world, for few of those cultures have been studied over time, but in the West it is clear that the equalitarian sexual ideology has made significant gains in the past 20 years. This is surely true among college-educated young people in the United States.[24] Admittedly, the newer equalitarian sexual ideology has not become dominant in all of its tenets in our society. In this regard, one recent study of the distribution of these tenets affords us considerable insight into the way sexual ideologies change.

TABLE 5.1   Major Sexual Ideologies and Their Tenets

NONEQUALITARIAN SEXUAL IDEOLOGY

1. Males are more competent than females in the exercise of power, and they should be dominant in the major social institutions.
2. Body-centered sexuality should be avoided by females.
3. Sexuality is a powerful emotion and one to be feared by females.
4. The major goal of sexual relationships for females is heterosexual coitus.

EQUALITARIAN SEXUAL IDEOLOGY

1. Males and females are equally competent in the exercise of power, and they should be treated as equals in the major social institutions.
2. Although person-centered sexuality is preferable, body-centered sexuality is acceptable for both males and females.
3. Sexual emotions are manageable by both males and females.
4. The major sexual goals for both males and females are physical pleasure and psychological disclosure.

This study was done in 1982 by Ilsa Lottes, a doctoral student at the University of Pennsylvania. Her respondents were from the New York–Philadelphia area and consisted of about 400 college and noncollege individuals.[25] It was found that most of these people could clearly be placed into one or another of our two basic sexual ideologies. That is, most respondents were consistent in expressing their adherence to a majority of either the equalitarian or the nonequalitarian sexual ideology tenets. Among college respondents, the support for the equalitarian sexual ideology was over 70%. Among the noncollege respondents, males were similarly supportive, but less than 40% of the noncollege females fell into the equalitarian sexual ideology. However, since this was not a representative sample, we cannot estimate what the results would be for the American population at large.

The most interesting finding of this study concerned the differences between male and female student adherents of the equalitarian ideology. These differences relate to the relative endorsement of each of the four tenets by males and females. In those males who were adherents of the equalitarian ideology, the weakest support was for tenet 1, which concerned the overall acceptance of gender equality. Only 68% of the equalitarian sexual ideology men supported this tenet. Over 80% of these same men gave support to the other three tenets. This means that such males were more likely to endorse the equalitarian version of tenets 2, 3, and 4 concerning sexuality, then would fully endorse the measure testing their overall gender equality in the major institutional areas of life. The 32% who did not endorse gender equality (tenet 1) would still be classified as adherents of equalitarian ideology because of their support for the three gender-equal tenets dealing directly with sexuality (tenets 2, 3, and 4). The implication here is that it is somewhat easier for males to accept gender equality in sexuality than to accept it in other life areas.

If we look at the female responses, something quite different emerges. For females who were classified as equalitarian adherents, the weakest support was for tenet 2, concerning the acceptance of body-centered sexuality. Only 52% of the equalitarian females supported tenet 2, whereas over 90% of them supported the other tenets. This means that females felt the most difficulty, despite their overall gender equality, in accepting body-centered sexuality.

What do these different patterns of belief for male and female adherents of the equalitarian sexual ideology tell us? They inform us that the relationship between gender equality and sexual equality differs dramatically for males and females.[26] That female equalitarian adherents have the most difficulty endorsing the tenet supporting body-centered sexuality suggests that this is the most difficult change for females to make in their sexual attitudes. Surely the centuries of training women to avoid body-centered sexuality would make acceptance of that form of sexuality, even as a possible choice, a difficult task. The equalitarian version of tenets 3 and 4 may be less difficult to accept because a woman can justify that choice by invoking love as her reason for not fearing sexuality and for accepting a wider variety of sexual behavior; but for tenet 2, no such qualification is possible, for it calls for the acceptance, as at least tolerable, of body-centered sexuality.

In contrast, the point of difficult transition to full acceptance of the equalitarian sexual ideology for males seems to be the endorsement of gender equality in all institutional areas. This is so even though for males the contrast between the lowest level of tenet endorsement and the average endorsement of the other three tenets is not as great as it was for females. Given male gender-role training, it is not surprising that the three tenets dealing with sexuality were the easiest to endorse. The acceptance of female equality in all institutional areas of society entails more attitudinal change for males than does the endorsement of the other tenets.

I believe what these findir is indicate is the differential gender sequencing of social changes that have been occurring in the West during the last 20 years. Women changed first into acceptance of greater gender equality and then altered their sexual customs to agree with their increased sense of gender equality. Because of the block toward body-centered sexuality that is present for them, 48% of these women have not fully made the change over. For men the situation is reversed. Their first change was toward more equalitarian acceptance of sexuality. Their last area of cultural resistance is the endorsement of greater gender equality. Indeed, 32% of these male adherents have still not made that ideological modification.

This portrait of an incomplete transition by adherents of the new equalitarian sexual ideology fits with my judgment about American society today: It is evidence of our changing sexual ideology, but it is also testimony that the change is far from completed. I would estimate that at least half of our adult population would still support many of the tenets of the nonequalitarian sexual ideology. They too are changing, however, and the findings of the study just cited give us a basis for predicting, for each gender, which tenets are likely to change first and which are likely to be the most recalcitrant.

I find it enticing to speculate whether this precise type of male-female difference applies to non-Western cultures. Would nonindustrialized societies also find that the same tenets are the most difficult to change for each gender? My hunch at the moment is yes! I say this because the basic power differentials between women and men are so widespread outside the Western world.

At the opening of this chapter I introduced overall cognitive and emotive ideologies. As stated earlier, I believe that the cognitive ideology is more likely to be the general ideology adhered to by a believer in the equalitarian sexual ideology. This is so for two reasons: first, because sexual ideologies are concerned with choices that evoke very strong emotions from people in most cultures, and, second, because the equalitarian sexual ideology grants a greater power to choose, especially to women. Therefore, given the assumption by the emotive ideology that humans have difficulty in controlling their emotions and making careful choices, I would assume that believers in the emotive ideology would be less likely to endorse the tenets that go with an equalitarian sexual ideology. The widespread cultural beliefs that assert the greater difficulty women have in controlling their emotions is further evidence of the strength of the emotive ideology and its congruence with the nonequalitarian sexual ideology. It would take an equalitarian sexual ideology and a cognitive ideology to counteract such belief systems. Indeed, there do seem to be logical implications relating our general ideologies and our specific sexual ideologies. I encourage others to test these implications using cross-cultural data.

A CROSS-CULTURAL TYPOLOGY OF SEXUAL IDEOLOGIES

The sexual ideologies themselves are composed of two basic dimensions: gender equality and sexual equality. Special insights can be gained if we build a model representing all the logical combinations of these two dimensions and then apply it cross-culturally. That typology is presented in Diagram 5.1.[27]

Let us first see if we can locate in the matrix presented in Diagram 5.1 the two major sexual ideologies we have been discussing. The nonequalitarian sexual ideology accepts dominance of males in both the gender and sexual area. So, it must be located somewhere in the row across gender equality that is labeled "Low, Male Dominant." Males also receive greater sexual rights in this ideology, and that leads us to the column heading under premarital sexual permissiveness that reads "High for Males Only." Now reading across and down to see where these two characteristics intersect, we find ourselves in type 7. This type of ideology is thus classified as male dominant in both gender scripts and sexual scripts, and that fits perfectly with our nonequalitarian sexual ideology.

The equalitarian sexual ideology is also easy to find. That ideology must be in the row that is high on gender equality and it must show sexual equality. That leaves only types 1 and 4 to possibly qualify. Type 1 is a rare type of society that accepts low premarital sexuality for both genders. The equalitarian sexual ideology, as I defined it, is basically a high sexually permissive type and will not fit with type 1. This leads us to type 4, which matches our definition of the equalitarian sexual ideology rather nicely.

We have located what I said were the two major sexual ideologies. What about the other ten types in our diagram? We can rule out six of them very quickly. Types 9, 10, 11, and 12 represent societies in which there is low gender equality because females are dominant. I know of no societies where females are dominant, and if there happens to be one or two out of the twelve hundred societies that have been

DIAGRAM 5.1 A heterosexual typology of gender and sexual equality.

	SEXUAL PERMISSIVENESS			
	LOW FOR BOTH GENDERS	HIGH FOR FEMALES ONLY	HIGH FOR MALES ONLY	HIGH FOR BOTH GENDERS
GENDER EQUALITY				
High	1	2	3	4
Low, Male Dominant	5	6	7	8
Low, Female Dominant	9	10	11	12

studied, that still is extremely rare. These types are included in the typology simply to show how selective are our cultures on this planet. So, for all practical purposes we can eliminate those four types. Types 2 and 6 can also be eliminated, since I know of no societies where females have greater sexual rights than males.

That leaves four types to be discussed: 1, 3, 5, and 8. Our Western Hebraic background was a type 7, in agreement with the nonequalitarian sexual ideology. After the advent of Christianity came at least a formal endorsement of type 1. That is, the Christian world professed belief in gender equality and in low sexual permissiveness for males and females. But what was the reality of that world? I think the presence of male dominance in all Western societies meant that we did not ever really have a gender-equal society. For some segments of society we might have had a type 5, but for most of the Western world even a type 5 society could not be achieved because, as we saw in Chapter 4, male gender power leads to male sexual rights. Equality in sexual rights was therefore not achieved any more than was equality in gender rights.[28] Thus, despite the early Christian rhetoric, the majority of groups in those societies would have fit a type 7 much closer than either a type 1 or 5.

The situation in the non-Western world is quite similar. Types 1 and 5 are rare forms of society. This is largely due to the almost universal presence of male dominance. This is not to deny that subgroups throughout the Western world do fully endorse and strive to live by a type 1 or a type 5 ideology.[29] Rather, I am simply asserting that they are in the minority and the trend is not toward their position.

In my judgment, the nonequalitarian sexual ideology (type 7) was and is the most common type of ideology in the history of our planet. The explanation of male power in Chapter 4 develops some of the reasons for the predominance of this type of sexual ideology. However, I also view a type 7 society as one that can be a transition toward type 4. Part of the pressure toward type 4 is due to the inconsistency created when gender equality begins to increase. Let me explain my conjectures on this point and indicate how types 3 and 8 are involved in this transition. I believe the reader will find it useful to refer to Diagram 5.1 to aid in following this discussion.

One kind of social movement away from type 7 is to shift toward type 8. This is perhaps easiest to grasp for Westerners, for we have been going in this direction for this entire century. By that I mean we have kept much of the male gender dominance but we have moved toward gender equality in sexuality. *I do believe that American women have in the last 20 years gained much more sexual equality than they have gender equality.*

Certainly there is still noticeable sexual inequality—especially in areas touched upon by tenet 2 (body-centered sexuality)—but over 80% of American women are now nonvirginal at marriage compared to about 50% in 1960.[30] Our present incidence of female nonvirginity is even higher in much of northern Europe.[31] Certainly, significant gains in gender equality have been made in the past 20 years, but the magnitude of the increase is significantly smaller than in the area of sexuality. Even now, only a small percentage of women are in the top positions in business, the professions, and government. During that entire 20-year period women earned only about 60% of what men did. Some gains have been made in those areas and more significant changes may well be made in the next decade or two. It takes time for the large enrollments in medicine, dentistry, and law to have an impact. Whatever the reasons may be, though, it does appear that more has changed in equality in sexuality than in gender equality.

There has also been a transition from type 7 to type 3. Here, I would judge that women would take this step, more quickly than men, for it involves the acceptance of full gender equality. I would expect women to be willing to grant themselves gender equality in the major institutional settings. Nevertheless, as the anti-ERA movement shows, this is certainly not an uncontested alteration. Yet I do believe it is a common one despite the fact that some women may feel threatened and resist such a change.

A movement from type 7 to type 3 would consist of major changes in gender equality but only minor changes in sexual equality. I would expect that some of the factors that retard change in sexual equality concern the difficulty some women find in accepting sexuality outside a stable affectionate relationship. Part of the reason for this reluctance may well be that there are still many men who would condemn such female body-centered sexuality, for it would make the woman's behavior less easily controlled. Some nonequalitarian sexual ideology males may also "use" sexually liberated women for their own pleasure but resist any serious relationships with them. The reality of such male reactions would strengthen the traditional female training against body-centered sexuality and create a roadblock to increased sexual activity.

Overall, I would contend that people who have moved from the ancient non-equalitarian sexual ideology (type 7) to types 3 and 8 are actually in transition to type 4. As noted, the pathways females and males take to type 4 are in many cases different. This is so because females find gender equality easier to accept and males find sexual equality easier to accept. Thus, each gender modifies the double standard in its own way. I believe the overall increases in sexual and gender equality, partial as they may be, are a catalyst in the movement toward type 4, the equalitarian sexual ideology.

This analysis of our cross-cultural typologies leads me to the same conclusions concerning the future dominance of the equalitarian sexual ideology as my analysis of the Lottes data earlier in this chapter. One can debate just how quickly we will move toward type 4. Indeed, some can assert that we will simply accept types 3 and 8 and not proceed toward the equalitarian sexual ideology. All I can do is state my judgment on this point and ask you to check back at the turn of the next century to see if I was correct.

This extended treatment of ideologies will perhaps encourage more people to try to operationalize and test these important influences on our lives. We have too long ignored this aspect of our sexual lives. We have been convinced that ideas are epiphenomena and that only economic and political pressures really influence us. The lasting grip of ideas is demonstrable in the preceding conclusions that point out how older ideologies restrain the speed with which we respond to changes in our gender and sexual scripts. For better or worse, older ideological tenets are an impediment in our movement toward new social structures.

PREMATURE EJACULATION: AN IDEOLOGICAL CONSTRUCT

Ideologies such as we have been discussing contain fundamental judgments about human nature and therefore about what is to be expected of people. In that sense, ideologies define what a particular group will think of as normal or abnormal behavior or attitudes. We have spoken of the basic tenets of the two sexual ideologies, but we have said little about the judging of sexual normality implied by these tenets. To understand more fully this very important point, I will attempt to expose some of the largely unspoken assumptions that are part of our sexual ideologies. I will start by examining an area of only modest controversy, but I will expand this to areas of highest debate. It is precisely in such emotionally charged areas that our ideological assumptions will be buried, and so that is where we must continue our "dig" toward discovering what comprises our notions of sexual normality. Our focus here will be on America, but I will extrapolate our conclusions to other cultures.

The issue I have chosen to start with is one of the more recent changes in our culture's approach to sexuality. It concerns our attitudes and behavior in regard to premature ejaculation. This is not an area of high controversy, and therefore it will be easier for us to set aside any prejudgments we may have and analyze it. I use this subject here to illustrate how ideology defines normality.

First, just what does premature ejaculation mean? Premature for whom? In some definitions, premature is measured simply by the speed with which orgasm occurs. In the American Psychiatric Association's definition it depends upon the male feeling anxious about his rapid ejaculation. The usual therapeutic definition of a premature ejaculator is a male who has orgasm after intromission in a short time span of, say, 20 seconds or so and who feels that something needs to be done to make the act more satisfying to both partners.[32] So, by some definitions premature does not necessarily mean premature for the person having the orgasm. In some definitions what is implied is that, not you, but your partner is not ready to have an orgasm. Also, the premature ejaculator is, of course, a male. The term for a female who reaches orgasm in a 20-second time period is *quick* or *responsive.* Virtually no concern is shown about such rapid female orgasmic behavior. It would seem that our culture assumes that females will not leave their partners unsatisfied but that the male may well do this to his partner.

To see how our ideological beliefs may color our view, transport yourself to a macho country like Brazil for a moment. Think about a conversation between two adult males wherein one says: "Last night I met a woman at a bar. Later we went to my apartment and made out. I was so turned on that I came just a few seconds after inserting!" What would his male friend say to him? I expect the most likely response would be, "A few seconds! That is tremendous. It must have been great—what a man you are!" I doubt very much if the friend would say, "A few seconds! You are a premature ejaculator and you better get yourself to a therapist!"

The reason that there would be little felt need for therapy is that Brazil is not as gender equal a society as the United States. Accordingly, there would be less concern for whether the female partner had a chance to reach orgasm and there would be admiration for male sexual potency as indicated by speed of orgasm. In such a society, a male who was slow in achieving orgasm would feel he had a problem, and his male friends might agree with that judgment. In fact, in our own country just a generation ago, the label *premature ejaculator* would be largely unknown and, relatedly, the reasoning supporting the label much less widespread.

The point I am making here is that the judgment that premature ejaculation is a problem that requires therapy is culturally based. As such, the "problem" depends on an equalitarian culture for its existence. This type of "health" problem is not like a broken leg, which would be recognized as a health problem in any society. We would all agree with the standard of physical health that requires the absence of any broken bones, but we have no such universally agreed upon standard when it comes to much of our sexual life. Therefore, premature ejaculation becomes a "health" problem only when our group accepts mutual sexual satisfaction of a certain sort as the standard of health or normality. Otherwise, the problem of premature ejaculation, from a societal point of view, does not exist.

Let us take this inquiry one step further and examine what the typical treatment for premature ejaculation has been in our society. The most common treatment is the *squeeze technique.* This involves the man informing the woman when he is close to orgasm and she then placing her thumb along the underside of the penis and pressing. This inhibits the orgasm. They then repeat this procedure and in this fashion the man learns that he can control his orgasm. The procedure is very effective in a rather short period of time. I am not questioning its efficacy— rather I am asking you to consider what the use of this sort of procedure symbolizes about our concept of sexual normality?

Logically one can think of several ways to handle premature ejaculation other than the sequeeze technique. For example, the female could achieve an orgasm prior to coitus by means of oral or manual sexuality. Why are these procedures not recommended more? I would suggest the reason is basically that we are a coitally centered society. The prime goal of sexuality is conceived to be coitus. Many Freudian analysts would argue that the normal psychosexual development is through a series of stages that leads to heterosexual intercourse.[33] The orthodox view contends that one starts out in infancy absorbed in oral sexuality, then proceeds to anal sexuality, then phallic, then latency, and finally genital sexuality.[34] Any failure to negotiate these stages leads to "abnormal" or "disturbed" sexual behavior such as in homosexuality, which, according to this view, is rooted in the inability to work out the latency phase. In terms of this psychoanalytic perspective, to focus upon homosexuality or even heterosexual oral, anal or manual sexuality would be a sign of failure to have progressed to the coital stage.

It is interesting to see how well this view of Freudians reflects the dominant culture in the Western world. Here, surely, is a theory shaped by the Western European culture in which it was formed. It was that culture that has for centuries stressed coitus as the ultimate sexual act. To the medieval Church any sexual act that could not lead to pregnancy was sinful. Masturbation, oral sexuality, anal sexuality, and homosexuality clearly fit that description and were condemned.[35]

Certainly one important basis of such a view was the conception of sexuality as a reproductive act more than a pleasurable act. But there is a more fundamental basis than that. Many societies wish to encourage heterosexual coitus, for they wish to encourage the production of more citizens for the state. Such additional citizens can be used for warriors, workers, and other social purposes.

In terms of kinship, many societies in the West and elsewhere encouraged coitus because it afforded them children who would eventually care for them in their old age. In this sense the Freudian emphasis upon heterosexual coitus reflects our societal background more than it does any empirically tested notion of "normality" or "abnormality." The so-called stages of Freudian psychosexual development are the stages that Western society expects its citizenry to go through. The same holds true for the emphasis on the squeeze technique—its therapeutic use reflects the acceptance of the priority of coitus in our society.

Let us go one step further, however, to examine the act of heterosexual coitus itself. It is upon inspection a sexual act structured to promote male orgasm much more than female orgasm. By definition it is not coitus if the penis is not contacted by the vagina. Yet contact with the clitoris is optional and often does not occur in the common positions of coitus. Is it any wonder that females have had much more trouble than males having orgasm during coitus? Unless there is deliberate manual contact with the clitoris during coitus, many women, perhaps a majority, have difficulty reaching climax. Consider how many males could achieve orgasm if the penis were not contacted. It would surely help to contact the area near the penis, like the testicles; even so, the achievement of orgasm would be made much more difficult for most males if there were no direct contact with the penis.[36]

To make matters even more difficult for female orgasm, coitus in the West and in other areas is very often an act that is orchestrated by males. At least on initial encounters, it is the male who moves the female into the coital positions that he prefers. Even on longer-term encounters it is most often the male who suggests coitus at a time when he is in the mood. Such control by the male ensures his satisfaction much more than that of the female.

Even the very counting of acts of intercourse in Western society is heavily male oriented. Think about two different sexual scenarios. Suppose we have a couple who engage in coitus for one hour. During that time the female has orgasms three times but the male has only one orgasm at the end of the hour. If that couple were asked how many times they made love that day, they would likely answer once—basing that answer on the male's final orgasm, which is the symbol of the end of the coital act.

Consider a second scenario of making love for one hour during which the male had three orgasms and the woman only one at the end of the hour. How would that couple respond? I would suggest that they might well report that they made love three times that day because once again the male climax is the measure of the coital act. It would be interesting to see if such "counting" would be the same in non-Western cultures. My bet would be that it would because so many of those cultures are also male dominant.

The obvious conclusion appears to be that coitus is a male-oriented sexual act, and thus any promotion of coitus as the ultimate act is hardly in the interest of gender equality. Yet it is precisely the belief in gender equality that defines premature ejaculation as a problem! Despite this, when we treat premature ejaculation by encouraging coitus as the context in which that problem must be resolved, we are promoting a male-oriented act to resolve a problem of gender inequity.

Clinicians and most individuals in treatment are not aware of this potential conflict because of the power of our ideological commitment to the coital sexual act as "normal" or "preferred." Even females in our Western culture will share this view and may prefer coital sexuality and blame themselves for any sexual difficulties they encounter. As we have just seen, these notions concerning preference for coitus are often rooted in our assumptions regarding the reproductive nature of sexuality and the dominance of males (see tenet 4). These notions are not part of any scientific theory of normality. Once again the importance of kinship and power structures for the understanding of sexuality is evidenced.

Finally, let me mention that our primate cousins afford us ample reason to expect rapid ejaculation in human males. The average male chimpanzee, gibbon or lemur takes less than 15 seconds to reach orgasm.[37] In fact, this coital brevity is one reason that Hrdy feels that female primates are not very selective of their male sexual partners. Female primates require a large number of male partners in order to achieve their own orgasm, which usually takes longer than a few seconds of thrusting. Hrdy believes that the view of a promiscuous male primate and a selective female primates is one that was imposed on biology by the Victorian thinking of the later nineteenth century and not by the realities of primate life.[38] This sounds quite plausible to me. In any case, if such rapid ejaculation is in our closest primate relatives, it would indeed be surprising if that same tendency was not present in some human primate males. We thus have reason at least not to view premature ejaculation as any sort of biological based "abnormality."

WHAT IS SEXUAL NORMALITY?

The important conclusion to be reached from our examination of premature ejaculation is that a great many of our social beliefs about sexual normality simply reflect our societal ideologies. These beliefs about sexual abnormality do not necessarily reflect any empirically based biological or psychological outcomes that inevitably lead to a general inability to perform sexually. To be sure, in a gender-equal coitally oriented society a rapidly ejaculating male would likely feel he had a "problem," but this is due to the norms that favor prolonged heterosexual coital behavior. The same feeling of discomfort would be true of a male who required ten minutes of coital thrusting to reach orgasm if he lived in a culture that stressed quick ejaculation. In East Bay in Melanesia, for example, most of the young men reach orgasm within 15–30 seconds after vaginal entry.[39] In that culture, a male who could not so perform would be considered to have a "delayed ejaculation" problem.

The conclusion seems obvious that if societal norms are our guidelines for psychological abnormality then any form of sexual behavior can be "abnormal." That being the case, we might do well to simply call such behavior nonconformist. It would seem to me that such a substitution of labels would alleviate a great deal of personal anxiety. Also, it would make it clearer that one can choose to be out of line on this or any issue with the dominant ideological positions. In short, awareness of normative nonconformity encourages the feeling that one may choose *not* to change, whereas the label *abnormality* imposes a pressure in the direction of change. Few people would want to be labeled abnormal, but many more would accept the label of nonconformist.

Surely, physiologically there are sexual conditions that do not depend on cultural norms and that are analogous to a broken leg in that they prevent the performance of any kind of desired sexual activity. This would be the case with certain defects in blood flow to the penis that prevent erection. It certainly is worth differentiating that situation from the case of a premature ejaculator. A problem in the physiological system can affect our sexuality, and that, of course, may be culture-free. Yet the specific type of examples I use here preclude such a broad physiological explanation.[40] Few would contend that premature ejaculation is due to some basic defect in physiology.

One illustration should suffice to show how easy it is to reify, or give greater reality than is warranted to some concepts of sexual "health or illness." Nicholas Groth in his 1979 book on rape discusses the sexual responses of the rapist. He notes that 3% of the rapists he studied were premature ejaculators.[41] Now just what does premature ejaculation mean in a rape situation?

If premature ejaculation were a disability like a broken leg, then it surely is appropriate to use that concept in this fashion. However, if the very concept of premature ejaculation simply means that the male reaches orgasm in coitus more quickly than the cultural norm dictates, then we have a quite different situation. Just what is the norm about orgasm during rape? Of course, we do not have norms that assert that a rapist must not reach orgasm in so short a time—that he should wait for the victim to reach orgasm!

That idea is preposterous, and so is the use of the label *premature ejaculation.* Groth's usage can only be attributed to an acceptance of quick orgasm as some type of "unhealthy" sexual index in and of itself. If someone who is a professional and who is sophisticated about rape can use a concept in this confusing fashion, then how much more likely is the general public to accumulate a laundry list of "unhealthy" sexual acts as a result of our promiscuous use of terms like *abnormal, unhealthy,* and *disturbed*?

Surely we all have strong preference in sexual behavior, and we also have sexual acts that we find heinous.[42] In my judgment, we can still severely condemn certain types of crimes without calling those acts proof of biological or psychological abnormality. We can express our values and insist on punishment and strive to effect change in the person in order to gain conformity to our beliefs. Some may not approve of such demands, but that is another issue.

My point here is that to use *abnormality* as interchangeable with acts that are violations of norms is to invite the politicalization of therapy. That outcome would make therapists the agents of the established power groups, for it would be therapists who would enforce conformity to the norms by labeling all such nonconformists as abnormal, dysfunctional, disturbed, or whatever other pejorative was in vogue at the moment.

We have seen this happen in totalitarian countries where people are sent to mental hospitals because they disagree with the dominant norms of the ruling party.[43] We cannot scientifically establish which forms of sexuality are "good" or "bad." We discussed in Chapter 1 what the problems are in attempting that. Consequently, unless we separate those acts that violate norms from those acts that violate scientifically established standards of biological or psychological normality, we will inevitably politicize our scientists and make their objectivity and fairness suspect.

Allow me to further illustrate my point concerning the distinction between labels of nonconformity and labels like abnormal or dysfunctional. Masters and Johnson's emphasis on couple commitment and communication as ways of removing roadblocks from the physiological and psychological operation of sexuality in stable relationships seems accurately based for large segments of our Western culture.[44] People who do not openly communicate their sexual needs and who do not establish a sense of security in their mates may well block the achievement of some levels of sexual enjoyment. However, this would not establish the absence of such commitment and communication as evidence of psychological abnormality. I do not believe Masters and Johnson would reach such a judgment. Rather, what their therapeutic approach asserts is that in cultures like the West, where stable marital relations with high commitment and open communication are valued, the lack of such interaction can block the achievement of certain aspects of sexual enjoyment.

We must remember that even in a Western culture, one could for any number of reasons decline to get involved in a stable relationship with commitment and open communication. Some might feel the personal benefits are not worth the loss of autonomy. Furthermore, one may argue as Vannoy does, that transient sexual encounters have higher "pure" sexual rewards and involve simpler negotiations with partners and for those reasons they may be preferable.[45] One may argue for such an unconventional choice even if it means that there will be more communication problems and more difficulty in establishing permanent relationships. Such difficulties hardly establish abnormality. All life choices involve costs as well as rewards. To justify the scientific use of terms like *abnormality*, one would have to show empirically that such lack of commitment and communication violates some scientifically established standard concerning psychological normality.

I do not categorically deny the possibility of using terms like *abnormal* in a scientific way despite the loose way these concepts are sometimes applied. In fact, I have a suggestion for a sociological definition of psychological abnormality. The science of biology is advanced sufficiently so that there are a reasonable number of established concepts of how the human body operates. This knowledge has enabled biologists to formulate concepts of abnormal bodily functioning, for example, when a virus enters the body and upsets the internal balance. Certainly individual physiological systems differ in their resistance to such a virus and in other ways as well, but there are general principles as to what constitutes a disturbance of the physiological system, and so we have a reasonable conception of disease or abnormality in terms of our bodies.

Psychology is a much younger science and several competing notions of normality exist. Let me add one more from the perspective of a sociologist. I start by recognizing that societal pressures to conform to particular ideological expectations can produce stress. Stress occurs when the individual is unable to achieve these internalized social goals. This is one very common reason for a person to seek therapy. In the case of premature ejaculation or other adjustment problems, the cause of stress is likely to be the felt dissonance between what one seeks and what one obtains, as I have detailed earlier.

To be sure, a "real" psychological problem exists here in the sense that the individual feels stressed, but the psychological meaning of that felt stress needs to be investigated. If, indeed, it is due to a nonconformity problem, it can be dealt with by accepting one's nonconformity *or* by changing oneself to become more conforming. The therapist can clarify and aid the patient toward such choices. This type of personal stress situation I would call a *conformity problem* and I would not use labels such as *abnormal, dysfunctional,* or *pathology* for such a condition. There is a temptation to use such labels, for they bear the prestige of the older, more established biological sciences. Still, I do believe that today many professionally trained therapists would hesitate to use them in the above instance.

There is another type of patient, though. In this case, perhaps the stress is due to some long-term basic cognitive or emotional disturbance in the person that is upsetting almost all the areas of that person's life. Then the question arises, do we have here more than a conformity stress-induced situation? It is in such an instance that we will find it useful to have objective criteria for the possible use of the term *abnormal.*

I suggest the following societal-level criteria for the use of the term *psychologically abnormal.* I would call abnormal those personal cognitive or emotional traits that disable the individual from functioning in *all* societies. In short, this would be a systemic personality disturbance. If the condition disabled the individual only in the native society, then he or she may simply be a nonconformist. However, if the characteristic is such that the person could not function in any type of society, then we have a different situation.

This definition makes it easier to delineate conformity problems from abnormality conditions. If a condition is a conformity problem, there will always be other groups or societies in which that behavior and the underlying traits would not be a problem. I mention East Bay as a society where the norm is rapid ejaculation. Also, in relation to open communication in marriage, there surely are many non-Western societies that play down such open communication. So, if we have societies with different ejaculatory and communication customs, then such behaviors must be within the normal range of individual cognitive and emotional abilities. That is, if we accept all societal customs as within the normal range of individuals, then only those individuals who cannot conform to any set of societal customs could be viewed as clearly unable to function in society. Short of this, people can still have problems of adjustment and feel stress in such areas, but we have no evidence that such people have a personality that could not operate in any society. All too often we test for abnormality by simply looking for a lack of fit with one society's ideology. To do so is to increase the likelihood of confusing conformity problems with general disabilities. The American Psychiatric Association's guideline suggests the use of the so called "value free" term *paraphilias* for those patterns of erotic arousal that differ from the "standard patterns."[46] I feel certain that most people would be more comfortable being called a non-conformist than a paraphiliac.

In essence I start with the premise that those basic personality characteristics (cognitive and emotional) that are promoted in any fully operating and ongoing society are within the limits of an undisturbed personality system. Accordingly, I am assuming that the label *disturbed* or *abnormal* personality means characteristics of a personality type unable to function in all social systems. If there are societies that socialize individuals to think and feel in ways that are condemned in our society, then there are societies in which those people can function; therefore those individuals do not have characteristics that make social life impossible for them. We may not like them, but they would not fit my societal criteria for psychological abnormality.

Now, one can ask, why use a societal-level measure of psychological normality? My answer to this is that personalities, as we know them, do not exist outside a societal setting. It is only by interaction with others that we learn to communicate, to understand others, to be able to form relationships, and to develop a conception of ourselves.[47] In this sense, psychological normality presupposes a social setting for its evaluation. I find it difficult to conceive of psychological normality outside of a social setting. For this reason I feel it is proper to offer a societal-level conception of psychological normality.

Applying my conception of normality, we would see the majority of sexual problems brought to therapists as the result of stress caused by conformity problems related to existing ideologies. Further, by my definition of normality, we would need to go beyond labeling a particular behavior. A judgment would have to be based on the cognitive and emotional state underlying that behavior. If that state were an emotional upheaval that was producing a total withdrawal or an indiscriminate violent assault on all other group members, then one could assume abnormality. This is so because it is inconceivable that such a cognitive and emotional state could be functional in any society. There are no societies that would accept a person who is totally withdrawn or a person who indiscriminately kills. Even warlike societies are quite select in whom they kill, and peaceful societies must be active to go about their daily tasks. The important point here is that particular sexual or other acts would not be automatically labeled abnormal. The yardstick of normality would be the potential integration of that action into a human society.

I do not pretend that my conception is simple to utilize or that it lacks any conceptual problems. We do not have full knowledge of all societies. What about theoretically possible societies, which do not now exist but could exist? A normal boundary should include them. How do we enable a patient to be a nonconformist and still avoid stress? What I have presented is but the broad outlines of a societal basis for conceptualizing psychological normality. Much more work is necessary to make this conception operational.

I do think, however, that this approach has advantages over some other views of normality. First, it does put forth an explicit model of the limits of a normal personality without depending on the ideology of any one society. Thus, it gives more opportunity for keeping the personal biases of our society out of our therapeutic judgments. Secondly, by its cross-cultural perspective this approach pressures psychologists to separate conformity problems from systemic personality problems that are more deeply rooted in cognitive and emotional disturbances. This is so because a cross-cultural approach forces awareness of alternatives and of the limits of one society's ideologies. Thirdly, this approach lessens the likelihood that specific acts will be labeled as abnormal, for it focuses upon the underlying cognitive and emotional states that may apply to many diverse acts.

In addition, this approach moves us away from building our notion of abnormality on a medical or biological model of disease or disorder and instead firmly roots our notion of normality in a broad societal framework. Much of the use of labels of abnormality stems from the fact that the study of sexuality began a hundred years ago within the medical profession.[48] Doctors are trained in the biological sciences and deal directly with diseases and so abnormality labels are part of their profession. Certainly it is important to keep the input of physicians, but it is also important to place sexuality into a societal framework. Finally, my approach presents individuals with a view of normality that they can understand and that may well reduce their anxiety about their problems, since, as I have said before, conformity problems are easier to accept than is the label *pathological disturbance* or paraphilia or anomolous behavior. The intent may be to use some of these terms in a "value free" fashion but the meaning to most people is judgmental.

As I see it, sexual therapists are not actually curing an "abnormal" or "dysfunctional" patient but are seeking instead to produce a patient who feels more comfortable with his or her sexual lifestyle. The more therapy is based on making one "normal," the more the patient is made to feel there is no choice. I believe that most sexual therapists produced by our university graduate programs today would agree with much of what I have said in this section. But there are others who would not; equally important, I suspect that the general public still thinks in terms of simple medical concepts of normality and abnormality.

Some psychologists would no doubt argue that there are general principles of personality functioning that can be utilized to arrive at judgments regarding sexual abnormality, and therefore my standard of the ability to function in some type of society is not needed. If psychological systems of normality are proposed, then the logical and empirical basis upon which the definitions of personal abnormality are based must be clearly explicated. Also, any psychological notion of abnormality would have to consider the ability of the person to operate in society. Thus, my notions would turn out to be at least one key element in any psychological notion of normality.

I am proposing a rather generous measure of normality. If we are to narrow it and assert other limitations on normality, we must ask for scientific reasoning and evidence. Extending the borders of the abnormal needs to be monitored so that it is not a facade for a particular ideological set of values.

This book is based on the premise that human sexuality has a crucial societal component that does indeed affect our sexual lives in major ways. We cannot assume that the same sexual act will have the same functional significance in different societal settings. In this sense virtually any sexual act can produce discomfort or stress in an individual due to social pressures and ideological beliefs. The reader will recall that there are societies wherein coitus begins at ages under ten for most children. The meaning of such child sexuality when it occurs with the guidance of close relatives and with societal approval is quite different than it would be in our own society today. The same could be said about virtually any sexual act. Therefore I believe we need to attend to the social context of a sexual act if we are to understand it and to judge its meaning scientifically. My suggestions are offered in that spirit. Surely this would be a scientific improvement over the vague notions of sexual normality that abound in our society today.[49]

SUMMARY AND CONCLUSIONS

Let us conclude this section by asking how the cognitive and emotive ideologies would apply to our discussion of sexual normality? It would seem to me that the more a group feels the need to control sexual behavior, the more they will use the term *abnormal* for whatever sexual behavior they dislike. Relatedly, the more one labels people who violate sexual norms as abnormal, the more one will want therapists to alter such people into greater conformity with their sexual norms.[50] In short, the use of nonconforming behavior as the basis for defining abnormality and the use of therapy to create conformity are related approaches. Both symbolize the desire to control and minimize choices and thus are characteristics of the emotive ideology.

Now, even though people endorsing the cognitive ideology do expand individual choices, they would surely have sexual behaviors that they would not include as legitimate choices and for which they, too, might utilize terms like *abnormal* or *unhealthy*. The key difference in these two general ideologies is in the scope of sexual behavior the ideology condemns and the willingness to restrict or expand that scope.

The specific sexual ideologies also relate to the question of normality. As we have seen, each sexual ideology has tenets that logically follow from the basic assumption of the ideology regarding gender equality. These beliefs spell out the specifics of what an adherent is likely to think of as normal behavior and, by inference, what is likely to be viewed as abnormal behavior. To illustrate, if one believes in tenet 2 of the nonequalitarian sexual ideology, then a woman who accepts body-centered sexuality may well be thought of as perverted or disturbed. The principle underlying the use of negative evaluations is that when someone violates our beliefs about preferable behavior, we are likely to respond by negatively labeling that person in some way.

Negative labeling is a common human tendency, and thus we should expect it to carry over even into our scientific usage. I have tried in this chapter to warn of this danger and to arm you with greater awareness of the ideological beliefs that exist. Since such ideologies embody our strongest values, they will serve as the source of our harshest condemnations of others. The next two chapters examine two areas of sexuality where very strong ideological feelings have been expressed: homosexuality and erotica. We will also see in those two areas the operation of the kinship and power aspects of sexuality. You have been prepared by what you have read so far. I hope that enables you to set aside temporarily whatever feelings you have on those issues in order to examine them as objectively as possible.

SELECTED REFERENCES AND COMMENTS

1. For an excellent introduction to the ideas of one of our greatest philosophers, Aristotle, see

McKeon, Richard (ed.), *The Basic Works of Aristotle*. New York: Random House, 1941.

2. Two of the finest sources for a general philosophical background concerning the power of ideas are

Randall, John Herman, Jr., *The Making of the Modern Mind*. Boston: Houghton Mifflin, 1940.

Woodbridge, Frederick J.E., *The Realm of Mind: An Essay in Metaphysics*. New York: Columbia University Press, 1926.

3. Some social scientists would feel that the cognitive ideology, with its emphasis on rational choice, is congruent with the exchange-theory orientation in sociology. For a brief statement of exchange theory see

Emerson, R.M., "Social Exchange Theory," in A. Inkeles, J. Coleman, and N. Smelser (eds.), *Annual Review of Sociology*. Palo Alto, Calif.: Annual Reviews, 1976.

4. Woodbridge, Frederick J.E., *The Realm of Mind: An Essay in Metaphysics*. New York: Columbia University Press, 1926.

5. The concept of rational choice is used here to mean choosing the most efficient means for a given end. This is the usual definition of that term. One can place value limitations on what means and ends are acceptable and still ask for the selection of the most efficient means to a given end from a set of means that fit some moral standard.

6. One of our creative anthropological observers has written an exciting book presenting what he calls "the meta science ideology" which he believes will aid in resolving problems in our societies around the world. I suggest you examine

Naroll, Raoul, *The Moral Order: An Introduction to the Human Situation*. Beverly Hills, Calif.: Sage Publications, 1983.

7. Those readers familiar with the social-contract theorists in philosophy will notice that such theories are relevant here. My entire discussion of ideology ties in with a great number of philosophical issues. I cannot here get involved in all of them, but once again I suggest one of my favorite reference works:

Edwards, Paul (eds.), *The Encyclopedia of Philosophy* (8 vols.). New York: Macmillan, Free Press, 1967.

8. Hobbes, Thomas, "Leviathan," in Frederick J.E. Woodbridge (ed.), *Hobbes Selections*. New York: Scribner's, 1930.

9. A synopsis of Goethe's thinking can be found in Volume 3 of the encyclopedia mentioned in note 7 above.

10. The cognitive approach in psychology accepts an interactive view of our cognitive and emotional selves. For a popular presentation of this perspective see

Ellis, Albert, and Robert A. Harper, *A New Guide to Rational Living*. N. Hollywood, Calif.: Wilshire, 1978.

11. For an overview of U.S. attitudes toward a variety of key areas, I suggest an examination of the results of the National Opinion Research Center's (NORC's) annual surveys. They select the key questions that have been asked over the years and check for current viewpoints. They have taken national samples since 1972, and their results are available at very low cost. For information write to

The Roper Center, Box U-164, The University of Connecticut, Storrs, CT 06268.

12. I did one of the first national surveys through NORC in 1963 and found at that time about 80% of the adult Americans thought premarital intercourse was always wrong. For an analysis of my 1963 study see

Reiss, Ira L., *The Social Context of Premarital Sexual Permissiveness*. New York: Holt, Rinehart & Winston, 1967.

13. Once again, the source for this is NORC's annual surveys.

14. Many people believe that the increases in premarital sexuality was a result of the awareness by young women that they had a chance to control pregnancy once the pill was available in 1960. This seems rather unlikely, since even in the most recent years (1984) the majority of teenagers were not using the pill and about half used nothing at their first coitus. The impact of the pill was most dramatic on married people and also on the sexual life of women in their 20s who were far beyond their first act of intercourse. For such women the pill may add an element of security, although even for these women other methods are replacing the pill today. We need to keep in mind that the condom and the diaphragm have

been available for over 100 years and that for groups that used them (like Jewish married couples), they were and are highly effective methods. The conclusion is that it is our values and attitudes that determine how well we use the contraceptive methods available. Secondly, the lack of modern contraception has not been a block for millions of people over many thousands of years from having premarital intercourse. See the following sources:

Reiss, Ira L., and Gary Lee, *Family Systems in America* (4th ed.). New York: Holt, Rinehart & Winston, (in press). (See especially Chapters 6 and 7.)

Bachrach, Christine A., "Contraceptive Practice among American Women, 1973–1982," *Family Planning Perspectives,* vol. 16, no. 6 (November–December 1984), pp. 253–260.

Zelnik, M., and J.F. Kantner, "Sexual Activity, Contraceptive Use and Pregnancy among Metropolitan-area Teenagers, 1971–1979," *Family Planning Perspectives,* vol. 12 (September–October 1980), pp. 230–237.

15. An earlier statement of my views on sexual ideologies can be found in the reference cited here. However, I was then speaking mainly of America and thus my presentation here differs somewhat. I wrote the article in 1980. It was one of my first steps toward writing this book.

Reiss, Ira L., "Some Observations on Ideology and Sexuality in America," *Journal of Marriage and the Family,* vol. 43, no. 2 (May 1981), pp. 271–283.

16. One important point to note about homosexual ideologies is that any tenet concerning gender power would be irrelevant. By definition homosexuals are of the same gender, and so the question of how to treat the opposite gender is not at issue. Gender is still indirectly involved in that gender-role training is reflected in the ways that male homosexuals act, which are distinct from the actions of female homosexuals. This is further discussed in the next chapter. Overall my estimate would be that young American male and female homosexuals generally would respond like young male and female heterosexuals and would be adherents of the equalitarian sexual ideology.

17. The data from Peggy Sanday allowed me to test for a relationship between the degree to which gender roles are segregated in a society and the status of women in that society. I reported in Chapter 4 that I found no significant correlation. This strengthens my reasoning that what matters is how socially important the tasks are that one's gender engages in, not whether the tasks are shared with the opposite gender.

18. In my initial statement on ideology in 1980 I utilized one additional ideological tenet that concerned using love as a purifier of sexuality. I did not feel this love tenet would hold up very widely cross-culturally and so I dropped it here. Also, tenet 2, concerning body-centered sexuality, implies the tenet I dropped; that is, if one rejects body-centered sexuality, it may well be because one feels that only love justifies sexuality, and sexuality without love is therefore unacceptable. My initial statement was contained in my presidential address at the October 1980 National Council on Family Relations meeting in Portland, Oregon.

19. The equalitarian ideology is congruent with both "permissiveness with" and "permissiveness without" affection standards. The nonequalitarian ideology fits with what I called the double standard. The original statement of these pemarital sexual standards comes from my 1960 book. In my 1967 book I used a scale measuring premarital sexual permissiveness to examine how these standards distributed in regional samples and a national sample of Americans. A great many studies have used my premarital sexual permissiveness scales. One was by DeLamater and MacCorquodale, who compared college and noncollege populations. The reader

may also wish to consult the 1970 and 1980 decade reviews of research and theory on premarital sexuality to gain a better overview of this area.

Reiss, Ira L., *Premarital Sexual Standards in America.* New York: Free Press, 1960.

Reiss, Ira L., *The Social Context of Premarital Sexual Permissiveness.* Holt, Rinehart & Winston, 1967.

Delamater, John, and Patricia MacCorquodale, *Premarital Sexuality: Attitudes, Relationships, Behavior.* Madison: University of Wisconsin Press, 1979.

Clayton, Richard R., and Janet L. Bokemeier, "Premarital Sex in the Seventies," *Journal of Marriage and the Family,* vol. 42, no. 4 (November 1980), pp. 759-775.

Cannon, Kenneth L., and Richard Long, "Premarital Sexual Behavior in the Sixties," *Journal of Marriage and the Family,* vol. 33, no. 1 (February 1971), pp. 36-49.

20. Carol Cassell develops this theme of how women use love to overcome sexual guilt in her book:

Cassell, Carol, *Swept Away: Why Women Fear Their Own Sexuality.* New York: Simon & Schuster, 1984.

21. The resistance of males to male homosexuality is reported in studies of swingers by Gilmartin and for males in general in Kinsey's work and in National Opinion Research Center polls.

Gilmartin, Brian, *The Gilmartin Report.* Secaucus, N.J.: Citadel Press, 1978.

Kinsey, Alfred C., Wardell Pomeroy, and Clyde Martin, *Sexual Behavior in the Human Male.* Philadelphia: Saunders, 1948.

22. We have evidence of such general increases in sexual activity from studies of birth control in marriage by Westoff. Newcomer and Udry report rates for adolescent populations. Also, Hunt offers us a not-so-representative national sample with evidence of increases in several areas. Finally, there are magazine surveys that, of course, do not represent the country but at least indicate that such increases are not very rare.

Westoff, Charles F., "Coital Frequency and Contraception," *Family Planning Perspectives,* vol. 6 (Summer 1974), pp. 136-141;

Hunt, Morton M., *Sexual Behavior in the 1970's.* Chicago: Playboy Press, 1974.

Wolfe, Linda, *Women and Sex in the 80's: The Cosmo Report.* Toronto: Bantam Books, 1981.

Tavris, Carol, and Susan Sadd, *The Redbook Report on Female Sexuality.* New York: Delacorte, 1977.

Newcomer, Susan F., and J. Richard Udry, "Oral Sex in an Adolescent Population," *Archives of Sexual Behavior,* vol. 14, no. 1 (February 1985), pp. 41-47.

23. Several studies in America have indicated a correlation between gender equality and premarital sexual permissiveness. I found such a relationship in four national samples of American adults taken by NORC. These were part of a study of causes of extramarital sexuality. Also, Jonathan Kelley, in a sample of Berkeley students, found the same relationship. In both instances the relationship became part of an explanation of sexual customs. See

Kelley, Jonathan, "Sexual Permissiveness: Evidence for a Theory," *Journal of Marriage and the Family,* vol. 40 (August 1978), pp. 455-468.

Reiss, Ira L., Ronald E. Anderson, and G.C. Sponaugle, "A Multivariate Model of the Determinants of Extramarital Sexual Permissiveness," *Journal of Marriage and the Family,* vol. 42 (May 1980), pp. 395-411.

24. Many studies in the professional journals support this conclusion. One sign of the increased legitimation of female sexuality is the vast increase in teenage female premarital sexuality. The journal *Family Planning Perspectives* has many articles on this topic. For a summary of three national surveys of teenage sexuality, see

Zelnik, M., and J.F. Kantner, "Sexual Activity, Contraceptive Use and Pregnancy among Metropolitan-area Teenagers, 1971-1979," *Family Planning Perspectives*, vol. 12 (September-October 1980), pp. 230-237.

25. This study did not have a representative sample. The students came from college classes whose instructors were willing to hand out the questionnaire, and the adults came from acquaintances of the researcher and her friends. Lottes used all five of the tenets that were in my 1981 article (see note 18). She also measured adherence to abstinence tenets I had devised. In this chapter I am interested predominantly in the majority of her respondents who were adherents of the equalitarian sexual ideology. My references to her study in the the text utilized the data contained in her 1983 paper interpreted to apply to my four tenets.

Lottes, Ilsa, "An Investigation of the Tenet Patterns of the Reiss Sexual Ideologies." Paper presented at the April 1983 Society for the Scientific Study of Sex Eastern Region meeting in Philadelphia.

Lottes, Ilsa, "Use of Cluster Analysis to Determine Belief Patterns of Sexual Attitudes," *Journal of Sex Research*, vol. 21 (November 1985), pp. 405-421.

Reiss, Ira L., "Some Observations on Ideology and Sexuality in America," *Journal of Marriage and the Family*, vol. 43 (May 1981), pp. 271-283.

26. Note the confusion in meaning that would occur here had we not clearly distinguished the meaning of *gender* and *sexual* in Chapter 2.

27. An early statement of my views on cross-cultural typologies was presented in February 1982 at a University of Iowa conference on the family. It was published the next year as

Reiss, Ira L., "Sexuality: A Research and Theory Perspective," pp. 141-147 in Peggy Houston (ed.), *Sexuality and the Family Life Span*. Iowa City: University of Iowa Press, 1983.

28. Bullough, Vern, *Sexual Variance in Society and History*. New York: John Wiley, 1976. (See Parts 1 and 2.)

29. It is important to specify which type of sexuality we are focusing upon in our typologies. The social situation may differ, for example, for premarital as compared to extramarital sexuality. Related to this point is a cross-cultural analysis by David Heiss that was aimed at seeing whether norms regarding the acceptance of sexuality for different age groups were consistent. He found norms in infancy, childhood, and adolescence to be related to each other in a positive direction. Adult norms tended to be the high point of restrictiveness. He did find considerable consistency in norms across age levels, but he also noted that sexual socialization can be inconsistent at different ages due to the structure of particular societies. See

Heise, David R., "Cultural Patterning of Sexual Socialization," *American Sociological Review*, vol. 32 (February 1967), pp. 726-739.

30. U.S. Department of Health and Human Services, National Center for Health Statistics, C.A. Bachrach and M.C. Horn, "Marriage and First Intercourse, Marital Dissolution, and Remarriage, U.S., 1982," *Advance Data from Vital and Health Statistics*, no. 107. Hyattsville, Md.: Public Health Service, April 1985.

31. Clement, Ulrich, Gunter Schmidt, and Margret Kruse, "Changes in Differences in Sexual Behavior: A Replication of a Study on West German Students (1966-1981)," *Archives of Sexual Behavior*, vol. 13, no. 2 (1984), pp. 99-120.

Money, John, and Herman Musaph (eds.), *Handbook of Sexology.* New York: Elsevier North-Holland, 1977.

32. Kaplan, Helen Singer, *The New Sex Therapy: Active Treatment of Sexual Dysfunction.* New York: Brunner/Mazel, 1974. (See especially pp. 298–299.)

American Psychiatric Association, *Diagnostic and Statistical Manual of Mental Disorders-III.* Washington, D.C.: APA, 1977.

Haeberle, Erwin J., *The Sex Atlas.* New York: Seabury Press, 1978. (pp. 260–262)

Lief, Harold I. (ed.), *Sexual Problems in Medical Practice.* Chicago: AMA, 1981. (See especially pp. 151–152.)

33. For a modified Freudian statement of this position see

Gadpaille, Warren J., "Research into the Physiology of Maleness and Femaleness," *Archives of General Psychiatry,* vol. 26 (March 1972), pp. 193-206.

Gadpaille, Warren J., "Psychosexual Development through the Life Cycle," Chapter 3 in Harold I. Lief (ed.), *Sexual Problems in Medical Practice.* Chicago: AMA, 1981.

34. For a brief and clear presentation of the stages of psychosexual development as Freud conceptualized them, see

Halberstadt-Freud, Hendrika C., "Freud's Libido Theory," Chapter 5 in John Money and Herman Musaph (eds.), *Handbook of Sexology.* New York: Elsevier North Holland, 1977.

35. Bullough, Vern L., and James Brundage, *Sexual Practices and the Medieval Church.* Buffalo: Prometheus Books, 1982.

36. Freud's theory of the vaginal orgasm has been rejected by most sexual therapists today. However, the recent discovery of the Grafenberg spot supports the possibility of vaginal contact producing orgasm. The Grafenberg spot is located on the anterior wall about two inches inside the vagina. Upward pressure pressures the duct connecting the urethra to the bladder and can in some women produce orgasm. In some of these cases, ejaculation of a fluid occurs. It is a matter of debate whether that fluid is mostly urine or if it is largely secretion from the duct itself.

Ladas, Alice Kahn, Beverly Whipple, and John D. Perry, *The G Spot: And Other Recent Discoveries about Human Sexuality,* New York: Holt, Rinehart & Winston, 1982.

37. Hong, Lawrence K., "Survival of the Fastest: On the Origin of Premature Ejaculation," *The Journal of Sex Research,* vol. 20, no. 2 (May 1984), pp. 109–122.

38. Hrdy, Sarah Blaffer, *The Woman that Never Evolved.* Cambridge, Mass.: Harvard University Press, 1981.

39. Davenport, William, "Sexual Patterns and Their Reguation in a Society of the Southwest Pacific," pp. 164-207 in Frank A. Beach (ed.), *Sex and Behavior.* New York: John Wiley, 1965. (See especially p. 185.)

40. There is a new-wave opinion supporting a biological view of homosexuality. This is commented upon in the next chapter.

41. Groth, A. Nicholas, *Men Who Rape: The Psychology of the Offender.* New York: Plenum Press, 1979. (See page 89.)

42. The best information we have on the seriousness of crimes (both sexual and otherwise) in the mind of the American public can be found in a national survey reported in

U.S. Department of Justice, Bureau of Justice Statistics. *Criminal Victimization in the U.S., 1981: A National Crime Survey Report,* NCJ-90208. Washington, D.C., November 1983.

43. For reports on such violations of human rights, see the publications by *Amnesty International.*

44. Masters, William H., and Virginia F. Johnson, *Human Sexual Inadequacy.* Boston: Little, Brown, 1970.

Masters, William H., and Virginia F. Johnson, *The Pleasure Bond.* Boston: Little, Brown, 1975.

45. Vannoy, Russell, *Sex Without Love: A Philosophical Exploration.* Buffalo: Prometheus Books, 1980.

46. American Psychiatric Association, *Diagnostic and Statistical Manual of Mental Disorders-III.* Washington, D.C.: APA, 1977.

47. The classic work describing the process by which the social self develops was published over 50 years ago.

Mead, George Herbert, *Mind, Self and Society.* Chicago: University of Chicago Press, 1934.

48. There are some good accounts of the beginnings of the so-called scientific study of human sexuality. See

Money, John, and Herman Musaph (eds.), *Handbook of Sexology.* New York: Elsevier North-Holland, 1977.

Robinson, Paul, *The Modernization of Sex: Havelock Ellis, Alfred Kinsey, William Masters and Virginia Johnson.* New York: Harper & Row, 1976.

Haeberle, Erwin J., *The Sex Atlas.* New York: Seabury Press, 1978.

49. The classic critique of virtually all use of the label *mental illness* was put forth by Thomas Szasz. My own position in this chapter is less radical but also seeks to limit the unscientific use of negative labels.

Szasz, Thomas, *The Myth of Mental Illness.* New York: Harper & Row, 1964.

The work of Ullerstam also sought to remove negative labels from most all sexual acts. Ullerstam was called the "smile on the face of the sexual revolution" by Yves de Saint-Agnes.

Ullerstam, Lars, *The Erotic Minorities.* New York: Grove, 1966.

50. Some alterations produce conformity through physical changes. I am not speaking here of simple cosmetic surgery. I recall a doctor in Ohio who in 1975-1977 altered the angle of the vagina by cutting the pubococcygeus muscle. The goal was to enhance clitoral contact in the male-on-top position. There were hundreds of wives who came to this surgeon for this operation in order to conform to their conception of normal sexual response and be able to achieve an orgasm in their husband's favorite position. This is a clear example of ideology altering anatomy.

CHAPTER SIX

THE SOCIETAL LINKAGES OF HOMOSEXUALITY

PERSPECTIVES ON HOMOSEXUALITY: THE HETEROSEXUAL BIAS

I deliberately used premature ejaculation to open up the discussion of ideology and normality in the last chapter. Since premature ejaculation is not viewed as horrendous, I thought my ideas would obtain a fairer hearing than if I began with a more controversial sexual act. Let us now turn to a sexual act that seven of every ten adult Americans judge to be "always wrong".[1] Is homosexuality an abnormal act? Remember, now, that I am not asking whether it is good or bad. That is a private moral judgment. Instead, I am asking whether there is a scientific concept of normality that homosexuality violates.

I spelled out my formulation of a sociological basis for a concept of psychological abnormality in the last chapter. If the characteristic in question would disable an individual from functioning in all societies, then I would apply the label *abnormal* to that characteristic. Psychological abnormality, in this view, is based upon the characteristic being universally socially destructive. According to this definition, as I will document in this chapter, homosexuality is not abnormal behavior. Of course, any sexual act, heterosexual or homosexual, can be used to express some personal abnormality, but nothing inherent in either homosexuality or heterosexuality is abnormal. In this section we will examine the belief put forth in various forms that heterosexuality is the normal sexual orientation, and anything else is therefore abnormal.

This is a sociological treatise, and thus the biological and psychological basis of what is being studied will not be tended to with as much care as will the societal foundations. My approach is not intended to imply that biological and psychological factors are causally irrelevant to the explanation of human sexuality. I surely do not believe that. My approach simply affirms my strong belief in the great value of a societal-level explanation of human sexuality. Of course, there are other causal factors that affect all aspects of our life but are outside of the purview of the sociologist. I will let others extoll the value of a biological or psychological approach to sexuality. In this book I deal with other approaches predominantly when they challenge or in other ways are relevant to the sociological view I am developing.

There are those who assert that if you do not support a biological causation view of homosexuality, you are exhibiting your prejudice against homosexuals. Such biological adherents reason that if homosexuality were conceived to be biologically caused, then people would not condemn homosexuals for they would know that homosexuals could not be changed in their sexual partner orientation. Two immediate responses need to be made to such assertions.

First—as a scientist one's interest is in discerning the causal nature of the situation, not whether the conclusions will lead to more or less societal prejudice. Of course, scientists are human beings and desire not to do harm to others, but their primary values as scientists assert that they must not distort or hide their findings. Some scientists might feel so strongly on an issue that they might refuse to publish their results and thereby place their private values above their professional scientific values. If a scientist distorted findings in order to promote a particular personal value, however, almost all other scientists would find that behavior totally unacceptable.

Accordingly, it would be scientifically unacceptable to assert that homosexuality is predominantly biologically caused when the evidence (to be discussed) does not support such a perspective. To be sure, those who politicize science might well condemn anyone who does not accept their causal viewpoint. As a scientist, I reject such politicizing of scientific work and reject pressures that condemn all but those results that one's private values support. That sort of approach leads to dogma, not knowledge. *It makes research unnecessary, for the important answers come from ideological beliefs and not from careful scientific research.*

One other point needs to be made about the current debate over the biological bases of homosexuality. I believe that those who dislike homosexuality will not change their feelings one iota if scientists were to assert that homosexuality is biologically caused. It is the homosexual activities and preferences that such people find objectionable, and that would remain the same. Analogously, we have had much racial prejudice in America, and surely whites are aware of the genetic basis of racial physical traits. Prejudice is generally based upon some conflict present in the lifestyles of different groups and not upon whether the causation is viewed as genetic. So, I would conclude that whether or not we accept a biological causation of homosexuality is irrelevant to the degree of prejudice that will exist toward homosexuality.[2] If a scientific perspective is followed, then instead of morally judging all who disagree, scientists can spend their time investigating the empirical support for the various competing explanations of homosexual and heterosexual orientations.

Let us start our exploration of homosexuality with some definitions. I would define *homosexual behavior* as sexual behavior between two individuals of the same gender. Also, I would define a *homosexual* as someone who prefers sexual relations with a person of the same gender and whose erotic imagery is of the same gender.[3] I use the gender and not the genetic sex of the individuals as the crucial distinction in homosexuality. We do not see the genetic sex of another person—we see their body type and their personality. Each culture selects from the genetic potential a set of physical and social characteristics and wraps the male and/or female gender-role label around them. It is the person's expression of gender and not their chromosomal makeup that may attract us sexually.

Note that there is a distinction between homosexual behavior and homosexual preference. One can engage in a homosexual act without preferring that act, just as one can engage in a heterosexual act without preferring that act. Also, one can have a cross- or same-gender preference without behaving in accord with that preference. A person may be heterosexual or homosexual in preference but abstain from all interpersonal sexual involvement.

The question of the normality of homosexuality is a universal question: Is there something that makes homosexuality in all societies evidence of some fundamental psychological problem in an individual that, like a broken leg, will prevent that individual from fully functioning in society? Some would hesitate even to search for an answer to this question, for they feel it implies that there is an abnormal personality type that goes with a homosexual orientation. This is certainly not my implication—the question of normality is raised because there are such strong ideological beliefs against viewing homosexuality as normal. Only by examining this question can we dispel, qualify, or confirm such beliefs. It is analogous to investigating the psychological implications of any individual orientation—like orthodox Christian, political democratic, or Marxist. We settle nothing by walking away from such investigations.

Let us examine some nonhuman species in order to gain a broader perspective on the question of homosexual orientation. In an examination of a wide range of nonhuman species of animals, R.H. Denniston concludes that[4]

> in the vertebrates, apparent homosexual behavior increases as we ascend the taxonomic tree toward mammals. . . . Frequent homosexual activity has been described for all species of mammals of which careful observations have been made. (Denniston, 1980: pp. 28, 34)

The noted comparative psychologist Frank Beach reports that homosexual behavior is present in all species of primates on which studies have been made.[5] It is clear, then, that homosexual behavior is far from a rare occurrence, especially in our cousins the nonhuman primates. The typical scenario for homosexual behavior in primates is for a male to assume the lordotic position in front of another male. This is called presenting behavior and involves putting the rear up in the air while bending over. The male bending over may well be mounted in such a situation.

In many instances these are acts of dominance and submission, not sexual acts. A defeated male may assume the lordotic position in front of the victor, and the mount by the victor may not have any obvious sexual elements. But in other cases we observe erection, anal penetration, and orgasm, which clearly is homosexual behavior, regardless of whether dominance is also present. Although less frequently reported, female homosexual behavior also is not uncommon in nonhuman primates.

The amount of homosexual behavior in nonhuman primates seems to be related to characteristics of the primates group. David Goldfoot and his colleagues report, for example, that when infant rhesus monkeys are raised only with other monkeys of the same genetic sex (called isosexual rearing), there occurs a notable increase in adult homosexual behavior.[6]

> Both males and females in the isosexual condition were characterized by a partial inversion of the manifestation of protosexual behavior. Isosexual males showed statistically less foot-clasp mounting and more presenting than heterosexual males. Conversely, isosexually reared females showed statistically more mounting and less presenting than heterosexual females. (Goldfoot et al., 1984: p. 395)

Goldfoot notes that males showed greater effects of the isosexual rearing than did females. This study clearly supports the role of learning in nonhuman primate homosexual behavior.

The evidence on human homosexuality also shows its common occurrence. Kinsey and other researchers report that about a third of Western males have engaged in homosexual acts to orgasm.[7] Most of these acts occur in the teenage years and involve mutual masturbation. The homosexual rates for females would be only about half or less of the male rates. We know much less about female homosexuals than male homosexuals both in America and cross-culturally.[8] However, some recent sources of information on lesbian couples in America are available.

One key point here is that when we look at 20-year-olds, the percentage who prefer homosexuality is but a fraction of those who have experienced it. I would estimate homosexual preference in America between 5% and 10% of males and probably half that percentage for females.[9] In this respect we are like the other primates, for they too have high proportions with homosexual behavior but rarely does this lead to homosexual preference.

The evidence of homosexuality as an almost universal occurrence in human and other species is so strong that no one can speak of homosexuality as an unusual or atypical act. Nevertheless, the common occurrence of an act does not establish its biological or psychological normality. However, if such common acts were destructive to group life, we should see evidence of that. I know of no such evidence for nonhuman primates. In further sections of this chapter I will show that homosexuality is an accepted element in a number of human societies and is there viewed as a behavior supportive of that society. First we need to examine some other areas related to the broad question of the normality of homosexuality.

If homosexuality is normal, why is heterosexuality universally preferred? In all species studied, very few individuals prefer homosexuality to heterosexuality, no matter how they were reared. Some psychiatrists and biologists have asserted that there is a "normal" biological basis for this preferential heterosexuality, and they generalize this assumed "natural heterosexual bias" to the human case as well.

I believe that is an unwarranted generalization. Nonhuman species are much more biologically controlled than we are. I have pointed out the impressive role of erotic imagery in human sexual behavior and showed how broad such preferences can be. One advantage of our larger frontal lobes is to afford us much greater imagination with which to plan our sexual lifestyles. Accordingly, it would seem that as you approach humankind, you find fewer biological controls on all parts of our social life.

As a sociologist I would start with the premise that in terms of orientation toward a sexual partner, humans are neutral at birth. That is, we have no genetic tendency to prefer someone of the same or the opposite gender. In fact, what the same or opposite gender looks like varies to some degree by culture. Cultures differ in their emphasis on thin or heavy body builds for both males and females; some cultures stress one type of hair, skin color, protruding buttocks (steatopygia), or particular genital size and texture. Therefore, humans could not have very precise genetically based preferences that would direct choice among such varieties of societal preferences.

Let us not forget the old "instinct" debates in the early decades of this century. It was Luther Lee Bernard, a sociologist, who in 1924 published his book on instinct and showed that over 14,000 human traits had been called instinctive.[10] He insisted that any scientific use of the term *instinct* or any assertion about genetic influence must be tied to evidence concerning specific genetic mechanisms that could produce a particular outcome. If eye color is genetic, we can locate the specific mechanisms. Can we do this for sense of humor, for sexual interest, for heterosexuality? Bernard's advice is indeed an excellent guidepost to follow in the area of sexuality, where all kinds of views abound concerning what we biologically inherit.

For nonhuman primates the situation may be somewhat different. It may well be that sexual odors of the female attract the male, and the sexual swelling of the female genitalia at estrus may also function in such a fashion. The female estrus cycle leads to a time each month when she will be most sexually aroused. The human situation is quite different. We have little evidence of olfactory arousal or of any specific time period during which the female is more sexually aroused.[11] Our sexual practices, erotic preferences, and courtship forms are much more varied than those in any other primate species. So, I would conclude that although there may be biological pressures which lead to heterosexual preferences in other primates, it does not follow that they are also operative in the human situation.

The argument over biological causation of homosexuality is an old one. Writing in 1896, Havelock Ellis referred to his acceptance of the biological perspective as a *new* approach.[12]

> Some authorities who started with the old view that sexual inversion is exclusively or chiefly an acquired condition . . . later adopted the more modern view. (Ellis, 1896/1954: p. 165)

The twentieth century once more reversed this judgment. Most researchers stress the importance of learning in the development of homosexuality. The evidence today establishes no clear basis to reject a largely learned view for homosexuality. In a review of the hormonal basis of homosexuality Garfield Tourney concluded:[13]

> The hormonal theory of sexual regulation, particularly in terms of orientation toward the sexual object, lacks evidence. . . . The hormones largely have their effect on end organ sensitivity while the libidinal urge or sexual drive may be largely psychological. (Tourney, 1980: pp. 41-42)

Further, in an examination of chromosomal differences in homosexuals, John Money concludes:[14]

> According to currently available evidence, the sex chromosomes do not directly determine or program psychosexual status as heterosexual, bisexual, or homosexual. . . . The hormones of puberty do not change the basic psychosexuality of a person. They simply activate and intensify it. (Money, 1980: p. 69)

The area of greatest speculation concerns possible prenatal effects on the human fetus that structure the brain in a fashion different than most fetuses of that genetic sex. We know very little about this in humans, however, and we have only speculations at present. I do not rule out such possibilities, but I feel that experiential causes, which we have seen do influence nonhuman primates, are even more important in the human case. We need not choose between a biological and a sociological explanation. Both viewpoints can produce explanatory theories.

I find biology, at least at this stage of its knowledge, to be largely mute on the question of why heterosexuality is preferred in human societies.[15] The assumption of a heterosexual bias that operates in our human genetic makeup is gratuitous and only an article of faith. Of course, heterosexual choice is necessary for reproduction, but a population of bisexuals would reproduce very nicely. It is true that those who were fully heterosexual might produce more offspring, but if such heterosexuals were not biologically different from bisexuals or homosexuals, they would not pass on this heterosexual orientation to their offspring. We would be well advised to look outside our genetic inheritance and search for possible societal explanations of why heterosexuality is preferred. I will develop my own societal-level explanation further on in this chapter, but first let us look at another explanation of homosexuality that asserts that the normal progression for humans is toward heterosexuality.

The Freudian approach to homosexuality still is influential, particularly in the psychiatric community. I have previously indicated my rejection of the orthodox version of this approach and asserted that it was more a reflection of turn-of-the-century Western society than of any scientifically supportable perspective. The fourth tenet of the nonequalitarian sexual ideology basically asserts the same position in its required focus on heterosexual coitus (see Chapter 5). The wide-spread influence of Freud makes it necessary to examine his position.

Freud himself did not call homosexuality an "illness." In his now-famous letter to an American mother he said:[16]

> Homosexuality is assuredly no advantage, but it is nothing to be ashamed of, no vice, no degradation, it cannot be classified as an illness. (Freud, 1921: p. 786)

However, Freud did refer to homosexuality as "perverse," and his followers seemed to view it as some sort of "abnormality." Part of the reason for this was Freud's assertion of the innate bisexuality of all humans. He viewed all of us as having the biological basis for going through a stage of homosexuality. This view rested in part upon embryological studies that show the remnants of the opposite genetic sex present in each infant. Freud reasoned that there must also be psychological remnants of each sex, and thus we are all bisexual. Clearly, such a perspective ignores the role of society in orienting us toward a sexual partner and it stresses the biological input. Freud felt that since humans are biologically bisexuals, they all have to work through the homosexual interest they have in order to become heterosexual. I should note that present-day biologists would reject any notion of an innate bisexuality in human genetic inheritance. In fact, as Judd Marmor has pointed out, so would many psychiatrists.[17]

According to Freud's psychosexual developmental theories, males were to work out their homosexual tendency during the oedipal stage by identifying with their father and his values. Males with a hostile or absent father and a dominating and seductive mother were unable to work through this stage and they therefore became homosexuals, unable to "advance" to the ultimate heterosexual level. Freud further believed that even those who worked through this stage had some latent homosexuality in them that could come out later in life. Most of his theory deals with male homosexuality, although he does offer an analogous explanation for female homosexuality.

I believe that the orthodox Freudian viewpoint is an expression of the widespread public belief that homosexuals were produced by "abnormal" family relationships. Most of the attempts to find such "pathological" family causes of homosexuality concluded that such descriptions apply only to a minority of homosexuals.[18] The well-known empirical work done by Bell, Weinberg, and Hammersmith reports that factors like detached hostile father, mother-dominated father, prudish father, unpleasant mother, negative relationship between parents, and other family-related factors are only weakly related to homosexuality. They stress that all such factors taken together account for only a minority of homosexual behavior.[19]

The most important direct influence on homosexual orientation in the Bell, Weinberg, and Hammersmith study was the presence of childhood gender noncon- formity. Childhood gender nonconformity was the best single predictor of adult homosexual preference. Gender nonconformity refers to being unlike the societal expectations for your gender. Bell and his colleagues measured this key variable by asking about childhood liking for typical male and female play activities and for self-judgments regarding childhood feelings of being masculine or feminine. They summed up this major finding by saying:[20]

> One of the major conclusions of this study is that boys and girls who do not conform to sterotypical notions of what it means to be a male or a female are more likely to become homosexual. (Bell, Weinberg, and Hammersmith, 1981: p. 221)

Bell, Weinberg, and Hammersmith conclude their report by saying that since family factors explained only a minority of the causes of gender-role noncon- formity, then the nonconformity might well be due to biological factors. Here, I would again respond by pointing out that such an assertion is without clear mean- ing until one locates specific biological mechanisms that can be shown to produce homosexual responses. Otherwise, it simply states the obvious—of course, homo- sexuality may be due to *unknown* biological causes, or to unknown psychological causes, or, to be sure, to unknown sociological causes. As long as the specific identity of the unknown possible cause remains unclear, we have added very little to our understanding of homosexuality.

Officially, the psychiatrists in 1973 removed homosexuality from their list of disorders, but they later added *egodystonic homosexuality*, a category that refers to homosexuals who are unhappy with their homosexual object choice.[21] There is no analogous category for egodystonic heterosexuality as a disorder; thus it is clear that psychiatrists are still eyeing homosexuality with suspicion.

It is interesting to note that although orthodox Freudians would contend that there is a biological basis for the tendency in all of us to go through a homosexual stage, they would also contend that we can learn to repress and not act upon these homosexual pressures. Thus, holding a biological causation position does not stop such psychiatrists from feeling that change is possible. This is important to state so that those who believe that the acceptance of biological causation will remove the desire to change homosexuals will see that this does not necessarily follow.[22]

Lest I leave the impression that all psychiatrists and psychologists view homo- sexuality as an abnormal condition, let me quote from Judd Marmor a well-known psychiatrist who has written extensively on homosexuality:[23]

In the final analysis, psychiatric categorization of the development of homo-sexual preference as a form of "disordered" sexual development is simply a reflection of our society's disapproval of such behavior, and psychiatrists, whether they realize it or not, are acting as agents of social control in putting the label of psychopathology upon it. . . . The labeling of homosexual behavior as a psychopathological disorder, or "perversion," however honestly believed, is an example of defining normality in terms of adjustment to social conventions. (Marmor, 1980: p. 396.)

Marmor's view here is quite congruent, as far as it goes, with my approach to nor-mality, which I explicated in the last chapter. It expresses my sociological judgment concerning the normality of homosexuality. The widespread notion that a hetero-sexual bias exists in our human makeup is simply a way of extolling the virtue of the dominant sexual partner orientation. As I have noted before, the heterosexual bias position is in accord with the fourth tenet of the nonequalitarian sexual ideology. As such, it is quite popular in the Western world; but from a scientific point of view, convincing evidence has not been presented.

A CROSS-CULTURAL OVERVIEW

Let us proceed toward the explanation of same- and cross-gender partner orienta-tions by examining how homosexuality operates in a variety of human societies. In many cultures although heterosexuality is favored, homosexuality is also encour-aged. Apropos of this are the Siwans in Africa, where every married male has a teen-age boy for anal intercourse but is also expected to be interested in sexual relation-ships with his wife. In our own heritage the Greeks, at least in the male aristocracy, combined homosexual and heterosexual behavior.

In light of the commonness of homosexual behavior, it would indeed be diffi-cult to believe that any rare sort of biological or psychological factor is necessary for its occurrence. This commonness leads one to ask further, are there entire societies that not only have homosexual behavior but prefer homosexuality over heterosexuality? Relevant to this query, I will describe one most interesting society.

Gilbert Herdt studied the Sambia in the highlands of New Guinea from 1974 to 1976.[24] Like many highland New Guinea societies, this one displayed a high degree of male dominance, hostility toward women, and rigid segregation of gender roles. The Sambia are a patrilineal society wherein men hunt and women garden. Traditionally, the Sambia have had a great deal of warfare with neighboring tribes. They often take wives from hostile villages and in return marry their female chil-dren to males in those villages (called "delayed marital exchange"). Girls marry when they are 12 to 15 years of age and boys are about 5 or 10 years older than the girls they marry.

They are a prudish society and forbid all heterosexual premarital coitus. Female genitalia even in infants is most often covered. Shame is used to control sexual behavior and attitudes. Virtually all marital coitus conforms to the male-on-top position. Fellatio is desired but cunnilingus is disparaged, as is heterosexual anal intercourse. All loss of semen is viewed as potentially dangerous and as weakening male strength. Therefore, marital coitus must be done in moderation.

The Sambia ritualize homosexuality in ways not common in most New Guinea groups. Other reports had spoken of such practices, but it was Herdt who studied and described these rituals in the greatest detail. Homosexuality in the Sambia was distinctive because of the length of time it involved in a male's life. Starting at about ages 7 to 10 boys would be introduced to a homosexual ritual that would be part of their life for the next 10 to 15 years. The Sambia believe that male children are vulnerable and that full masculinity is difficult to achieve. In order for male children to be able to produce sperm and impregnate their wives, these boys must ingest semen orally from mature males.

Such a belief, causally relating sexual maturity to childhood sexuality, is not uncommon. I mentioned this general type of belief in the Lepcha and Tiwi societies, where it was believed that female childhood sexuality promoted female pubertal development. People in these societies notice that children have sexual encounters and afterward puberty does occur, and this sequencing verifies to them their causal perspective. Such reasoning is, of course, an example of what the philosophers would call the "after this, therefore, because of this" fallacy.

In Sambia this homosexual ritual is the mechanism by which semen is transferred from older males to prepubertal boys. The ceremony is described by Herdt as a "penis and flute" ceremony. Bamboo flutes are played and they are also used to illustrate the mechanics of fellatio. The belief is passed on that fellatio causes the boy's penis to grow to the size of the older male whom he is fellating. In addition, if he partakes of sperm every day for several years, he will be strengthened and be able to eventually produce his own sperm. Note that this homosexual ritual is viewed as preparing the male for being able to impregnate his wife in heterosexual coitus. In addition, it is the way in which other manly traits of strength and courage are obtained. So Herdt is quite correct when he states that

> transitional homoeroticism is the royal road to Sambia manliness. (Herdt: 1981: p. 3)

In accord with their modest view of sexuality, these homosexual acts are not carried out in a group setting but rather occur outdoors when the two males are alone.

When the boy reaches the age of 15 or so, he then becomes the insertor for younger males. The age difference is important, for it is not proper for two boys the same age to engage in fellatio. It is also believed not proper for friends to engage in fellatio, but it is acceptable for enemies to do so. This fact plus the age difference in insertor and insertee would lead one to believe that interpersonal power is involved in these ritual relationships just as it is in future marital heterosexual relationships. In marriage the male will be the insertor and the dominant one. The hostility present in male-female relationships is congruent with the accent on dominance in such sexual interactions.

After marriage and parenthood the male must cease all homosexual relationships and does not participate in the ritual that leads to such behavior. Herdt estimates that "no more than 5% of the entire male population" become preferentially homosexual in their behavior (p. 252). We have no measure of how many males may be utilizing homosexual erotic imagery in their heterosexual behavior, but the implication is that it would be few. One of the attitudes that helps stop homosexual fellatio for married men is the belief that the wife's vagina infects the man's penis.

> To introduce the penis (contagiously infected by the wife's vagina) into a boy's mouth would be a dangerous, polluting act. Most men do in fact become exclusively heterosexual after marriage. (Herdt: 1981: p. 252)

Herdt points out that this form of *transitional* homosexuality has been found in other Melanesian societies such as the New Hebrides, Kiwai Papuans, Keraki Papuans, Baruya, Etoro, Kaluli, and Marind-Anim.[25]

The length of time occupied by these practices seems long in the Sambia case, but in the Etoro, who also live in New Guinea, there seems to be an equally long involvement in such homosexual preparation for heterosexual manhood. Further, the fear of loss of strength through heterosexual coitus is perhaps even stronger in the Etoro.[26] The Etoro actually forbid heterosexual coitus for over 200 days a year as a control on bodily weakness due to semen loss. These people note that after orgasm a man is out of breath, and they compare that to an old man who seems frequently to be out of breath. Then they relate the two events by saying that it is heterosexual coitus that ages one and leads to old men being out of breath.

Fears about the weakening effects of homosexual interactions are not as common, for homosexual acts are not seen as taxing one's strength as much as heterosexual acts. Still, homosexuality is supposed to be a youth's preparation for adult heterosexuality, and thus adult males endanger themselves if they continue to participate in homosexuality.

As we have seen, these societies have an endorsement of homosexual behavior for at least a time in a man's life. Yet we must be aware that most men would define the homosexual behavior as a masculinizing event and one that prepares them for heterosexual behavior. In that sense the societal focus still seems to be on heterosexuality, but with a great deal of anxiety involved. Also, we must distinguish the acceptance of homosexual behavior from the acceptance of a preference for homosexual behavior. Herdt, in talking of the Sambia, sums up this view by saying that

> homosexual behaviors do not equal a homosexual identity. They themselves would not accept that label, for their experiences lead mostly to exclusive heterosexuality and fatherhood. (Herdt: 1981: p. 319)

Despite their heterosexual priorities, these Melanesian societies would surely think of homosexual behavior as perfectly normal and acceptable. In fact, they would unquestionably call it an essential part of their life as a man. Therefore, the Sambia represent a type of society in which homosexual behavior is viewed as normal. There would be no belief in Sambia, as there is throughout the West, supporting the abnormality of homosexuality. Unfortunately, little has been written about female homosexuality in these cultures, and so I cannot make any comparative analysis.[27]

Let us look at cultures we are somewhat more familiar with, such as those in Polynesia, South and North America, North Africa, or the Mediterranean. In these cases we will find less, but still some, male homosexuality that is in part at least thought of as acceptable.

I have already mentioned that in Polynesia each village may have a mahu, or a male who may be a transvestite in that he can choose to dress like a woman. This male is also believed to be a homosexual in his behavior and preference. It is considered acceptable for males to engage in homosexual behavior with the mahu, providing this is not their preferred mode of behavior. Levy describes this practice as still present in modern Tahiti.[28]

Many North American Indian societies allow cross-dressing, or transvestitism. This is often called by the French name of berdache. We cannot be sure of the degree of association of such transvestite customs with homosexual behavior.[29] In some societies there is also the possibility of a change in gender, similar to what we spoke of in Chapter 4. In the Mohave Indian society there was the possibility of genetic males and females reversing their assigned gender and becoming an alyha (female) or a hwame (male). They could then engage in sexual relations with someone of the same genetic sex but who was in the cultural role of a member of the opposite gender. Thus, although such a couple would belong to the same genetic sex, they would have a heterosexual relationship according to the gender they had adopted.[30] This change in gender was often marked by an initiation ceremony. These people could marry. There were some restrictions, for a hwame could not be a leader in war or in the tribe. Whatever sexual behavior occurs after this change in gender is accepted as normal by the Mohave. By my definition of homosexuality, the sexual behavior following such changes in gender would be heterosexual. In our society the same would be true in the case of a marriage of a genetic male transsexual and someone of the male gender. The important distinction of genetic sex and gender is highlighted in these examples. It is gender and not genetic sex that determines homosexual and heterosexual behavior.

In a review of cross-cultural homosexual practices, J. M. Carrier makes the important distinction between the insertor and insertee male homosexual roles.[31] He points out that in many South American, North African, and Mediterranean societies the male who is the insertor in oral or anal sexuality is not stigmatized, but the male who is the insertee is viewed as effeminate.[32] There is thus the judgment that the insertee role is a female role and unacceptable for adult males. In many cases if the insertee is a boy, then even the insertee act is more acceptable, for a boy would not be judged by adult male standards.

Consider how this set of attitudes compares to those we have just examined in Sambia and elsewhere in Melanesia. There, too, it was an older teenage or adult male who had oral intercourse with a prepubertal boy. This was acceptable for both. Yet if an adult male were to play the insertee role, his behavior would be unacceptable. An adult male must play the dominant role. In ancient Greece adolescent boys were sexual partners who played the insertee role while the adult male played the insertor role.

One generalization here appears to be that it is acceptable to play the insertor role when the partners are "not men".[33] Partners who are young boys or effeminate men are alike in being conceived as "not men," and that makes homosexual behavior acceptable, especially for the insertor. In most of these societies as noted, if an adult male played the insertee role, he would be condemned and would be labeled effeminate. Once an adult male insertee is labeled effeminate, he becomes an acceptable "not man" partner for insertors. This is so even though the insertee is often viewed as behaving improperly.

The masculine gender role most often restricts what sexual behaviors are acceptable in accord with a cultural definition of masculinity. (Recall our discussion of tenet 4 in the last chapter.) There seems to be social pressure for keeping the male emphasis on heterosexually and at least in part integrating sexuality with marriage and parenthood. Carrier sums up this viewpoint thus:

> Exclusive homosexuality, however, because of the cultural dictums concerning marriage and the family, appears to be generally excluded as a sexual option even in those societies where homosexual behavior is generally approved. For example, the two societies where all male individuals are free to participate in homosexual activity if they choose, Siwan and East Bay, do not sanction exclusive homosexuality. (Carrier, 1980: p. 118)

In sum, it seems that many societies accept homosexual behavior under specific conditions. Also, there is widespread acceptance of homosexual preference for certain periods of one's life, in specific types of relationships. But few, if any, societies seem to promote homosexual preference as the main form of sexuality for most individuals for most of their lives.

The common occurrence and acceptability of homosexuality without any obvious consequences that produce psychological or societal distress supports the view that homosexual behavior is normal for our species and for human societies. Much of the data applies only to males, but what we have said generally fits what little we know of female homosexuality as well. The one difference seems to be that female homosexuality is less subject to such strong hostility in most societies. The dominance of the male societal role may lead to the exertion of more societal pressure on males to avoid even the appearance of a submissive femalelike role. We have seen that in many cultures around the world this pressure does not exclude all homosexual behaviors. Some forms of male homosexuality are viewed as proper for males, but some seem to symbolize the lower position of women and are culturally proscribed.

NEW EXPLANATIONS:
TWO PATHWAYS TO HOMOSEXUALITY

We have dealt with social forces that restrain the popularity of homosexuality. Another question concerns what social forces encourage homosexuality. As part of my examination of homosexuality cross-culturally, I analyzed the Standard Sample to ascertain which societal characteristics were associated with the prevalence of homosexuality. My warnings in earlier chapters concerning the limitations of these data are even more applicable to the codes developed for homosexuality. I used the code by Broude that indicated the frequency of homosexuality in a society.[34] Her data applied only to male homosexuality. I carefully examined in a variety of ways the cross-cultural data from the Standard Sample. Only a few variables showed consistent and strong relationships to the frequency of homosexuality in a society. Note that I am speaking here only of males and only of homosexual *behavior*, not of homosexual *preference*. My results are presented in Diagram 6.1.

Diagram 6.1 indicates that those societies with more class stratification have more homosexual behavior and that those societies with high mother-infant involvement and low father-infant involvement also have more homosexual behavior. This diagram, like those in earlier chapters, is a causal diagram hypothetically presenting the variables in a time sequence going from the earliest causes on the left to the outcome explained on the right. As usual, only those variables and those paths that met all the statistical tests of significance are presented. (See Appendix A.)

A Freudian looking at this diagram might conclude that it supports the Freudian view that homosexuality is promoted by a close-binding mother and an absent or hostile father who together make the working out of the oedipal complex difficult. I have an alternative explanation that is much more sociological. Societies with high mother and low father involvement in infant care are often high male-dominant societies. The high mother and low father involvement with infants is a concomitant of the male-dominated system that in agriculture stipulates that fathers work the fields and get involved in the power structure instead of tending to their infants. In support of this interpretation, note that Diagram 6.1 does indicate a positive relationship of homosexuality with highly stratified societies. We

DIAGRAM 6.1   Causes of male homosexual behavior.

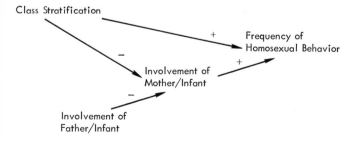

know that stratified societies are high on male dominance, and that is consistent with my thesis.[35]

My position is that in male-dominant societies, the greater the rigidity in the male gender role, the greater the likelihood of producing male homosexual behavior.[36] If we grant that societies stress heterosexuality, then it makes sense to look for some of the causes of homosexuality in the way heterosexuality is promoted. This is a useful perspective both for societies that are hostile to homosexuality, as we are, or societies that encourage some homosexuality, like the Sambia.

I view sexuality, whether heterosexual or homosexual, as easy to accept because of its pleasure and disclosure aspects. Therefore, homosexuality may occur as an alternative or support for heterosexuality, as in the case of the Sambia society. But homosexuality may also occur because of difficulty or dislike for the heterosexual orientation, as in the United States and in much of Western Europe. Please keep in mind that I am discussing mostly homosexual *behavior* here. Such behavior may lead to homosexual preference, but the causal connections there require separate attention.

In a male-dominant society with low father involvement in infant care, the odds are increased of finding a male child growing up with little help in modeling his role after his preoccupied father. In such a society the male role is sharply delineated from the female role in terms of what is and is not permitted. Thus, the male gender role and its heterosexual component is more difficult to learn than it would be in a society that is less male dominant and less rigid in gender-roles. In addition, the more narrow and rigid a gender role is, the more likely individuals will find that role uninteresting and unpleasant. Individuals represent a wide range of interests and abilities; therefore, the narrower the gender role, the greater the proportion of people who will not be compatible with such a role.

In accord with this reasoning, I would suggest that the causal importance of mother-infant and father-infant involvement is rooted in the combination of gender-role segregation and male dominance that they reflect. The segregation of roles is rigidifed when you add the element of male dominance. Male dominance will motivate males to guard and preserve their specialized gender behavior more carefully because it expresses their cultural dominance.

In an equalitarian and less segregated gender-role system, there would be much overlap as to what each parent would do; therefore the low participation of either parent would not matter as much in terms of learning gender roles. Where gender roles are segregated and unequal, then it does matter if the bearer of the dominant and very distinct father role is not often present. In such a case, gender-role acquisition by the male child would be more difficult and the outcome could well be to make that child feel like a gender nonconformist. The feeling of being out of step in terms of the requirements of one's gender role may lead to peer criticisms and to a young person feeling negative about the heterosexual aspects of the gender role. These events could make homosexual behavior more likely. The reader will recall that Bell and his colleagues concluded that such gender noncon-formity on the part of children was the strongest predictor of homosexuality.[37]

Another socialization difficulty may occur when parents are radically differ-ent than peers in terms of heterosexual permissiveness. This may also lead to chil-dren feeling they are not conforming to their gender role. An illustration of this in American society would be when the antiheterosexual puritanism of parents pre-vented a male or a female from joining his or her peers in heterosexual activities. This, in turn, may lead to such youngsters feeling out of place in their gender roles in general and thus more likely to believe they are unable to participate in hetero-sexual courtship activities. Psychiatrist Judd Marmor endorses such a causal nexus:[38]

> A common finding in the backgrounds both of lesbians and male homo-sexuals is a strong antiheterosexual puritanism, stemming from either or both parents, that tends to color heterosexual relationships with feelings of guilt or anxiety. (Marmor, 1980: p. 17)

If we apply what I have said so far about pathways to homosexuality in a society like ours, we would conclude that our loosening up of gender roles and our greater acceptance of heterosexuality by parents as well as peers should have decreased the amount of homosexuality in America. Probably the most common opinion today is that homosexuality has not decreased in America. If we accept that common opinion, how do we reconcile this situation with our theory?

First let me note that the causes discussed above are both negative routes. That is, they are ways of becoming homosexual because of some problem with heterosexuality. But there are also *positive pathways* to homosexuality that I have not discussed. In a less gender-rigid and more sexually permissive society a person could feel freer to experiment with homosexuality, and that could well increase homosexual behavior. Such experimentation will produce the impression of greater homosexuality, but it may not establish any increase in homosexual *preference*— just an increased acceptance of homosexual *behavior*. That is what I judge the pre-sent situation to be in America.

I am not making an invidious comparison between homosexuality and heterosexuality and saying that without negative labeling of heterosexuality, homo-sexuality will not be preferred. Rather, the support for heterosexuality is so immense in all societies (even the Sambia) that only a small percentage will be able to resist the cultural pressures favoring heterosexuality. In that sense an increase in homosexual behavior is no guarantee of an increase in homosexual preference. Where the gender role encompassing heterosexuality is simple to achieve, it will be easier to return from any homosexual experimentation and conform to the hetero-sexual pressures present in the society.

Negative pathways to homosexual behavior apply predominantly to societies like those in the West, which are generally critical of homosexuality. Only in a homosexually hostile or indifferent society do we have to invoke some weakness in the heterosexual training as the cause of homosexual behavior. In this sense, almost all of our theories of homosexuality are culture bound, for they assume the absence of support for homosexual behavior. Some of these theories may have relevance for our type of society, but we need to start to develop explanations that apply to societies that are supportive of homosexual behavior. That is what I shall now attempt to do.

For societies like the Sambia, I would suggest a different interpretation of the causal relationships in Diagram 6.1. I have noted that societies with low father-infant involvement and high stratification typically are male-dominant societies. Such societies are likely to have male kin groups organized around both descent and residence (see Diagram 4.1 for findings on this point). The presence of such male kin groups may encourage males to identify more with each other. As in Sambia, this can be associated with a view that females are of less importance and inferior to males. Such a belief system could then more easily promote acceptable sexual relationships among men. This seems to be a more likely outcome than in a society lacking in male kin groups and male dominance. There is some empirical support for this position, for I do find that in the Standard Sample those societies high on the presence of male kin groups have more homosexual behavior than those societies medium or low on male kin groups. (See the correlation matrix, Exhibit A.1, in Appendix-A.) This fits with the experimental research results of isosexual rearing of rhesus monkeys referred to earlier in this chapter (see note 6).

An interesting question that may arise here in the reader's mind concerns Western and Middle Eastern societies that also have high male dominance and emphasis upon male kin groups. Is the causal path suggested here a second more accepted route for the promotion of homosexual behavior in such societies? I think that the use of young boys or "feminine" adult males as insertees in homosexual behavior in many of these societies is congruent with this causal pathway notion. It may well be that sexual relations with "not men" are the way Western and Middle Eastern cultures have of informally accepting homosexuality for men who think of themselves as heterosexuals. In some of these societies this may be further encouraged by restrictive heterosexual customs. So, to this extent, we could say that this pathway to homosexuality, at least informally, also operates in the West. Note that this pathway stresses the fit of homosexuality with the heterosexual customs of that society. In this sense *the presence of male kin groups does not establish competing customs but integrates homosexual customs with the dominant heterosexual emphasis.*

Of course, my explanations for both the homosexually rejecting and accepting types of societies are speculative and require much further testing. Yet they do make sense of the relationships in Diagram 6.1. There is one unifying theme in both types of explanations. It is the perceived fit with heterosexuality that is the basis for the attitude toward homosexuality. Those societies that perceive a mutual support of homosexuality and heterosexuality have different ways leading to homosexuality than those societies that perceive a hostility among the two major sexual orientations.

Accordingly, I offer two different types of explanations for homosexual behavior. Since we now know that many societies accept homosexual behavior, it would indeed be strange if precisely the same causal factors would produce such behavior in two such different social settings. Regardless of the accuracy of my explanations, it is time we insisted on explanations that are specific to the social context of homosexuality. The biological and Freudian explanations we examined earlier derive from a society that asserts that homosexuality is an unnatural act. They are not adequate explanations for even that type of society, and they are totally inappropriate for the Sambia type of society.

I further suggest that the same two pathways to male homosexuality exist for female homosexuality. Lesbianism can occur due to rigid female gender roles and/or due to the presence of supportive female groups. Analogously, in supportive societies the lesbian activity is likely to be construed to be integrated with heterosexual behavior in the long run. The work of lesbianism by Deacon (see footnote 27) supports this perspective. Since there is so little reporting on lesbianism, I cannot elaborate more here, but I do feel that there are theoretical reasons to expect that comparable explanations will apply to male and female homosexuality.

KINSHIP AND GENDER: STRUCTURAL SUPPORT FOR HETEROSEXUALITY

Given the common occurrence of both homosexual and heterosexual behavior in human societies, one key question is, why aren't all human societies fully acceptant of homosexual and heterosexual behaviors? Humans are unique among the primates in the amount of exclusive homosexuality we have. Yet the point that almost everyone ignores is that humans are also unique in the amount of exclusive heterosexuality we have. Why are we so exclusive in our sexual choices? I think we are ready to answer that question now.

One set of reasons has been given: Heterosexuality is tied to the production of children, and children are considered desirable in virtually all societies. Even though many societies do not support a scientific view of the biological connection of coitus and pregnancy, they still see the connection of heterosexuality and children as existing in some fashion. Marriage is universally seen as the legitimation of parenthood, and parenthood in all cultures is expressed in the heterosexual kinship terms of mother and father. Thus, heterosexuality is almost certain to be encouraged. Children are also seen as the social security of one's old age and as the source of future supplies of warriors and workers. So, the heterosexual marital unions that produce children are valued for these reasons.

Gender roles are defined in terms of cross-gender (heterosexual) partner preferences. In good part this, also, is an outcome of marriage customs giving substance and meaning to the male and female gender roles. Gender roles are everywhere constructed with the marriage and family component writ large. No society has gender roles that omit conceptions concerning how that gender should behave and think in the area of marriage and the family. Thus, gender roles will most often either organize homosexual customs so as to make them supportive of marriage and family roles, as in the Sambia example, or restrict homosexuality in ways that they believe will prevent it from interfering with those roles.

We have seen that this dependency of gender role upon marriage customs does not mean that societies will condemn homosexual behavior; rather, it means that their acceptance of it will depend on its being integrated with the existing cross-gender sexual orientation.[39] Sexuality, as I have described it, has the power to bind people together through their mutual physical and psychic pleasures. Most societies have used this power of sexuality to maintain the types of relationships they want. The importance of sexuality and the importance of marriage thus combine to produce a cross-gender sexual preference in virtually all societies we know about.

In some cases the societal desire to use sexuality to promote desired relationships can encourage homosexual relationships. This was the case among soldiers in some early Greek societies, where homosexuality was encouraged as a way to strengthen the willingness to fight for each other in combat. Nevertheless there are two sides to a boundary: It includes those within, but it also excludes those outside. Thus, when a religious institution or a political group wants to establish sharp boundaries separating it from others, there is pressure to exclude and thereby more clearly establish a distinct identity.[40] Many religious and political groups historically excluded homosexuals and viewed them quite negatively. In this sense, the custom of social boundary marking would be another cause of hostility toward "outside" groups such as homosexuals.

I will put forth another, somewhat more speculative, reason for the preference in society for cross-gender sexual partners. In almost all cultures we know about, males are given the more assertive, dominant, and aggressive role in the society (see Chapter Four). Given this fact, sexually joining two males would often involve placing two assertively trained individuals together, and a clash of wills over sexuality would therefore be more likely. Note that one of the most common settings cross-culturally for male homosexuality is when one male is older and therefore dominant over the other. Disputes over power are less likely in such a setting. Evidence from the Western world indicates that male homosexuals are not usually sexually exclusive and that in time, the sexual encounters between long-term homosexual mates become infrequent.[41] Part of this is surely due to a search for variety, but it may also be due to a desire to avoid conflict and perhaps to find a sexual relationship with others that permits the kind of dominance or submissiveness that is preferred.

The same speculative reasoning concerning gender training in assertiveness exists for lesbian relationships. Placing two females together in a typical male-dominated society would be placing two individuals together who are low on sexual assertiveness, and this might lead to low levels of sexual initiation by either partner. In fact, studies of lesbian couples do indicate just such low rates of lesbian sexual interaction compared to male homosexuals or to heterosexual couples.[42]

My thinking here is that in a male dominant society it is easier to unite in sexuality individuals who differ in their dominance desires and that given most societal norms, this is more likely to be a male and a female. Some of the research on friendships indicate that in the Western world, at least, male-male friendships are not as high on self-revelation as are male-female friendships.[43] Male friends seem competitive and often relate only superficially. It is true that female-female friendships are high on self-revelation, but the problem of who initiates sexuality is not solved simply by high self-revelation.

In sum, I do believe that the major supports of heterosexuality are in marriage and gender constraints. Nonetheless, the dominance aspect of gender roles is worthy of our examination as a secondary cause. It should be understood, though, that even in male-dominated societies there are great differences in assertiveness and dominance within the male and within the female gender, and so, if desired, a difference in assertiveness can be achieved homosexually.[44] It still follows, however, that if society trains men and women generally to be different in assertiveness and in dominance, then a difference in assetiveness will be easier to achieve in matches involving both genders as compared with one-gender unions.

SUMMARY AND CONCLUSIONS

The evidence from human and nonhuman societies supports the normality of homosexuality as a form of sexual expression. I hope our cross-cultural examination has given the reader some appreciation for the particular ways in which ideology, kinship, and power structure the integration of homosexuality in a society. To refer to our typology of general ideologies (see Chapter 5), I would say the Western world has taken an emotive ideological stance toward homosexuality and views homosexuality as a path that should not be offered as a choice. There has been some softening of this opposition. We do have half the states with consenting-adult laws. However, in terms of sexual ideologies, the Western world still seems to persist in endorsing tenet 4's stress on a heterosexual focus. We seem aware of only one way to focus on heterosexuality. In a sense the Sambia society also focuses upon heterosexuality; but instead of using avoidance as their means, they use the method of integrating homosexuality as a pathway to heterosexuality.

Perhaps of greatest importance in the comparative sociological approach to homosexuality is the awareness of the ways our society restrains even the nature of our scientific explanations. The view of homosexuality as a distortion of proper heterosexuality is analogous to our belief that communism is a distortion of proper political development. The provincialism of many of our therapeutic approaches to homosexuality should be obvious by now. My two interpretations of Diagram 6.1 can serve as a catalyst toward the growth of distinct theories for explaining homosexuality in different societal contexts. Yet there is also a need for a unified theoretical explanation. I hope the reader has noticed that I have explained homosexuality in both types of societies by reference to our kinship and gender systems—the same systems which explain heterosexual partner choices. All of this is the beginning of a unified, abstract explanation of all our sexual partner choices.

The examination of homosexuality in this chapter used the three basic societal linkage areas of kinship, power, and ideology that were developed in earlier chapters. By knowing that these areas are linked to all sexual customs, I found it was easier to search for explanations of different homosexual customs. I deliberately chose this area because of its centrality to a sociological understanding of sexuality and also because it is a controversial area that certainly illustrates how our ideological beliefs can color our understanding. The next chapter will continue to challenge your ability for dispassionate analysis. In the process it will display a few more components of my sociological explanation. Having come this far, I think you will enjoy the challenges of the next chapter, on the topic of erotica.

SELECTED REFERENCES AND COMMENTS

1. The National Opinion Research Center's (NORC's) annual survey of a representative sample of 1500 adult Americans is the source of information on attitudes toward homosexuality. The reader may have noticed that I also use this source for attitudes toward other sexual acts, such as premarital and extramarital coitus. For a quick assessment of national attitudes it is as good as any available source. However, for in-depth probing of such attitudes other research is preferable because NORC is aimed at covering a large number of attitude areas and it cannot cover each area in depth.

2. In a recent article Frederick Whitam noted that in the societies he checked, the percentage who preferred male homosexuality stayed within the 5–10% range. He assumes that this regularity affirms the biological basis of homosexuality. I would take issue with such a judgment. In order to establish a biological base in a scientific sense, one must locate specific biological mechanisms, not merely find a regularity. The reason for this becomes clear when we realize that there is a well-established regularity in the percentage of people around the world who enter into marriage—over 90%. Is getting married a biologically determined act? In many countries a quite similar proportion of males are employed outside the home. Does that make such male employment biologically based? There may be some biological base for homosexuality, but it won't be established by anything short of finding the specific linkages to biological mechanisms. I am striving to establish the societal base of sexuality by establishing the specific linkages to societal mechanisms. One cannot ask for less in the case of any biological, psychological, or other explanatory claims. For Whitam's views see Whitam, Frederick L., "Culturally Invariable Properties of Male Homosexuality: Tentative Conclusions from Cross-cultural Research," *Archives of Sexual Behavior,* vol. 12, no. 3 (May 1983), pp. 207–226.

3. In the case of nonhuman species, I would substitute the words *genetic sex* for gender in my definition of homosexuality. This necessity further indicates the vast overlay of societal learning that is involved in our sexuality as compared to

our primate cousins. This is not to deny learning has a place among other primates—it surely does—but that place is much smaller in importance.

4. The quote by Denniston comes from his chapter in Marmor's book on homosexuality. This book is one of the finest of the recent books on homosexuality. It contains chapters by people in various disciplines. Marmor himself is a psychiatrist, but not one who conforms to Freudian notions. He argues that homosexuality is rooted in biological, sociopsychological, and cultural factors.

No one can really argue with such a global assertion—there surely must be "some" roots in all three of those areas. By the same token, such a global statement, popular as it is, tells us very little of the specific ways in which these three levels operate. Some of the individual chapters in Marmor's book partially spell that out. My attempt in this chapter is to develop in some detail the sociological factors involved.

Denniston, R.H., "Ambisexuality in Animals," Chapter 1 in Marmor, Judd (ed.), *Homosexual Behavior: A Modern Reappraisal.* New York: Basic Books, 1980. © 1980 by Basic Books, Inc., Publishers. Reprinted by permission of the publisher.

5. Frank Beach is an authority on cross-species sexual behavior. See Chapter 11 in

Beach, Frank A. (ed.), *Human Sexuality in Four Perspectives.* Baltimore: Johns Hopkins University Press, 1977.

6. Goldfoot, David A., K. Wallen, D.A. Neff, M.C. Mcbriar, and R.W. Goy, "Social Influence upon the Display of Sexually Dimorphic Behavior in Rhesus Monkeys: Isosexual Rearing," *Archives of Sexual Behavior.* vol. 13, no. 5 (October 1984), pp. 395–412.

7. Sources for the prevalence of homosexual behavior in males and females in America can be found in Kinsey's work. Kinsey reports that 37% of the males and 13% of the females in his study reported having at least one homosexual orgasm. We lack more recent behavioral estimates, although we have good attitudinal measures in the research surveys by NORC. In England Michael Schofield's work is worth examining.

Kinsey, Alfred C., Wardell Pomeroy, and Clyde Martin, *Sexual Behavior in the Human Male.* Philadelphia: Saunders, 1948.

Kinsey, Alfred C., Wardell Pomeroy, Clyde Martin, and Paul Gebhard, *Sexual Behavior in the Human Female.* Philadelphia: Saunders, 1953.

Schofield, Michael, *Sociological Aspects of Homosexuality: A Comparative Study of Three Types of Homosexuals.* Boston: Little, Brown, 1965.

8. Recent reviews of homosexuality cross-culturally do contain some valuable information and some good references. The list that follows should be a good start for the interested reader:

Carrier, J.M., "Homosexual Behavior in Cross-cultural Perspective," Chapter 5 in Judd Marmor (ed.), *Homosexual Behavior: A Modern Reappraisal.* New York: Basic Books, 1980.

Davenport, William H., "Sex in Cross Cultural Perspective," Chapter 5 in Beach, Frank A. (ed.), *Human Sexuality in Four Perspectives.* Baltimore: Johns Hopkins University Press, 1977.

Whitehead, Harriet, "The Bow and the Burden Strap: A New Look at Institutionalized Homosexuality in Native North America," Chapter 2 in Sherry B. Ortner and Harriet Whitehead (eds.), *Sexual Meanings: The Cultural Construction of Gender and Sexuality.* Cambridge: Cambridge University Press, 1981.

There are also books dealing with lesbian communities, lesbian couples, and theories about lesbians. I will mention only a few that are relevant to a sociological understanding. In all but the first book only sections deal with lesbianism.

Wolf, Deborah Goleman, *The Lesbian Community,* Berkeley: University of California Press, 1980.

West, D.J., *Homosexuality Re-examined.* Minneapolis: University of Minnesota Press, 1977. (See especially Chapter 7.)

Paul, William, J.D. Weinrich, J.C. Gonsiorek, and M.E. Hotvedt, *Homosexuality: Social, Psychological and Biological Issues.* Beverly Hills, Calif.: Sage Publications, 1982. (See especially chapters 21, 22, and 23.)

Saghir, Marcel T., and E. Robbins, *Male and Female Homosexuality.* Baltimore: Williams & Wilkins, 1973.

Blumstein, Philip, and Pepper Schwartz, *American Couples.* New York: Morrow, 1983.

9. Of course, such estimates are subject to error, but my estimates are the same as those made independently by Judd Marmor. See page 7 in

Marmor, Judd (ed.), *Homosexual Behavior: A Modern Reappraisal.* New York: Basic Books, 1980.

10. For additional arguments on the need to identify specific biological mechanisms in any assertion of causation, see my comments in note 2. The classic work by Bernard was

Bernard, Luther Lee, *Instinct.* New York: Holt, Reinhart & Winston, 1924.

11. Many studies have been undertaken to detect a correlation of time during the menstrual cycle with sexual desire. The results are highly contradictory, and so I conclude that there is no clear pattern.

12. Although I have great respect for the contribution Ellis made toward promoting the use of anthropological data and his avoidance of moral judgments about sexual behavior, I cannot resist informing the reader of some of Ellis's less scientific views about homosexuality. In his work on homosexuality he made a point of telling the reader that he believed that male homosexuals often could not whistle whereas female homosexuals were able to whistle and both were alike in their preference for the color green! The lack of an explanatory framework is obvious in his willingness to accept these features as informative. For an introduction to his work see the following:

Ellis, Havelock, *Psychology of Sex: A Manual for Students.* New York: New American Library, 1954.

Grosskurth, Phyllis, *Havelock Ellis: A Biography.* New York: Knopf, 1980.

13. Tourney, Garfield, "Hormones and Homosexuality,"Chapter 2 in Judd Marmor (ed.), *Homosexual Behavior: A Modern Reappraisal.* New York: Basic Books, 1980. © 1980 by Basic Books, Inc., Publishers. Reprinted by permission of the publisher.

14. Money, John, "Genetic and Chromosomal Aspects of Homosexual Etiology," Chapter 3 in Judd Marmor (ed.), *Homosexual Behavior: A Modern Reappraisal.* New York: Basic Books, 1980. © 1980 by Basic Books, Inc., Publishers. Reprinted by permission of the publisher.

15. For an overview of the place of hormones in sexual behavior, see

Goy, R.W., and D.A. Goldfoot, "Hormonal Influences on Sexually Dimorphic Behavior," Chapter 9 in R.O. Greep and E.B. Astwood (eds.), *Handbook of Physiology: Endocrinology* (vol. 2, sec. 7, part 1). Baltimore: Williams & Wilkins, 1973.

16. Freud, Sigmund, "Letter to an American Mother," *American Journal of Psychiatry,* vol. 102 (1921), p. 786.

17. For a fuller expression of Marmor's qualification of Freud, see the Overview and Epilogue sections in his book

Marmor, Judd (ed.), *Homosexual Behavior: A Modern Reappraisal.* New York: Basic Books, 1980.

18. One such recent examination takes an intriguing position contending that the pattern of distant or hostile father is a *result* of finding homosexuality in a child in a homophobic society. The distancing of the father is, in this view, not a cause of homosexuality and would not occur in a society that was less condemnatory of homosexuality.

Whitman, Frederick L., and Michael Zent, "A Cross-cultural Assessment of Early Cross-gender Behavior and Familial Factors in Male Homosexuality," *Archives of Sexual Behavior*, vol. 13, no. 5 (October 1984), pp. 427–440.

19. Bell, Alan P., Martin S. Weinberg, and Sue Kiefer Hammersmith, *Sexual Preference: Its Development in Men and Women*. Bloomington: Indiana University Press, 1981. (See in particular Chapter 17.)

20. For information on this see Chapters 7 and 14 in the Bell, Weinberg, and Hammersmith book listed in note 19.

21. American Psychiatric Association. *Diagnostic and Statistical Manual of Mental Disorders-3*. Washington, D.C.: APA, 1977.

22. On a personality level, it may be that the popularity among homosexuals of a biological determination of homosexuality may rest upon the ability of this view to relieve the guilt that our society imposes on homosexuals. Our society's critical attitude toward homosexuality can easily make those who engage in homosexual acts feel that they are doing something wrong. A shared belief that such actions are biologically determined could reduce that self-blame.

23. Marmor, Judd (ed.), *Homosexual Behavior: A Modern Reappraisal*. New York: Basic Books, 1980. © 1980 by Basic Books, Inc., Publishers. Reprinted by permission of the publisher.

24. Herdt, Gilbert, *Guardians of the Flutes: Idioms of Masculinity*. New York: McGraw-Hill, 1981.

25. For a broader view of homosexuality in Melanesia see:

Herdt, Gilbert (ed.), *Ritualized Homosexuality in Melanesia*. Berkeley: University of California Press, 1984. In some of these societies the males who are homosexually involved later on exchange sisters as their wives.

26. Kelly, Raymond C., "Witchcraft and Sexual Relations: An Exploration in the Social and Semantic Implications of the Structure of Belief," pp. 36–53 in Paula Brown and Georgeda Buchbinder (eds.), *Man and Woman in the New Guinea Highlands*. Washington, D.C.: American Anthropological Association, 1976.

27. There is one account of institutionalized lesbianism which I have come across that may be of interest.

Deacon, A.B., *Malekula: A Vanishing People in New Hebrides*. London: George Routledge, 1934.

28. Levy, Robert I., *Tahitians: Mind and Experience in the Society Islands*. Chicago: University of Chicago Press, 1973.

29. The reader should distinguish between the concepts *homosexual, transvestite,* and *transsexual.* We have already defined *homosexual.* A transvestite is a person who cross-dresses, that is, dresses as does the opposite gender and gains erotic pleasure from that. It is problematic as to whether transvestites also are homosexual in behavior. In American society, most reports indicate that is not commonly the case. However, in other cultures the situation may well be different. In distinction from a transvestite, a transsexual is a person who feels encased in the wrong body and wants an operation to effect the change to the opposite genetic sex's body and to the gender role that goes with that genetic body. See the Glossary for further information on these and related concepts.

30. Devereux, G., "Institutionalized Homosexuality of the Mohave Indians," *Human Biology*, vol. 9 (1937), pp. 498–527.

For a general analysis of such customs see

Whitehead, Harriet, "The Bow and the Burden Strap: A New Look at Institutionalized Homosexuality in Native North America," Chapter 2 in Sherry B. Ortner and Harriet Whitehead (eds.), *Sexual Meanings: The Cultural Construction of Gender and Sexuality.* Cambridge: University of Cambridge Press, 1981.

31. Carrier, J.M., "Homosexual Behavior in Cross-cultural Perspective," Chapter 5 in Judd Marmor (ed.), *Homosexual Behavior: A Modern Appraisal.* New York: Basic Books, 1980. © 1980 by Basic Books, Inc., Publishers. Reprinted by permission of the publisher.

32. Carrier mentions a novel on sexual behavior in Morocco where there is a dialogue concerning a male who seeks anal intercourse indiscriminately with women, old men, and young boys. His companion asks him why he does this, and he answers that it is okay, for he is doing it *to them* and finally he says: "A zook is a zook. What's the difference? I niki it." (*niki* means fuck; *zook* means ass). This statement reveals much about the attitudes that prevail toward homosexuality from the insertor's viewpoint. See

Tavel, R., *Street of Stairs.* New York: Olympia Press, 1968. (See p. 53.)

33. The concept "not men" comes from

Karlen, Arno, "Homosexuality in History," Chapter 4 in Judd Marmor (ed.), *Homosexual Behavior: A Modern Reappraisal.* New York: Basic Books, 1980.

34. Sanday also had a measure of homosexuality for societies in the Standard Sample. My examination of Sanday's measure of homosexuality raised serious doubts in my mind of its utility. I then spoke to Sanday, and she shared my misgivings and advised me not to use it. Thus, I was left with only Broude's measure.

35. One other point that needs comment: The relationship in Diagram 6.1 between class stratification and mother-infant involvement was negative, that is, the more stratification, the less mother-infant involvement. This is an unexpected result, but if we remember the negative relationship in Diagram 4.1 between agriculture and mother-infant involvement, it may become clearer. Agriculture encourages stratification by providing enough food for more people to reside permanently in one place. At the same time, this means more births for mothers and necessitates help in childcare from older children, grandmothers, and others. In that way both agriculture and stratification promote less involvement of the mother with her infants than was the case in hunting and gathering societies. The reader should keep in mind, though, that mothers in stratified, agricultural societies still do much more with infants than do fathers. The diagram shows that father involvement relates negatively to mother involvement so low father involvement counteracts the influence of class stratification on mother involvement.

36. There is an interesting cross-cultural study of 21 societies that reports a positive relationship between gender-role rigidity and violence. The requirement for males to be violent may also make conformity to the male role difficult. See

McConahay, Shirley A., "Sexual Permissiveness, Sex-Role Rigidity, and Violence across Cultures," *Journal of Social Issues,* vol. 33, no. 2 (1977), pp. 134–143.

37. For the detailed tables and diagrams of their study see

Bell, Alan P., Martin S. Weinberg, and Sue Kiefer Hammersmith, *Sexual Preference: Statistical Appendix.* Bloomington: Indiana University Press, 1981.

38. Marmor, Judd (ed.), *Homosexual Behavior: A Modern Reappraisal.* New York: Basic Books, 1980. © by Basic Books, Inc., Publishers. Reprinted by permission of the publisher.

39. For a psychological approach to this area see

Langevin, Ron, *Erotic Preference, Gender Identity, and Aggression in Men: New Research Studies.* Hillsdale, N.J.: Erlbaum, 1985.

40. Davies, Christie, "Sexual Taboos and Social Boundaries," *American Journal of Sociology*, vol. 87, no. 5 (March 1982), pp. 1032–1063.

41. McWhirter, David P., and Andrew M. Mattison, *The Male Couple: How Relationships Develop.* New York: Prentice-Hall, 1984.

42. Saghir, Marcel T., and E. Robins, *Male and Female Homosexuality.* Baltimore: Williams & Wilkins, 1973.

Blumstein, Philip, and Pepper Schwartz, *American Couples.* New York: Morrow, 1983.

43. Bell, Robert R., *Worlds of Friendship.* Beverly Hills, Calif.: Sage Publications, 1981.

Brain, Robert, *Friends and Lovers.* New York: Basic Books, 1976.

44. Recent research supports the finding that homosexual males score higher on femininity measures than do heterosexual males, but it should be clear that homosexuals still identify with their own genetic sex. The possible place of such scores in an explanation of cross or same gender preferences needs to be explored. Transsexual males score much higher than any male group on femininity, but they, of course, do not identify with their own genetic sex. See

Langevin, Ron, *Erotic Preference, Gender Identity, and Aggression in Men: New Research Studies.* Hillsdale, N.J.: Erlbaum, 1985.

CHAPTER SEVEN

EROTICA

Pathway to Sexuality or Subordination?

PORNOGRAPHY OR EROTICA:
WHAT YOU SEE IS WHAT YOU GET

The reader may think that now that we have dealt with homosexuality, we have handled the most controversial of areas. I do believe that, especially among intellectuals, the issue of erotica is more controversial. Intellectuals would very largely agree concerning the normality of homosexuality. They would be considerably more divided on the issue of erotica.

Even the choice of the term *erotica* as opposed to *pornography* is controversial, and so perhaps we should begin there. By now everyone must know that the word *pornography* comes from the Greek "pornograph" meaning stories about prostitutes. It has taken on a negative connotation over the centuries and today includes all materials involved with lustful ideas. The word *obscenity* is often used interchangeably with *pornography*, but it has a legal meaning. In American law the obscene is that part of pornography which has been judged to be illegal. To be so judged, the work must be offensive to community standards, appeal to prurient interests (lustful cravings), and lack serious scientific, educational, literary, political, or artistic value. The work must meet all three criteria to be declared obscene and therefore not protected by our First Amendment rights to free expression. This is one of the very few exceptions to the protection offered by the First Amendment to all expressions of ideas. Many court cases have tested whether a particular erotic movie or book is obscene by these criteria. Usually court decisions about obscenity are difficult to arrive at and are unclear.

In the 1970s some feminist groups began to formulate a distinction between pornography and erotica. They declared as pornographic those portrayals of women that they felt "subordinated" or "objectified" or "degraded" women in sexually explicit situations. They reserved the terms *erotica* for those sexually explicit portrayals they felt did not do these objectionable things to women. There is much controversy on this entire issue within the feminist movement. In 1979 Women Against Pornography (WAP) was formed, and this group has pushed for expanded legal restrictions on a wide variety of books and films they judged to be pornographic. In 1984 the Feminist Anti-Censorship Taskforce (FACT) was established in opposition to the position of WAP.

The distinction drawn by some feminists in the 1970s between pornography and erotica appeared to be simply a moral statement of their personal preference. Those who adopted such a distinction were in effect saying, "I like this type of sexual excitement, but I find this other type degrading." This is clearly not a scientific distinction. Technically speaking, the term *erotica*, from the Greek, refers to sexual love or sexual excitement. What is erotic to one person may be a matter of indifference or offense to another. It is our cultural training and our ideological beliefs relevant to sexuality that set up the sexual scripts that shape our erotic responses. The labeling of particular erotic scripts as "bad" or "pornographic" is a clear attempt to impose one's own sexual scripts upon others.

What is the most nonjudgmental term to use to describe the entire realm of sexually explicit materials in a society? To help make this selection, compare for a moment the term *fornication* with the term *premarital intercourse*, or the term *adultery* with the term *extramarital intercourse.* In both instances, the first term is a moralistic term with biblical origins while the second is an attempt to apply a descriptive, scientific term. I believe that *pornography* has become a negatively evaluated term much like *fornication* and *adultery.*

Therefore, I propose to call by the term *erotica* all materials that seem designed predominately for sexual arousal. The usage agrees with that of others such as William Fischer and Elizabeth Allgeier.[1] Accordingly, the term *erotica* as used here simply refers to presentations that are sexually exciting to the typical audience at which the work is aimed. This usage also stresses the social nature of sexual excitement, that what may arouse and please one group of people may not arouse and may even displease another group. In this book all such materials shall be called erotica. If one dislikes a particular erotic form, that form can be called "bad" or "degrading" erotica. To label particular erotica as pornographic adds little to simply saying it is morally unacceptable to that viewer. Further, by having one overall term like *erotica*, we avoid building private sexual preferences into our terminology.

Much of the present controversy in America over erotica is a result of the chagrin and anger felt when others use what are felt to be "degrading" sexual stimuli for their sexual arousal. Of course, those using that stimuli may well not think of it as degrading, but they still are expressing a different choice of erotica. Such diverging erotic standards are part of the nature of a complex human society. We could find analogous sharp differences if we compared political beliefs or religious beliefs. Our morality enters into our judgment of all social activity, and surely sexuality is not excluded from that human tendency. The reader is, of course, free to find all erotica offensive or to find none of it bothersome. Our task here is not to judge what is moral but to explain how and, most importantly, why others arrive at their judgments.

Other uses of ideological beliefs in conceptions of erotica are quite obvious. There are those who would control a great deal of erotica because they feel people are usually influenced by it in a "harmful" direction; yet others feel that people are not so influenced by it and can intelligently choose here as they do elsewhere. Clearly, those two positions reflect our basic emotive and cognitive ideologies. In accord with these positions are pronouncements regarding what is "abnormal" or "normal" erotica. Epithets such as "sick" or "deranged" are frequently heard as accusations against those whose sexual scripts differ from their own. It should be clear at the outset that all Americans are in agreement in wanting to discourage those forms of erotica that are certain to lead to "harm" to others. The heart of the erotica debate centers on whether one believes that particular forms of erotica produce harm to others.

In a broad sense erotica would include anything that was designed to arouse us sexually. Nevertheless, our concern in this chapter is with a special type of erotica, namely, commercial erotica. More specifically, most of what I shall discuss concerns erotic movies—those rated X or beyond. A minority of such films contain obvious physical violence—like a sadistic rape or a brutal beating of a woman. A 1984 book by Robert Rimmer listed about 10% of the 650 films he examined as containing "deviational sadistic, violent and victimized sex."[2] We shall have something to say about such films, but it is well to realize at the outset that they are not representative of X-rated films. As further evidence of this let me quote Dr. Thomas Radecki, chairperson of the National Coalition on Television Violence (NCTV):[3]

> NCTV has found the 1984 summer Hollywood movies to contain the highest amount of violence ever, 28.5 violent acts per hour, with PG movies containing some of the highest levels of violence. X-rated movies actually contain far fewer murders and even fewer rapes than PG or R-rated material. (Radecki, 1984: p. 43)

I will briefly describe a typical X-rated film. This is the type of film that is used in much of the research I shall discuss here. This film has a very thin plot, the acting is unimpressive, and the scenes focus upon oral, anal, and coital acts with extensive closeups of that action. The acts are mostly heterosexual, and when they are homosexual, unless the film is made specifically for male homosexuals, the focus is upon lesbian sexual acts. This avoidance of male homosexuality is due to the strong attempt to appeal to Western heterosexual males' lustful feelings in these films. Little or no physical violence against women occurs in the vast majority of these films. There may be some status differences in the male and female roles portrayed, but physical force rarely enters in obvious ways into the sexual action. I believe that this is the most common form of erotic film today. It is hardcore in that erections and vulvas are shown frequently and usually joined.[4] We will discuss at length erotic films with violence, but the foregoing describes what the typical erotic theatergoer is exposed to.

EROTICA AND VIOLENCE:
THE EXPERIMENTAL RESEARCH EVIDENCE

President Johnson set up the United States Commission on Obscenity and Pornography in the late 1960s. After two years of examining research evidence, this 19-person commission's majority report was that no harm was done by "pornography":[5]

> If a case is to be made against "pornography" in 1970, it will have to be made on grounds other than demonstrated effects of a damaging personal or social nature. Empirical research designed to clarify the question has found no reliable evidence to date that exposure to explicit sexual materials plays a significant role in the causation of delinquent or criminal sexual behavior among youth or adults. (Report of the Effects Panel of the commission, 1971, p. 139)

Similar reports had been submitted by advisory commissions in other countries. Although Congress and President Nixon refused to change any laws, it seemed that the scientific question was at least temporarily resolved.

This temporary scientific resolution did not last long. Shortly after the nine-volume report of this commission we began to see the exploration of the connection between violent erotica and aggression against women. These new researchers pointed out that the commission had not sufficiently checked the differential impact of violent as opposed to nonviolent erotica, nor did they adequately explore the potential violent outcomes of viewing erotica. There had been earlier studies of the impact on children of violence on television, and that helped inspire further exploration of a possible connection between viewing erotic films and violence against women in society.

The new researchers were largely trained in psychology and used the experimental methods taught in that discipline. They obtained volunteer college males and placed them in a situation wherein a female confederate of the experimenter would anger these subjects. This could be done in a number of ways. One common method was to tell the subject that if he did a task a certain way, he would avoid an electrical shock and then to have the female confederate give the shock even when the subject did the task properly. Then with the subject angered, and therefore emotionally worked up, the researchers would show an erotic film. After the film the subject would be given an opportunity to administer a shock to the female confederate who had previously angered the subject. The students who were exposed to the erotic film were then compared to another group who had the same experience with the confederate but had not seen the film. The goal was to see if viewing the erotic film increased the likelihood of administering a shock to the female confederate. The results of these early experiments were inconclusive. Such inconclusiveness is not uncommon even today. Researchers in this area disagree a great deal as to the findings that are established.[6]

Some experimenters thought that what was needed in order to discern the impact of the films was encouragement about giving shocks to the female confederate. They felt that perhaps the college male volunteers were on their good behavior for the experimenter. So, they verbally encouraged giving the shock, and in the experiment they offered the subjects a second chance to administer the shock. Still the differences between the control group (who did not see the erotic film) and the experimental group (who did see the erotic film) were not impressive.

Some of the early experiments in the 1970s indicated that softcore erotica, like *Playboy*, actually *reduced* the liklihood of an aggressive response.[7] So the hardcore erotica was used in the newer experiments, and in some cases researchers then went a step further and showed erotic films with violence in them. In many cases the latter would be a rape scene in which the woman was beaten and raped. There was also the question of whether the dosage was too small, and so eventually massive doses of such films lasting up to several hours a day for several weeks were employed. With these alterations, the difference between the control and experimental groups was much more visible in many of the experiments.

Now, there were problems of determining just which of the several conditions of the experiment produced the increased willingness to give the shock. Donnerstein and Malamuth were two of the researchers who designed experiments to see if it was the erotica or the violence that was most important. They designed experiments in which one group saw a violent erotic film, a second saw a nonerotic violent film, a third saw an erotic, nonviolent film, and a fourth control group saw neither an erotic nor a violent film. The results indicated that erotic films by themselves without the presence of physical violence against women was not the factor producing the willingness to administer the shock. In point of fact, many of the films used by Donnerstein were not X-rated but rather were R-rated films seen on cable TV and in typical theaters. It seemed clear that the addition of physical violence to the film was the main causal factor. As Donnerstein put it:[8]

> As we have seen . . . it is the aggressive content of pornography that is the main contributor to violence against women. In fact, when we remove the sexual content from such films and just leave the aggressive aspect, we find a similar pattern of aggression and asocial attitudes. (Donnerstein, 1984: p. 79)

These results would seem to leave us with the view that if anything promotes violence, it is the viewing of violence. But life is not that simple. Zillmann has conducted some fascinating experiments that further qualify even this seemingly obvious conclusion. Zillmann compared the impact of erotica of various types and concluded that one major explanatory factor is the degree to which the viewer reacts pleasantly or unpleasantly to what is seen. He discovered that if the erotica—whatever type it was—was reacted to with a pleasant emotional state, then the likelihood of aggression was actually *reduced.* Whereas if the viewer reacted to erotica—whatever type it was—unpleasantly, then the likelihood of aggression was *increased.*

Thus, Zillmann suggests that it is not the objective content of the film that is important but the subjective emotional response to it. If one viewer is disgusted or frightened by a film, aggression is more likely. If another viewer is pleased and entertained by a film, aggression is reduced. *Most strikingly we find that whether the film was erotic or not does not matter.*

To test these ideas, Zillmann showed an eye-operation film that was assumed to lead to displeasure for most viewers and compared it with an erotic film featuring bestality, which was also assumed to be unpleasant to most viewers. He found no difference in the aggression produced! Then he showed a film with scenes from a rock concert, which he assumed would lead to a pleasant reaction, and compared it to explicit coital scenes, which he also assumed would be viewed as pleasant. Again he found that in both instances the viewers were low on aggression. He sums up his views by saying that:[9]

> Sexual drive evidently does not have a uniform effect on aggressive behavior, and the diversity of modifications that sexual stimulation can produce consequently cannot be accurately predicted from the mere fact of sexual stimulation. (Zillmann, 1984: p. 133)

In the light of Zillmann's work, conclusions on the impact of erotica need to be further specified. In addition to the qualifications of previous researchers concerning the importance of prior anger, the length of the exposure, the encouragement to aggression, and the presence of physical violence, we must add the hedonic value of the exposure to the viewer. The complexity of this situation points to the need to avoid glib conclusions about the violent outcomes of viewing erotica.

Besides searching for aggressive outcomes of erotica, some research has inquired about attitudinal consequences of erotica. Their aim was to discern if males become more "callous" or lacking in "respect" for women as a result of viewing erotica.[10] These researchers used the same experimental procedures I described earlier, but instead of seeing if an electric shock was administered, the outcome they now looked for was a higher score on Don Mosher's "callousness" scale or a higher score on belief in "rape myths" as measured by Burt's scale.[11]

Zillmann reports that attitudinal effects of viewing erotica are still measurable three weeks after exposure. The increased callous attitudes toward women is measured by increased support for beliefs that women are useful mainly as sexual objects. It is interesting to note that Zillmann reports similar "callous" changes in female subjects' attitudes toward other females.[12] Other changes were observed in less favorable attitudes regarding gender equality, less severe punishments recommended for rape, and perceptions that a wider range of sexual relations are commonly occuring in society.

Zillmann's experiments, which involved massive exposure over a six-week period, also found that over this time period males became less critical of erotic films and less in favor of legal proposals to restrict erotic films. The subjects also came to be "habituated" by the films; that is, they tended to react less strongly to the films as time went on. All this indicates that the films were changing the viewer's attitudes.

Let's pause for a moment now and evaluate the experimental findings on aggressive behavior and attitude changes related to erotic films. First, I would sum up by saying that the exact specification of conditions that might produce particular outcomes is of primary importance. The type of film (violent only, erotic and violent, or just erotic) makes a great deal of difference, as we have seen. Also, the individual's reactions hedonically to the film affects the outcomes. Secondly, there does seem to be a change in attitudes when individuals are exposed to massive amounts of even nonviolent erotica, but just how "real" are these changes in behavior and attitudes in the experiment? How lasting are they, and do they predict future aggressive behavior against females?

In order to start to answer these queries, we must tend to the question, how valid are the results of all these experiments? Let us start with the reports of attitude changes such as those by Zillmann. We must consider the possibility that volunteer college males would not be fully candid when asked about rape myths, callousness to women, and gender equality *prior* to being exposed to the erotica. They might at that early point in time hesitate to endorse the callous statements that portray women merely as sexual objects. Nevertheless, after being exposed week after week to erotic films by the experimenter, they may feel more willing to open up and reveal how they actually felt all along.

I am suggesting that it is possible that the attitude change measured before and after exposure is really a change in willingness to reveal. In addition, this willingness may increase because the subjects sense the support of the experimenters for just such revelations. These possibilities have yet to be resolved by any research work, and so we must reserve final judgment.

Let us examine the question of the permanency of such attitudinal changes. Just how deep and lasting are such changes? Zillmann did the longest follow-up to date, and that was just three weeks after the end of the experiment. He did find that the attitude changes were still measurable at that time, but he also recognized the need for longer-term follow-up. Nevertheless, there is some additional evidence on the fixity of these attitude changes.

Malamuth and Check reported on their debriefing procedures and results.[13] Such debriefings are required by the federal government granting agencies because the researchers assert the possibility that these films can increase the subjects' aggression and increase their negative attitudes toward women. Thus, all subjects are supposed to be debriefed shortly after the experiments in order to return them to their original attitudinal state. Malamuth and Check used a short procedure for this purpose. They gave the subjects a one-page statement that informed them that the attitudes of women in the films they saw were not typical; that is, they were told that women are not as sexually receptive as these films portray, nor do they quickly become aroused when a male attempts to rape them. In addition, the experimenters spoke to the men briefly on this same point.

The unexpected finding is that after this simple debriefing, the significant differences in attitudes between the experimental and control groups relevant to women disappeared completely. Actually, the exposed males were even less callous in their final attitudes than men who were in the control group and had not been exposed to any erotica! Now how does one interpret such results? One can simply say that these very short debriefings are quite effective. An alternative explanation is that the altered attitudes were never deeply rooted. As I noted earlier, it is possible that attitude changes both during the experiments and afterward were encouraged by a desire to say what the subjects thought was wanted by the researchers. Whether this "experimenter effect" is applicable or not, however, it does seem that the attitude changes were not deeply rooted.

Just how much outside social interaction with males and females it would take to have the same neutralizing effect as the debriefing is unknown. But without strong support in their daily lives for their "new" callous attitudes, it surely would seem unlikely that any such new attitudes would prevail. These findings lead to the conclusion that with day-to-day support for callous attitudes the films would hardly matter and without that support they would not likely have any lasting impact. In short, the power and longevity of such attitude changes as have been observed is questionable.

Consider next the behavioral implications of this erotica research: Do such films lead to violent acts against women? By way of preface the reader should remember that most of the causal connection of the film and aggressive behavior toward the female confederate was attributed to the negatively evaluated violence in the film and not to the erotica. Other researchers, like Zillmann, would argue that erotica, even if not violent, could promote the same aggression, particularly if the film was perceived as unpleasant by the viewer. There are still others who believe that even if there is no physical violence, but if a power difference in favor of the male is portrayed, that will in itself promote physical aggression against women. We have little to support this view, and I mention it only to indicate that nonviolent erotica has not been given a clean bill of health by all researchers.

It is also well to keep in mind that some people define as violent any form of presentation that represents a sexual relationship in which the male has more prestige or power than his female partner. Such usage of the concept of violence is hardly scientific and is best guarded against. Its source is a moral condemnation of gender inequality and the consequent assignment of negative connotations to all that signifies such inequality. Of course, one may study the consequences of gender power inequality without calling such situations violent. This is precisely what we did in Chapter 4.

Overall, the experiments we have discussed have shown that under some conditions (surely not fully understood today) some types of erotica do lead a college student volunteer to give a shock to a female confederate who earlier had angered him. The question I am raising here is, what can we conclude from this concerning the likelihood of rape or other physical attacks against women? I believe it is a long jump in logic and in evidence from the experiments to any statement about what is likely to happen in the outside world. Allow me to elaborate.

The social setting in which the individuals who view erotica are embedded is an important datum. To judge the consequences of any activity, one must have some idea of what alternative activities would occur if this one did not happen. If, for example, a group of 18-year-old males were not to go to an X-rated film, what would they do? Would they be exposed to conversations and events that would promote a different set of gender and sexual attitudes? In short, whatever beliefs are held about women among a group of 18-year-old males would likely be expressed when these males got together. Such views might well be just as "crude" and "debasing" and "subordinating" of women as those that might be in some erotic films. Therefore, the judgment about the impact of erotic films needs to be informed by what would be the alternate outcome if such films were not seen.

The reader might well raise the issue as to what produces the basic values that reflect the desire to go to an erotic film or to talk bluntly about sexual experiences over a pitcher of beer. The basic values are outgrowths of the ways in which males and females relate in our society. I believe the pursuit of commercial erotica is simply one of the social scripts that exists for finding pathways to the altered state of sexual arousal. To be sure, for a few it may be a means of expressing dominance or aggressive fantasies against women. But I would argue that for the great majority of males who go to an erotic film, the motivation is physical pleasure.

Certainly the erotic script, like all scripts, will contain values that reflect whatever male dominance exists in our society, but that is a common element even in nonsexual scripts, and it is not that but rather the explicit erotic character of the film that is essential in attracting the viewer.[14] Remember that the plots in such films are quite thin. The focus of such films is on genitalia, not on character development. We will talk more of this later, but in order to help answer the question of possible violent outcomes, let's now look at evidence from nonexperimental research.

EROTICA AND VIOLENCE:
THE NONEXPERIMENTAL RESEARCH EVIDENCE

Studies have been made that examine the experiences of sex offenders with erotica in their formative years. The Kinsey Institute published one such study some 20 years ago and found that sex offenders in jail actually had less exposure to erotica than did prisoners who were in jail for other offenses.[15] The backgrounds of sex offenders revealed parents who were puritanical and narrow in their approach to sexuality. Consequently, these future sex offenders were less exposed to explicit erotica when they were growing up than were other youngsters.

More recent studies have found similar results when comparing those imprisoned for sex offenses with those imprisoned for other offenses. At the University of Minnesota, Professors David Ward and Candace Kruttschnitt in 1983 undertook a comparison study of three matched groups of males: (1) those in jail for sex offenses, (2) those in jail for other offenses, and (3) those not in jail. In 1984 I helped examine some of these data and found that those in jail for sex offenses had had no greater exposure to erotica than those in the other two matched groups. These results were presented by Kruttschmitt at a City Council hearing in Minneapolis in March 1984. One might question how representative Minnesota is of the nation, but as I indicated above, similar findings have been consistently reported from other researchers.

Specific studies of rapists have been made to see if they had been more exposed to erotica than other men. Most of these studies have not found any such difference. Gene Abel, a therapist who has dealt extensively with rapists, made a comparison of his own.[16] He compared those rapists who had extensive exposure to erotica to those rapists who had little exposure to erotica. His goal was to see if those exposed the most to erotica would commit the most violent types of rape or rape more frequently. Abel's results indicated very little in the way of differences between these two groups of rapists.

I am not trying to imply that erotica is totally irrelevant to crimes of sexual violence. There are a few sex offenders who state that they obtained the idea for exactly how to commit a rape murder from some film or magazine. To be sure, these are very few in number; but they do occur. However, once more we must raise the question, what would have occurred had these males not encountered the erotic films or magazines that detailed the way a rape murder could be carried out? Did the erotica cause the violence, or was the person already violently inclined and therefore sought out the erotica? Without erotica would such men have never been violent against women?

What we do know is that there are individuals who claim that a film triggered their response. Recall that it was John Hinckley who said he was pushed in the direction of attempting to assassinate President Reagan by seeing the film *Taxi Driver*. Incidentally, this was not an X-rated film. Also, in 1983 the networks played the film *The Deer Hunter* (also not an X-rated movie), which described some violent events in Vietnam. In one scene a game of Russian roulette was being played with real bullets. Within a week after that film was shown on television, the press reported that over a dozen young teenage boys had died playing Russian roulette. There were millions who saw the film and did not react this way. Yet one could still assert that this film was one causal factor in the deaths of those boys.

The fact of the matter is that for a very small proportion of highly suggestive viewers, a wide range of films may trigger a violent reaction. I must quickly add that it is also quite likely, however, that for such people there will very often be other events that can trigger some tragic reaction. The choice confronting the public is the degree to which they want to stop all forms of communication that may trigger violence in a very few. In order to protect the First Amendment rights of free expression, the courts have ruled that only those forms of expression that have a "virtual certainty" of producing potential harm can be banned.[17]

Our culture has historically relatively strongly supported freedom of expression. Despite this fact, we have placed more restrictions in the area of sexuality than in almost any other form of expression. As I have noted earlier, Supreme Court decisions have stated that erotica that violates community standards can be banned if it has no serious value in other important parts of our life. In addition, in 1982 we joined many other Western countries in banning all forms of child erotica regardless of whether it could be shown to be legally obscene. This was done on the grounds that children do not have the ability to defend themselves legally against abuse that might occur in the creation of child erotica. So, we have typically come down hard on erotica. This is surely due, in part, to our conservative sexual heritage, which includes a view of sexuality as something dangerous and evil that must be controlled (recall tenet 3 of the nonequalitarian sexual ideology).

The question raised by the new legislative proposals on erotica is not whether we should remove some of the standard First Amendment rights from erotica—that we have already done in our Supreme Court rulings—but whether we should extend and increase these restrictions. This is a personal value choice for each of us to answer. The review of evidence in this chapter is relevant to such a decision.

If we are concerned with the possible promotion of violence, the evidence from erotica research and other sources indicates that if any type of mass media presentation can lead to violence, it is the direct portrayal of violence.[18] Even the exact causal operation of this connection is in dispute. We know, though, that there is much more widespread viewing of violence against women and men on television in R- and PG-rated movies than in X-rated erotica. As I have documented earlier in this chapter, only a small segment of erotica contains any portrayal of physical violence matching that on television or in other movies. Furthermore, the audiences at erotic films are but a small percentage of those attending to other more widespread forms of mass media.

WHO GOES TO EROTIC FILMS?

As part of my examination of the issue of the impact of erotica, I analyzed national data concerning who attends X-rated movies. Since we are concerned with whether such movies encourage the subordination of women, it is important to find out if those who attend are more opposed to gender equality. NORC (the National Opinion Research Center) takes annual surveys of a representative group of Americans 18 and older every year. One of the questions NORC often asks in these surveys concerns attendance at an X-rated movie during the past year.

I was able to examine six national surveys done between 1973 and 1983.

About one fifth of all the respondents said they went to an X-rated movie during the past year. There were, as expected, more males than females attending (25% of males versus 14% of females). Almost half of those who went were under 30, and almost all the others were under 60 years of age. About 60% were married. I divided the respondents into those with less than a high school education, those who were a high school graduate, and those with more than a high school education. For each of these three groups the respective percentages of those who went to an X-rated movie in the past year were 13, 20, and 24. So, a higher proportion of those with at least some college education went to an X-rated movie in the past year.

Then I compared those who went to an X-rated movie with those who did not in terms of several questions that measured gender equality. Table 7.1 has those precise questions and the response breakdown by whether the respondent attended an X-rated movie in the last year.

TABLE 7.1   Gender Equality and X-Rated-Movie Attendance

	ATTENDED	DID NOT ATTEND
1. Do you agree or disagree with this statement? Women should take care of running their homes and leave running the country up to men. (% yes)	19%	32%
2. If your party nominated a woman for president, would you vote for her if she were qualified for the job? (% Yes)	90%	79%
3. Do you approve or disapprove of a married woman earning money in business or industry if she has a husband capable of supporting her? (% approve)	81%	72%
4. Tell me if you agree or disagree with this statement: Most men are better suited emotionally for politics than are most women. (% agree)	34%	45%

SOURCE: NORC surveys: 1973, 1975, 1976, 1978, 1980, and 1983.

The percentage difference on all four questions is enough to be significant on statistical tests. This indicates, then, that those who do go to an X-rated movie are more, not less, gender-equal than those who do not go. I checked these results separately for each year, for males and females, and for each education level, and the differences remained significant in all these subgroup comparisons. This indicates that these results are not simply an outcome of an unusual year or just applicable for males or just applicable to college-educated people.

As a further indication of the type of people who attend an X-rated movie, I examined questions on abortion and found that 46% of those who went and 34% of those who did not go approved of abortion for a "women who wants it for any reason." This fits with other research indicating that more gender-equal individuals are accepting of a woman's right to have an abortion.[19] On questions of erotica itself the people who went to an X-rated movie were more likely to believe that erotica provided information and less likely to say that sexual materials lead to a "breakdown of morals" or to rape, and they were more opposed to additional laws against erotica.

These data argue against the view that erotica leads to attitudes supporting the subordination of women. It surely seems that many people who go to X-rated movies do not view those movies as degrading to women. These people seem to be high on gender equality, and it is difficult to believe they would participate in and defend an activity they believed lowered the value placed on women.

Of course, the NORC surveys do not have information on exactly what X-rated movies these people attended, nor do my results preclude there being a minority of people who attend such movies who do lose respect for women. The data do show, however, that on the average the people who do *not* go to such movies are *more* likely to be gender-nonequal. This lack of equality is certainly not due to exposure to erotica.

It would seem that much of the support for the opposition to many commercial forms of erotica comes from people who also oppose gender equality. For them, this is a matter of preserving what they feel is the proper relation of the genders and the proper expression of sexuality. In addition to this conservative group we have a radical feminist group also supporting legal restrictions on commercial erotica. To this subgroup of feminists, their stand is a political matter of fighting against what they feel is a degrading portrayal of women. They seek support for what they define as gender equality. This surely is not a major goal for the conservatives.

The Indianapolis ordinance that was designed to restrict erotica was introduced in 1984 by Councilwoman Beulah Coughenour, a Republican and a leader in Indiana in the fight *against* ERA![20] The radical feminists and the conservatives who support such restrictive legislation have one goal in common: They seek legally to restrain the forms of commercial erotica that are allowed. Yet their reasons for doing this are strikingly different and opposed. Nowhere is the clash of ideologies in our country more obvious than on gender equality, and yet we have in such legislation a pragmatic coalition.

The radical feminist opposition to many forms of commercial erotica stems from the gender-based reasons I discussed earlier in this chapter. These women are acutely aware that many males value women only for the physical pleasure they can derive from them. For women who are seeking equality, this body-centered focus of men is a constant denigration of their self-worth. The body-centered focus ignores the many other contributions to society that women make. It is that narrow view of women which so angers the radical feminists.

In addition, radical feminists, despite their gender equality, were socialized into our traditional gender roles when they were growing up. That traditional exposure may well have made these women likely to value a stable, person-centered sexuality and devalue the more pleasure-centered varieties that erotica often emphasizes (tenet 2 again). This early socialization plus their gender equality values probably led to the attempt to separate the erotica they liked from that which they disliked and call the latter pornography. In time it has led some to support the Indianapolis type of ordinance which restrains a wide variety of erotica that is supposed to subordinate women. Even nude photos that focused upon one part of the female body were labeled exploitive and called pornographic and included in the erotica that the ordinance would restrain. Clearly, the goal is to formulate in law what to this segment of feminists is gender-equal erotica.

They assumed that anyone who could enjoy an erotic scene that they interpreted as subordinating women must not be a gender-equalitarian person. I believe they have misread the meaning of erotica to most men. In my judgment, the erotica focus for most men is not to degrade women but to obtain physical pleasure from viewing explicit sexual scenes. The NORC data showing that men who see X-rated movies are actually more gender-equal than those who do not would appear to support this conclusion

Betty Friedan, the founder of the National Organization of Women has argued against restrictive legislation. She advises feminists:[21]

> Get off the pornography kick and face the real obscenity of poverty. No matter how repulsive we may find pornography, laws banning books or movies for sexually explicit content could be far more dangerous to women. The pornography issue is dividing the women's movement and giving the impression on college campuses that to be a feminist is to be against sex. (Friedan, 1985: p. 98)

Sexual restrictions on women has for millennium been seen as a way to "protect" women from the "degrading" influences of sexuality. Protective motives have been used to restrict female paid employment and access to birth control.

Note that very little of the outcry against erotica refers to the degrading or devaluing or exploiting of males in erotica. After all, males are in erotic films, and if such activity is "dehumanizing" or "exploitive of the human body," then this would apply to them as well. But males are not mentioned because the attention is on gender inequality, and males are the group in power and thus are not felt to require help. As I see it, the radical feminists' opposition to erotica is not basically an opposition to open sexuality—they would accept that if it were placed in what they defined as an equalitarian context. It is at its roots an opposition to what they judge to be a nonequalitarian view of sexuality. But, as I have noted earlier, there is a real question as to the accuracy of their judgment regarding what is nonequalitarian erotica.

The traditionalists who also support the control of erotica come at this issue from an altogether different perspective. They oppose commercial erotica because they feel that the sexuality involved is offensive to decency and modesty, as they define those terms. They would speak out equally strongly against homosexuality in ways opposed by most of the radical feminists. They would also be more restrictive on abortion and more "profamily" on many issues that would sharply distinguish them from most feminists.

It is not the gender inequality that the conservatives oppose in commercial erotica but the open display of sexuality. If gender inequality were displayed in some nonsexual context, such as on questions about abortion, daycare, working mothers, or women priests, such conservatives would not feel any need to speak out. In fact, many of them would actively support nonequalitarian positions on such issues.

So, we have a union of conservatives, who oppose the open sexual display, and radical feminists, who oppose not the openness but the gender inequality, as they see it, in those sexual portrayals. There are not many other issues where these two groups would be allies. I expect their union to be brief, for on the fundamental issue of gender equality they are indeed poles apart. As one indication of this radical difference I note that in Suffolk County, New York the conservatives have taken the model of the Indianapolis anti-erotica legislation and revised it to reflect a profamily and antigay position.[22]

EROTICA: A CROSS-CULTURAL VIEW

It is time to get a broader perspective on erotica. To do that I will present an overview on the place of erotica in the subordination of women, whether that subordination entails physical violence or just social subordination.[23] In Chapter 4 we discussed at length the issue of gender equality. I pointed out there how sociologists measure the relative power of men and women by looking at their roles and influences in the major settings of the family, economic, political, and religious institutions. If one is constantly exposed to women as subordinates in all these institutions in terms of the influence they wield, then it is easy to understand why even young children would perceive women as being less powerful.

To the extent that women move into more equal positions of power in these basic institutions, we can expect such perceptions of female subordination to alter. Our "significant others," that is, our close friends, kin, and lovers shape and reinforce our attitudes toward men and women.[24] These individuals are exposed to the same daily view of females being low on power in virtually all our major institutions. There is thus systematic reinforcement of the relative power of each gender. Change is surely possible, but just being determined to change things without altering the social position of women in the major institutions would be largely illusory.

Now let us confront the question of the place of erotica in the subordination of women. Just how much influence on the subordination of women does erotica have? I believe the research we examined earlier in this chapter and our awareness of the institutional sources of power lead to the conclusion that erotica has very little influence on the subordination of women in society. Erotica, as we are speaking of it here, is largely a commercial enterprise. The aim of such erotica is not social stability nor social reform but sexual excitement in exchange for money. The customer, here as in all of our markets, can select from a variety of products. Almost all these products reflect felt demand, and if that demand does not materialize, the product will cease to be manufactured. In short, erotica largely mirrors the socialization of those who use it.

One can discern changes toward greater gender equality in erotic films over the past decade or two. Just as an illustration, shortly after the straight movie *Nine to Five* appeared, an erotic film called *Eight to Four* that parodied it was made. Both films followed the same story line of a male chauvinist boss in an office and of his eventually being put in his place by his female employees. This same sort of use of common popular themes can be seen in other hardcore erotica films, such as *Urban Cowgirls* modeled after *Urban Cowboys*. My point here is that erotic films reflect what is of interest to potential viewers much more than they shape the direction of that interest. Such films, then, are more accurately viewed as simply an echo of the society in which we live. That being the case, as our society has become more gender-equal, so have our erotic films.

Most of the direct sources of a group's power are in that group's specific institutional integration as reflected in employment positions and ties to political groups. The viewing of erotica can hardly be conceptualized as comparable in importance to such fundamental forces. It would be easy to think of many other noninstitutional activities that would likely display conventional gender-role attitudes with considerably more influence. One need only think of television and nonerotic films. Each of these occupies far more of our time than erotic films and each surely in its own way imparts a gender-nonequal message.

As a way of analyzing the relationship of erotica to gender equality, let us examine other societies to see what role erotica plays in shaping gender roles. Do we find that those societies with the most lenient attitudes toward erotica are those with the greatest degree of gender inequality?

Quite the contrary is the case in the West. Those societies like Sweden and Denmark that contain a wide array of erotica easily available are the *most* gender-equal countries in the Western world. It would be much more difficult to obtain erotica in countries like Spain and Belgium, and those countries are much *less* gender equal. The data are not available for a more systematic, detailed check of all Western societies, but what we do know hardly evidences any causal impact of erotica at all. In fact, as cited earlier, contrary evidence indicates that restrictions on erotica are much more common in gender-nonequal societies. It is apparent that nonequalitarian countries do not need open erotica to maintain inequality, and gender-equal countries are not moved from their equality by the abundance of erotica. Quite frankly, erotica seems a rather impotent element in the social construction of gender.

One careful check of the relation of erotica to the subordination of women was done in Denmark by Berl Kutchinsky.[25] Denmark opened up its laws on written erotica in 1967 and on visual erotica in 1969. Kutchinsky compared the rate of sex offenses between 1967 and 1973 and found there was no increase in rape. He did find an 85% reduction of sexual offenses against small children in Copenhagen during that six-year period. Other sex offenses remained stable. It is relevant to point out here that in West Germany a similar check was made after the law changed, and a 59% reduction in sex offenses against small children was found. Kutchinsky speculates that perhaps for child sex offenders, the easy availability of magazines portraying child sexuality lessened some offenders' felt need for abusing children. I will not pursue the implications of this because our focus here is upon sex offenses against adult women. In that regard, there was little change in such offenses that could be attributed to the opening up of the laws restricting erotica.[26]

Kutchinsky also reports that after 1969 the sales of erotic materials fell by two thirds. It seemed that the Danish public had been quickly satiated in their curiousity and most did not use commercial erotica to any great extent. Kutchinsky calls this the "banana boat syndrome." He is referring here to the rush to buy bananas in Denmark when they again became available after the Second World War. That also did not last very long.

We have another interesting case study in Japan. After the Second World War Japan intensified its laws on erotica to conform with what they thought the United States would approve. They wished to emulate us in technology and so wanted to maintain good relations by not offending us with their erotica. While our laws have liberalized in the past 40 years, the Japanese laws have not altered much and still ban visual display of pubic hair or adult genitals. But as long as this ban is technically observed, much more is allowed than would be true in the United States. In Japan, for example, nudity in mass magazines (but no public hair or genitalia) is common and public television shows are more sexually explicit.

The one characteristic that interests us most here is that in both film and novel in Japan there is a recurrent theme of bondage and rape.[27] Abramson and Hayashi state:

> Of particular note in Japanese pornography (film and novel) is the recurring theme of bondage and rape. Although Japanese movies are much less explicit than their American and European counterparts, the plot often involves the rape of a high school girl. This theme is also evident in the cheap erotic novels (with titles like *Gang-raped Daughter*) and sexual cartoons. In fact, one of the best ways to ensure the success of a Japanese adult film is to include the bondage and rape of a young woman. (Abrahamson and Hayashi, 1984; p. 178)

One might suspect that with that form of erotica so widespread, if erotica is causal, Japan would have a very high rape rate. In actual fact, Japan has one of the lowest rates of any industrialized country in the world.[28] In Japan, as in all cultures, the messages sent out by erotica are mediated through the shared attitude structure of the people. In the case of Japan there is a strong socialized sense of responsibility, respect, and commitment. Relatedly, shame plays a powerful role in Japan. The Japanese view erotic rape and bondage films as a cathartic escape valve that provides vicarious satisfaction for unacceptable behavior.

One important lesson of the Japanese case is that the erotic is not a direct pathway to imitation. There is always a filtering system and counterinfluences. To be sure, the Japanese generally internalize more controls than do Americans, but that is not to say we have none. No people simply imitate what they see and hear. To illustrate, the Western world has amongst its citizens those who endorse a sado-masochistic sexual style with its extensive exposure to violence.[29] Yet very little unwanted violence occurs among such people. This is so because almost all sado-masochists are seeking pleasure, even if the pathway is through pain. They interpret their sexual relations in those terms and avoid unwanted violence. They demonstrate that if we communicate with one another, we have customary ways of using our ability to evaluate and choose and thereby interpret and organize our experiences in ways that are compatible with our values. At times this thought seems to get lost in the erotica debate.

In nonindustrialized cultures little systematic information on erotica is available. However, one study on modesty by William Stephens is relevant here.[30] The Presidential Commission on Obscenity and Porongraphy sponsored Stephens's study of cross-cultural information pertaining to "obscenity" and sexual modesty. He studied 92 nonindustrialized societies using the Human Relations Area Files.[31] He found that peasant societies, more than tribal societies, were restrictive in terms of sexual modesty as indicated by the insistence on covering the body. These peasant societies also had the strictest codes regulating premarital and marital sexual conduct.

Stephens studied the telling of sexual jokes and obscene stories and reports:

> The peoples who seem most preoccupied with sexual joking and obscenity are not those who appear to have the most to [release], but those who should have the least. They tend strongly to be the most sexually free, the least constrained by taboo and modesty rules. (Stephens, 1972: p. 8)

Stephens believes that the control of the older, tribal "immodesty" resulted from the increase in deference and patriarchy that occurred with the advent of agriculture. He believes that more democratic and gender-equal cultures have fewer restrictions on sexuality. Such a lack of sexual restrictiveness goes with more acceptance of a blunt, direct approach to sexuality. The ease with which a people engage in sexuality does not seem to reduce their erotic focus nor their gender equality.[32]

Of greatest interest to us here is his finding that these highly permissive, immodest groups were usually gender-equal. In talking of these groups, he states that

> In all [these] groups, however, the status of women appears to have been relatively high, and family relations fairly equalitarian. (Stephens, 1972: p. 15)

This is additional evidence of a lack of connection of acceptance of erotica with gender inequality. In fact, once again the evidence seems to indicate that tolerance of erotic variety goes with gender equality. Of course, erotica in these cultures will not be identical with our types of erotica. Nevertheless, their erotica does include genital focus, concentration on orgasm, blunt sexual jokes, attention to female body parts, and centering on physical pleasures. All this is also common in our erotica.

Violent forms of erotica are not mentioned by Stephens, but one can still ask about the association of open-erotica cultures with high rape rates. The evidence here is again negative for if we look at the cultures Stephens classifies as high on erotica, we find they are generally ranked low on rape rates.[33] Once more what associations we do find cross-culturally show a connection of erotica with low violence and with gender equality. I do not interpret such findings as evidence that erotica is productive of gender equality. Rather, I think more gender-equal societies are less restrictive on female sexuality, and part of such acceptance of female sexuality is a greater willingness to openly enjoy erotic images of many sorts.

THE STANDARD SAMPLE: EXPLANATION OF RAPE

Since the issues revolving around erotica do bring into question the possible relationship to rape, it is well to deal with rape more directly at this point. My comments should have indicated to the reader that I do not accord much causal power to erotica in producing rape or almost any other major societal outcome. But if I deny erotica a role in the production of rape, then what societal facts would I involve? In order to answer this question, I did examine the Standard Sample and search for social factors that could be tentatively viewed as causally related to the frequency of rape in a society.

I start with the proposition that regardless of the form or extent of erotica in a society, those groups with low power will be most easily abused. Thus, cultures in which women have the least power should be cultures in which rape is most common. I tested this basic proposition using the Standard Sample. Both Broude and Sanday coded societies for rape proneness. Broude was able to code 31 societies on frequency of rape, while Sanday coded 95 societies using a somewhat broader definition, which included the use of rape in ceremonies or as a threat against women.[34]

It is important to note at the outset that both of these researchers disagree with Susan Brownmiller's view of rape as a crucial weapon that men have universally used to intimidate women.[35]

> Rape . . . is nothing more or less than a conscious process of intimidation by which all men keep all women in a state of fear. (Brownmiller, 1975: p. 5)

Both Broude and Sanday found about half their societies were low or absent on evidence of rape, and in many of the other societies it did not appear that rape was socially supported as a universal threat to intimidate women. Brownmiller overlooks the fact that males have always had strong kinship reasons to protect their daughters and wives from sexual violence by other men.[36] For this reason there are strong pressures working against the use of rape as a means of female exploitation. A view of "all" men as rapists is more a politicization of this area of research than it is a scientific statement.

Sanday does report that both machismo and interpersonal violence were characteristics of societies that had high rates of rape.[37] She concludes that these are two basic causes of rape. I examined her data together with those of other researchers and found that the causal nexus was more complex than that. I used another measure of violence in order to see if a particular way of coding that variable made a difference in the causal picture obtained. Marc Ross had gathered data on several measures of violence.[38] I took four of his measures, which covered (1) the presence of local community conflict, (2) the commonness of physical force, (3) internal warfare, and (4) external warfare. Surprisingly, I found that *none* of these measures significantly correlated with the frequency of rape as measured by either Broude or Sanday.

I then further examined Sanday's measure of interpersonal violence and discovered that even it did not correlate with rape frequency as measured by Broude. Sanday's measure of violence showed a signficant correlation only with her own measure of rape. These results made me feel that the seemingly obvious causal connection between the presence of violence in a culture and the presence of rape needed further exploration. Even if one accepts Sanday's measures as valid and rejects those of Broude and Ross, it still seems advisable to search for other, possibly more important, causes of rape given this questionable support for the violence measure. For those who favor the importance of violence, it would be well to refine the meaning and the measurement of violence.

To search for other causal variables, I constructed and tested a causal diagram, like those I have used in Chapters 3, 4, and 6. This diagram analyzes the connections of two other causes in addition to the general violence in a culture. I wanted to see which of these three variables was the most influential on rape proneness when we remove any possible influence of the other variables. Causal diagrams answer precisely that question and contain only those variables that have their own "net" or "independent" influence.[39] The results are in Diagram 7.1.

The statistical analysis showed that macho attitudes and belief in female inferiority influenced the occurrence of rape in a society.[40] This finding is suppor-

DIAGRAM 7.1 Predictors of rape.

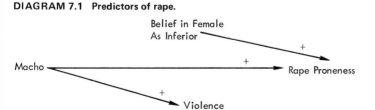

tive of my position that the lower the status of females, the more likely they would be mistreated. The reader should realize that although the relationship of belief in female inferiority and rape is statistically significant, this does not mean that all groups with a belief in female inferiority will have high rape rates. It simply means there is a tendency in that direction—not a certainty.

Macho beliefs also appear as a somewhat powerful variable. It is a measure of the degree to which the male role endorses physical aggressiveness, high risk taking, and a casual attitude toward sexuality. The relationship to the belief in female inferiority did not quite make the required level of significance (see Appendix A, Table A.5). The relationship between these two variables in Diagram 4.1 was significant, although there we used Whyte's measure of machismo and here we are using Sanday's measure. It is possible, though that there is no causal relationship between these two variables and what correlation there is simply results from their both being products of a male-dominant culture. At the very least, given the findings in this diagram, we cannot be sure that macho beliefs themselves produce the belief in female inferiority. Macho beliefs in the diagram also shows a significant correlation with greater violence in a society. This seems reasonable given the aggressive element in such macho beliefs. Yet endorsement of aggression and casual sexuality need not imply endorsement of a belief in female inferiority. This is surely a point worth further investigation.

The diagram does not indicate any causal connection of violence with rape even though, as I have indicated, such a connection does shows up when using Sanday's measure of violence.[41] The lack of support for this connection in the codes of other researchers makes this causal path questionable. Indeed, I would have thought that any culture that supported violence in other areas would support it in violence against women. It seems that this is not the full story, and perhaps particular beliefs relevant to the protection of females prevents this connection from being as common as one might think. The lack of a clear connection of violence customs with rape is one of the most surprising results of my cross-cultural analysis. I certainly hope that some of my readers will explore this area via additional research.

Surely a machismo view of the male gender may encourage men to view sexuality in an aggressive way. In this view, sexuality can be a way of getting back at someone. If the rapist did not conceive of sexuality this way, he would not use a sexual act to express his anger and power needs. One of the distinctive differences between rapists and other violent men is that rapists express their violence in sexual terms.[42] There are also reports indicating a sexually restrictive upbringing of rapists, low empathic ability, and an aggressive macho-male conception. From a cross-cultural perspective the key point is that the support for a machismo orientation rests on the power of male kin groups in a society. That power, as we saw in Chapter 4, is rooted, in part, in the kinship system. Our measure of male kin groups in Diagram 4.1 was the presence of patrilineal descent and patrilocal residence, and both are kinship terms. From a sociological perspective aggression derives more from group organization than from biology and thus male groups are important elements.

Of course, I am aware that there are many other variables that I could not consider, for they were not coded by anyone for the Standard Sample. Also, we need more precise ways to measure some key variables such as machismo.[43] However, this analysis has shown that the variables in Diagram 7.1 are likely some of those central in producing rape. This affords the reader at least a beginning of the answer to the question of what produces violence against women.

EROTIC FANTASIES AND GENDER ROLES

One very important question that we must address here concerns the reasons why males and females in our society view erotica in such very different ways. If erotica is largely a reflection of our gender roles, then perhaps the answer lies somehow in that realm. Males do often seem to favor, or at least not to be offended by, the hardcore erotica. Females very often seem to be offended, particularly by hardcore erotica. Why this difference?

We might start by realizing that most erotica has historically been aimed at arousing males. Men have paid the money to purchase the books, films, and more recently video cassettes, and so the products have been aimed at their erotic satisfaction. That might help explain why women would be bored or indifferent to such erotica but not why some women would feel hostile toward such erotica.

To understand female hostility to male erotica we need to grasp the essence of the major theme of the majority of erotica. I believe that theme is a fantasy story of women who are sexually insatiable and are thus incapable of resisting any type of male sexual advance. Male erotic films show that in a matter of seconds, regardless of the approach of the male, the woman is overcome by her sexual passion and willingly participates in all sorts of sexual activities. Given a society in which males are trained to be the sexual initiators and in which males therefore often feel rejected by females who are not sexually interested in them, is it any wonder that this insatiable female fantasy would be so popular?

Erotica thus portrays women with their negotiating or bargaining power removed. In this sense it is analogous to rape, except that in rape that negotiating power is removed by the threat of the male, whereas in fantasy it is removed by the woman's raging sexual passions. Surely some women viewers resent this loss of choice in erotic films, especially when the scenario does not conform with their own notions of the proper way to promote erotic feelings. Allow me to elaborate on this point.

What is one of the most common female sexual experiences in our society? It is to be sexually pressured to cooperate with male sexual desire. Related to this, women know that males often want only their own sexual interests satisfied and value little else in their sexual partners. This makes women at times feel used and exploited and devalued. Many women deal with this situation by demanding affection before sexual performance in order to gain reassurance that they are valued in nonsexual as well as sexual ways. Such typical gender-role pressures also tend to make women more likely to view sexuality as an act of making oneself vulnerable to another person while at the same time making it likely that males will view sexuality as the taking of pleasure. Surely this sets the stage for potential conflict.

Given this common scenario in male-female sexual interaction, it is not surprising that women would be offended by much of erotica, for to be portrayed as having no bargaining power is to be helpless to resist a male advance that is unwanted. Erotic films also remind women of the male emphasis on body parts, and this may arouse whatever insecurities women have regarding the attractiveness of their own bodies. Perhaps this uncertainty about one's own body is part of the greater distrust of body-centered sexuality by females.[44] The body-centered aspect of many erotic films may also remind some females that they are valued by many men only for their physical attractiveness. This narrow perspective may infuriate them when it is presented boldly on the screen.

Note that men are not so bothered when females concentrate upon male bodies. The reason is, I believe, that men know that they are valued in our society for much more than their bodies, and thus any emphasis on their bodies does not preclude other sources of self-worth. The situation for women is different, for although they are valued in other ways—as wives, daughters, and mothers—they are not as valued in the other major institutions that deal with power, like the political and economic institutions. Once again, the structure of one's gender role influences the reaction to erotica.

In a sense males and females are in a double bind—they want sexual pleasure in life, but they also want their sexual partner to value them as special. We have touched on this point in our discussion of jealousy in Chapter 3. Stressing the importance of selecting a sexual partner is one way for people to feel that they are special, but that very selectivity reduces the ease with which one can obtain sexual partners. Females in this bind are trained to strengthen their discretionary desires and concentrate on one man, and males are trained to strengthen the quick-pleasure aspect of that double bind and indulge. This gender difference is surely partly based on the dominant position of males, and it does create a different emphasis on sexual pleasure, or body-centered sexuality by males as compared to females.[45]

Women in particular are placed in a position where males are seeking to have sexual relationships with them, but these same males want their importance verified by the discretion exercised by their partner. Thus, women are pressured to be both very selective and very sexually responsive. Some of this same dual demand is placed on males by females, but with one important difference: In a male-dominant culture, the greater social censure for any violation of these desires will be visited upon women. Thus, women feel more constrained, and as a way of integrating their attitudes and behaviors, they are more likely to endorse a disapproving view of casual sexuality.

The conflicting objectives of selectivity and pleasure seeking are present in homosexual relations as well. Male homosexuals more strongly favor physical pleasure values while female homosexuals more strongly support selectivity values.[46] In this sense homosexuals very much reflect the gender roles of the society in which they were reared.

If my thesis is correct and erotic fantasies reflect the desires that are part of one's gender role, for example, for males this would be wanting to be accepted as a sexual partner, then what about female erotic fantasies? The most common complaint heard from women is that current hardcore movie erotica does not have enough romance or plot or building up of a relationship prior to the sexual encounter. This complaint surely fits with the stress on commitment in the female role (recall tenet 2 of our nonequalitarian sexual ideology).

In one sense female erotic fantasy may be based on the same principle as male erotic fantasy. By this I mean that it is enhanced by removing the negotiating power of one's sexual partner. This is not done by making the male sexually insatiable but instead by making the male romantically obsessed.[47] It is love or attraction of an intense personal sort which in this female fantasy renders the male helpless to resist. He must pursue her, give her what she desires, and treat her properly. The female sexual role is compatible with that scenario, and she can relax her sexual constraints and feel safe under those conditions. In this fashion, if the erotic film is romantic or at least shows that the male has a special interest in one particular female, then she can with little internal conflict project herself into the plot of the erotic story or film and allow herself to become aroused.

I am not arguing that love will not arouse males and raw erotica will not arouse females. We have experimental evidence indicating that males and females can be aroused by very similar scenarios. One recent study indicates that both genders are most aroused when the plot shows that the female initiates the sexual activity.[48] This would be compatible with the male desire for a complying female and it would be compatible with the female desire not to be pressured into sexual activity. Females can be aroused by a pure erotic story providing that the female is seen as choosing to act sexually and is not being pressured in a distasteful way by the male just to satisfy his erotic needs. Likewise, males can be aroused by a romantic story if the male is not shown to be trapped in the relationship by the romantic feelings. So, if the social setting of the fantasy is congruent with one's gender role, then the basic turn on becomes the explicit sexual activity.[49] But both genders fail to respond as easily when the setting violates their gender's sexual guidelines.

Our gender roles define power differences between males and females, and since sexuality is a valued goal, we have the potential for conflict among males and females concerning the achievement of this goal. Given the gender differences in power and the attractiveness of sexual pleasure, it is not at all surprising that dominance and submissiveness would be eroticized and expressed in our fantasies, although in different ways by males and females. Fantasies of power or submission seem quite common. One very important point here concerns the degree to which people make the distinction between erotic fantasy and reality. If that distinction is not made and the erotic fantasy is unacceptable as reality, the individual can be frightened. On the other hand, if fantasy and reality are distinguished, then one is aware that we can fantasize things we will never do in reality. The fantasy is thereby defused and its power to frighten removed. The Japanese's empahsis on rape fantasies and their ability to accept that as only a fantasy is a case in point, as is the reports by women of erotic forced-sexuality fantasies.

Males who have difficulty understanding why some women are not aroused by particular erotic themes might do well to speculate about what erotic themes would turn off men. For heterosexual males the answer would be to show them an erotic male homosexual film. In this instance, the heterosexual male viewer would be unwilling to project himself into this type of erotic scene, for he would feel that it is not the type of erotic turn on compatible with his male role. In any analogous fashion, much of hardcore erotica presents scenarios in violation of female sexual roles and makes identification with such fantasies difficult for many women.

If we do not seek to understand the societal reasons for the lack or presence of erotic response, we may easily attribute motives that are unrealistic. Some females may, for example, believe that the films that center on male sexual plea-sure—even though usually lacking in physical violence—are expressions of male desires to subordinate women. We see some reflection of this female sensitivity to being exploited in the finding that wives, more than husbands, worry about oral sexuality being a service to the other person and wonder if they are being used.[50]

> We think the meaning of oral sex is different for men and women. While many women may enjoy fellatio, others see it as a form of submissiveness, even degradation. . . . In cunnilingus, the male partner is not as likely to perceive the act as symbolizing sexual obedience, because he is apt to be the more powerful partner. (Blumstein and Schwartz, 1983: pp. 233–234)

Blumstein and Schwartz also make the point that lesbian women do not think of oral sexuality as involved with obedience or subjugation. This further indicates that those feelings are connected with the interface of male and female gender roles.

I would assert that there is a power element in erotica inherent in the desire to have the sexual partner do what would turn one on.[51] But that is not the same as a desire to subordinate or to devalue either gender. The goal is to gain physical and psychic pleasure from a sexual relationship. To most viewers an erotic film is a fantasy way to enjoy themselves, not an expression of their disregard for the opposite gender.

Bearing on this same point, experiments that have been done on reactions to the use of force in a sexual film indicate that the great majority of men and women are turned off if the film portrays a woman who is being hurt and who shows clearly that she dislikes it.[52] Despite that, both women and men respond with arousal to such a scene when the woman in a matter of a few seconds changes from opposition to total sexual surrender. The males who are the most aggressive prefer such "reversal" surrender scenes to consenting erotic scenes. For this minority of males, arousal is not blocked because of the opposition of the female partner. Again, given our somewhat macho male-gender roles, such a connection is not entirely surprising. I should add here that this connection arises from the basic macho type of gender role. It has been around a long time and is surely not a result of viewing an erotic film. In fact, it's social support was much stronger *prior* to the open erotica era of the last 20 years.

Sadomasochism is certainly relevant to an understanding of the relation of power to sexuality. Current research on sadists and masochists indicates that they typically do not seek to impose unwanted pain on each other. Most often they are involved in a mutually satisfying encounter. The masochist controls the sadist, and often there is a code word used which indicates the occasion when the masochist really wants the sadist to stop.[53] To such individuals, subordination is the fantasy pathway for reaching sexual satisfaction, but subordination need not be a reality of their day-to-day relationships.

Sadomasochistic relationships illustrate how aggressive erotic actions can be utilized as erotic fantasy without leading to unwanted violence. This would support a perspective that stresses that people can distinguish fantasy from reality and that they can channel their desires for dominance and submission into sexual scripts that avoid unwanted violence.

This is not to deny that a small segment of both genders may resent the power over their sexual satisfaction that the culture bestows on the opposite gender. Males may resent that women can deny them their type of sexual gratification, and women may resent that males deny them the type of erotic scenario they seek. Most of us, however, negotiate our way through the intricacies of our gender roles and find sufficient satisfactions. A few may give up and begin to dislike and devalue the opposite gender, and perhaps many others have minor amounts of such feelings.

It may be from such disillusionment that some of the distortions of the erotic meanings of others is born. Those who accurately see the erotic perspective that activates other people's desires are more likely to understand and to accept them. It is relevant here to note that homosexuals are less turned off by heterosexuality that heterosexuals are by homosexuality.[54] I believe this is in good part due to the greater exposure and understanding that homosexuals have regarding heterosexuality than vice versa. We need a great deal more research here to gain precise understandings of how we each learn our own and others' erotic understandings. This is a vital area, for our mutual satisfaction depends upon our ability to understand and enhance each other's erotica.

Clashes over commercial erotic enjoyment may be ameliorated by the phenominal growth in the videocassette market today. Males like to watch erotic videos at home with a female partner, and that means they want a type of sexual script depicted that will also turn on their partner. This means more erotic pleasuring according to female gender-role conceptions. So the new erotic videos seek to have more gender-equal sexual pleasuring illustrated and more relaxed person-centered themes as the setting for the hardcore sexual encounters.[55] In this way the pressures of the marketplace will likely lead to erotic films that appeal more to both genders.

SUMMARY AND CONCLUSIONS

Let me review where we have traveled in our examination of erotica. We have examined the proposition that erotica of various sorts makes women more sub-ordinate to men by presenting women as predominantly sexual objects to be used by men. My general conclusion is that erotica, like most of the mass media, simply reflects what exists in our overall society and if it were eliminated other customs with similar reflections would likely take its place. As we have seen, there is very little indication that commercial erotica is a prime mover in the area of gender inequality, or anywhere else for that matter. Nevertheless, we need to ask ourselves what is the most effective way to contain that erotica we do not like. Should we outlaw it, protest publicly, write against it, learn to tolerate it or what? These are private moral choices that remain even if erotica is seen purely as a matter of taste.

The position of women in our central institutions is the key basis of whatever power and status they have in any society. If change is desired, that is where it can be made. One thing that can be done is to stress the value of women beyond their sexual attractiveness. We can point to the skills they possess, their intellectual abilities, their talents, and their general value to society.

Therefore, if we are interested in lessening the subordination of women in Western societies, it would seem a futile gesture to attack various forms of erotica. As I have noted, the commercial erotica industry is largely a reflection of whatever relationships exist between men and women in the outside society and the great majority of it is non-violent. We can strive to smash that mirror if we want, but it will not change the reality reflected. If we could press a button and wipe out all erotica that anyone thought lowered the status of women, what would change? I submit that very little would change. The next day the position of women in busi-ness, politics, religion, education, and the family would remain basically the same. Therefore, to change female status, it would be far more effective to work, as many are, at changing the laws or customs that restrict female entry into the top positions in our social institutions.

All societies seem to have forms of erotica that celebrate the human body in terms of the gender roles of that culture. There is no way to stop that, for if we did remove all such body-oriented stimuli, we would lessen the likelihood of sexuality occurring. After all, it is the union of two bodies that is the essential ingredient in a sexual encounter. If the body is not eroticized, why would people engage in sexual relationships of any kind? Remember that even a touch on the genitals is not auto-matically felt to be sexual—it depends on the sexual scripts one has internalized. Sexuality is an altered state, and therefore we need extensive sexual scripts to help us achieve it. We may, of course, continue to argue for what we feel are "better" sexual scripts, but we must also be aware that those judgments change. If we do not like something out there in society, such as gender inequality, it is probably much more effective to go after changing that directly in its institutional base. That may be the more difficult path but it is much more effective than going after a weak reflection like commercial erotica.

The implication of my findings on the Standard Sample is that the direct causes of rape involve the status of women and the presence of machismo attitudes on the part of men. If we think it takes an aggressive, tough, unemotional person to gain leadership—if we treat the society as the marines treat a platoon—then we are promoting a machismo orientation. This approach justifies aggressiveness as the pathway to achieving what one is seeking in the sexual or any other arena.

Finally, if we tie this machismo orientation exclusively to the male gender, we can expect to enhance the already high male tendencies in the aggressive direction. Changes in the basic institutions of politics and economics to accommodate a less macho orientation would be effective in raising female status. Such changes would alter the male and female gender roles in ways that would make them more mutually supportive. I have suggested in this chapter that it is the clash of our different gender roles that is the fundamental cause of our differences concerning erotica and that conflict introduces stresses into our sexual relationships.

We can generalize the findings in Diagram 7.1 and say that action is more likely to be taken aganst a group in direct proportion to its status in the society and to the aggressivity that is sanctioned. It was no accident that during the Second World War we imprisoned Japanese-American citizens and not German and Italian Americans. The Japanese were viewed by many Americans as of lower status, and therefore it was easier to treat them unequally. The history of black-white relationships in this country would lend further support to the proposition that low-status groups are the recipients of the greatest violence.

I do believe that our general ideologies and our sexual ideologies, and the importance of male kin groups and our gender-role concepts, all afford major insights into the intense debate about the impact and meaning of erotica. Related to this is a fear element in sexuality that is especially strong in the emotive ideology. It is that fear which promotes a restrictive approach to erotica. The cognitive ideology also has some of this fear, for this fear is based on the high value we all place on sexuality. Were we indifferent or nonchalant about sexuality, neither ideology would be so involved. But we view sexuality as a vital part of our personal life, and thus we are vulnerable to bouts of anxiety concerning it. The non-equalitarian ideology with its tenet (3) concerning the great power of sexuality to mislead exacerbates our fears. I have tried to demonstrate in this chapter that such fear is encouraged by the politicizing of sexuality by some alarmists.

Before we leave this chapter, let me mention that there is a third general ideology, which I have not yet commented upon anywhere in this book. That is the ideology of social science. That ideology applies only to the part of one's life occupied by a scientific role. Even for a scientist this is not usually a majority of one's lifespace. In this sense the ideology of social science does not give us guidance in all of our everyday relationships. Rather, as I discussed in Chapters 1 and 2, it affords one an additional way of understanding our everyday relationships. The emphasis in the scientific ideology on reason and understanding makes it clearly a close relative of the cognitive ideology; but since science does not apply to all areas of life, it is much more specialized than the broader cognitive ideology.

The ideology of social science stresses the imparital study of social phenomena and the publication of research results and explanations so others can critically examine them and develop more accurate theories to explain our social lives. I have tried to follow this scientific ideology in this chapter and throughout this book. This is not an easy task, for all of us have our own value judgments. Yet if we are to provide a perspective other than that offered by the dominant ideologies of our culture, we must work toward this goal of scientific understanding. If I have encouraged you to look at least briefly at some of our most controversial issues from the perspective of social science, then I am content.

SELECTED REFERENCES AND COMMENTS

1. The use of the term *erotica* in place of *pornography* is becoming increasingly common. See
Allgeier, Elizabeth Rice, and Albert R. Allgeier, *Sexual Interactions.* Lexington, Mass.: Heath, 1984.
Fisher, William A., "Gender, Gender Role Identification, and Response to Erotica," Chapter 12 in Elizabeth Allgeier and Naomi McCormick (eds.), *Changing Boundaries: Gender Roles and Sexual Behavior.* Palo Alto, Calif.: Mayfield, 1983.

2. I wrote to the Kinsey Institute for an estimate of the proportion of X-rated films that displayed physical violence against women. In their reply they used the same source I cite here:
Rimmer, Robert H., *The X-Rated Videotape Guide.* New York: Arlington House, 1984.
For a recent analysis of adult magazines with similar results, see
Winick, Charles W., "A Content Analysis of Sexuality Explicit Magazines Sold in an Adult Bookstore," *Journal of Sex Research,* vol. 21, no. 2 (May 1985), pp. 206–210.

3. Thomas Radecki, in *"Film Comment,"* vol. 20, no. 6 (November/December 1984.)

4. Hardcore and softcore are common distinctions made in erotica. By hardcore I mean films that show erections and vulvas. Softcore shows nudity and simulated sexuality.

5. The original report of the president's commission was followed by nine volumes of research on which the report was based. The summary statement I quoted is from
Report of the Commission on Obscenity and Pornography. Washington, D.C.: GPO, 1971.

6. For a review of the research that followed the president's commission's report, see the chapters cited here.
Donnerstein, Edward, "Pornography: Its Effect on Violence against Women," Chapter 2, and
Byrne, Donn, and Kathryn Kelley, "Pornography and Sex Research," Introduction in

Neil M. Malamuth, and Edward Donnerstein (eds.), *Pornography and Sexual Aggression.* Orlando, Fla.: Academic Press, 1984.

7. Donnerstein published a study indicating that softcore erotica, like *Playboy*, actually lessened aggressive responses. Others have found the same results. For Donnerstein's work here, see

Donnerstein, Edward, Marcia Donnerstein, and Ronald Evans, "Erotic Stimuli and Aggression: Facilitation or Inhibition," *Journal of Personality and Social Psychology,* vol. 32, no. 2 (1975), pp. 237–244.

Despite such findings Baron and Straus recently reported that sales of magazines like *Playboy* are highest in states where rape is highest. However, the authors suggest that such a finding may simply reflect that more open sexual attitudes promote both the magazine sale as well as the frustration or anger in those men who feel offended by the changes or who feel left out. Baron and Straus also found that where sales of *Playgirl* were high, rape rates were high. This finding fits with the interpretation that such correlations are *not* causal.

Baron, Larry, and Murray A. Straus, "Sexual Stratification, Pornography, and Rape in the U.S., " Chapter 7 in Neil M. Malamuth and Edward Donnerstein (eds.), *Pornography and Sexual Aggression.* Orlando, Fla.: Academic Press, 1984.

Yllo, Kersti, "The Impact of Structural Inequality and Sexist Family Norms on Rates of Wife-Beating," *International Journal of Comparative Social Welfare,* vol. 1, no. 1 (Fall 1984), pp. 16–29.

8. Edward Donnerstein, "Pornography: Its Effect on Violence against Women," Chapter 2 in Neil M. Malamuth and Edward Donnerstein (eds.), *Pornography and Sexual Aggression.* Orlando, Fla.: Academic Press, 1984.

9. Zillmann's recent book is an excellent source to consult for a full development of his theoretical perspective. The quote is from that book:

Zillmann, Dolf, *Connections between Sex and Aggression.* Hillsdale, N.J.: Erlbaum, 1984.

10. The original measure of callousness was developed by Donald Mosher for the President's Commission on Obscenity and Pornography. Mosher has recently developed what he considers a much better measuring instrument for a concept he now calls a "macho personality constellation." He describes it and presents evidence of its validity in the following article:

Mosher, Donald L., and Mark Sikin, "Measuring a Macho Personality Constellation," *Journal of Research in Personality,* vol. 18 (1984), pp. 150–163.

11. For a discussion of the measurement of rape myths, see the article that follows. In this and all such measuring instruments, the question of validity must be addressed. The reader may want to judge for himself or herself how well this instrument measures rape myths.

Burt, Martha R., "Cultural Myths and Supports for Rape," *Journal of Personality and Social Psychology,* vol. 38, no. 2 (1980), pp. 217–230.

12. Zillmann, Dolf, *Connections between Sex and Aggression.* Hillsdale, N.J.: Erlbaum, 1984, pp. 187–193.

13. Malamuth, Neil M., and James V.P. Check, "Debriefing Effectiveness Following Exposure to Pornographic Rape Depictions," *Journal of Sex Research,* vol. 21, no. 1 (February 1984), pp. 1-13.

Check, James V.P., and Neil M. Malamuth, "Can There Be Positive Effects of Participation in Pornography Experiments?" *Journal of Sex Research,* vol. 20, no. 1 (February 1984), pp. 14–31.

14. The terms *accident* and *essence* are concepts used by, among others, the ancient Greek philosopher Aristotle. The essence of something consists of that without which the thing would not be what it is, whereas the accidental properties

are those that can be altered and yet the thing remains the same. The essence of sexuality is its connection to physical pleasure and self-disclosure, while an accidental quality would be what clothing is considered sexually exciting. In erotica the essence is sexual excitement, while whether men control women in the films is but one of many accidental properties. For more on Aristotle's exact usage see

Edwards, Paul (ed.), *The Encylopedia of Philosophy,* vol. 1. New York: Macmillan, 1967.

15. Gebhard, Paul H., J.H. Gagnon, W.B. Pomeroy, and C.V. Christenson, *Sex Offenders: An Analysis of Types.* New York: Harper & Row, Pub., 1965.

16. Abel is a therapist with some unique data on rapists. He operates a clinic that guarantees anonymity to any sex offender who wishes to come in for treatment. Thus, he treats a wider range of rapists than would be found in a prison situation. For some insight into his work, I recommend the articles cited here:

Abel, Gene G., David H. Barlow, Edward B. Blanchard, and Donald Guild, "The Components of Rapists' Sexual Arousal," *Archives of General Psychiatry,* vol. 34 (August 1977), pp. 895-903.

Abel, Gene G., Judith V. Becker, Edward B. Blanchard, and Djenderedjian, "Differentiating Sexual Aggressives with Penile Measures," *Criminal Justice and Behavior,* vol. 5, no. 4 (December 1978), pp. 315-332.

Abel, Gene G., Judith V. Becker, William D. Murphy, and Barry Flanagan, "Identifying Dangerous Child Molesters," pp. 116-137 in R.B. Stuart (ed.), *Violent Behavior: Social Learning Approaches to Prediction, Management and Treatment.* New York: Brunner/Mazel, 1981.

17. The reader should be aware that some violent sexual films may *reduce* the likelihood of violence by showing the horror of sexual violence. One such film was "Salo" by Felini.

18. The National Commission on the Causes and Prevention of Violence was one of the early commissions dealing with the relation of mass media and crime. It indicated causal connections of media violence to real-life violence. The report led to psychologist Leonard Berkowitz's writing a controversial article in the early 1970s that inspired much of the recent research on violence.

19. For excellent reporting on abortion and contraception research examining their relationship to other variables, I suggest the reader browse through a recent year or two of the journal *Family Planning Perspectives.* I find it one of the best sources of this type of information available. For specific reports on the association of conservatism in general with attitudes toward abortion, see

Granberg, D., and B.W. Granberg, "Abortion Attitudes: 1965-1980: Trends and Determinants," *Family Planning Perspectives,* vol. 12 (September-October 1980), pp. 250-261.

Walfish, S., and M. Myerson, "Sex Role Identity and Attitudes toward Sexuality," *Archives of Sexual Behavior,* vol. 9 (June 1980), pp. 199-205.

Luker, Kristen, *Taking Chances: Abortion and the Decision Not to Contracept.* Berkeley: University of California Press, 1975.

Luker, Kristen, *Abortion and the Politics of Motherhood.* Berkeley: University of California Press, 1984.

20. *Los Angeles Times,* December 31, 1984. The ordinance was declared unconditional for being in violation of First Amendment rights by Judge Sarah Evans Barker on November 19, 1984. The case has been appealed by the City of Indianapolis.

21. Betty Friedan, "How to Get the Women's Movement Moving Again," *New York Times Magazine,* November 3, 1985, p. 26. See also the editorial in: *New Directions for Women,* (January-February 1985).

I testified regarding the scientific evidence on the proposed Minneapolis Ordinance on pornography in March 1984. That ordinance was vetoed by Mayor Fraser and was very similar to the Indianapolis Ordinance on which I later prepared an affidavit which incorporated the scientific evidence.

22. See page 13 of *New Directions for Women,* (January-February, 1985).
For a recent book criticing the censorship approach see Burstyn, Varda (ed.), *Women Against Censorship.* Vancouver: Douglas & McIntrye, 1985.

23. I use the term *subordination* in its common meaning of placing one group in a position of lesser worth in relation to another group.

24. The widely used concept of significant other is derived from
Mead, George Herbert, *Mind, Self and Society.* Chicago: University of Chicago Press, 1934.

25. There are several articles one could read by Kutchinsky. I will list just a few here:
Kutchinsky, Berl, "The Effect of Easy Availability of Pornography on the Incidence of Sex Crimes: The Danish Experience," *Journal of Social Issues,* vol. 29, no. 3 (1973), pp. 163-181.
Kutchinsky, Berl, "Eroticism without Censorship: Sociological Investigations on the Production and Consumption of Pornographic Literature in Denmark," *International Journal of Criminology and Penology,* vol. 1 (1973), pp. 217–225.
Kutchinsky, Berl, "Obscenity and Pornography: Behavioral Aspects" (In press).

26. The availability of hardcore commercial erotica in America does not show a clear correlation with rape rates. For example, rape rates doubled during the 1960s when only mild increases in available erotica were occurring. In the 1970s the rape rate increased considerably, but not as sharply as the dramatic increases in the availability of erotica.

Trends in rape rates are complicated by the fact that most rapes go unreported. In this connection, there has been a recent investigation of the relation between the proportion of rape that is reported and changes in gender-role equality. As gender roles have become more equal, women have been more willing to define as rape some types of physical force used by their dates. So, a good deal of the increase in rape rates in America may well be the result of such recognition by women that what was occurring on some of their dates was legally rape. A great deal of rape is precisely such date or acquaintance rape, and thus any change in willingness to report such events would seriously affect rape rates. See
Faison, Rebecca, and James D. Orcutt, "Trends in Sex Role Attitudes and Reporting of Rape Victimization, 1973–1980." Paper presented at the 1984 meeting of the Society for the Study of Social Problems in San Antonio, Texas.

These authors used "victimization" rates as evidence of the amount of rape that was actually occurring, whether or not it was reported. Victimization rates are estimated by interviewers asking about the occurrence of crimes that were not reported to the police. The reader may wish to look at some recent victimization reports.
U.S. Department of Justice, Bureau of Justice Statistics. *Criminal Victimization in the U.S., 1981: A National Crime Survey Report,* NCJ-90208. Washington, D.C., November 1983.
U.S. Departent of Justice, Bureau of Justice Statistics. *Report to the Nation on Crime and Justice: The Data,* NCJ-87068. Washington, D.C., October 1983.

27. Abramson, Paul R., and Haruo Hayashi, "Pornography in Japan: Cross-cultural and Theoretical Considerations," Chapter 6 in Neil M. Malamuth and Edward Donnerstein (eds.), *Pornography and Sexual Aggression.* Orlando, Fla.: Academic Press, 1984.

28. The comparative rape rates are given on pages 180–181 of the reference in note 27.

29. Weinberg, Thomas, and G.W. Levi Kamel (eds.), *S and M: Studies in Sadomasochism*. Buffalo: Prometheus Books, 1983.
I should note that in psychology it is learning theory that stresses external influences on people. Psychodynamic approaches stress inner drives. See Chapter I in: Bandura, Albert. *Aggression: A Social Learning Analysis*. Englewood Cliffs, N.J., Prentice-Hall, 1973.

30. Stephens, William N., "A Cross Cultural Study of Modesty," *Behavior Sciences Notes*, Vol. 1 (1972), pp. 1–28.

31. The Human Relations Area Files are the original files on cultures around the world founded by George Peter Murdock at Yale University during the 1930s. These files consist of index cards by topic for a few hundred cultures. It was out of this file that the Standard Sample eventually was developed.

32. It is enlightening to remember that even highly permissive cultures have fantasies about the availability of "total" sexual satisfaction. Malinowski reports on the Trobrianders' belief in an island inhabited by sexually insatiable women called Kaytalugi and an erotic paradise called Tuma where one's spirit goes after death.
Malinowski, Bronislaw, *The Sexual Life of Savages in N.W. Melanesia*. New York: Harvest Books, 1929. (See especially pp. 419–437.)

33. Many of the Pacific cultures like the Samoans, Tikopians, and Tiwi Islanders have low rape rates. For a very high rape society see
LeVine, R.A., "Gusii Sex Offenses: A Study in Social Control," *American Anthropologist*, vol. 61 (1959), pp. 965–990.

34. Sanday, Peggy Reeves, "The Socio-cultural Context of Rape: A Cross-cultural Study," *Journal of Social Issues*, vol. 37, no. 4 (1981), pp. 5–27.
Broude, Gwen J., and Sarah J. Greene, "Cross-cultural Codes on Twenty Sexual Attitudes and Practices," *Ethnology*, vol. 15 (October 1976), pp. 409–429.

35. Many writers on rape have rejected the extremism of Brownmiller's view that males are naturally programmed for rape. In addition to Sanday's study (cited in note 34), there is an interesting work by Julia and Herman Schwendinger. Julia Schwendinger was one of the founders of the first rape crisis center in America (Bay Area Women Against Rape, or BAWAR).
Schwendinger, Julia R., and Herman Schwendinger, *Rape and Inequality*. Beverly Hills, Calif.: Sage Publications, 1983. (See in particular Chapter 5.)
The original thesis by Brownmiller is contained in
Brownmiller, Susan, *Against Our Will*. New York: Simon & Schuster, 1975.

36. In connection with the ideas in Chapter 3, I examined the relationship of husband's sexual jealousy to violence and found it to be a significant positive relation. However, wife's sexual jealousy had no relation to violence in a culture. This supports the perspective that males have the power to enforce their desire to protect certain relationships.

37. A psychological analysis of the anger and power motives of rapists has been done by Groth. In addition, Prescott has done some cross-cultural work that is compatible in that it stresses that cultures that deprive people of physical affection (touching and sexuality) will be high on violent acts like rape. For these two presentations see
Groth, Nicholas A., *Men Who Rape: The Psychology of the Offender*. New York: Plenum Press, 1979.
Prescott, J.W., "Body Pleasure and the Origins of Violence," *Futurist* (March–April 1975), pp. 64–80.

38. Ross, Marc Howard, "Political Decision Making and Conflict: Additional Cross-cultural Codes and Scales," *Ethnology,* vol. 22 (April 1983), pp. 169–192.

39. The net or independent correlation of a variable is the correlation it displays to another variable when you keep all other possible causal variables constant. This procedure means that any correlation that was due to these other variables is removed and only the distinctive influence of this variable remains. Consult any statistics book on multiple correlation for further information and consult my Appendix A.

40. In Diagram 7.1 I used the machismo and rape measures from Sanday, the violence measure from Ross, and the belief in female inferiority measure from Whyte. Had I used the female status measure from Sanday, the results would be different. Her measure of female status did not show any significant relation to her measure of rape. Martin Whyte had criticized Sanday's female status measure. Since he spent his entire book on measuring female status, I chose to use one of his measures instead of Sanday's.

41. Another point on the relation of violence to rape in Sanday's data: If you simply do a correlation of these two variables, there is a significant relationship. However, if we simultaneously look at violence, female status and machismo (all from her data) as three influences on rape, the situation changes. The relation of violence to rape then becomes much weaker. See Appendix A for more details.

Relevant to this point is the work by Baron and Straus. Using a 50 state analysis they also failed to find a significant correlation between violence rates and rape rates. We often tend to assume that two disliked factors will be related but it seems questionable in this case. We need to avoid prejudging such possible relationships and instead study them carefully. See note 7 for reference to the Baron and Straus study.

42. Langevin, Ron (ed.), *Erotic Preference, Gender Identity, and Aggression in Men: New Research Studies.* Hillsdale, N.J.: Erlbaum, 1985. (See especially Chapters 1 and 2.)

Langevin, Ron, *Sexual Strands: Understanding and Treating Sexual Anomalies in men.* Hillsdale, N.J.: Erlbaum, 1983. (See especially Chapter 12.)

43. Mosher's new conceptualization is referenced in note 10.

44. The Glossary in this book defines body-centered and other terms. I first used and explained body-centered and person-centered sexuality in:

Reiss, Ira L., "The Treatment of Premarital Coitus in Marriage and Family Texts," *Social Problems,* vol. 4, no. 4 (April 1957), pp. 334–338.

45. Females stress affection in their premarital standards. I conceptualize premarital sexual standards into four categories: (1) the double standard, (2) permissiveness with affection, (3) permissiveness with and/or without affection, and (4) abstinence. Standards 2, 3, and 4 are single standards; that is, their rights and duties apply equally to males and females. For example, permissiveness with affection affirms the acceptability of coitus when either a male or female is involved in a stable, affectionate relationship. Females endorse this standard the most, whereas males are more likely to accept the permissiveness with or without affection standard. For a full explanation see

Reiss, Ira L., *Premarital Sexual Standards in America.* New York: Free Press, 1960.

Reiss, Ira L., *The Social Content of Premarital Sexual Permissiveness.* New York: Rinehart & Winston, 1967.

46. This difference between male and female homosexuals has been reported in many studies. See my discussion in Chapter 6. In addition, I recommend the

following two sources for those who wish to read more about such male and female differences:

Saghir, M.T., and Robins E., *Male and Female Homosexuality: A Comprehensive Investigation.* Baltimore: William & Wilkins, 1973.

Blumstein, Philip, and Pepper Schwartz, *American Couples.* New York: Morrow, 1983.

47. The erotic romantic novel is estimated to have 20 million women readers in America. According to Coles and Shamp, the basic theme is of an older man who takes advantage of a young woman's love for him and sexually abuses her. Later he falls in love with her, and then she leaves him. It is interesting to note how little we ever think about female erotica. Our cultural view of female and male roles make the male the sexual initiator, and thus we focus on his erotica and often fail to conceptualize female forms of erotica. For an interesting analysis of female erotica see

Coles, Claire, and M. Johanna Shamp,"Some Sexual, Personality, and Demographic Characteristics of Women Readers of Erotic Romances," *Archives of Sexual Behaviors,* vol. 13, no. 3 (1984), pp. 187–209.

48. This significant piece of research is reported in

Garcia, Luis T., K. Brennan, M. DeCarlo, R. McGlennon and S. Tait, "Sex Differences in Sexual Arousal to Different Erotic Stories," *Journal of Sex Research,* vol. 20, no. 4 (November 1984), pp. 391–402.

49. There are several popular books on erotic fantasies of men and women. Nancy Friday has written some such books, but they are journalistic and for a mass audience. There also has been some scientific work on fantasy. I suggest starting with the following works:

Barbach, L.G., and L. Levine, *Shared Intimacies: Women's Sexual Experiences.* New York: Anchor Press, 1980.

Hariton, B.E., et al., "Women's Fantasies during Intercourse: Normative and Theoretical Implications," *Journal of Consulting Clinical Psychology,* vol. 42 (June 1974), pp. 313–322.

Pickard, Christine, "A Perspective on Female Responses to Sexual Material," Chapter 6 in Maurice Yaffe and Edward C. Nelson (eds.), *The Influence of Pornography on Behaviour.* London: Academic Press, 1982.

50. For an insightful account of the ambivalence women feel about oral sexuality, see

Blumstein, Philip, and Pepper Schwartz, *American Couples,* pp. 231–237. New York: Morrow, 1983.

51. Sartre, a twentieth century French philosopher, stressed the surrender of independence involved in a sexual encounter. He suggested that sexuality turns each person into a lust-controlled object of the other. Ultimately, Sartre felt, sexuality was aimed at nothing less than a total control over the other person's freedom by trapping that person in his or her own lustful desires. Clearly, this thesis stresses the power element in sexuality.

Stoller, an analyst, puts his views on this point as follows:

Sadomasochism is, I think, a central feature of most sexual excitement. My hunch is that the desire to hurt others in retaliation for having been hurt is essential for most people's sexual excitement all the time but not for all people's excitement all the time .... the dynamics of sexual excitement, which unfortunately express for most people the theme of harming one's erotic object in order to get revenge or otherwise undo painful experiences from infancy on. (Stoller, 1979: pp. 113, 220)

I think both these writers are more curious about the personality system than the social system. Their understanding of sexuality is quite different from mine. I would stress, as the key source of the power element in sexuality, the gender-role conceptions in a society and the sexual scripts they orchestrate. In sexual encounters a person may well be acting out the power dimension of his or her gender role or seeking to compensate in fantasy for some aspect of that gender role. Yet Sartre and Stoller stress conscious and unconscious personality needs as the source of the power element in sexuality. For my interest, they ignore too much of the societal setting in which such psychological elements obtain their essential meaning. Nonetheless, these authors are still well worth reading, for even I will admit that there is more in the world than what sociologists think about. I will also cite a philosophical and historical approach to sexuality by Foucault. I must admit however, that I found it most difficult to follow the argumentation of Foucault.

Sartre, Jean-Paul, Being and Nothingness (Trans. Hazel Barnes). New York: Philosophical Library, 1956. (See especially pp. 379–412.)

Stoller, Robert J., *Sexual Excitement: Dynamics of Erotic Life.* New York: Simon & Schuster, 1979.

Foucault, Michael, *History of Sexuality: Volume One: An Introduction.* New York: Vintage, 1980.

52. Neil Malamuth is closely identified with research into the arousal produced by various presentations of aggression against women. See the following for a recent summary:

Malamuth, Neil M., "Aggression against Women: Cultural and Individual Causes," Chapter 1 in Neil M. Malamuth and Edward Donnerstein *(eds.), Pornography and Sexual Aggression.* Orlando, Fla.: Academic Press, 1984.

53. There are some new sources that view sadomasochistic behavior in terms of its social dimensions and lifestyle activities instead of in terms of its unconscious psychological meaning. For such a view see

Weinberg, Thomas, and G.W. Levi Kamel (eds.), *S and M: Studies in Sadomasochism.* Buffalo: Prometheus Books, 1983.

54. Langevin, Ron (ed.), *Erotic Preference, Gender Identity and Aggression in Men: New Research Studies.* Hillsdale, N.J.: Erlbaum, 1983.

Langevin, Ron, *Sexual Strands: Understanding and Treating Sexual Anomalies in Men.* Hillsdale, N.J.: Erlbaum, 1983 (see Chapter 4).

55. Rimmer, Robert H., *The X-Rated Videotape Guide.* New York: Arlington House, 1984 (see especially Chapters 1, 2, and 3).

There are several women making erotica movies for women. For example, look at the movies of Candida Royal and Steffani Martin-Landis. The latter recently sponsored the first New York Women's Erotic Film Festival.

CHAPTER EIGHT

A SOCIOLOGICAL THEORY OF HUMAN SEXUALITY

SOCIOLOGY: A SINGULAR PERSPECTIVE

The reader can start to relax now. We are nearing the end of our journey. We have one final task: to integrate and specify, as best we can, the sociological explanation of human sexuality developed in this book. To be sure, this is no mean task. But it is essential to present succinctly an overview of the key features of my theoretical position. Although at this stage in our theoretical development there will of necessity be many gaps, it is still crucial to leave the reader with as clear a perspective as possible concerning the sociological explanation of human sexuality developed in this book. The ground must be prepared for future theoretical growth.

I will seek to accomplish this goal in three phases. First, I will present briefly three basic assumptions that underlie my sociological approach. Secondly, I will relate in narrative form the sociological theory of sexuality that I have developed. This will be an informal, discursive presentation. I will conclude this section with a summary diagram revealing the broad overview of the key elements involved in this sociological explanation. This narrative account will be divided into four sections relevant to the three linkage areas and to social change.

The third phase consists of a more precise, formal presentation of the same explanatory schema in the format of 25 explanatory propositions. These propositions will contain the bulk of the reasoning and empirical relationships that are derivable from the narrative account of my sociological theory. I will organize these 25 propositions into the same four major divisions as were present in the narrative account. Each of these four propositional sets will contain interrelated propositions.

By following this mode of increasingly specific explanation, I mean to satisfy the curiosity of the more general rather as well as that of the more specific professional.

BASIC ASSUMPTIONS UNDERLYING THE PROPOSITIONS

All theoretical explanations are based upon certain, often unspoken, assumptions about the world in which we live. My theoretical approach is no exception. Most of these assumptions have been mentioned at least briefly, but it is useful to group them together in one place.

Assumption One

I assume that the scientific approach is one way to understand social reality. This does not rule out the possibility of religious or other philosophical approaches to reality. Rather, it asserts that I am founding my explanation in the scientific realm. By science I mean systematized knowledge based upon observation and experimentation that is directed toward explaining and predicting the phenomenon studied. Accordingly, it is assumed here that there is an objective reality that can be scientifically explained. The epigraph to this book clearly states my view on this matter. Lest you think this is an incontestable assumption, recall that philosophers have debated this very point for centuries despite the fact that most Westerners fully accept this assumption.

Assumption Two

I accept a modified hedonistic view of human behavior. I assume that all human behavior is motivated by the pursuit of pleasure and the avoidance of pain. The important point here is that all behavior is self-oriented. However, I modify the more radical hedonistic perspective by asserting that people's selves vary in the degree to which they incorporate the welfare of others as a source of pleasure and pain. Social life is based upon our ability to internalize the welfare of others to the point that we feel rewarded when they are rewarded. It is by such absorption of others into ourselves that the boundaries separating people are partially removed. Our most important social relationships attempt to unite people in just this way. Most of us learn in our sexual behavior to incorporate at least partially the pleasures of others as our own pleasures. Even so, it is in good part our basic nature as creatures who pursue self-oriented pleasures of all sorts that makes sexuality so important to us.

Assumption Three

I assume that societal-level causes are major influences on our sexual life-styles. I further assume that factors such as biological and psychological causes are central when comparing individuals but not of first importance when comparing societies. For example, there is no a priori reason to presume that one society is different from another in the biological makeup of its population. Thus, I conclude that among societies, differences in sexuality will be due to sociological forces. Hence, in the examination of lifestyles of societies or groups, sociology is clearly central to any explanation.

I am sure that I must be making other philosophical assumptions, but the three stated here are the most obvious ones that underlie my sociological explanation of sexuality.

A NARRATIVE STATEMENT OF THE THEORY

Sexual Bonding:
Antecedents of Kinship and Gender

Once I asserted the sociological or societal level as the chosen level of explanation I needed to formulate a clear definition of sexuality from that perspec-tive. I defined sexuality as consisting of those shared cultural scripts that are designed to produce erotic arousal that in turn will produce genital response. The idea behind this definition is not just that sexuality is learned but that it is learned from the societal scripting of the erotic life of individuals.

Here and throughout the book I am searching for broad, universally valid definitions, concepts, and explanations. It is equally important, though, to explain the variation regarding how societies operate within these universal parameters. I have used, among other things, my causal analyses of the Standard Sample in various chapters to help in arriving at explanations of such societal variations.

I further explained human sexuality by proposing that for all societies genital response most often leads to significant levels of physical pleasure and self-dis-closure. These two consequences give sexuality importance in all societies regardless of the level of socially acceptable sexual permissiveness. This importance stems from the interpersonal-bonding potential produced by the pleasure and disclosure characteristics of sexuality. All societies judge interpersonal bonding to be impor-tant, for such bonding is the structural foundation of a society. Societies organize the bonding power of sexuality so as to enhance socially desired relationships and avoid socially undesired relationships.

To illustrate: sexual bonding is encouraged in marital relations that tie together individuals from different social groups, whereas sexual bonding is dis-couraged in parent-child relationships to avoid role conflict and jealousy and also to encourage young people to seek mates from other groups and thereby build alliances that can be helpful.[1] In the extramarital area, some societies stress the pleasure aspects of sexuality in order to keep self-disclosure to a minimum and thereby discourage any stable, personal bonding outside of marriage.[2] In some societies, like the Sambia, homosexuality is encouraged as part of a desired male-bonding process and a preparation for heterosexuality. Only a few societies attempt to discourage sexuality in all settings outside of marriage. Not so long ago, the United States was one of those societies.

The rudimentary forms of kinship can be viewed as deriving from and being supported by the sexual bonding of individuals who nurture offspring. The socially defined descent relationship between children and parents can be seen as an out-come of a stable sexual relationship between the parents. In that sense, the tie to the offspring develops from those who remain to socialize the child. Those stable adults would most often include the biological mother of the child and also her mate. It is the stable sexual bonding of the parents that I conceptualize as the social support network into which the newborn child is placed. Stability does not necessi-tate a life time but it does imply a number of years. Other adults, such as the mother's brother or the mother's mother, may be very important once the produc-tion of children begins, but it is the presence of a stable sexual mate that establishes the relationship basis for the start of parenthood.

The reader will recall that I do not view the importance of the sexual relation-ship as reducible simply to its reproductive consequences. In fact, I have stressed the greater importance of the consequences of physical pleasure and self-disclosure. Sexuality can bond and will be judged as important even when there are not any reproductive consequences. Surely homosexuality has bonding power without reproductive outcomes. It is the potential of sexuality to create lasting human relationships that makes it likely that couples will stay together long enough to produce and nurture a newborn. The pleasure and disclosure aspects of sexuality can act as a catalyst to the development of increasing self-disclosures regarding shared nonsexual pleasures that can further create a stable bond. In that sense the bonding nature of sexuality leads to its high valuation and to the possibility of reproduction occurring and conventional kinship ties developing. In this fashion, sexual bonding helps creates the support system needed for the newborn to survive.

As the kinship system with its generational ties develops, gender roles also are formed. In order to accomplish the nurturance of the newborn and maintain the satisfying bonds derived from the sexual relationship, some pattern of task assign-ment for male and female must be developed. It is through this process of the social assignment of task and power relationships that the rudiments of societal gender roles are hypothesized to be formed.

Sexuality and the Power of Each Gender

One outcome of this desire to maintain important sexual bonds is the linkage of sexuality in marriage to power and jealousy. The ability to control sexuality depends on one's power. Power, in turn, depends on one's role in the major insti-tutions: the political, religious, family, and economic institutions. The specific roles in the family assigned to males and females can define the degree of freedom each gender has to participate in other institutional roles and thereby restrict or expand that gender's potential societal power. In effect, the societal sculpturing of gender roles that centers females more than males in the family institution is the key basis of the lesser power females are given in virtually all the other societal institutions. Nevertheless, we should not lose sight of the power inherent in kinship ties themselves. The greater the kin ties for women, the less likely that women will be sexually abused. This is so because the woman's kin will offer unified protection against such abuse. This can be noted particularly in matrilineal societies.

Power influences access to the important sexual possibilities in a society. Power legitimates access to whatever pleasures of life are present in that culture. Thus, the greater the power of one gender, the greater that gender's sexual rights in that society. These greater sexual rights of men may show up in the increased likelihood of sexual abuse of women. In addition, the powerful have more ability to organize gender roles in ways that further stabilize their power in the basic institutions. This has typically been accomplished by encouraging men to participate more in the political and economic systems and women more in the family system. In addition, male power in other institutions may flow over into the kinship roles and strengthen their influence even in marital and family relationships.

Sexuality and Ideology

As a society stabilizes its institutional structure, it will develop a set of deeply rooted beliefs about the nature of human beings. These beliefs are the logical foundations of more specific notions of good and bad, normal and abnormal. These firmly held beliefs about human nature are what we have called ideologies. Such ideologies will have relevance to all the major institutions in a society and to all important relationships, including, of course, sexual relationships. Thus, sexuality will have an ideological base deriving from its ideological linkages in society. The basic dimensions of sexual ideologies revolve about levels of gender equality and sexual permissiveness. These are the two basic issues that men and women face everywhere in their sexual relationships; that is, how equal will the relationship be, and how much sexual permissiveness will each gender be allowed. Differences in sexual ideology and in power are linked to different attitudes toward erotica. In this sense, attitudes toward erotica are linked to one's position in a social system.

Heterosexuality and homosexuality are interdependent in that one is defined in terms of the other. Homosexuality can be defined as another acceptable part of sexuality that is integrated with the kinship and gender concepts of the society, or it can be defind as a competitive pathway that must be guarded against. Contrast the Sambia and the United States to visualize these two alternatives. In both cases, homosexuality and heterosexuality are defined in terms of each other, but with quite different resolutions.

The centrality of heterosexuality in human societies is directly derivable from its linkages with kinship and gender roles. Acceptable sexual behavior, whether it be homosexual or heterosexual, is fundamentally defined in terms of its degree of compatibility wth the basic kinship and gender conceptions of a society.

Social Change and Societal Linkages

In sum, then, the universal linkages of sexuality in society occur in the areas of kinship, power, and ideology. As noted, in kinship, the linkages to sexuality will be found in the jealousy mechanisms protecting sexual bonding in marriage. In the power area the crucial sexual linkages are to gender roles. Such gender roles are seen as developing out of the kinship structure, which in turn was derived from sexual bonding. Finally, the specific ideological areas involving sexuality will concern notions of normality centering upon equality and permissiveness, for those issues are central in kinship and gender relationships. *So the linkages of sexuality to kinship, power, and ideology are here specified as being ties to marital jealousy, gender roles, and concepts of sexual normality.* It is important to be explicit here because kinship, power, and ideology are broad aspects of society, and it is well to be more precise regarding exactly where the linkages to sexuality will be found. It is by means of an examination of these universal linkage areas that the specific explanations of sexuality are derived. Through these explanations we can understand the variations that occur in these linkage areas in different societies.

The kinship, power, and ideology linkages of sexuality are, of course, causally tied to other important parts of the social system. In particular, the economic institution, consisting of the type of subsistence (hunting, agriculture, industry), is influential in terms of change. This is so because the economic institution is viewed in rational terms as a means to the end of providing subsistence. Accordingly, societies are often willing to change the economic system if new subsistence opportunities present themselves. Change is not quite as easy in the political, religious, and family institutions.[3]

I do not deny that the causal relationship between parts of the society may be a two-way relationship and that this eventually needs to be carefully examined. This is so, even though most of my diagrams and other parts of my explanation have been presented as predominantly one-way processes. I do believe, however, that the direction I have posited is the most powerful. However, that does not deny the possibility of a reverse influence of a more minor sort in at least some areas. The relative power of each causal direction is a matter for empirical study. Changes in kinship can influence the economic or political institution, as well as vice versa. Further, despite my view that the economic institution is the most flexible, the relative importance for change of any one institution in a society is an empirical question that needs to be investigated for each major social change. In the specific propositions presented in the next section, four are explicitly put forth as bidirectional (propositions 16, 17, 24, and 25).

It is not possible to present a precise overview of my explanation in one diagram. However, it may be helpful for the reader to examine an abstract graphic portrayal of my overall sociological perspective in Diagram 8.1.

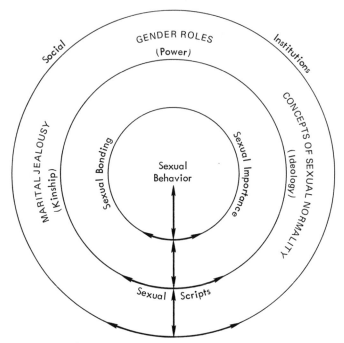

DIAGRAM 8.1 Sociological overview of human sexuality.

This diagram basically asserts that sexual behavior, due to its bonding qualities, acquires social importance and thereby becomes linked in specific ways with
kinship, power, and ideology, all of which shapes our sexual scripts and is, in turn,
linked to the basic social institutions in a society. As the arrows on the diagram
indicate, all the causal relationships in one circle and among circles potentially flow
both ways. Thus, a change in the economic or political system can affect the type
of power roles given to each gender, and that may affect the sexual scripts and
thereby alter sexual behaviors. This diagram is no substitute for the specific theoretical statements that follow. Still, the diagram orients one's thinking in a sociological
direction. It represents the broad theoretical space into which the specific propositions will be placed in the next section of this chapter.

THE PROPOSITIONAL STRUCTURE OF THE THEORY

Now I will list particular explanatory statements (propositions) organized within
the four areas that I have discussed in the preceding narrative statement of my
theoretical position. The initial statements in each set are the broader "premises,"
or the logical bases, for other statements that follow. Accordingly, many of the
statements are logically related to each other. Presenting the propositions in this
more precise form, should make the theoretical structure I am building more
apparent and should better serve as a basis for future theorizing and research.

Propositions on Sexual Bonding
as the Antecedent of Kinship and Gender roles

1. Societies judge stable social relationships as of great importance.
2. Societies view physical pleasure and self-disclosure as the building blocks of stable social relationships.
3. Physical pleasure and self-disclosure are the common outcomes of sexual behavior.
4. Therefore, sexual behavior will be seen as important due to its ability to promote stable relationships.
5. Such stable bonding between genetic males and females produces a context for the nurturance of offspring.
6. Stable heterosexual relationships are the rudimentary bases for husband-wife and parent-child roles; and thus, in this sense, kinship and gender roles are derivative from the bonding properties of sexual relationships.
7. Important social relationships are culturally defined in ways that are intended to institutionalize protective mechanisms.
8. Therefore, marital sexuality will involve jealousy norms concerning the ways, if any, to negotiate extramarital sexual access without disturbing the existing marriage relationship.

The presentation of these eight propositions in statement form should help the reader grasp the logical interrelations that exist among these propositions. Some of the propositions are clearly derivative from the proposition or propositions immediately preceeding them, and for those I have inserted the word *therefore* in the statement of the proposition. Consider proposition 4: The first three propositions imply proposition 4. Propositions 1 and 2 assert that stable social relationships are valued and that physical pleasure and self-disclosure are two important ways to promote such stability. Statement 3 then affirms that sexual behavior leads to physical pleasure and self-disclosure, which we have already asserted promotes stable relationships. It then follows that sexual behavior will be viewed as important because of its potential role in the maintenance of long-term relationships.

Reflect upon proposition 8. It logically follows from proposition 7. If the importance of a relationship determines the protection it receives, then it follows that since marital sexuality is everywhere highly valued, it will receive protection in the form of jealousy customs. In cultures where marital sexuality is most highly valued, that protection will be at its apogee, but it will be present in considerable amount in all cultures. Proposition 8 is a specific application of the more general assertion made in proposition 7.

Propositions on Sexuality
and the Power of Each Gender

9. The authorized power of a group is basically utilized to obtain valued social goals.

10. Therefore, since sexuality is a valued social goal, as a group gains power there will be increased sexual privileges in that group's sexual scripts, its erotica, and its ability to avoid sexual abuse.
11. A group's overall prestige in a society is in good part derived from its power in the major social institutions.
12. Common residence of a group increases the feelings of solidarity and, relatedly, the power of that group.
13. Therefore, the gender whose descent group reside together will achieve more power than other genders and its members will experience less sexual abuse.
14. The greater the use of specialists in the major social institutions, the greater the difficulty in participating fully in more than one institution.
15. Thus, the greater tie of the female to the nurturance of the newborn, the greater the limits on her participation in nonfamily institutions and the lower her social power in those institutions vis-à-vis males.[4]

Once again the propositions beginning with the word *therefore* (10, 13, and 15) are special cases of the more general proposition that precedes them. In proposition 15 we have an example of how institutional specialization in the family lowers the power that type of person is likely to have in other institutions. Thus, proposition 15 is a specific instance of what the more general proposition 14 states. Scientific explanation expands by means of just such logically derivative propositions as propositions 10, 13, and 15. If empirical testing shows that a logically deduced proposition such as proposition 10, 13, or 15 is empirically supported, then one has more confidence in the general propositions from which they were derived.

Propositions on Ideology and Sexuality

16. Ideologies reflect and reinforce the social values operative in each of the major institutions.
17. Therefore, to the extent that a gender's dominance is structured into the operant values of the basic institutions, ideologies will support the greater power of that gender and assign it greater rights in those institutional areas.
18. General ideologies of a culture will be productive of specific sexual ideologies that reflect compatible ideological assumptions.
19. Therefore, in a culture where one gender is dominant in the general ideology, that gender will be granted greater sexual privileges incorporated in that culture's sexual ideology and in the sexual scripts and erotica preferences of each gender.
20. Homosexual and heterosexual behaviors will each be accepted to the degree that the society defines them as integrative with the basic gender characteristics in the accepted ideologies.
21. The more rigid and narrow the gender ideology, the greater the nonconformity to the sexual aspects of such a gender role.

One value of specifically stating these propositions is that we can discern more precisely what variables one needs to measure and what the specific nature of the proposed relationship is like (positive or negative; one-way or two-way). Ultimately, such explicit propositions make it possible to interrelate propositions that have the same variable in common or are logically related in other ways.

Propositions on Social Change and Sexuality

22. That institution that stresses flexibility the most will be the most likely to initiate change in other basic institutions.
23. Therefore, since the economic institution is the most flexible, economic changes will be a key catalyst for changes in society.
24. Changes in economic or other nonkinship institutions have a feedback (two-way) causal relationship with changes in marital jealousy, gender roles, and sexual ideologies.
25. Changes in marital jealousy. gender roles, and sexual ideologies have a feedback causal relation with changes in sexual behavior.[5].

Each of these 25 propositions can be presented in terms of individual diagrams. I have composed a first approximation of such diagrams for those who are interested and placed them in Appendix B. For the general reader, the diagramatic representation of each proposition is not needed and therefore is not covered here.

THE PROPOSITIONS:
THEIR UNITY AND DERIVATION

Although far from fully spelled out there are logical interrelationships that tie together all four sets of propositions.[6] In one sentence: *The importance of sexuality in human relationships is the basis for the boundaries placed upon sexuality and for those in power seeking sexual rights that become part of the ideologies and the elements in any social change in sexual customs.* Thus, there is a comprehensive logical and empirical unity to these propositions. It will take much additional theorizing and research to clear away more of the conceptual underbrush and define more precisely the various interstices. Nevertheless, I will make a start in that process here.

Each of the four theoretical areas starts with broad general propositions. I have noted that those propositions are the premise or the logical starting point for some other propositions in that set which relate more specifically to sexuality.[7] In this fashion I hope to afford the reader a more coherent grasp of how the specific propositions on sexuality fit into the context of other, more general sociological propositions.

Many of the propositions were inductively arrived at after the reading and research I did for this book. Others were deduced from more general propositions. I could have logically elaborated these propositions, stated them more formally, and thereby created a much larger number of them.[8] But they are sufficient in number and in formality for my purposes of establishing the foundation of a basic sociological explanation of human sexuality. Nevertheless, the reader should be aware that there are other propositions that can be deduced from these and that other sociological propositions exist with which these 25 propositions can be interrelated.

One value of presenting my theoretical position in the format of logically interrelated sets of testable propositions is that it delineates the structure of the explanation being proposed and makes testing and elaboration that much easier. Each proposition is offered with the *ceteris paribus* qualification, that is, the assumption is that all else is equal. Thus, equally powerful groups should have equal access to sexuality (proposition 10) but if one of the powerful groups consists of monks who have taken an oath of chastity they will not fit that proposition so well. In such a case, all else is clearly not equal.

There are interrelationships of the propositions across the four separate sets that the reader can logically derive. Proposition 10, for example, asserts that group power relates to the sexual rights of that group. If so then group power ought to relate to the protective jealousy customs discussed in propositon 8. Additionally, proposition 10 is logically related to proposition 4. This is so because it is the importance of sexuality that makes those in power seek sexual rights. Propositions 17 and 11 both concern the influence of a group in the basic institutions and thus are interrelated through that common focus. These are but a few of the points at which the propositions in any one set logically and empirically relate to those in the other three sets. I leave it to others to tease out further the possible interrelationship among these four sets of propositions. This is one direction for future theoretical work to pursue and thereby extend and elaborate the web of propositions in this sociological explanation.[9]

These 25 propositions comprise the basic logical and propositional structure of my theory. Nevertheless, they are not all inclusive of the ideas put forth in this book. I have sought to minimize complexity and have left out some specific explanatory ideas that do not easily relate to these sets of propositions. Other propositions are logically implied by these propositions but they are not explicitly stated. To illustrate, proposition 10 asserts that the powerful will have less sexual restraints. From this general statement we can deduce that if anyone is going to be restricted from body centered sexuality it will be the less powerful. Since women are generally less powerful than men, we can further conclude that they will be more restricted from such body centered sexuality. Note that this deduction is in accord with tenet 2 of the nonequalitarian sexual ideology.

In the five causal diagrams in this book I have presented some specific empirical tests based upon analysis of the Standard Sample which are relevant to several of these propositions.[10] A good number of the 25 propositions stated in this chapter were partially derived from an examination of those causal diagrams. Rather than burden the reader here with the detailed derivations I include my comments about them in the Selected References and Comments section at the end of this chapter.[11]

I will mention here that I did not take each concrete two variable correlation in the causal diagrams and make it into one of my propositions. Instead I sought to make the propositions somewhat more abstract and general and more easily related to general sociological propositions. There is a clear theoretical advantage to a proposition having greater scope of applicability. But my major reason for being more abstract was that I wanted the propositions to represent those more general relationships which I had logically derived *after* contemplating the theoretical implications of the findings in each diagram. I felt that was preferable to simply accepting every specific correlation between two concrete variables as a separate proposition. Given the limitations of the available data, it seemed wiser not to just literally accept all correlations in every diagram at face value.

Finally, I should add that the propositions are far from being simply based on the five causal diagrams. They derive largely from general sociological theory, from other cited sources on industrial and nonindustrial societies, from logical fit with a prior theoretical position, and from my general theoretical intuition. There surely is a personal, almost esthetic aspect to any theory. Fortunately, this is all subject to future testing, verification and alteration by myself as well as others.

There is always the possibility of someone developing a different theoretical explanation that more parsimoniously explains the same reasoning and empirical findings using different propositions than mine. Science is the tentative possession of partial truths. When you are certain you have the final explanation you have departed from the scientific realm. I encourage others to present their alternative or additional propositions.[12]

Some specific concepts beg for elaboration. Propositions 9 to 15 all deal with power, and some of the ideology propositions (17 and 19) also relate to power. Surely, then, there is a pressing need for a more developed theory of social power than that presented in this book. Power was a major causal variable in many of my explanations. A more formalized theory of social power would allow for more precise formulation and testing of the many propositions relating power to sexuality. The concept of normality is another crucial area begging for further clarification. I have commented upon the need for other conceptual clarifications elsewhere in this book. Our theories are only as clear as our concepts, and therefore conceptual clarification is a most strategic area for future work.

I believe that my propositions specify the major sources of the societal determinants of our sexual customs. In addition to simply pointing to kinship, power, and ideology as universal linkages, we have traveled some distance in showing how specific segments of these linkages interrelate with each other. More than that, this sociological theory allows us to explain variation in the ways these universal linkages operate in different societies and to account for changes in them. That is, we can state the conditions under which jealousy will be stronger (proposition 7 and 8 and others) or female power stronger (propositions 13 to 17 and others). Accordingly, we can predict what specific alterations in a society would affect sexual life-style outcomes. If you carefully read over these propositions, you will become more aware of their potential for explaining variation in sexual customs in present societies.

I have mentioned that the Standard Sample is but one source of these propositions. A great deal of other data and ethnographic accounts were consulted, and modern industrial societies were examined as well as other types. I do believe that these 25 propositions apply to all types of societies and to a variety of sexual areas. To illustrate, they can be used to analyze premarital sexuality in America. Does proposition 7, concerning protective mechanisms, apply to premarital sexual relationships? Surely premarital sexuality has jealousy-provoking situations—particularly in important stable sexual relationships. It would be necessary to specify more precisely the conditions that maximize such an outcome, but the proposition does seem generally applicable. Likewise, the propositions on power and gender (propositions 9 to 15) could be checked to see if our premarital sexual customs also reflect gender power differentials. I suspect that there is generally less of a gender gap in power in the premarital period than in the marital period. We could develop specific propositions to explain this.

We know that unmarried people share the tenets of our sexual ideologies (see Chapter 5), and so we assume that our general ideology influences our sexual ideology as asserted in proposition 18. The specific differences in sexual standards premaritally as compared to extramaritally could be explored. Finally, the role of economic factors in the rapid changes in premarital sexuality in the 1965-1975 decade can be explored to see if it is compatible with propositions 22 to 25. Does, for example, the increased ability of women to earn income contribute to their greater interpersonal power in ways compatible with propositions 15 and 24? Overall, my judgment is that the evidence would support the explanatory power of these propositions for premarital sexuality in America and would lead us toward the development of additional and more specific propositions. Specification and elaborations of precisely this sort are what is needed to develop further the social applicability for this explanation of sexuality.[13]

Clearly, there are many loose theoretical threads that demand further examination. My goal is, not closure of the theoretical search for a societal-level explanation, but the opening up of this exciting endeavor. I present you here with a rough map that contains some of the explanatory keys related to human sexuality. I hope this will lure many of you to set forth and refine this map and further unearth the treasure that lies within.

CODA

This has been a five-year journey for me—one of the most complex I have ever taken in my academic career. By the same token, it has been one of the most satisfying. In a sense, the denser the jungle, the greater the pleasure in finding your way out. When I started on this project I surely could not have predicted the theoretical form this book has taken. The joy I am now experiencing comes from the knowledge that I was able to progress toward the goal of understanding how human sexuality is knit into the social fabric.[14]

I have made it clear that in terms of developing a scientific explanation of human sexuality, each science is at its best when it, to paraphrase Voltaire, tends to its own garden.[15] All sciences have had generations in which to develop their methodology, their particular theoretical explanations, their techniques of analysis, and their central explanatory concepts. If one tries to combine theoretically all the major scientific disciplines that study sexuality, then each area loses some of this knowledge and expertise that has been developed over many years. I know of no individual who can keep up with everything in even one of these disciplines, let alone in all of them. What we often end up with in multidisciplinary scientific theorizing is a watering down of all the fields that are combined.[16]

On the other hand, I am not proposing that other fields have no value for a sociological or societal-level explanation of sexuality. I certainly have used knowledge from psychology and biology in this book. But I have used knowledge from these fields only when it has thrown additional light on the development of a distinctive sociological explanation. Most importantly, the major sexual differences that appear across cultures and within one culture across time evidence that there is a great deal that requires a special societal-level explanation. I have focused my energy on developing just such sociological explanations.

Even so, I would not object to an attempt by others to integrate the specific scientific explanations from psychology and biology with my sociological approach. However, I would also not hold out much hope for a successful outcome because at this stage in our scientific understanding of human sexuality each science has too little to offer toward such an integrated perspective. Perhaps when each of the various sciences concerned with sexuality has a deeper understanding of human sexuality, we may more profitably combine our explanatory schemas. The sociological explanation is the newest and is therefore the most in need of domestic nurturance before it seeks to mate with other explanatory schemas. Even then, I am not at all convinced that viable "offspring" will be possible from such unions.

Despite my emphasis on specialization for those doing research and theory work I particularly do not want to discourage the use of materials from other disciplines by those in applied professional fields in education, social work, and therapy. I think that therapists dealing with sexual problems can learn much about the possible place that kinship, power, and ideology may have in the problems their patients or clients present to them. Having a broad cross-cultural approach can be very useful to a therapist—as I have noted in my discussion of normality in Chapter Five. In addition, the therapist or sex educator will benefit by knowing the research and theory coming out of biology and psychology. Therapists can find much in such knowledge that will inform their work with clients and patients.

Nevertheless, in applied fields like therapy, as in the basic sciences, I do not think this knowledge will be the building stones of a theory of effective therapy. A theory concerning therapy must be built on the expertise of the professionals in that field. Other fields are helpful in interpreting some of the problems brought by patients and in suggesting which therapeutic techniques will work best. That is undoubtedly of considerable value. It is still the case however, that the essential ingredients of a therapeutic approach are built predominantly upon the expertise of the therapist qua therapist. Therefore, although I would strongly encourage the seeking of multidisciplinary knowledge by practitioners, I would not encourage a search for an integrated multidisciplinary explanation of sexual therapy. A theory about sexual therapy explains therapy and not sexuality.

As I mentioned in the opening chapters, science does not seek to define nor explain total reality. Philosophy deals with such imponderables. Each science specializes both in the substance of interest and in the level of analysis utilized. As further evidence of the value of such a specialized approach, I would point out that it has been just such single disciplinary work that comprises the bulk of the research and theory contribution made in this century to the study of human sexuality.[17]

Given my focus upon sociology, one may justifiably ask why I have relied so heavily on anthropological studies. Cultural anthropology is a social science discipline very similar to sociology. The basic difference is that anthropology focuses more on a cross-cultural approach and is somewhat less demanding in terms of quantitative methods. Of first importance is that the level of analysis and the concepts utilized are very much alike in both disciplines. In my thinking, when that occurs, from a theoretical perspective, you have but a single discipline. In fact my approach in this book is often called comparative sociology which is indeed very difficult to distinguish from cultural anthropology. The focus upon the societal level of explanation in both comparative sociology and cultural anthropology is strikingly similar. For that reason I consider sociology and cultural anthropology sibling disciplines. In many universities they are still in one unified department.[18]

Much is still left unsaid here and, in some instances, unexplored. There are many areas of sexuality upon which I have touched only lightly. I have focused upon those areas of sexuality that have at least a modicum of cross-cultural research in the published literature and are relevant to a societal-level explanation. My first goal was to find the societal linkages to sexuality that would apply to all societies, and thus I had to follow where this objective led me. My objective in this book was a societal-level theoretical explanation of sexuality and not an encyclopedic coverage of all key sexual topics.

My explanations will, I hope, be a start toward an understanding of even those areas of sexuality that I have not directly explored. The advantage of formulating a cross-culturally valid broad explanation of sexuality is that logically such an explanation should have implications even for those areas of sexuality not fully examined. Also, if the theory is weak in any direction, future research on such areas can point the weakness out and new theoretical elements can remedy that problem.

My wish is that having made the effort to organize the key societal linkages and their theoretical ties to the patterns of human sexuality, I will have provoked enough interest to encourage more people to join the development of this sociology of human sexuality. The causal search is neverending, for causal solutions are always tentative.[19] The primal scientific instinct is to challenge, not to accept. It must always be that way if we are to find reliable and valid answers to our quest.

Theoretical space is free to all. So come and examine, reason about, question, and qualify what I have done. I do hope that what I have said is of value to all who work in the area of human sexuality in whatever capacity. There is also relevance to those who have a personal, but not a professional, interest in understanding sexuality. My propositions can be elaborated so as to afford usable and relevant knowledge for many commonly raised questions. For one thing, you should now be more aware of alternative sexual systems and know something more about the costs and rewards of each in terms of your own set of values. This breadth of knowledge should afford you a deeper understanding of the social basis of the many disputes in our society concerning sexual jealousy, erotica, homosexuality, gender power, and sexual normality. The explanation of something as important as human sexuality must be complex, but the operation of theory is to simplify and thereby point to the patterns that exist in what William James called that "booming, buzzing, confusion" labeled reality.

I have one final suggestion. It would be far more helpful to the improvement of our *scientific* understanding if we minimize politicizing the scientific investigation of sexuality. There is a place for pleading our special moral concerns, and it is in our many private roles as citizens. I believe that we need also to respect the importance of the attempt to do impartial, fair, scientific analysis. I am sure that such scientific knowledge and understanding can aid us in our applied and political goals as well as in purely scientific ways. With this in mind, we may well find it profitable to allow this new sociological perspective an opportunity to demonstrate its potential in our lives.

There are those who will say that my findings verify much of the Marxist position or of the feminist positions that have recently been taken. Some may even think I have also found support for aspects of Freudian or sociobiological approaches. As I see it, my theory and my empirical data in their general outline and in their specifics do not comfortably fit with more than pieces of any of these older approaches.

Of course, some overlaps do exist—some rather striking ones such as the importance of social power in structuring sexual customs—but there is one rather important distinction to bear in mind: I have no allegiances to the dogmas of any other position as to how power or other social factors operate. I have strong loyalty to a sociological, societal-level explanation. That is my only dogma. Lacking allegiances to these older approaches, my explanation is freer to take the wisdom of all these approaches and thereby enhance the societal explanation of human sexuality.

I thank you all for your coming along with me on this exploratory voyage. I hope it will be but one of many voyages for you into the fascinating puzzle of human sexuality. Perhaps you will be able to advance us further into the labyrinth that contains the means of deciphering our human sexuality. I wish us all the best of good fortune in the future development of this sociological enterprise. We have nothing to lose but our preconceptions and we have a new understanding to gain.

SELECTED REFERENCES AND COMMENTS

1. There are other reasons for incest taboos, such as the potential abuse of the child due to the power differential with parents. This was briefly discussed in Chapter 4. Anthropologists in particular have analyzed the societal reasons for incest taboos. A perusal of the journal *American Anthropologist* would be a good place to start for the interested reader.

2. In America we have tied sexuality to notions of power and aggression so much that we may believe that all societies also do that. However, other Western countries do not give the same aggressive meaning to sexuality. For example, I spent the year 1975–76 in Sweden at Uppsala University and explored the way sexuality was conceptualized in Sweden. Just as one comparison, in America if you have been given a raw deal in buying something, you can say you were "fucked," which means the same as saying you were "treated badly." In Sweden the word for sexual intercourse cannot be used in that fashion. This indicates to me that sexuality itself in Sweden may be less likely to be used as a way of treating someone badly. Our conceptualization of the meaning of sexuality is reflected in our everyday usage and would reward any examination.

3. The economic institution need not always be the most flexible or important institution in a society. In this sense it would likely be wise to follow Alice Schlegel's advice and search for which institution is the most influential in a particular society. In my propositions, I do endorse the idea of ranking the influence of each of the major institutions. This would eventually lead to our being able to formulate more precise propositions. For an excellent discussion of "central" instituions and gender stratification cross-culturally, see

Schlegel, Alice, "Toward a Theory of Sexual Stratification," Chapter 1 in Alice Schlegel (ed.), *Sexual Stratification: A Cross Cultural View*. New York: Columbia University Press, 1977.

4. Some of Chafetz's propositions on power and gender are congruent with mine.

Chafetz, Janet. *Sex and Advantage: A Comparative Macro-Structural Theory of Sex Stratification*. Totowa, N.J.: Rowman & Allanheld, 1984.

5. Logically, I should also consider change caused by forces external to a particular society. For simplicity sake I have not entertained any propositions concerning that in my theory. Colonialism, war, and trade are but a few of the means by which external forces may alter a particular society.

6. I call all these theoretical statements by the term *proposition*, but clearly not all the statements are of the exact same sort. However, all the statements are subject to empirical testing, relate two or more variables, and are part of the logical structure of my overall theoretical position. For excellent coverage of the use of propositions in social science theory, see the following references:

Hoover, Kenneth R., *The Elements of Social Scientific Thinking* (3rd ed.). New York: S. Martin's Press, 1984.

Wallace, Walter L., *Principles of Scientific Sociology*. New York: Aldine, 1983.

Zetterberg, Hans L., *On Theory and Verification in Sociology*. New York: Tressler Press, 1954.

Reynolds, Paul Davidson, *A Primer in Theory Construction*. Indianapolis: Bobbs-Merrill, 1971.

Chafetz, Janet S., *A Primer on the Construction and Testing of Theories in Sociology*. Chicago: F.E. Peacock, 1978.

Hage, Jerald, *Techniques and Problems of Theory Construction in Sociology.* New York: John Wiley, 1972.

Burr, Wesley, R. Hill, I. Nye, and I.L. Reiss," Metatheory and Diagraming Conventions," Chapter 2 in W. Burr, R. Hill, I. Nye, and I.L. Reiss (eds.), *Contemporary Theories about the Family.* Vol. 1, New York: Free Press, 1979.

Freese, Lee (ed.), *Theoretical Methods in Sociology.* Pittsburgh: University of Pittsburgh Press, 1980.

7. The premise one starts with is logically called an axiom or postulate. In a strict sense such premises are not emprically testable. From such axioms one can deduce theorems that are themselves testable. If the theorems are not shown to be false, then we have more faith in the premises of our thinking. Clearly, we are far from any complete axiomatic theory. Also, theory can proceed in other ways. It is well, in any case, to examine empirically and logically all aspects of any theoretical position—even those called premises. Even mine!

Lee Freese's theoretical writings are particularly relevant to this point. Although he stresses axiomatic theory more than I would, his ideas are worth examining. See

Freese, Lee (ed.), *Theoretical Methods in Sociology.* Pittsburgh: University of Pittsburgh, 1980.

8. Propositions 5 and 6 concern speculative evolutionary notions. Of course, one may be skeptical about those without rejecting the propositions concerning present-day societies.

9. The concepts in each of the 25 propositions need to be able to be precisely measured, and thus careful definitions and measurement procedures are necessities. For a somewhat technical statement of conceptualization and measurement I recommend

Blalock, Hubert M., Jr., *Conceptualization and Measurement in the Social Sciences.* Beverly Hills, Calif.: Sage Publications, 1982.

10. For a philosophical article by a quantitative scientist on the problem of cross-cultural data, see

Campbell, Donald T., "Degrees of Freedom and the Case Study," *Comparative Political Studies,* Vol. 8, no. 2 (July 1975), pp. 178–193.

11. In the examination of the Standard Sample, I sought to causally explain five sexually relevant outcomes: (1) beliefs that females are inferior; (2) sexual jealousy reactions of husbands; (3) sexual jealousy reactions of wives; (4) homosexual frequency; and (5) rape proneness. I will note some of the ways in which these analyses related to the propositions discussed in this chapter. The analysis of marital sexual jealousy (Diagrams 3.1 and 3.2) brought out variables like the importance placed on property in a culture as a predictor of the degree of husband sexual jealousy. I took the emphasis on property to be a measure of male power and therefore conceived of the association of that variable with husband sexual jealousy as partial support for propositions 8 and 10. Also, the relation of male kin groups to husband sexual jealousy is congruent with proposition 13's emphasis on the importance in sexuality of kin group power.

In Diagram 4.1 I interpreted the positive relationship of a belief in female inferiority to the degree of mother involvement with infants to be supportive of propositions 14 and 15, which point out how involvement with the family lowers one's power in other institutions. This same point is supported by the negative relationship in Diagram 4.1 between male kin groups and father-infant involvement. The male kin group promotes male power and that reduces participation in childcare roles. That diagram also is consistent with proposition 16 which asserts that institutional values will be reflected in ideological beliefs. The belief in the female's basic inferiority is reflective of the female's limited power outside the family.

Proposition 24 asserts the power of the economic institution in terms of gender roles and that too is illustrated by the place of agriculture in Diagram 4.1. Note however, that proposition 24 asserts that a two way causal relationship exists. All my causal diagrams presented only one way causation. The reason for that is that two way causation is much more difficult to test for and demonstrate. The path analytic techniques are much simpler if one way causation is assumed. Nonetheless, I deliberately implied in several of my 25 propositions that causation was bidirectional. We cannot examine everything at once and the steps taken in this book are preparatory for more complex causal analysis at a later date.

My interpretation of Diagram 6.1 on homosexuality is expressed in part in proposition 21. The association in Diagram 6.1 of the extent of class stratification and of strong mother-infant involvement with the prevalence of homosexual behavior fits with the notion that rigid gender roles promote homosexual behavior especially in cultures like the U.S.

Propositions 10 and 13 are logically related to the relationships found in Diagram 7.1 concerning rape proneness. Those propositions imply that having low status and weak kin ties can increase the chances of sexual abuse. This is consistent with the association of a belief in female inferiority with rape proneness. I did not include a proposition directly on machismo and rape because it is not clear to me just how separate machismo is from other measures of male power, and propositions 10 and 13 already make the point concerning the relation of male power to rape. The lack of any clear tie of violence rates to rape rates also kept me from formulating any propositions in this area.

The causal diagrams, as can be seen in my discussion, do not answer a great many of the questions that arise in our thinking. They were but one of several sources for the propositions in this chapter.

12. A few new cross-cultural codes deserve attention. I did not feel they were essential for me to analyze at this time, but they are worth examining. See in particular

Barry, Herbert, and Alice Schlegel, "Measurements of Adolescent Sexual Behavior in the Standard Sample of Societies," *Ethnology.* Vol. 23, no. 4 (October 1984), pp. 315-330.

Mosher, Donald L., and Mark Sikin, "Measuring a Macho Personality Constellation," *Journal of Research in Personality.* Vol. 18 (1984), pp. 150-163.

Frayser, Suzanne G., *Varieties of Sexual Experience.* New Haven, Conn.: HRAF Press, 1985.

13. Some readers of this book may be familiar with my earlier theoretical work and may wonder how that ties in with this book. I commented upon this in note 6 in Chapter One and note 48 in Chapter Four. In my 1967 book I had developed a theoretical explanation of premarital sexuality that I called the autonomy theory. This theory, in its briefest form, asserted that "the degree of acceptable premarital sexual permissiveness in a courtship group varies directly with the degree of autonomy of the courtship group and with the degree of acceptable premarital sexual permissiveness in the social and cultural setting outside the group" (Reiss, 1967: p. 167). Two key causes of premarital sexuality are identified in that statement: the social and cultural setting and the autonomy of the courtship group.

My current theoretical effort spells out the factors that affect "the degree of acceptable sexual permissiveness in the social and cultural setting." In this sense, this book is an extension, on a much broader scale, of my earlier work. What of the autonomy notion itself, though? As I noted in Chapter Four, note 48, autonomy of a group is in a sense a measure of its power. A courtship group that is boxed in by parental regulations, religious edicts, political laws, and lack of money is low on autonomy and low on power. To be autonomous a group needs to be freed from such influences, and that means a reduction of the ability of these external groups to affect the lifestyle of the courtship group. Since the power dimension has shown itself to be such a major influence in my current work, this earlier statement of autonomy may be able to be integrated with a fuller analysis of the role of power in sexuality. I hope others will help me to explore my autonomy theory and seek further to integrate it with my current theory. For now, I merely want to let the reader know that the idea is not forgotten nor is it alien to my current theorizing.

I have also done theoretical work on extramarital sexuality. I did utilize measures of the major social institutions in that explanation. The sociological theory in this book is a global sociological explanation. As such it should be inclusive of my theoretically narrower explanations of both premarital and extramarital sexuality. I do plan at a later date to deal with these interrelationships. Some key references to this earlier work follow:

Reiss, Ira L., *The Social Context of Premarital Sexual Permissiveness.* New York: Rinehart & Winston, 1967.

Reiss, Ira L., and Brent C. Miller, "Heterosexual Permissiveness: A Theoretical Analysis," Chapter 4 in W. Burr, R. Hill, I. Nye, and I.L. Reiss (eds.), *Contemporary Theories about the Family* (vol. 1). New York: Free Press, 1979.

Reiss, Ira L., Ronald E. Anderson, and G.C. Sponaugle, "A Multivariate Model of the Determinants of Extramarital Sexual Permissiveness," *Journal of Marriage and the Family,* vol. 42 (May 1980), pp. 395–411.

14. The difference between a sociological-level explanation and a psychological-level explanation can be seen in some of Broude's work. In an examination of the double standard in extramarital sexuality, Broude concludes that

> the double standard is interpreted as a reflection of both male fears of sexual betrayal and male concern over sexual adequacy. (Broude, 1980; p. 181)

This is a psychological-level explanation stressing individual fears of adequacy. It is not necessarily in conflict with a sociological-level explanation, but it clearly is different. In contrast with Broude, I interpret the double standard in extramarital sexuality as a reflection of a social structure that places males in the top power positions in most societal institutions.

Broude, Gwen J., "Extramarital Sex Norms in Cross-cultural Perspective," *Behavior Science Research,* vol. 15, no. 3 (1980), pp. 181–218.

15. Voltaire, *Candide and other Writings.* New York: Random House, 1956. (See especially p. 189.)

16. I have developed my thinking on this topic in the following article:

Reiss, Ira L., "Trouble in Paradise; The Current Status of Sexual Science," *The Journal of Sex Research.* Vol. 18, no. 2 (May 1982), pp. 97–113. (See the May 1983 issue of this journal for a response to my paper and my rebuttal.)

17. For a discussion of this point see the article cited in note 16. To obtain a general view of the study of sexuality 25 years ago see:

Ellis Albert and Albert Abarbanel (eds.), *The Encyclopedia of Sexual Behavior* (2 vols.). New York: Hawthorn, 1961.

18. Anthropology has specialities that are unique to it, for example, physical anthropology and archeology. Sociology also has special approaches, such as the micro approach. The micro approach focuses upon human interaction in small groups. Some of that was used in this book, particularly in our discussion of jealousy and erotica and sexual scripts. However, my overall unit of analysis was the

society or the major institutions in a society. That is called a macro or comparative approach. Other sociologists may identify as Marxists or phenomenologists, and that further distinguishes them. In sum, then, when I say sociology and anthropology are alike in their level of analysis I am speaking of cultural anthropology and macro comparative sociology.

A micro sociological approach is one that also can be further explored. Such an approach would focus upon socialization and the interactive processes by which people learn their sexual scripts. Such a micro sociological approach could be theoretically linked with the macro theory I am developing. The work of Simon and Gagnon cited in the Bibliography is relevant here.

19. It was David Hume who, over 200 years ago, made science aware of the tentativeness of its causal assertions. In sociology it was Robert MacIver who was one of the first sociologists to examine carefully the notion of social causation. See

Hume, David, *An Enquiry Concerning Human Understanding.* LaSalle, Ill.: Open Court, 1952. (Originally published in 1777.)

MacIver, Robert M., *Social Causation.* New York: Ginn, 1942.

APPENDIX A

METHODOLOGICAL NOTE
ON THE STANDARD SAMPLE

Each time I presented the findings from the Standard Sample I discussed in the text and in the "Selected References and Comments" section of the relevant chapter the specific variables used and some of the problems involved. Thus, I have discussed some of the validity and reliability problems of the Standard Sample data. Nevertheless, it is necessary to do three more things: (1) present an overview of the Standard Sample data and how I utilized them; (2) list the codebook wording of the variables used and their frequency breakdown, and (3) give the reader a matrix of the correlations of these variables, and more specific statistical data on the five causal diagrams in the book. This will afford you a better understanding of my findings and, in addition, it will make it much easier for those who desire to replicate or expand upon my findings.

THE UTILIZATION OF THE STANDARD SAMPLE:
AN OVERVIEW

By now the reader is aware that the Standard Sample is a subset of the Ethnographic Atlas. In 1969 Murdock and White selected what they felt were the best-described 186 nonindustrialized cultures representative of the six major culture regions of the world.[1] The sample cultures divide as follows into these six regions:

Sub-Saharan Africa: 28 societies
Circum-Mediterranean: 28 Societies
East Eurasia: 34 Societies
Insular Pacific: 31 Societies
North America: 33 Societies
South and Central America: 32 Societies

These societies were selected by the quality of the ethnographic coverage. The attempt was also made to avoid societies with a great deal of historical contact with each other in order to gain a more representative and broader view of the culture area. The societies chosen represented 51 independent linguistic families. The major types of subsistence in the Standard Sample is representative of those in the non-industrialized world in general.

To avoid acculturation effects from contact with Europeans, the societies are described at the earliest period for which satisfactory ethnographic data are available. Most of the societies were studied between 1851 and 1950. For an exact location of the societies I suggest looking at the maps in the original article by Murdock and White.

The reader should bear in mind that these 186 societies represent the non-industrialized societies of the world. No comparable sample of industrialized societies with similar information is available. In this book I have utilized small samples of industrialized societies or individual society studies in order to develop my ideas on the industrialized world. In addition, I have used some well-described nonindus-trialized societies not included in this Standard Sample. Some, like the Sambia, were only very recently studied and were therefore not in the Standard Sample. Of course, those additional nonindustrialized societies were not part of the five causal diagrams I presented. They were brought into my discussions because they were good-quality ethnography and they had special value for our understanding human sexuality cross-culturally. I began to use the Standard Sample to examine some general causal notions that I had developed from my own in-depth reading of industrialized and nonindustrialized societies. I do not want to exaggerate the importance of the Standard Sample data for my theory. Although it surely added a great deal to my knowledge, my goal was the sociological understanding of human sexuality, and that extends far beyond the confines of the data in the Standard Sample.

My approach to the data in the Standard Sample was to select those coded variables that were most relevant for searching out the societal linkages of sexuality. In many cases I started by examining a variety of variables and selected from those the ones that seemed most appropriate. In some instances, as mentioned in previous chapters, I found codes that contradicted each other. In such cases I sought to find the codes that seemed the most valid. I arrived at this judgment, when possible, by checking "known cases." If I knew some cultures very well, for example, I would see how each source had coded those cultures and choose the source that con-formed most closely to my conception of those societies. In other instances I chose on the basis of which source provided the most complete set of coded categories. In yet others I would choose on the basis of which source coded a sufficient number of societies for me to carry out the necessary statistical analysis.

On occasion I had to exclude variables that were measured inappropriately for testing my hypotheses. I had, for example, to drop a measure of male dominance because that measure included rape frequency in the society as an index of male dominance. This made it impossible for me to examine whether male dominance was related to rape frequency. In some cases I dropped measures because they did not distinguish males from females on behavior or attitude measures of sexuality. Knowing that most societies have noticeable elements of a double standard in sexuality, I could not confidently use a measure of sexuality that did not yield separate information on males and females.

In all these ways I was using my own knowledge and my own judgment in the selection of variables. However, the reader should not be too alarmed at my possible bias because the number of variables on sexuality was so small that in most instances I had to take what was available and no choice was possible. I will present here the variables I found most useful in my analysis. Those who wish can go to the original sources to seek for additional variables and make their own validation judgments.

KEY VARIABLES AND THEIR FREQUENCY DISTRIBUTION

I list here the name of the variable as given in the original codebook of the author or authors and follow it in parentheses by the name I used for it in this book. All variables have been arranged so that the categories are coded from low on the variable to high on the variable when applying my label for the variable. The variable wording is from the original sources, as are the answer categories, except in those cases where the categories consisted of a large number of numerical scores (interval data). In those instances, for simplicity sake, I have trichotomized the answer categories. I list the frequency distribution of responses for each category of each variable. Finally, I place an identification letter in front of each variable number so the reader can easily note the source of that variable.[2] For the Standard Sample, in front of the variable number I place the letters SS; for Broude, B; for Whyte, W; for Ross, R; for Hupka, H; and for Sanday, S.

	NUMBER OF SOCIETIES CODED	PERCENTAGE OF ALL SOCIETIES CODED
(SS)1. NON-MATERNAL RELATIONSHIPS-INFANCY (MOTHER-INFANT INVOLVEMENT)		
a. Most care, except nursing, is by others	1	0.6

b. Mother's role is significant but less than all other combined	2	1.2
c. Mother provides half or less of the care	10	6.2
d. Principally mother, other have important roles	63	38.9
e. Principally mother, others have minor roles	81	50.0
f. Almost exclusively the mother	5	3.1
Total Number of Societies Coded	162	100.0

(SS)2. ROLE OF FATHER: INFANCY (FATHER-INFANT INVOLVEMENT)

a. No close proximity	8	5.2
b. Rare instances of close proximity	27	17.5
c. Occasional or irregular close proximity	72	46.8
d. Frequent close proximity	44	28.6
e. Regular, close relationship or companionship	3	1.9
Total Number of Societies Coded	154	100.0

(SS)3. MARITAL RESIDENCE AND DESCENT (MAKE KIN GROUPS)

(The above variable was coded by combining the responses to the marital residence and descent variables so that a society that was neither patrilocal or patrilineal received a low code, a society that was either patrilocal or patrilineal but not both received a medium code; and a society that was both patrilocal and patrilineal received a high code.)

a. Low on male kin groups	62	33.3
b. Medium on male kin groups	53	28.5
c. High on male kin groups	71	38.2
Total Number of Societies Coded	186	100.0

(SS)4. WILDPLANTS, HUNTING, FISHING, ANIMAL HUSBANDRY, AGRICULTURE (EXTENT OF AGRICULTURE)

(This variable was coded from the specific codes for the above-listed five types of subsistence in order to derive those societies in which agriculture was dominant over all other types of subsistence.)

a. Agriculture not greater than other forms of subsistence	59	33.3
b. Agriculture greater than other forms of subsistence	118	66.7
Total Number of Societies Coded	177	100.0

(SS)5. CLASS STRATIFICATION (CLASS STRATIFICATION)

a. Absence among freemen	76	41.3
b. Wealth distinctions	42	22.8

c. Elite (based on control of land or other resources)	3	1.6
d. Dual (hereditary aristocracy)	38	20.7
e. Complex (social classes)	25	13.6
Total Number of Societies Coded	184	100.0

(SS)6. NORMS OF PREMARITAL SEX BEHAVIOR OF GIRLS (FEMALE PREMARITAL HETEROSEXUAL PERMISSIVENESS)

a. Insistence on virginity	38	30.9
b. Prohibited but weakly censured and not infrequent	32	26.0
c. Allowed, censured only if pregnancy results	17	13.8
d. Trial marriage, promiscuous relations prohibited	3	2.4
e. Freely permitted, even if pregnancy results	33	26.8
Total Number of Societies Coded	123	100.0

The preceding six variables came from the Standard Sample.[3] As the reader can see, there was only one direct question on sexuality. Clearly, I needed more sources, and so I went to the ethnographic literature to search for those who might have added new codes for the cultures in the Standard Sample. I came across five such sources. I next list the key variables from those sources, starting with Broude.[4]

(B)7. FREQUENCY OF PREMARITAL SEX, MALE (MALE PREMARITAL HETEROSEXUAL FREQUENCY)

a. Uncommon: males rarely or never engage in premarital sex	13	12.7
b. Occasional: some males engage in premarital sex but this is not common or typical	11	10.8
c. Moderate: not uncommon for males to engage in premarital sex	18	17.6
d. Universal or almost universal: almost all males engage in premarital sex	60	58.8
Total Number of Societies Coded	102	100.0

(B)8. FREQUENCY OF EXTRAMARITAL SEX, MALE (MALE EXTRAMARITAL HETEROSEXUAL FREQUENCY)

a. Uncommon: men rarely or never engage in extramarital sex	10	19.6
b. Occasional: men sometimes engage in extramarital sex, but this is not common	6	11.8

c. Moderate: not uncommon for men to engage in extramarital sex	29	56.9
d. Universal or almost universal: almost all men engage in extramarital sex	6	11.8
Total Number of Societies Coded	51	100.0

(B) 9. FREQUENCY OF EXTRAMARITAL SEX, FEMALE (FEMALE EXTRAMARITAL HETEROSEXUAL FREQUENCY)

a. Uncommon: women rarely or never engage in extramarital sex	15	28.3
b. Occasional: women sometimes engage in extramarital sex, but this is not common	9	17.0
c. Moderate: not uncommon for women to engage in extramarital sex	23	43.4
d. Universal or almost universal: almost all women engage in extramarital sex	6	11.3
Total Number of Societies Coded	53	100.0

(B)10. FREQUENCY OF RAPE (HETEROSEXUAL RAPE FREQUENCY)

a. Absent	8	25.8
b. Rare: isolated cases	10	32.3
c. Common: not atypical	13	41.9
Total Number of Societies Coded	31	100.0

(B)11. FREQUENCY OF HOMOSEXUALITY (FREQUENCY OF HOMOSEXUAL BEHAVIOR)

a. Absent, rare	40	58.0
b. Present, not uncommon	29	42.0
Total Number of Societies Coded	69	100.0

The next two variables come from Whyte.

(W)12. IS THERE A GENERALLY HIGH VALUE PLACED ON MALES BEING AGGRESSIVE, STRONG, AND SEXUALLY POTENT, MACHISMO ? (MACHISMO EMPHASIS)

a. Little or no emphasis	22	27.2
b. Moderate emphasis	33	40.7
c. Marked emphasis	26	32.1
Total Number of Societies Coded	81	100.0

(W)13. IS THERE A CLEARLY STATED BELIEF THAT WOMEN ARE GENERALLY INFERIOR TO MEN? (BELIEF IN FEMALE INFERIORITY)

a. No such belief	66	71.0
b. Yes	27	29.0
Total Number of Societies Coded	93	100.0

The next code comes from Ross.

(R)14. LOCAL CONFLICT; PHYSICAL FORCE; INTERNAL WARFARE; EXTERNAL WARFARE (VIOLENCE)

(This is a combined variable composed of the four variables listed. It was composed by giving one point for each of the four questions answered with a high response. See the specific reference from Ross in note 3 for the exact wording of each of the four questions. I counted a high response for Local Conflict as categories 1 and 2; a high response for Physical force as category 1; a high response for Internal Warfare as Categories 1 and 2; and a high response for External Warfare as category 1.)

a. Lowest	21	23.3
b. Low	24	26.7
c. Low moderate	20	22.2
d. High moderate	16	17.8
e. High	9	10.0
Total Number of Societies Coded	90	100.0

The next six variables are from Hupka.

(H)15. WIFE'S SEXUAL JEALOUSY (WIFE'S SEXUAL JEALOUSY)

(Codes go from low to high on a scale of zero to 36 according to the severity of punishment for the person involved weighted by the impact on the marriage. For convenience sake, I trichotomize the scores here. In the regression runs all such interval variables were, of course, run fully open.)[5]

a. Low = 0–12	9	23.1
b. Medium = 13–24	24	61.5
c. High = 25–36	6	15.4
Total Number of Societies Coded	39	100.0

(H)16. HUSBAND'S SEXUAL JEALOUSY (HUSBAND'S SEXUAL JEALOUSY)

(Coded the same as question 15.)

a. Low = 0–12	8	10.0
b. Medium = 13–24	27	33.8
c. High = 25–36	45	56.2
Total Number of Societies Coded	80	100.0

(H)17. PROPERTY (IMPORTANCE OF PROPERTY)

(This is coded from zero to 36 depending on the importance placed on property. For convenience sake, I trichotomize the scores here.)

a. Low = 0–12	19	23.7
b. Medium = 13–24	40	50.0
c. High = 25–36	21	26.3
Total Number of Societies Coded	80	100.0

(H)18. PROGENCY (EMPHASIS ON PROGENY)

(This variable measures the emphasis on legitimate children and their importance to parents. It is measured by scores of 0–36. For convenience sake, I trichotomize the results here.)

a. Low = 0–12	20	25.0
b. Medium = 13–24	37	46.3
c. High = 25–36	23	28.7
Total Number of Societies Coded	80	100.0

(H)19. PAIRBONDING (IMPORTANCE OF MARRIAGE)

(This variable measures the emphasis placed on marriage in a society. It uses a scale of 0–36. For simplicity sake, I trichotomize the responses here.)

a. Low = 0–12	19	23.7
b. Medium = 13–24	36	45.0
c. High = 25–36	25	31.3
Total Number of Societies Coded	80	100.0

(H)20. SEXUAL GRATIFICATION (HETEROSEXUAL RESTRICTIVENESS)

(This variable measures restrictions on premarital, extramarital, and postmarital heterosexuality on a scale of 0–36. For simplicity sake, I trichotomize the responses here.)

a. Low = 0–12	25	31.3
b. Medium = 13–24	23	28.8
c. High = 25–36	32	40.0
Total Number of Societies Coded	80	100.00

The final set of questions comes from Sanday.

(S)21. AGRICULTURE (PREVALENCE OF AGRICULTURE)

(This variable was adopted by Sanday from the Standard Sample data.)

a. Not practiced	31	19.9
b. Practiced but confined to nonfood crop	3	1.9
c. Unimportant, less than 10%	17	10.9
d. Significant, more than 10% but less than any other	8	5.1

e. More than any other but less
   than 50%   34   21.8
f. More than all other subsistence
   techniques combined   63   40.4
Total Number of Societies Coded   156   100.0

(S)22. SEGREGATED FEMALE TECHNOLOGICAL ACTIVITIES (SEGREGATED FEMALE TECHNOLOGY)

(This variable uses a 50-item scale devised by G.P. Murdock and C. Provost and measures the percentage of all technological activities performed predominantly or exclusively by females.[6] Sanday's scores run from 9 to 73. For the sake of covenience, I have trichotomized the item here.)

a. Low = 9–30   36   21.1
b. Medium = 31–52   101   64.7
c. High = 53–73   19   12.2
Total Number of Societies Coded   156   100.0

(S)23. SEXUALLY INTEGRATED TECHNOLOGICAL ACTIVITY (GENDER-INTEGRATED TECHNOLOGY)

(This variable measures the percentage of all technological activities equally performed by both genders. It uses the same scale as in variable 22. Sanday's scores range from zero to 35. For convenience, I have trichotomized the responses here.)

a. Low = 0–12   113   72.4
b. Medium = 13–24   38   24.4
c. High = 25–35   5   3.2
Total Number of Societies Coded   156   100.0

(S)24. STRUCTURE(S) WHERE MALES CONGREGATE ALONE, OR MALES OCCUPY SEPARATE PART OF HOUSEHOLD, OR SHARP CEREMONIAL SEGREGATION OF THE SEXES (MALE STRUCTURES)

a. Absent   24   21.6
b. Present   87   78.4
Total Number of Societies Coded   111   100.0

(S)25. IDEOLOGY OF MALE TOUGHNESS, MACHISMO (MACHO)

a. Absent   21   19.4
b. Present   87   80.6
Total Number of Societies Coded   108   100.0

(S)26. INCIDENCE OF RAPE—OR EVIDENCE OF RAPE AS BEING AN ACCEPTED PRACTICE (HETEROSEXUAL RAPE PRONENESS)

a. Never, rare   45   47.4
b. Reported as present, no report
   of frequency or suggestion that
   incidence is moderate; description
   such that clearly cannot be
   classified as rare   33   34.7

c. Institutionalized (rape an
accepted practice which is used
to punish women or is part of

a ceremony)	17	17.9
Total Number of Societies Coded	95	100.0

(S)27. DEGREE OF INTERPERSONAL VIOLENCE (INTERPERSONAL VIOLENCE)

a. Mild or absent	44	33.6
b. Moderate	46	35.1
c. Strong	41	31.3
Total Number of Societies Coded	131	100.0

(S)28. FEMALE STATUS SCALE SCORE (FEMALE STATUS)

(This is basically a measure of the degree to which females produce subsistence and possess some power outside the domestic sphere. I have provided arbitrary labels.)

a. Lowest	11	8.3
b. Low	9	6.8
c. Low Moderate	5	3.8
d. Moderate	13	9.8
e. High Moderate	23	17.3
f. High	41	30.8
g. Highest	31	23.3
Total Number of Societies Coded	133	100.0

These 28 variables are the major ones referred to in this book. Sixteen of them comprise the variables in the causal diagrams.[7] Twelve other variables are here because they are mentioned in the book in some significant fashion. I have two measures of the presence of agriculture, for example, for that is an important causal variable. I checked out my statements on the role of agriculture using both of them and thereby increased the confidence in the results. The same is true of the two measures of rape, violence, machismo, female status, and male kin groups. The precise variable I ended up using can be discerned by the variable label in the diagram.

There are also variables that were not so useful but are important in my discussion of findings. The sexual restrictiveness variable of Hupka, for example, tried to cover too many areas of sexuality with one measure. Since I discuss the problems with this variable in Chapter 3, I felt it belonged here for the reader to see its composition. The progeny variable of Hupka did not work out as an explanatory factor either, but it is included because many people believe that jealousy is based upon a fear of illegitimate offspring. The lack of support for that view in the progeny measure is important to recognize, and so I included it here for emphasis and possible further testing by others. In addition, I did not find Sanday's female status measure very useful and used Whyte's measure instead, but I still include both here. I include two measures of violence, for the results differ—as I mention in Chapter 7—depending on which one you use.

In sum, then, the presence of a variable in this appendix does not mean it is being recommended. Rather, it is present if it is seen as important in the checking of the explanations tested in this book. These 28 were selected from a much larger number of variables after a long series of careful checks. It is hoped that some of the readers will continue to mine these data together with the new data that come forth regularly in this field.

PROCEDURES AND STATISTICS
IN THE CAUSAL DIAGRAMS

I started my analysis of the data by examining bivariate tables of these 28 variables and many others. My initial objective was to search for patterned ways each variable related to the others and thereby derive additional plausible hypotheses to test. To illustrate, it was from such examination that I noted the ways in which the various measures of male power seemed strongly associated with the measures of sexuality and consequently formulated some power explanations that became part of the causal diagrams later tested.

I examined many of these associations using other variables as controls to see if the relationship was general or limited to specific social contexts. I noted, for example, that an emphasis on male kin groups was associated with a belief in female inferiority, and I checked to see if this held up in polygamous as well as in monogamous societies, in unstratified as well as stratified societies, and so on. This relationship held up in all these societal contexts. This finding itself required the development of reasons for the broad scope under which the relationship of the presence of male kin groups associated with a belief in female inferiority.

The next step was to test some relationships involving more than two variables. Here, I soon ran into the problems associated with missing data. The reader can note the large differences in the number of societies coded on each of the 28 variables—the range being from 31 to 186 societies. This means that if you ran a traditional multiple regression you would only retain the lowest number of societies coded on any of the variables used in the regression. The missing-data problem also meant that you could not utilize as many variables in a single multiple regression as your theoretical interests might dictate; the more variables used, the more likely you will reduce the number of societies that have all of them coded.

I utilized some ways of minimizing these limitations. First, I did all my multiple regressions using both listwise and pairwise deletion. Listwise deletion, the traditional approach, reduces the total number of cases to that of the least answered variable; but pairwise deletion takes each two-variable regression independently and, therefore, does not drop those cases that have not been coded on all the variables. I always compared the results of both deletion methods, although for the diagrams in the book I used the pairwise deletion results. In the majority of cases, no difference was evident in the listwise and pairwise results.[8] That is important because it increased my confidence in my results.

In addition, I also broke down my causal analysis into smaller segments than I otherwise would. There are 16 different variables in my five causal diagrams. Had the number of cases with information permitted, I would have tried to develop one causal diagram involving most of them; but there was no way that I could really test such a large diagram using the number of responses I had on each variable. Instead, my diagrams include a total of between 4 and 7 variables. However, the causal diagrams I used did have some variables in common, and thus one can easily speculate as to how two or more such causal patterns might fit together.

To begin with I did only regular multiple regressions of the variables in each of the five sets that were to become the five diagrams in the book. This enabled me to note what the net effect of each variable was on the dependent variable in that set. Then I thought that it would be much more meaningful if, in addition, I could test some ideas concerning the temporal sequence of influence among the several variables in each set of variables. So, I designed some causal sequences asserting a temporal order among the variables. The five causal diagrams in this book present the results of a series of multiple regressions aimed at discerning if the actual relationships among the variables fit into those proposed causal patterns. Such causal diagrams are helpful in building explanations much more than using only one multiple-regression analysis for each set of variables. There are other analysis techniques besides multiple regression which I might have tried but the missing data problem would interfere there also. Further, these data are crude measures and I felt that it would be best to not become too technically involved but rather to do a careful first examination of these data and leave it to others to proceed beyond that if they wish.

As a general background of the causal analysis it may be helpful to examine the bivariate correlations among the variables in any particular diagram. As an aid in doing this I present the correlation matrix for all 28 variables in Exhibit A.1. The reader may be interested in examining the correlations between variables supposedly measuring the same concept. The reader can also note how a particular bivariate correlation holds up when it is inserted into a multiple-regression analysis in the diagrams.

Following the matrix are five tables, one for each of the five diagrams. The relative strength of each relationship and its statistical probability is listed for each regression in each diagram. The first regression in each table is all one would have had if simple multiple regression were used in place of path analysis. It is important to present this information so as to further specify the nature of the support for these causal diagrams.[9] Causal relationships are not something that one "proves"; rather, one examines proposed causal relationships to see how well they meet various statistical tests. If they are not shown to be in error by these tests, then our confidence is increased, but we never reach certainty.

EXHIBIT A.1 Pearson Correlation Matrix for Standard Sample*

	1	2	3	4	5	6	7	8	9	10	11	12	13	14	15	16	17	18	19	20	21	22	23	24	25	26	27	28
1		-.28	.09	-.15	-.13	-.01	.20	.00	-.07	.11	.27	.35	.31	.06	.13	.13	.07	.12	.22	.07	-.19	.11	.07	.00	.13	.14	.09	-.07
2			-.21	-.13	-.09	.16	.11	.03	.06	-.37	-.24	-.33	-.22	-.22	.09	.13	.00	-.11	-.18	-.07	.08	-.18	.08	-.28	-.34	-.16	-.21	-.01
3				.18	.18	-.17	-.08	-.11	-.07	.11	.24	.19	.28	.15	.22	.30	.02	.17	.19	.04	.21	-.10	.12	.18	.11	.19	.18	-.17
4					.37	.01	.13	.12	-.07	-.18	.18	-.09	.10	.00	-.20	.03	.10	-.03	.02	-.13	.92	-.30	.05	.31	.05	.15	.07	.10
5						-.25	-.01	-.27	-.38	-.18	.35	-.09	.25	.06	-.15	.12	.11	.05	.24	.01	.38	-.35	.00	.17	.01	-.06	.13	.07
6							.62	.47	.38	.21	.12	.10	-.11	-.10	.44	-.18	.06	-.28	-.32	-.52	-.06	.02	.03	-.11	-.01	-.07	.01	-.02
7								.61	.37	.22	-.08	-.04	-.02	.02	.40	.20	.22	-.11	.09	-.45	.01	-.04	.00	-.02	.09	-.07	.11	.12
8									.88	-.19	-.20	-.37	-.17	.20	.33	.09	-.03	.07	.00	.00	-.01	-.05	.12	.20	.05	.11	.16	.29
9										.32	-.28	-.24	-.35	.27	.22	.03	.03	.02	-.09	.00	-.10	.01	-.06	.17	.02	.00	.25	.29
10											-.12	-.28	.13	.07	-.36	.17	-.26	.03	-.13	.12	-.20	.00	-.06	.14	.06	.44	.36	.06
11												.78	.44	.26	.07	.09	.21	-.11	.05	-.30	.25	-.30	.04	.31	.14	.32	.05	-.08
12													.32	.13	.00	.15	.05	.03	.17	.40	.13	-.06	-.01	.17	.10	.50	.20	.22
13														.51	.39	.10	-.02	.17	.14	.34	.13	.12	.09	.11	.14	.21	.51	-.13
14															.10	.27	-.24	-.23	-.05	.15	-.05	-.20	.17	.31	.19	.14	.05	-.10
15																.64	-.14	-.06	.18	.50	.37	.09	.17	.14	.37	.14	.32	-.08
16																	.36	.25	.37	.21	.14	-.01	.12	.26	.14	.50	.20	-.21
17																		.31	.41	.43	.17	-.19	-.10	.26	.09	.20	.51	-.13
18																			.30	.41	.09	-.01	.04	-.11	-.05	.22	.05	-.21
19																				.19	-.03	.18	.04	-.11	-.21	.22	.03	-.10
20																					-.08	.20	.05	-.10	.18	.03	.18	.03
21																						.30	.07	.21	.12	.00	.11	-.05
22																							-.27	.07	.04	-.10	.01	.02
23																								-.14	.18	.07	.06	.03
24																									.45	.26	.24	.06
25																										.42	.49	-.23
26																											.47	-.22
27																												-.20
28																												

*My labels for each variable number are 1 = mother-infant involvement; 2 = father-infant involvement; 3 = male kin groups; 4 = extent of agriculture; 5 = class stratification; 6 = female premarital sexual permissiveness; 7 = male premarital sexual frequency; 8 = male extramarital sexual frequency; 9 = female extramarital sexual frequency; 10 = rape frequency; 11 = frequency of homosexual behavior; 12 = machismo emphasis; 13 = belief in female as inferior; 14 = violence; 15 = wife's sexual jealousy; 16 = husband's sexual jealousy; 17 = importance of property; 18 = emphasis on progeny; 19 = importance of marriage; 20 = sexual restrictiveness; 21 = prevalence of agriculture; 22 = segregated female technology; 23 = gender-integrated technology; 24 = male structures; 25 = macho; 26 = rape proness; 27 = interpersonal violence; 28 = female status. I have left off the letter prefix from the numbers of each variable in this matrix.

A complete description of each variable is contained earlier in this appendix.

Even the nontechnically trained reader can gain additional information from these tables. I suggest first looking down the column headed "significance level" in each of the five tables. If the notation there is listed as .10 or less, the relationship is considered a rare enough event to be called significant. Those relationships that met this statistical test appear on my chapter diagram represented by a line with an arrow connecting the two variables involved. You will note that many of the possible relationships do not come out significant. They were not all expected to come out significant. Rather, I designed causal diagrams, close to the final ones presented in the book, and expected only certain "paths" or relationships to come out significant.

The "path coefficients" column in Tables A.1 to A.5 presents the standardized regressions (called betas) and allows one to judge the relative strength of relationships in any one diagram. The higher the beta, the stronger that particular relationship. Each table has between 3 to 6 dependent variables and each of them have one or more predictor variables in the next column. There is a beta for each predictor variable with each dependent variable. There is also an "R Sq" for each regression on a dependent variable. R Sq stands for the amount of variance in the dependent variable explained by all the predictor variables. That measure varies

TABLE A.1   Significance Levels and Path Coefficients for Diagram 3.1 on Husband's Sexual Jealousy*

DEPENDENT VARIABLE**	PREDICTOR VARIABLES	SIGNIFICANCE LEVEL	PATH COEFFICIENTS (BETA)
Husband's Sexual Jealousy: R Sq. = .284	Female Premarital Sexual Perm.	.545	−.077
	Import.-Marriage	.041	.273
	Import.-Property	.052	.254
	Male Kin Group	.038	.254
Female Premar. Sexual Perm.: R Sq. = .100	Import.-Marriage	.017	−.316
	Import.-Property	.115	.221
	Male Kin Groups	.378	−.116
Import-Marriage: R Sq. = .206	Import.-Property	.000	.410
	Male Kin Groups	.049	.203
Import.-Property: R Sq. = .001	Male Kin Groups	.828	−.025

*This note applies to all five tables. The significance levels and the betas are based on pair-wise deletion. The significance limit was set at .10. A .10 level in multiple regression is a two tail test and thus it is equal to a .05 level on a one tail test as in Pearson correlations. All relationships were checked by listwise deletion as well. I used a stepwise backward-regression method. For the variables that did not make the .10 level of significance, I present the statistics based on the final equation in which they appeared. I use my variable titles, sometimes in abbreviated form, for all the variables.

**The numbers of the variables in the first regression in this table starting with the dependent variable, are H16 by SS6, H19, H17, SS3. For the exact wording of any variable consult the listing in this appendix.

TABLE A.2   Significance Levels and Path Coefficients for Diagram 3.2 on Wife's
Sexual Jealousy*

DEPENDENT VARIABLE	PREDICTOR VARIABLES	SIGNIFICANCE LEVEL	PATH COEFFICIENTS (BETA)
Wife's Sexual Jealousy: R Sq = .317	Female Premarital Sexual Perm.	.009	.501
	Import.-Marriage	.100	.303
	Import.-Property	.644	−.082
	Male Kin Groups	.053	.357
Female Premar. Sexual Perm.: R Sq = .100	Import.-Marriage	.017	−.316
	Import.-Property	.115	.221
	Male Kin Groups	.378	−.116
Import-Marriage: R Sq = .206	Import.-Property	.000	.410
	Male Kin Groups	.049	.203
Import.-Property: R Sq = .001	Male Kin Groups	.828	−.025

*The numbers of the variables in the first regression in this table are H15 by SS6, H19, H17, SS3. Check the listing in this appendix for the exact wording of any variable.

from zero to 1.0, and the higher it is, the more variance explained in the dependent variable. The more variance explained by the independent or predictor variables, the more accurately we could predict change in the dependent variable. My major interest here is theoretical and not prediction, and therefore I do not stress how much variance I explain but rather whether the relationships came out significant and fit with a particular explanatory schema.[10] I realize some of this may be complex for those who haven't used these techniques. Any standard statistics text will be quite helpful.

Basically, a causal diagram is an attempt to portray accurately the actual correlations among the variables. I could have presented additional statistics and thereby further detailed the nature of my statistical findings. I refrained from doing this because I feel the data from the Standard Sample that I am using are crude, and it is best to treat the analysis of such data as a pilot study for arriving at causal notions that will be tested further in future research. Perhaps others will be able to test my explanations more precisely with additional data and codes.

I hope some of the readers will have sufficient interest to further explore my findings on the Standard Sample. New data codes are developed all the time. The lack of detailed analysis of sexual customs by many ethnographers has led to sexuality, even for the Standard Sample societies, being inadequately described. This inadequate coverage of sexuality inevitably leads to coding problems because with inadequate data, reliable and valid codes are indeed hard to come by. I tried to deal with this problem by selecting the best variables available, but there still are many problems. However, my reading of current anthropological work indicates that this situation is being remedied. In part this is so because of the greater influence today by anthropologists with an interest in gender and sexuality. For

TABLE A.3 Significance Levels and Path Coefficients for Diagram 4.1 on Female Gender Inequality*

DEPENDENT VARIABLE	PREDICTOR VARIABLES	SIGNIFICANCE LEVEL	PATH COEFFICIENTS (BETA)
Belief in	Machismo Emp.	.033	.253
Female	Mother-Inf. Involvement	.031	.257
Inferiority:	Father-Inf. Involvement	.716	−.044
R Sq. = .233	Class Stratification	.008	.301
	Male Kin Groups	.154	.162
	Ext. Agriculture	.607	.061
Machismo	Mother-Inf. Involvement	.021	.275
Emphasis:	Father-Inf. Involvement	.030	−.257
R Sq. = .181	Class Stratification	.492	−.079
	Male Kin Groups	.296	.120
	Ext. Agriculture	.479	−.082
Mother-Infant	Father-Inf. Involvement	.000	−.301
Involvement	Class Stratification	.260	−.098
R Sq. = .111	Male Kin Groups	.440	.064
	Ext. Agriculture	.021	−.189
Father-Infant	Class Stratification	.482	−.059
Involvement	Male Kin Groups	.013	−.206
R Sq. = .042	Ext. Agriculture	.250	−.096
Class	Male Kin Groups	.091	.121
Stratification	Ext. Agriculture	.000	.344
R Sq. = .148			
Male Kin Groups	Ext. Agriculture	.016	.180
R. Sq. = .032			

*The numbers of the variables in the first regression in this table are W13 by W12, SS1, SS2, SS5, SS3, SS4. The reader can consult the listing of the variables earlier in this appendix for the exact wording.

TABLE A.4 Significance Levels and Path Coefficients for Diagram 6.1 on Male Homosexual Behavior*

DEPENDENT VARIABLE	PREDICTOR VARIABLES	SIGNIFICANCE LEVEL	PATH COEFFICIENTS (BETA)
Frequency-	Mother-Inf.		
Homosexual	Involvement	.007	.321
Behavior:	Father-Inf.		
R Sq = .224	Involvement	.296	−.127
	Class-Strat.	.001	.390
Mother-Inf.	Father-Inf.		
Involvement	Involvement	.001	−.290
R sq = .100	Class-Strat.	.062	−.152
Father-Inf.	Class-Strat.	.248	−.094
Involvement:			
R Sq = .009			

*The numbers of the variables in the first regression in this table are: B11 by SS1, SS2, SS5. Consult the listings of questions earlier in this appendix for the exact wording of any variable.

TABLE A.5 Significance Levels and Path Coefficients for Diagram 7.1 on Rape Proneness*

DEPENDENT VARIABLE	PREDICTOR VARIABLES	SIGNIFICANCE LEVEL	PATH COEFFICIENTS (BETA)
Rape Proneness: R Sq. = .355	Violence	.680	.083
	Belief-Female Inferior	.029	.432
	Macho	.080	.337
Violence:	Belief-Female Inferior	.899	−.027
R Sq = .134	Macho	.086	.366
Belief-Female Inferior: R Sq = .036	Macho	.155	.191

*The numbers of the variables in the first regression in this table are S26 by R14, W13, S25. The reader may consult the listing of the exact wording of variables earlier in this appendix.

industrialized societies we also have need for a firmer database upon which to examine our explanations. Here, too, I am encouraged by some of the recent research that even the U.S. government agencies have undertaken.[11]

I wish to end this technical appendix by reminding the reader that the ultimate goal of scientific research is explanation. So, if the details of the data overwhelm you once in a while, remember that they are the bases for developing more accurate and useful explanations of human sexuality.

SELECTED REFERENCES AND COMMENTS

1. Murdock, George P., and Douglas R. White, "Standard Cross Cultural Sample," *Ethnology,* vol. 8 (October 1969), pp. 329–369.

2. The sources for the 28 variables are
Whyte, Martin King, "Cross-cultural Codes Dealing with the Relative Status of Women," *Ethnology,* vol. 17 (April 1978), pp. 211–237.
Broude, Gwen J., and Sarah J. Greene, "Cross-cultural Codes on Twenty Sexual Attitudes and Practices," *Ethnology,* vol. 15 (October 1976), pp. 409–429.
Ross, Marc Howard, "Political Decision Making and Conflict: Additional Cross-cultural Codes and Scales," *Ethnology,* vol. 22 (April 1983), pp. 169–192.
The raw data and codes from Hupka and Sanday were sent to me upon request. They are unpublished, but these authors have analyzed these data in the following publications:
Sanday, Peggy Reeves, "The Socio-cultural Context of Rape: A Cross-cultural Study," *Journal of Social Issues,* vol. 37, no. 4 (October 1981), pp. 5–27.
Hupka, Ralph, "Cultural Determinants of Jealousy," *Alternative Lifestyles,* vol. 4 (August 1981), pp. 310–356.
The data from the Standard Sample were purchased on a computer tape from HRAF (the Human Relations Area Files) in New Haven, Connecticut. Anyone wishing these data can contact HRAF, and anyone wishing the Sanday or Hupka data

will have to contact them for permission. Sanday is a professor at the University of Pennsylvania, and Hupka is a professor at California State University in Long Beach.

3. Variables SS4, SS5, and SS6 are codes from the Ethnographic Atlas. Since the Standard Sample is a subset of the atlas, any codes available for the atlas can be used on the Standard Sample.

4. The frequencies given for each variable are in a few instances slightly different than those presented by the sources I consulted. I carefully checked such differences and reconciled them as best I could. They were differences only of one or two cases in a particular category of response.

I should clarify further the reasons for many of the codes not being available for all 186 societies. Whyte took a 50% sample of the 186 societies and thus chose to use only 93 of the societies. Ross also chose a 50% sample of the 186 societies in his coding and found 3 of them uncodable and so ended up with 90 societies. Hupka obtained his societies from the HRAF files and came up with only 80 cultures that were in the Standard Sample. Sanday found only 156 societies of the Standard Sample were sufficiently codable for her purposes. Broude also found that many of the societies in the Standard Sample lacked sufficient information on enough of her variables to be useful. She used between 31 and 102 societies for the codes I used in this book.

5. Hupka's coding schema is described in the following paper:

Hupka, Ralph B., and James M. Ryan, "The Cultural Contribution to Emotions: Cross-cultural Aggression in Romantic Jealousy Situations." Paper presented at the meetings of the Western Psychological Association, Los Angeles, 1981.

6. Murdock, George P., and Caterina Provost, "Factors in the Division of Labor by Sex: A Cross-cultural Analysis," Chapter 10 in Herbert Barry and Alice Schlegel, (ed.), *Cross-cultural Samples and Codes*. Pittsburgh: University of Pittsburgh Press, 1980.

7. The numbers of the variables that were not used in any of the diagrams are 7, 8, 9, 10, 18, 20, 21, 22, 23, 24, 27, and 28.

8. There were 53 path coefficients checked in these five diagrams. Listwise and pairwise deletion methods agreed on 46 of them. There are problems with using listwise or pairwise deletion procedures with these data. But my use of both and final reliance on pairwise is in line with current views. See:

Anderson, Andy B., A Basilevsky, and D.P.J. Hum, "Missing Data: A Review of the Literature," Chapter 12 in Peter H. Rossi, James D. Wright, and Andy B. Anderson (eds.), *Handbook of Survey Research*. New York: Academic, 1983.

9. In some instances the dependent variables I used in my regression analysis were dichotomies. I did use other statistical techniques, including tabular analysis, to check for any distortion this may have produced. As far as I could tell, the use of dichotomies as dependent variables did not distort my findings.

10. All my causal diagrams assume asymmetrical relationships, that is, oneway causation. Of course, reality may well in some cases involve two-way causation or a "feedback loop." The assumption of asymmetry is simply a convenient way to make a first approximation in a causal diagram. I do not view it as the final word.

For the reader interested in the many intricate issues connected with causal analysis in the social sciences, I suggest the followng brief selections:

Freese, Lee, (ed.) *Theoretical Methods in Sociology*. Pittsburgh: University of Pittsburgh Press, 1980.

Bailey, K.D., "Evaluating Axiomatic Theories," pp. 48–71 in E.F. Borgatta and G.W. Bohrnstedt (eds.), *Sociological Methodology*. San Francisco: Jossey-Bass, 1970.

Costner, H.L., and R. Leik, "Deductions from Axiomatic Theory," pp. 49–72 in H. Blalock, Jr. (ed.), *Causal Models in the Social Sciences*. Chicago: Aldine, 1971.

11. A recent government study, the National Survey of Family Growth (cycle 3), included within it questions on the timing of first sexual intercourse. Not too long ago the government would have avoided such questions. I consider this a very positive step toward improved knowledge regarding human sexuality. I believe it will aid us in dealing with the many problems related to sexuality. See

U.S. Department of Health and Human Services, National Center for Health Statistics, C.A. Bachrach and M.C. Horn, "Marriage and First Intercourse, Martial Dissolution, and Remarriage: U.S., 1982," no. 107. Hyattsville,Md.: Public Health Service, April 1985.

APPENDIX B

DIAGRAMMATIC PRESENTATION OF THE PROPOSITIONS

There are some readers who would like to see the 25 propositions from Chapter Eight presented in diagrammatic form. By this I mean simply one diagram for each proposition. It is not my intent to try to interrelate all 25 propositions in one diagram even though that would be a most valuable undertaking for it would reveal interrelationships and missing propositions. I leave that serious task for the future. Below are the 25 propositions, individually diagramed. It will be helpful to consult the verbal presentation in Chapter 8 for any futher clarity about each proposition.

1. Stability of a Relationship $\xrightarrow{+}$ Importance of a Relationship

2. Physical Pleasure & Self Disclosure $\xrightarrow{+}$ Stable Social Relationship

3. Sexual Behavior $\xrightarrow{+}$ Physical Pleasure and Self Disclosure

4. Stable Sexual Relationship $\xrightarrow{+}$ Judged as Important

5. Stable Heterosexual Relationships $\xrightarrow{+}$ Nurturance of Newborn

6. Stable Heterosexual Relationships $\xrightarrow{+}$ Kinship Customs
   $\xrightarrow{+}$ Gender Roles

7. Importance of Social Relationship $\xrightarrow{+}$ Institutionalized Protective Mechanism

8. Importance of Marital Sexuality $\xrightarrow{+}$ Protective Jealousy Customs

9. Power of Group $\xrightarrow{+}$ Attaining Valued Social Goals

10. Power of Group $\xrightarrow{+}$ Group sexual Rights in: Sexual Scripts, Erotica, & Avoidance of Sexual Abuse

11. Power of Group in Key Institutions $\xrightarrow{+}$ Prestige of Group in Society

12. Common Group Residence $\xrightarrow{+}$ Power of Group

13. Common Resident Descent Group $\xrightarrow{+}$ Power of Descent Group
$\xrightarrow{-}$ Sexual Abuse

14. Institutional Specialization $\xrightarrow{-}$ Power of Specialist in Other Institutions

15. Female Specialization in Family $\xrightarrow{-}$ Female Power in Other Institutions

16. Operant Institutional Values $\xleftarrow{+}\rightarrow$ Type of Ideologies

17. Institutionalized Gender Dominance $\xleftarrow{+}\rightarrow$ Gender Dominant Ideology

18. Type of General Ideology $\xrightarrow{+}$ Type of Sexual Ideology

19. Gender Dominant in Basic Ideology $\xrightarrow{+}$ Gender Dominant in: Sexual Ideology, Erotica Preference, & Sexual Scripts

20. Integration with Gender Ideology $\xrightarrow{+}$ Acceptability of Heterosexuality and Homosexuality

21. Rigidity of Gender Ideology $\xrightarrow{+}$ Sexual Non-Conformity

22. Institutional Flexibility $\xrightarrow{+}$ Initiator of Change in Other Institutions

23. Economic Changes $\xrightarrow{+}$ Change in Other Institutions

24. Change in Non-Kinship Institutions $\xleftarrow{+}\rightarrow$ Change in Marital Jealousy, Gender Roles, and Sexual Ideologies

25. Changes in Marital Jealousy, Gender Roles, and Sexual Ideologies $\xleftarrow{+}\rightarrow$ Changes in Sexual Behavior

There is an obvious need for conceptual definition in order to test these propositions. A start on this can be obtained by looking up some of these concepts in the Glossary and Index to this book. In some instances I had to make slight changes in the proposition in order to better diagram it. For those who will seek to refine, expand and interrelate these propositions: Good Luck! Please inform me of your results.

GLOSSARY

The definitions and explanations offered here are based on the usage of the terms in this book. In most cases that is very similar to how the terms are used elsewhere, but by no means is this always the case. I have tried to include all the key concepts for which I felt an easy reference would be helpful to the reader.

Abnormal: Those characteristics that disable an individual from functioning in all types of human societies.

Altruism, Selfishness: Altruistic behavior is behavior in which the welfare of others is internalized as part of the actor's own welfare to the degree desired by that society. Behavior is labeled as selfish when the actor has not fused the welfare of others with his or her own welfare to the degree desired by that society. The distinction thus turns on the composition of the self, not on whether the action is self-oriented. All actions are presumed here to be self-oriented.

Aggression: Aggressive behavior aims at inflicting injury of some sort, verbal or physical, on others.

Androgen: A type of hormone that promotes male genitalia development and functioning as well as promoting the secondary characteristics (growth of beard, for example) that accompany genetic male maturation. The term *androgen* includes testosterone, aldosterone, and androsterone.

Anthropology: The field that studies human social life in a variety of cultural settings. As used here the focus is upon what American anthropologists call cultural anthropology and what the British anthropologists call social anthropology. However, the broader field of anthropology includes archeology, linguistics, and physical anthropology.

Assumption, Scientific: Fundamental assertions about the nature of the world we scientifically study. Such statements are not empirically testable, for they are the starting point of our reasoning. An example would be the assumption that the world is knowable through the senses.

Autonomy, Individual: Refers to the degree to which one is not controlled by outside pressures but permitted to rule oneself. The same term may be applied to parts of a society. For example, universities in America are generally not highly restricted by political and economic pressures, and thus American universities are high on autonomy.

Axiomatic Theory: At its simplest level it is a type of scientific explanation that involves stating premises that are assumed to be true and then logically deducing from those premises relationships that can be empirically tested.

Bestiality: Sexual relationships between a human and a nonhuman animal. Also called zoophilia.

Biology: The science that studies life processes of organisms. Included here would be physiology, anatomy, endocrinology, and primatology.

Bisexual: A person who is relatively equally sexually attracted to the same and opposite genders.

Body-Centered Sexuality: Sexual interaction focused upon the body of the partner rather than the personality of the partner.

Bonding: A strong emotional attachment between two individuals.

Bridewealth: A common marriage custom wherein the groom presents some gifts to the bride's family. Also known as brideprice.

Cause: One or more conditions that are necessary and sufficient for the production of some effect. A necessary condition is one that must occur if the effect is to occur. A sufficient condition is one that is always followed by the effect. A condition may be necessary but not sufficient to produce the effect. Drug experimentation may, for example be necessary but not sufficient to produce addiction. A condition may be sufficient but only one of the ways to produce the effect, and thus it is not necessary. Loss of all one's blood, for example, is a sufficient cause of death but not the only cause and so not necessary. Rarely do we find conditions that are necessary and sufficient in social science. Causal analysis, like politics, is the art of the possible and the probable.

Causal Diagram: A diagram that presents the causally related variables in time sequences, usually with arrows drawn to indicate the causal direction (or directions), and showing whether the relationship is positive, negative, or otherwise. One type of causal diagram would be what sociologists call a path diagram.

Chromosomal Sex: Genetic sex usually symbolized by the presence of XX(female) or XY(male) genes in the chromosomes of the individual and present in all body cells.

Clitoridectomy: The surgical removal of the clitoris or portions thereof.

Coding, Research: A research procedure aimed at placing into clear categories responses obtained on a particular measure. For example, you may ask people how often they go to church and then divide their answers into several categories from zero to every day. That process of creating categories and putting answers into them is called coding. It is an essential part of quantitative research.

Cognitive Ideology: A lifeview that emphasizes the place of intellectual activity and choice in human decision making.

Correlation: The relationship of a change in one variable to a change in other variables. If only two variables are related, the correlation is bivariate; if more than two, multivariate. All causally related variables are correlated, but not all correlations are causal. Going to college, for example, may be correlated with obtaining high-paying jobs, but it may well not be the college education that caused college people to obtain high-paying jobs. Rather, it may be that college people come from wealthier families to begin with and would get better-paying jobs even if they did not go to college.

Coverture: A feudal doctrine adopted into English common law that asserted that after marriage a woman must turn over all her property and money to her husband. From that point on the woman was unable to engage in legally binding contracts, and even her children legally belonged to her husband. Starting in the nineteenth century, the laws in the United States gradually rescinded such restrictions.

Culture: The social "inheritance" of a group, that is, the shared ways of thinking, feeling, and believing that are passed down from one generation to another. The term is also used to indicate a total society or group, particularly a small nonindustrialized society. It does *not* refer only to music and art.

Culture: Covert, Overt: Covert culture consists of those shared ways of thinking, feeling, and believing that are usually not directly communicated but whose presence can be detected by long-term residence in a group. Those elements of culture that are explicitly stated in obvious ways comprise overt culture.

Cultural Scripts: Normative statements shared by a group concerning the ways individuals in specific social roles should act, think, and feel.

Cunnilingus: Oral stimulation of the female genitalia.

Custom: A shared way of interacting socially that has been present in a group for a generation or more.

Deductive: A type of logical reasoning that starts with a general proposition and derives less general, lower-level propositions consistent with it. For example, "Sexual customs are viewed as important in all societies. The United States is a society. Therefore, U.S. sexual customs will be viewed as important." Such deductive reasoning is an essential part of axiomatic theory.

Definitions: Nominal, Operational, Real: There are three types of definitions. There is a nominal definition, which simply states that we agree to use these particular words to describe some phenomenon. The definition of *tiglon* as an offspring of a tiger and a lion is a nominal definition. It does not claim to be "true" but merely to be a convenient way to refer to such offspring. There are also operational definitions, which simply assert the specific measurements one will use to define a concept. An example would be using dollars of income to measure social class. Finally, there are real definitions, which attempt to get at the essence of a phenomenon. My definitions of sexuality and family are two examples of real definitions found in the glossary. Real definitions relate a term that has some shared social meaning to its definition. In this sense, a real definition asserts a proposition and thus can be tested empirically. One way of testing a real definition is to see if the common meaning of a term is identified with the definition of that term you have formulated. Do people think of sexuality when you refer to genital response? Real definitions, then, do have truth value and can be part of a logical system of inferences. All three types of definition are important in scientific work.

Dichotomy: The division of a class or category into two mutually exclusive groups, for example, rich and poor, black and white, male and female.

Disclosure: The degree to which one reveals parts of the self that are not obvious or widely known.

Double Standard: The judging of the same act by two different standards for two different groups, for example, allowing males more premarital heterosexual rights than females.

Dowry: A gift made at marriage by the bride to her husband.

Dysfunctional: A part of a social system that disrupts the operation of another part of that system. Abortion is dysfunctional for adoption, for example, since unwanted babies are the supply source for adoptions.

Emotions: Primary, Secondary: Primary emotions are those considered to be universal and basic, such as anger, fear, happiness, surprise, disgust, and sadness. Secondary emotions are those derived from some combination of these primary emotions, for example, jealousy.

Emotive ideology: A lifeview that asserts the priority of emotions in the decision making of humans.

Empirical: That which is derived from observation or experimentation.

Endocrine System: An integrated set of glands, such as the thyroid or the adrenal, that secret directly into the bloodstream. Our hormones are produced by such glands.

Endocrinology: The scientific study of the physiology of the endocrine glands.

Equalitarianism: A doctrine asserting the similar worth of all groups of people. Also called egalitarianism.

Equality, Social: Usually the equality of a group is measured in terms of the relative degree of power of that group in the major social institutions.

Erotic: That which arouses sexual desire.

Erotica: Literature of art that is intended to arouse sexual desire. Sometimes called pornography.

Erotica: Hardcore, Softcore: Hardcore erotica is that which explicitly displays the genitalia in states of sexual excitation and the behaviors accompanying such states. Softcore erotica may display genitalia but not in states of sexual excitement and often only simulates sexual behaviors.

Essence: That without which the thing being described would not exist, that is, its intrinsic and indispensable properties. Part of the essence of sexuality is erotic arousal and genital response. A person lacking that would not be experiencing the essence of sexuality.

Estrogen: A hormone present in much larger quantities in females that promotes the growth of female secondary sex characteristics, such as breasts.

Ethnographer: A person who studies a society and describes it for others. Usually the society is a nonindustrialized society and is not native to the ethnographer. Cultural anthropologists are ethnographers.

Ethnographic Atlas: The collection of computer-useable information on some 1200 cultures developed by George Peter Murdock.

Exchange Theory: An explanatory schema concerning human behavior that emphasizes the individual balancing of computed rewards and costs in the making of decisions.

Family Institution: The normative ways in which a small kinship group performs the key function of nurturant socialization of the newborn.

Fantasy: The creation of mental images through imagination, association, and invention.

Fellatio: The oral stimulation of the penis.

Feminism: The doctrine that asserts that women deserve equal rights with men in all spheres.

Freudianism: A set of beliefs derived from the ideas of Sigmund Freud (1856–1939). Basic among them are the importance of the unconscious, the stages of psychosexual development (oral, anal, and phallic), and, relatedly, the efficacy of helping patients resolve problems by exploring their earliest experiences.

Functional: A part of a social system that tends to support another part of that system. For example, norms supporting autonomy for teenagers tend to support their premarital sexual experiences.

Gender: A cultural construct applied to the newborn usually according to their genital appearance. Some cultures have more than just the male and female gender, and some allow for change of gender.

Gender Identity: Self-definition as a male or female (or other genders if the society has them).

Gender Role: The set of rights and duties given by a particular society to those occupying the specific gender categories in that society. Such rights and duties apply to behavior and attitudes in all the major life areas of that society.

Group: A number of individuals who have a "we" feeling, common norms, and patterned relationships with each other.

Group Marriage: A marriage in which there are multiple mates of more than one gender—a form of polygamy.

Hedonism: The philosophy that asserts that all people pursue pleasure and seek to avoid pain. This view goes back to Greek philosophers like Epicurus but was popularized in the eighteenth and nineteenth centuries by British utilitarian philosophers like Jeremy Bentham and John Stuart Mill. Mill added to the pursuit of pleasure a concern for producing the greatest amount of good by human actions. Many subtypes of hedonism have developed over the years.

Heterosexual: Cross-gender (male-female) sexual thoughts, feelings, or behaviors. Those who prefer this orientation are called heterosexuals.

Homosexual: Same-gender sexual thoughts, feelings, or behaviors. Those who prefer this orientation are called homosexuals.

Hormones: Internal secretions of endocrine glands.

Human Relations Area Files (HRAF): The original cross-cultural files started by George Peter Murdock in the late 1930s. Topics of interest on cultures were indexed on cards covering the information on that topic for all available cultures. Out of this endeavor came the Ethnographic Atlas and then the Standard Sample.

Hypothalamus: A structure at the base of the brain that can affect the hormonal balance in our bodies as well as our emotional behaviors. It controls the pituitary gland, which in turn regulates our entire endocrine system.

Ideology: The fundamental beliefs of a group concerning human nature. The cognitive and emotive ideologies are illustrative. There are more specific ideologies: for example, sexual ideologies assert the level of equality and permissiveness that agree with the nature of each gender as defined by that culture.

Inductive: A type of reasoning that starts with finding specific relationships and then logically derives a more general explanatory statement that will subsume the more specific statements. It is reasoning from the particular to the general. For example: "Sexual attitudes predict sexual behavior. Political attitudes predict political behavior. Thus, attitudes predict behavior." There is a probabilistic nature to inductive reasoning, as you can see in the example, and the need for empirical testing is obvious.

Infibulation: A custom that usually involves surgical removal of the clitoris and parts of the labia and the sewing up of the remaining labia so that coital access to the vagina is most difficult, if not impossible.

Institution: An accepted, normatively defined means by which individuals in specific social roles fulfill some crucial requirements of the society. An example would be the family institution composed of the ways in which kin groups nurture the newborn.

Institutionalized: The development of stable, predictable patterns of social interaction based upon a common normative agreement. The result of such institutionalization is the basic set of institutions that we find in all societies.

Isomorphism: The degree to which two things are seen as identical in form, for example, a map and the territory being mapped.

Jealousy, Sexual: A boundary-setting custom developed for limiting sexual access to those relationships that a group defines as important. On an interpersonal level it is a felt threat from an outsider to an important relationship in which one is involved and produces feelings of anger and fear.

Kinship: A social relationship defined either by belief in descent ties (parent-child or sibling ties) or affinal ties (in laws via marriage). In some societies there also are fictive kin ties, such as those with godparents.

Levirate: A custom that decrees that when an older brother dies, his younger brother should marry the widow.

Linkages, Social: The focus here is upon the ways in which one part of a society is connected to another part. To illustrate: in this book we have often spoken about how the differential social power of the genders is linked to the sexual customs of the genders.

Lordotic: A common position for primate sexual intercourse in which the female bends over with her rear in the air and the male mounts her from behind.

Love: A strong emotional attachment to another person. The exact specifications permitting the feeling to be called love depends on the cultural definition that prevails in one's group. The term is also used sometimes in connection with objects, ideas, and Gods.

Machismo: A characteristic of male gender roles that stresses male physical aggressiveness, high risk taking, and casual sexual relations with women. Men with this orientation are called macho.

Macro, Micro: In sociology these are two levels of analysis. A macro level of analysis searches for relationships among the larger segments of the society, such as between the political and economic institutions. Macro sociologists also compare entire societies with each other and are called comparative sociologists. A micro level of analysis searches for relationships within a single institution or within the smaller segments of society, such as friendship groups. Micro sociologists are closer to psychology, while macro sociologists are closer to anthropology in their conceptual interests.

Mahu: In Polynesian societies there often was one male in each village who was a transvestite and was called a Mahu. Most writers assume that the Mahu preferred homosexuality. The Mahu was a casual sexual outlet for some of the heterosexual males of the village.

Marital Institution: This institution consists of the normative ways in which husband and wife roles legitimate parenthood.

Marriage, Cross-Cousin: A cross-cousin is a child of your parent's sibling of the opposite gender. A common form of marriage would be matrilateral cross-cousin, wherein the male child would marry his mother's brother's daughter. Patrilateral cross-cousin marriage is rarer and involves the male child marrying his father's sister's daughter.

Marxism: The explanatory schema derived from the works of Karl Marx (1818–1883) stressing the important role of the economic institution in the creation of exploitative ruling groups. There are many varieties of adherents today.

Matriarchy: A society in which the major sources of power are in the hands of the female gender.

Matrilineal: A descent system that traces descent only through one of the four grandparents, namely, one's mother's mother.

Matrilocal: A residence system in which a bride brings her husband to live with her in or near her parental home. The term *uxorilocal* is also used.

Mobility: Geographic, Social: Geographic mobility refers to movement in physical space, as from one city to another; social mobility refers to movement in social space, as from one social class to another.

Nadle: A third gender in the Navajo culture. Members of this gender are those who are dissatisfied with the male or female gender role as well as those born with ambiguous genitalia.

Normality: Normality is the appropriate label for all characteristics except those that would disable an individual from functioning in all types of human societies.

Normative: Refers to being shaped by norms.

Norms: Norms are standards for behavior that are shared by the members of a group.

Nurture: The giving of emotional response and/or support.

Objectivity, Scientific: The state of being unbiased by private moral values in the conduct of scientific research. Fairness and impartiality are the goals of scientific research. Objectivity is another word for the accepted orientation towards scientific explanations.

Obscenity: This is a legal concept that in the United States implies that the erotic materials appeal to the prurient interest, violate community values, and have no serious scientific or other value.

Oceanic Kiss: An ancient way of kissing in Polynesia that emphasizes placing your face to the cheek of the other person and smelling his or her skin.

Ockham's Razor: The position that one should prefer the simpler to the more complex explanation. Named after a fourteenth-century British Franciscan.

Orgasm: A subjectively experienced significant peak of physical pleasure during sexual relationships.

Orgasm Disclosure Ratio: For a given time period it is the number of people who have seen you experience an orgasm divided by the total number of people with whom you are socially interacting.

Path Analysis: A type of causal analysis developed in genetics and economics and now widely used in sociology. The attempt is to determine the fit of a particular causal ordering of variables with the relationships that exist in your data set. It is based upon multiple-regression techniques.

Patriarchy: A society in which the major sources of power are controlled by males.

Patrilineal: A system of tracing descent in which only one of the four grandparents is the direct line of descent, specifically, one's father's father. Also called aganatic descent.

Patrilocal: A system of residence wherein after marriage the husband brings his bride to live with or near his parents. The term *virilocal* is also used.

Person-centered Sexuality: Sexual interaction focused upon the broad range of traits making up the basic personality of one's partner.

Polyandry: A marriage system in which there is one wife and multiple husbands.

Polygamy: A marriage system in which there are multiple mates of at least one gender. Polyandry, polygyny, and group marriage are all forms of polygamy.

Polygyny: A marriage system in which there is one male and multiple wives.

Polynesia: An area of the Pacific Ocean forming a triangle between Hawaii on the north, New Zealand on the south, and Easter Island on the east. Melanesia and Micronesia are other island areas just west of a line drawn from New Zealand to Hawaii.

Pornography: The popular term for what we call in this book erotica.

Postulate: A general term in theory building for a statement that is the beginning point of a line of reasoning. From such a statement one can deduce more specific propositions. For example, "The greater the social interaction level of a group, the greater its cohesiveness and relative power compared to other groups." From that postulate one may deduce that the professional group or the religious group or any specific group that interacts the most will be the most powerful. That deduction can then be tested empirically. Sometimes the concept *axiom* is used interchangeably with *postulate*.

Power: The ability of a person or group, against resistance, to influence another person or group. Power supported by norms is called legitimate or authorized, and the exercise of influence that is not so supported is called unauthorized power.

Proposition: A general term in theory building that refers to a statement relating two or more variables in a specific fashion. For example, "The greater the power of a group, the greater the likelihood that they will possess what is valued in that society." Propositions are the prime element in theory construction in science.

Psychology: The science that studies individual thoughts, feelings, and behaviors. There are many specializations within psychology, and in recent decades the importance of the social context for understanding the individual has been stressed.

Rational: The ability to reason; often operationalized by the ability to choose the most efficient means to a given end.

Reality: Erotic, Everyday: Erotic reality consists of the way the world is experienced when one is erotically aroused. Everyday reality refers to the way the world is experienced when one is not erotically aroused. For example, the way one would treat another person may well vary by whether or not one is erotically aroused by that person.

Regression, Multiple: A form of multivariate analysis used when there are three or more variables. It allows one to discern the net affect of each independent variable on the dependent variable and to examine each relationship in greater detail than the use of only a correlation coefficient would permit.

Relativism: A philosophical perspective that stresses the lack of universally valid conclusion concerning which perspective is better. This viewpoint can be applied beyond the field of ethics to any perspective on the world.

Reliability: The degree to which one can achieve the same results in a repeat measurement of a research instrument or scale. It is a measure of consistency and lack of ambiguity. A test may be reliable but not valid. That is, it may yield the same measurements time and again but not be measuring what it is supposed to measure. (Ask any student about this!)

Roles: Roles are the rights and duties that go with occupying a particular position in the social structure. Thus, a student has the right of attending class and the duty to take exams. One can speak of role performance as well as role expectation.

Sadomasochism: The combination of sadism and masochism. Sadism refers to obtaining sexual pleasure from inflicting pain on others, while masochism refers to obtaining sexual pleasure from receiving pain from others.

Science: Systematized knowledge based on observation and experimentation that is aimed at explaining and predicting the phenomenon studied.

Sensual: Pertaining to effects on any of the senses. Thus, *sensual* is broader than *sexual*. We can sensually appreciate a fine dinner but have no sexual response. All sexual responses would involve the senses in some fashion and thus be one type of sensual response. The reverse is obviously not true.

Sex: One's genetic or chromosomal sex. For example XX (female) or XY (male).

Sexual or Sexuality: From a societal point of view, those behaviors and attitudes that are part of a society's cultural scripts aimed at erotic arousal and genital response. The two major outcomes of sexuality are physical pleasure and self-disclosure.

Sexual Abuse: On a societal level this would consist of those sexual acts that are negatively sanctioned. On a personal level it would be those unwanted sexual acts that are imposed.

Sexual Scripts: Those cultural scripts that are aimed at erotic arousal.

Social Class: A category of people within a stratified society who share similar socioeconomic status and life chances.

Social Psychology: A scientific field that is part of both psychology and sociology that stresses understanding the ways in which the social system affects the individual, particularly in small-group settings such as in love or friendship groups.

Social System: An interrelated set of statuses and roles. This can be as broad as a society, with major institutions interrelated, or it can be as small as a single group, with individual member roles interrelated.

Society: A group with a shared culture and social roles structured for the occupants of the key positions in the major institutions. It is assumed that all major institutions will be present in a society; at a minimum that would include political, economic, family, and religious institutions.

Sociobiology: This term is used to refer to an explanatory approach that emphasizes the importance of biological evolutionary processes in shaping present social systems. For example, sociobiologists often say that males are more interested in a variety of partners than are females because it was to their evolutionary advantage to impregnate as many partners as possible and thereby increase the survival of their own traits. In contrast, a sociologist would stress group training and power differentials as the source of such a male-female difference.

Sociology: The science that studies human societies. It is broader than economics and political science, for it studies not only those institutions but others and the overall society thereby created. It overlaps a great deal with cultural anthropology, although it is generally more rigorous in its use of scientific methodology and less cross-cultural. There is some overlap with psychology, particularly for micro-oriented sociologists.

Sodomy: Usually refers to male homosexual anal intercourse. However, in our legal system sodomy can mean any "unnatural sexual act," and that could be construed to include heterosexual anal intercourse, oral sexuality, homosexuality in general, and heterosexuality in "unusual" positions.

Sororate: The marriage custom that states that when a sister dies, the surviving sister will marry the widower.

Standard Cross-cultural Sample: Also called the Standard Sample. A sample of 186 societies chosen by Murdock and White in 1969 as the best-described representative sample of the nonindustrialized cultures of the world. Many codes describing these cultures were formulated in 1969, and since then many have been added. The Standard Sample data are available on computer tape.

Statistically Significant: This means the relationship you are examining is rare enough so that you can rule out the effect of sampling and accept the relationship found as worthy of further investigation.

Status: Often used as an equivalent of social prestige or honor. Also indicates the rights and duties related to a position with a socially assigned amount of prestige. Roles are the dynamic acting out of the rights and duties connected with such a position.

Stratification, Social: A ranking of statuses and roles in a social system. Each rank has significant differences in power and prestige and may consist of people who identify with each other and share a common subculture. Such a rank can be called a social class or a social caste, depending on whether one's position is based on achievement or on ascription at birth.

Structure: A pattern or design in the relationship of parts in a system. In sociology, we speak of social structure meaning the patterned way in which the key institutional roles are interrelated. The structure of a marriage would entail the roles of husband and wife and the cultural prescriptions concerning how they are to interrelate. Sometimes the term *system* is interchanged with structure. The key difference is that those who use the term *system* focus on the dynamic aspect of the interrelations, while those use the term *structure* focus more on its stable form.

Subjectivism: A philosophical position that contends that our knowledge is produced by our own mind. The external world in such a view is either denied or viewed as unimportant. The term is also used to support a relativistic ethical position.

Subordination: The placing of a group or class in a lower rank relative to another group or class.

System: This is a general term simply referring to an interrelated set of parts. To illustrate: One may speak of the family system and thereby refer to the interrelation of husband-wife and parent-child roles, or one may speak of the interrelations of our major social institutions as a system.

Theory, Scientific: An interrelated set of propositions that explain the phenomena being examined. Theories can be tested by making predictions logically based upon them. They can be refined by examining them in a variety of social contexts to see if they vary. They can be refuted by an alternative explanation that is simpler or more accurate in its predictions. The ultimate goal of all science is to explain the world by developing sound theoretical statements.

Transsexual: An individual who feels that he or she is trapped in the body of the wrong genetic sex. Some such individuals undergo surgery to integrate their body with their gender preferences.

Transvestite: An individual aroused by dressing in the costumes of the opposite gender.

Universal, Social: An assertion about social life that holds in all societies. Examples would be "Nurturance of the newborn is always done by a small kinship group" or "Sexuality is always societally shaped." It is usually assumed that if such a practice is universally present, it likely is universally necessary for the survival of society. However, additional evidence and reasoning beyond universal presence are needed to establish such universal necessity.

Validity: The extent to which a measuring instrument measures what it purports to measure, is its validity. If you say you are measuring racial prejudice by an attitude scale, the validity can be examined if we have individuals whose prejudice level we believe we know. We can then administer the attitude scale to see if these individuals score in accord with our knowledge. If they do, we would to that extent affirm the validity of our measuring instrument.

Value, Social: That which a group feels ought to be desired. For example, in America, freedom, equality, love, and democracy are values. It is from such values that norms or standards for behavior are constructed.

Value Hierarchies: A group usually ranks its values to indicate which are more important. The resultant ranking of values is what is called a value hierarchy.

Value, Importance of: The further up the hierarchy of values, the greater the importance of a value. We assume that sexuality is always high on a society's hierarchy even when that society is striving to restrict sexuality to marriage.

Value Judgment: This is a statement about the world that is made in such a way as to imply how one ought to behave and that is stated in a fashion not scientifically testable. For example, "If you do not go to church, you will go to hell" is a value judgment. It instructs you how you ought to behave, and there is no scientific way to test it.

Variable: A concept defined so that its magnitude may be measured. For example, family size, degree of stratification, and level of sexual permissiveness are all variables, for they all can be quantitatively measured.

Variable: Dependent, Independent: A dependent variable is that which a researcher is trying to explain. In a causal framework it is the effect. An independent variable is that which is associated with some outcome. In a causal framework it would be a cause. Independent variables are sometimes called predictor variables.

BIBLIOGRAPHY

ABEL, GENE G., DAVID H. BARLOW, EDWARD B. BLANCHARD, and DONALD GUILD, "The Components of Rapists' Sexual Arousal," *Archives of General Psychiatry*, vol. 34 (August 1977), pp. 895-903.

ABEL, GENE G., JUDITH V. BECKER, EDWARD B. B. BLANCHARD, and DJENDEREDJIAN, "Differentiating Sexual Aggressives with Penile Measures," *Criminal Justice and Behavior*, vol. 5, no. 4 (December 1978), pp. 315-332.

ABEL, GENE G., JUDITH V. BECKER, WILLIAM D. MURPHY, and BARRY FLANAGAN, "Identifying Dangerous Child Molesters," Chapter 6 in R.B. Stuart (ed.), *Violent Behavior: Social Learning Approaches to Prediction, Management and Treatment*. New York: Brunner/Mazel, 1981.

ABRAMSON, PAUL R., and HARUO HAYASHI, "Pornography in Japan: Cross-cultural and Theoretical Considerations," Chapter 6 in Neil M. Malamuth and Edward Donnerstein (eds.), *Pornography and Sexual Aggression*. Orlando, Fla.: Academic Press, 1984.

ALLGEIER, ELIZABETH RICE, and ALBERT R. ALLGEIER, *Sexual Interactions*. Lexington, Mass.: Heath, 1984.

AMERICAN PSYCHIATRIC ASSOCIATION, *Diagnostic and Statistical Manual of Mental Disorders-III*. Washington, D.C.: APA, 1977.

ANDERSON, ANDY B., A. BASILEVSKY, and D.P.J. HUM, "Missing Data: A Review of the Literature," Chapter 12 in Peter H. Rossi, James D. Wright, and Andy B. Anderson (eds.), *Handbook of Survey Research*. New York: Academic, 1983.

APPIGNANESI, RICHARD, *Freud for Beginners*. New York: Pantheon Books, 1979.

ARONOFF, JOEL, and WILLIAM D. CARNO, "A Re-examination of the Cross-cultural Principles of Task Segregation and Sex Role Differentiation in the Family," *American Sociological Review*, vol. 40 (February 1975), pp. 12-20.

ASHER, HERBERT B., *Causal Modeling*. Beverly Hills, Calif.: Sage Publications, 1976.

BACHRACH, CHRISTINE A., "Contraceptive Practice among American Women, 1973-1982," *Family Planning Perspectives*, vol. 16, no. 6 (November 1984), pp. 253-260.

BAILEY, K.D., "Evaluating Axiomatic Theories," pp. 48–71 in E.F. Borgatta and G.W. Bohrnstedt (eds.), *Sociological Methodology*. San Francisco: Jossey-Bass, 1970.

BANDURA, ALBERT, *Aggression: A Social Learning Analysis.* Englewood Cliffs, N.J.: Prentice-Hall, 1973.

BARBACH, L.G., and L. LEVINE, *Shared Intimacies: Women's Sexual Experiences.* New York: Anchor Press, 1980.

BARON, LARRY, and MURRAY A. STRAUS, "Sexual Stratification, Pornography, and Rape in the U.S.," Chapter 7 in Neil M. Malamuth and Edward Donnerstein (eds.), *Pornography and Sexual Aggression.* Orlando, Fla.: Academic Press, 1984.

BARRY, HERBERT, and ALICE SCHLEGEL, "Measurements of Adolescent Sexual Behavior in the Standard Sample of Societies," *Ethnology*, vol. 23, (October 1984), pp. 315–330.

BEACH, FRANK A. (ed.), *Human Sexuality in Four Perspectives.* Baltimore: Johns Hopkins University Press, 1977.

BECKER, GEORGE, "The Social Regulation of Sexuality: A Cross-cultural Perspective," Unpublished paper, 1984.

BELL, ALAN P., MARTIN S. WEINBERG, and SUE KIEFER HAMMERSMITH, *Sexual Preference: Its Development in Men and Women.* Bloomington: Indiana University Press, 1981.

BELL, ALAN P., MARTIN S. WEINBERG, and SUE KIEFER HAMMERSMITH, *Sexual Preference: Statistical Appendix.* Bloomington: Indiana University Press, 1981.

BELL, ROBERT R., *Worlds of Friendship.* Beverly Hills, Calif.: Sage Publications, 1981.

BENJAMIN, HARRY, *The Transsexual Phenomenon.* New York: Julian, 1966.

BERNARD, LUTHER LEE, *Instinct.* New York: Holt, Rinehart & Winston, 1924.

BERNDT, RONALD and CATHERINE BERNDT, *Sexual Behavior in Western Arnhem Land,* New York: Viking Fund, 1951.

BLALOCK, HERBERT M., JR., *Causal Models in the Social Sciences.* Chicago: Aldine, 1971.

BLALOCK, HERBERT M., JR., *Conceptualization and Measurement in the Social Sciences.* Beverly Hills, Calif.: Sage Publications, 1982.

BLUMSTEIN, PHILIP, and PEPPER SCHWARTZ, *American Couples.* New York: Morrow, 1983.

BOTTOMORE, TOM, *Marxist Sociology.* New York: Holmes & Meier, 1975.

BOURGUIGNON, ERIKA (ed.), *A World of Women.* New York: Praeger, 1980.

BRAIN, ROBERT, *Friends and Lovers.* New York: Basic Books, 1976.

BRANDES, STANLEY, "Like Wounded Stags: Male Sexual Ideology in an Andalusian Town," Chapter 6 in Sherry B. Ortner and Harriet Whitehead (eds.), *Sexual Meanings: The Cultural Construction of Gender and Sexuality.* Cambridge: Cambridge University Press, 1981.

BROUDE, GWEN J., and SARAH J. GREENE, "Cross-cultural Codes on Twenty Sexual Attitudes and Practices," *Ethnology*, vol. 15 (October 1976), pp. 409–429.

BROUDE, GWEN J., "Extramarital Sex Norms in Cross-cultural Perspective," *Behavior Science Research*, vol. 15, no. 3 (1980), pp. 181–218.

BROWNMILLER, SUSAN, *Against Our Will.* New York: Simon & Schuster, 1975.

BULLOUGH, VERN L., *Sexual Variance in Society and History.* New York: John Wiley, 1976.

BULLOUGH, VERN L., "Age at Menarche: A Misunderstanding," *Science*, vol. 213 (July 17, 1981), pp. 365–366.

BULLOUGH, VERN L., and JAMES BRUNDAGE, *Sexual Practices and the Medieval Church.* Buffalo: Prometheus Books, 1982.

BURAWOY, MICHAEL, "The Resurgence of Marxism in American Sociology," Introduction in *Marxist Inquiries; Studies of Labor, Class and States.* Chicago: University of Chicago Press, 1982.

BURR, WESLEY R., I. NYE, R. HILL, and I.L. REISS, "Methatheory and Diagramming Conventions," Chapter 2 in Burr, W., I. Nye, R. Hill, and I. Reiss (eds.), *Contemporary Theories about the Family,* (vol. 1). New York: Macmillan, 1979.

BURSTYN, VARDA (ed.), *Women Against Censorship.* Vancouver: Douglas & McIntrye, 1985.

BURT, MARTHA R., "Cultural Myths and Supports for Rape," *Journal of Personality and Social Psychology*, vol. 38, no. 2 (1980), pp. 217–230.

BUUNK, BRAM, "Jealousy in Sexually Open Marriages," *Alternative Lifestyles*, vol. 4, no. 3, (August 1981), pp. 357–372.

BUUNK, BRAM, and RALPH B. HUPKA, "Autonomy and Togetherness in Close Relationships: A Study of Seven Nations," Paper presented at the meeting of the National Council on Family Relations, St. Paul, Minnesota, October, 1983.

BUUNK, BRAM, and RALPH B. HUPKA, "Cross Cultural Differences in the Elicitation of Sexual Jealousy," *Journal of Sex Research* (In press).

BYRNE, DONN, and KATHRYN KELLY, "Introduction: Pornography and Sex Research," Introduction in Neil M. Malamuth and Edward Donnerstein (eds.), *Pornography and Sexual Aggression*. Orlando, Fla.: Academic Press, 1984.

CAMPBELL, DONALD T., "Degrees of Freedom and the Case Study," *Comparative Political Studies*, vol. 8, no. 2 (July 1975), pp. 178–193.

CANNON, KENNETH L., and RICHARD LONG, "Premarital Sexual Behavior in the Sixties," *Journal of Marriage and the Family*, vol. 33, no. 1 (February 1971), pp. 36–49.

CARRIER, J.M., "Homosexual Behavior in Cross-cultural Perspective," Chapter 5 in Judd Marmor (ed.), *Homosexual Behavior: A Modern Reappraisal*. New York: Basic Books, 1980.

CASSELL, CAROL, *Swept Away: Why Women Fear Their Own Sexuality*. New York: Simon & Schuster, 1984.

CHAFETZ, JANET, *A Primer on the Construction and Testing of Theories in Sociology*. Chicago: F.E. Peacock, 1978.

CHAFETZ, JANET, *Sex and Advantage: A Comparative, Macrostructural Theory of Sex Stratification*. Totowa, N.J.: Rowman and Allanheld, 1984.

CHECK, JAMES V.P., and NEIL M. MALAMUTH, "Can There Be Positive Effects of Participation in Pornography Experiments?" *Journal of Sexual Research*, vol. 20, no. 1 (February 1984), pp. 14–31.

CLAYTON, RICHARD R., and JANET L. BOKEMEIER, "Premarital Sex in the Seventies," *Journal of Marriage and the Family*, vol. 42, no. 4 (November 1980), pp. 759–775.

CLEMENT, ULRICH, GUNTER SCHMIDT, and MARGRET KRUSE, "Changes in Sex Differences in Sexual Behavior: A Replication of a Study on West German Students (1966–1981)," *Archives of Sexual Behavior*, vol. 13, no. 2 (March 1984), pp. 99–120.

COLES, CLAIRE, and M. JOHANNA SHAMP, "Some Sexual, Personality, and Demographic Characteristics of Women Readers of Erotic Romances," *Archives of Sexual Behavior*, vol. 13, no. 3 (May 1984), pp. 187–209.

COMFORT, ALEX, *The Anxiety Makers: Some Curious Preoccupations of the Medical Profession*. London: Thomas Nelson, 1967.

CONANT, JAMES B., *On Understanding Science*. New Haven, Conn.: Yale University Press, 1951.

CONSTANTINE, LARRY, "Jealousy: Techniques for Intervention," Chapter 18 in Gordon Clanton and Lynn G. Smith (eds.), *Jealousy*. Englewood Cliffs, N.J.: Prentice-Hall, 1977.

CONSTANTINE, LARRY, and JOAN CONSTANTINE, *Group Marriage*. New York: Macmillan, 1973.

CONSTANTINE, LARRY L., and FLOYD M. MARTINSON (eds.), *Children and Sex: New Findings, New Perspectives*. Boston: Little, Brown, 1981.

COSTNER, HERBERT L., and ROBERT LEIK, "Deductions from Axiomatic Theory," pp. 49–72 in H. Blalock, Jr. (ed.), *Causal Models in the Social Sciences*. Chicago: Aldine, 1971.

CRANO, WILLIAM D., and JOEL ARONOFF, "A Cross-cultural Study of Expressive and Instrumental Role Complementarity in the Family," *American Sociological Review*, vol. 43 (August 1978), pp. 463–471.

CROMWELL, RONALD E., and DAVID H. OLSON (eds.), *Power in Families*. New York: Halsted Press, 1975.

DALY, MARTIN, MARGO WILSON, and SUZANN J. WEGHORST, "Male Sexual Jealousy," *Ethology and Sociobiology*, vol. 3, (1982), pp. 11–27.

DANIELSSON, BENGT, *Love in the South Seas*. New York: Reynal, 1956.

DAVENPORT, WILLIAM, "Sexual Patterns and Their Regulation in a Society of the SW Pacific," Chapter 8 in Frank A. Beach (ed.), *Sex and Behavior*. New York: John Wiley, 1965.

DAVENPORT, WILLIAM H., "Sex in Cross Cultural Perspective," Chapter 5 in Frank A. Beach (ed.), *Human Sexuality in Four Perspectives*. Baltimore: Johns Hopkins University Press, 1977.

DAVIES, CHRISTIE, "Sexual Taboos and Social Boundaries," *American Journal of Sociology*, vol. 87, no. 5 (September 1982), pp. 1032–1063.

DAVIS, MURRAY, *Smut: Erotic Reality/Obscene Ideology*. Chicago: University of Chicago Press, 1983.

DEACON, A. B., *Malekula: A Vansihing People in New Hebrides*. London: George Routledge, 1934.

DEGLER, CARL, *At Odds: Women and the Family in America from the Revolution to the Present*. Oxford: Oxford University Press, 1980.

DELAMATER, JOHN, and PATRICIA MACCORQUODALE, *Premarital Sexuality: Attitudes, Relationships, Behavior.* Madison: University of Wisconsin Press, 1979.

DENNISTON, R.H., "Ambisexuality in Animals," Chapter 1 in Marmor, Judd (ed.), *Homosexual Behavior: A Modern Reappraisal.* New York: Basic Books, 1980.

DEVEREUX, G., "Institutionalized Homosexuality of the Mohave Indians," *Human Biology,* vol. 9 (1937), pp. 498-527.

DIAMOND, MILTON, and ARNO KARLIN, *Sexual Decisions.* Boston: Little, Brown, 1980.

DONNERSTEIN, EDWARD, "Pornography: Its Effect on Violence against Women,"Chapter 2 in Neil M. Malamuth and Edward Donnerstein (eds.), *Pornography and Sexual Aggression.* Orlando, Fla.: Academic Press, 1984.

DONNERSTEIN, EDWARD, MARCIA DONNERSTEIN, and RONALD EVANS, "Erotic Stimuli and Aggression: Facilitation or Inhibition," *Journal of Personality and Social Psychology,* vol. 32, no. 2 (1975), pp. 237-244.

DOUGLAS, NIK, and PENNY SLINGER, *Sexual Secrets: The Alchemy of Ecstasy.* New York: Destiny Books, 1979.

EDWARDS, PAUL (ed.), *The Encyclopedia of Philosophy,* (8 vols.) New York: Macmillan, 1967.

EINSTEIN, ALBERT, and LEOPOLD INFELD, *The Evolution of Physics: The Growth of Ideas from Early Concepts to Relativity and Quanta.* New York: Simon & Schuster, 1950.

EINSTEIN, ZILLAH R. (ed.), *Capitalist Patriarchy and the Case for Socialist Feminism.* New York: Monthly Review Press, 1979.

ELLIS, HAVELOCK, *Psychology of Sex: A Manual for Students.* New York: New American Library, 1954. (Originally published in 1933.)

ELLIS, ALBERT, and R.A. HARPER, *A New Guide to Rational Living.* N. Hollywood, Calif.: Wilshire, 1978.

ELLIS, ALBERT, and ALBERT ABARBANEL (eds.), *Encyclopedia of Social Behavior* (2 vols.). New York: Hawthorn, 1961.

ELWIN, VERRIER, *The Baiga.* London: John Murray, 1939.

ELWIN, VERRIER, *The Muria and Their Ghotul.* New York: Oxford University Press, 1947.

ENGELS, FRIEDRICH, *Socialism: Utopian and Scientific.* New York: International, 1935.

ENGELS, FRIEDRICH, *The Origin of the Family, Private Property, and the State.* Chicago: Charles H. Kerr, 1902. (Originally published in 1884.)

ETIENNE, MONA, and ELEANOR LEACOCK (eds.), *Women and Colonization: Anthropological Perspectives.* New York: Praeger, 1980.

EVANS-PRITCHARD, E.E., *Kinship and Marriage among the Nuer.* London: Oxford University Press, 1951.

FAISON, REBECCA, and JAMES D. ORCUTT, "Trends in Sex Role. Attitudes and Reporting of Rape Victimization, 1973-1980," Paper presented at the 1984 meeting of the Society of the Study of Social Problems in San Antonio, Texas.

FINKELHOR, DAVID, *Sexually Victimized Children.* New York: Free Press, 1979.

FISHER, WILLIAM A., "Gender, Gender Role Identification, and Response to Erotica," Chapter 12 in Elizabeth R. Allgeier and Naomi B. McCormick (eds.), *Changing Boundaries: Gender Roles and Sexual Behavior.* Palo Alto, Calif.: Mayfield, 1983.

FORD, C.S., and FRANK A. BEACH, *Patterns of Sexual Behavior.* New York: Harper & Row, 1951.

FOUCAULT, MICHAEL, *History of Sexuality: An Introduction.* New York: Vintage, 1980.

FRAYSER, SUZANNE G., *Varieties of Sexual Experience.* New Haven, Conn.: HRAF Press, 1985.

FREESE, LEE, (ed.), *Theoretical Methods in Sociology.* Pittsburgh: University of Pittsburgh Press, 1980.

FREUD, SIGMUND, *Three Contributions to the Theory of Sex.* New York: Dutton, 1962. (Originally published in 1905.)

FREUD, SIGMUND, "Letter to an American Mother," *American Journal of Psychiatry,* vol. 102 (1921), p. 786.

FREUD, SIGMUND, *Civilization and Its Discontents.* New York: Doubleday Anchor Books, 1958. (Originally published in 1930.)

FRIEDAN, BETTY, "How to Get the Women's Movement Moving Again," *New York Times Magazine* (November 3, 1985), p. 26

GADPAILLE, WARREN J., "Research into the Physiology of Maleness and Femaleness," *Archives of General Psychiatry,* vol. 26 (March 1972), pp. 193-206.

262

GADPAILLE, WARREN J., "Psychosexual Development through the Life Cycle," Chapter 3 in Harold I. Lief (ed.), *Sexual Problems in Medical Practice.* Chicago: AMA, 1981.

GAGNON, JOHN H., "Female Child Victims of Sex Offenses," *Social Problems,* vol. 13 (Fall 1965), pp. 176-192.

GAGNON, JOHN H., and WILLIAM SIMON, *Sexual Conduct.* Chicago: Aldine, 1973.

GARCIA, LUIS T., K. BRENNAN, M. DECARLO, R. MCGLENNON, and S. TAIT, "Sex Differences in Sexual Arousal to Different Erotic Stories," *Journal of Sex Research,* vol. 20, no. 4 (November 1984), pp. 391-402.

GEBHARD, PAUL H., J.H. GAGNON, W.B. POMEROY and C.V. CHRISTENSON, *Sex Offenders: An Analysis of Types.* New York: Harper & Row, Publ., 1965.

GILMARTIN, BRIAN, *The Gilmartin Report.* Secaucus, N.J.: Citadel Press, 1978.

GOLDFOOT, DAVID A., K. WALLEN, D.A. NEFF, M.C. MCBRIAR, and R.W. GOY, "Social Influences upon the Display of Sexually Dimorphic Behavior in Rhesus Monkeys: Isosexual Rearing," *Archives of Sexual Behavior,* vol. 13, no. 5 (October 1984), pp. 395-412.

GOLDFOOT, DAVID, H. WESTERBORG-VAN-LOON, W. GROENEVELD, and A. KOSS SLOB, "Behavioral and Physiological Evidence of Sexual Climax in the Female Stump-Tailed Macaque (Macaca Arctoides)," *Science,* vol. 208 (June 27, 1980), pp. 1477-1479.

GOODALE, JANE C., *Tiwi Wives: A Study of the Women of Melville Island, North Australia.* Seattle: University of Washington Press, 1971.

GOODY, JACK, *Production and Reproduction: A Comparative Study of the Domestic Domain.* Cambridge: Cambridge University Press, 1976.

GOODY, JACK, and S.J. TAMBIAH, *Bridewealth and Dowry.* Cambridge: Cambridge University Press, 1973.

GORER, GEOFFREY, *Himalayan Village: An Account of the Lepchas of Sikkim,* (2nd ed.). New York: Basic Books, 1967.

GOY, R.W., and D.A. GOLDFOOT, "Hormonal Influences on Sexually Dimorphic Behavior," Chapter 9 in R.O. Greep and E.B. Astwood (eds.), *Handbook of Physiology: Endocrinology* (sec 7, col. 2, pt. 1). Baltimore: Williams & Wilkins, 1973.

GRANBERG, D., and B.W. GRANBERG, "Abortion Attitudes: 1965-1980: Trends and Determinants," *Family Planning Perspectives,* vol. 12 (September-October, 1980), pp. 250-261.

GREEN, RICHARD, *Sexual Identity Conflict in Children and Adults.* New York: Basic Books, 1974.

GROSSKURTH, PHYLLIS, *Havelock Ellis: A Biography.* New York: Knopf, 1980.

GROTH, A. NICHOLAS, *Men Who Rape: The Psychology of the Offender.* New York: Plenum Press, 1979.

GUTTENTAG, MARCIA, and PAUL F. SECORD, *Too Many Women?* Beverly Hills, Calif.: Sage Publications, 1983.

HAEBERLE, ERWIN J., *The Sex Atlas.* New York: Seabury Press, 1978.

HAGE, JEROLD, *Techniques and Problems of Theory Construction in Sociology.* New York: John Wiley, 1972.

HALBERSTADT-FREUD, HENDRIKA C., "Freud's Libido Theory," Chapter 5 in John Money and Herman Musaph (eds.), *Handbook of Sexuality.* New York: Elsevier North-Holland, 1977.

HARITON, BARBARA E., and JEROME L. SINGER, "Women's Fantasies during Intercourse: Normative and Theoretical Implications," *Journal of Consulting Clinical Psychology,* vol. 42 (June 1974), pp. 313-322.

HARLOW, HARRY F., "The Heterosexual Affection System in Monkeys," *American Psychologist,* vol. 17 (January 1962), pp. 1-9.

HEISE, DAVID R., *Causal Analysis.* New York: John Wiley, 1973.

HEMPEL, CARL G., "Fundamentals of Concept Formation in Empirical Science," pp. 1-93 in Otto Neurath (ed-in-chief), *International Encyclopedia of Unified Science,* (vol. 2, no. 7). Chicago: University of Chicago Press, 1952.

HERDT, GILBERT, *Guardians of the Flutes: Idioms of Masculinity.* New York: McGraw-Hill, 1981.

HERDT, GILBERT (ed.), *Ritualized Homosexuality in Melanesia.* Berkeley: University of California Press, 1984.

HOBBES, THOMAS, *Leviathan* in Frederick J. E. Woodbridge (ed.), *Hobbes Selections.* New York: Charles Scribner's Sons, 1930.

HONG, LAWRENCE K., "Survival of the Fastest: On the Origin of Premature Ejaculation," *The Journal of Sex Research*, vol. 20, no. 2 (May 1984), pp. 109–122.

HOOVER, KENNETH R., *The Elements of Social Scientific Thinking* (3rd ed.). New York: St. Martin's Press, 1984.

HRDY, SARAH BLAFFER, *The Woman That Never Evolved*. Cambridge, Mass.: Harvard University Press, 1981.

HUME, DAVID, *An Enquiry Concerning Human Understanding*. LaSalle, Ill.: Open Court, 1952.

HUNT, MORTON M., *Sexual Behavior in the 1970's*. Chicago: Playboy Press, 1974.

HUPKA, RALPH B., "Cultural Determinants of Jealousy," *Alternative Lifestyles*, vol. 4, no. 3 (August 1981), pp. 310–356.

HUPKA, RALPH B., and JAMES M. RYAN, "The Cultural Contribution to Emotions: Cross-cultural Aggression in Romantic Jealousy Situations," Paper presented at the meeting of the Western Psychological Association, Los Angeles, 1981.

HUPKA, RALPH B., "Jealousy: Compound Emotion or Label for a Particular Situation?" *Motivation and Emotion*, vol. 8, no. 2 (1984), pp. 141–155.

HYDE, JANET, *Understanding Human Sexuality*. New York: McGraw-Hill, 1979.

IM, WONG-GI, R., STEFANIE WILNER, and MIRANDA BREIT, "Jealousy: Interventions in Couples Therapy," *Family Process*, vol. 22 (June 1983), 311–219.

JOURARD, SIDNEY M., *Self Disclosure: An Experimental Analysis of the Transparent Self*. New York: John Wiley, 1968.

KAPLAN, HELEN SINGER, *The New Sex Therapy: Active Treatment of Sexual Dysfunction*. New York: Brunner /Mazel, 1974.

KARLEN, ARNO, "Homosexuality in History," Chapter 4 in Judd Marmor (ed.), *Homosexual Behavior: A Modern Reappraisal*. New York: Basic Books, 1980.

KELLEY, JONATHAN, "Sexual Permissiveness: Evidence for a Theory," *Journal of Marriage and the Family*, vol. 40 (August 1978), pp. 455–468.

KELLY, RAYMOND C., "Witchcraft and Sexual Relations: An Exploration in the Social and Semantic Implications of the Structure of Belief," pp. 36–53 in Paula Brown and Georgeda Buchbinder (eds.), *Man and Woman in the New Guinea Highlands*. Washington, D.C.: American Anthropological Association, 1976.

KINSEY, ALFRED C., WARDELL POMEROY, and CLYDE MARTIN, *Sexual Behavior in the Human Male*. Philadelphia: Saunders, 1948.

KINSEY, ALFRED C., WARDELL POMEROY, CLYDE MARTIN, and PAUL GEBHARD, *Sexual Behavior in the Human Female*. Philadelphia: Saunders, 1953.

KUTCHINSKY, BERL, "The Effect of Easy Availability of Pornography on the Incidence of Sex Crimes: The Danish Experience," *Journal of Social Issues*, vol. 29, no. 3 (July 1973), pp. 163–181.

KUTCHINSKY, BERL, "Eroticism without Censorship: Sociological Investigations on the Production and Consumption of Pornographic Literature in Denmark," *International Journal of Criminology and Penology*, vol. 1 (1973), pp. 217–225.

KUTCHINSKY, BERL, "Obscenity and Pornography: Behavioral Aspects." (In press).

LADAS, ALICE KAHN, BEVERLY WHIPPLE, and JOHN D. PERRY, *The G Spot: and Other Recent Discoveries about Human Sexuality*. New York: Holt, Rinehart & Winston, 1982.

LANGEVIN, RON, *Sexual Strands: Understanding and Treating Sexual Anomalies in Men*. Hillsdale, N.J.: Erlbaum, 1983.

LANGEVIN, RON (ed.), *Erotic Preference, Gender Identity, and Aggression in Men: New Research Studies*. Hillsdale, N.J.: Erlbaum, 1985.

LEE, GARY, *Family Structure and Interaction: A Comparative Analysis*. Minneapolis: University of Minnesota Press, 1982.

LEIK, ROBERT K., and WALTER R. GOVE, "Integrated Approach to Measuring Association," Chapter 10 in Herbert L. Costner (ed.), *Sociological Methodology, 1971*. San Francisco: Jossey-Bass, 1971.

LEVINE, ROBERT A., "Gusii Sex Offenses: A Study in Social Control," *American Anthropologist*, vol. 61 (1959), pp. 965–990.

LEVINE, ROBERT A., and BARBARA B. LEVINE, "Nyansongo: A Gusii Community in Kenya," pp. 15–202 in Beatrice B. Whiting (ed.), *Six Cultures: Studies of Child Rearing*. New York: John Wiley, 1963.

LEVI-STRAUSS, CLAUDE, *The Elementary Structure of Kinship*. Boston: Beacon Press, 1969.

LEVY, ROBERT I., *Tahitians: Mind and Experience in the Society Islands*. Chicago: University of Chicago Press, 1973.

LIEF, HAROLD I. (ed.), *Sexual Problems in Medical Practice*. Chicago: AMA, 1981.

LOTTES, ILSA, "The Use of Cluster Analysis to Determine Belief Patterns," *Journal of Sex Research,* vol. 21 (November 1985), pp. 405–421.

LOTTES, ILSA, "An Investigation of the Tenet Patterns of the Reiss Sexual Ideologies." Paper presented at the April 1983 Society for the Scientific Study of Sex meeting in Philadelphia.

LUKER, KRISTIN, *Taking Chances: Abortion and the Decision Not To Contracept.* Berkeley: University of California Press, 1975.

LUKER, KRISTIN, *Abortion and the Politics of Motherhood.* Berkeley: University of California Press, 1984.

LURIA, ZELLA, and MITCHEL ROSE, *Psychology of Human Sexuality.* New York John Wiley, 1979.

LYONS, HARRIET, "Anthropologists, Moralities, and Relativities: The Problem of Genital Mutilations," *The Canadian Review of Sociology and Anthropology,* vol. 18 (November 1981), pp. 499–518.

MACCOBY, ELEANOR E., and CAROL JACKLIN, *The Psychology of Sex Differences.* Stanford, Calif.: Stanford University Press, 1974.

MACIVER, ROBERT M., *Social Causation.* New York: Ginn, 1942.

MALAMUTH, NEIL M., "Aggression against Women: Cultural and Individual Causes," Chapter 1 in Neil M. Malamuth and Edward Donnerstein (eds.), *Pornography and Sexual Aggression.* Orlando, Fla.: Academic Press, 1984.

MALAMUTH, NEIL M., and JAMES V.P. CHECK, "Debriefing Effectiveness Following Exposure to Pornographic Rape Depictions," *Journal of Sex Research,* vol. 21, no. 1 (February 1984), pp. 1–13.

MALAMUTH, NEIL M., and EDWARD DONNERSTEIN (eds.), *Pornography and Sexual Aggression.* Orlando, Fla.: Academic Press, 1984.

MALINOWSKI, BRONISLAW, *The Sexual Life of Savages in N.W. Melanesia.* New York: Harvest Books, 1929.

MARMOR, JUDD (ed.), *Homosexual Behavior: A Modern Reappraisal.* New York: Basic Books, 1980.

MARSHALL, DONALD, and ROBERT C. SUGGS, *Human Sexual Behavior.* New York: Basic Books, 1971.

MARTIN, M. KAY, and BARBARA VOORHIES, *Female of the Species.* New York: Columbia University Press, 1975.

MASTERS, WILLIAM H., and VIRGINIA F. JOHNSON, *Human Sexual Response.* Boston: Little, Brown, 1966.

MASTERS, WILLIAM H., and VIRGINIA F. JOHNSON, *Human Sexual Inadequacy.* Boston: Little, Brown, 1970.

MASTERS, WLLIAM H., VIRGINIA JOHNSON, and ROBERT KOLODNY, *Human Sexuality.* Boston: Little, Brown, 1982.

MAYHEW, BRUCE H., "Structuralism Versus Individualism. Part One: Shadow Boxing in the Dark," *Social Forces,* vol. 59, no. 2 (December 1980), pp. 335–375.

MCCONAHAY, SHIRLEY A., and JOHN B. MCCONAHAY, "Sexual Permissiveness, Sex Role Rigidity, and Violence across Cultures," *Journal of Social Issues,* vol. 33, no. 2 (April 1977), pp. 134–143.

MCKEON, RICHARD (ed.), *The Basic Works of Aristotle.* New York: Random House, 1941.

MCWHIRTER, DAVID P., and ANDREW M. MATTISON, *The Male Couple: How Relationships Develop.* Englewood Cliffs, N.J.: Prentice-Hall, 1984.

MEAD, GEORGE HERBERT, *Mind, Self and Society.* Chicago: University of Chicago Press, 1934.

MEAD, MARGARET, *Growing Up in New Guinea.* New York: Morrow, 1930.

MERNISSI, FATIMA, *Beyond the Veil: Male-Female Dynamics in a Modern Muslim Society.* Cambridge, Mass.: Schenkman Books, 1975.

MESSENGER, JOHN C., *Inis Beag: Isle of Ireland.* New York: Holt, Rinehart & Winston, 1969.

MESSENGER, JOHN C., "Sex and Repression in an Irish Folk Community," Chapter 1 in Donald S. Marshall and Robert C. Suggs (eds.), *Human Sexual Behavior.* New York: Basic Books, 1971.

MITCHELL, GARY, *Behavioral Sex Differences in Nonhuman Primates.* New York: Van Nostrand Reinhold, 1979.

MONEY, JOHN, "Genetic and Chromosomal Aspects of Homosexual Etiology," Chapter 3 in Judd Marmor (ed.), *Homosexual Behavior: A Modern Reappraisal.* New York: Basic Books, 1980.

MONEY, JOHN, and HERMAN MUSAPH, *Handbook of Sexology.* New York: Elsevier North-Holland, 1977.

MONEY, JOHN, "The Conceptual Neutering of Gender and the Criminalization of Sex," *Archives of Sexual Behavior,* vol. 14, no. 3 (June 1985), pp. 279–290.

MOSHER, CLELIA, *The Mosher Survey.* New York: Arno Press, 1980.

MOSHER, DONALD L., "Three Dimensions of Depth and Involvement in Human Sexual Response," *Journal of Sex Research,* vol. 16 (February 1980), pp. 1–42.

MOSHER, DONALD L., and MARK SIKIN, "Measuring a Macho Personality Constellation," *Journal of Research in Personality,* vol. 18 (1984), pp. 150–163.

MURDOCK, GEORGE P., "Ethnographic Atlas: A Summary," *Ethnology,* vol. 6 (April 1967), pp. 109–236.

MURDOCK, GEORGE P., and DOUGLAS R. WHITE, "Standard Cross Cultural Sample," *Ethnology,* vol. 8 (October 1969), pp. 329–369.

MURDOCK, GEORGE P., and CATERINA PROVOST, "Factors in the Division of Labor by Sex: A Cross-sultural Analysis," Chapter 10 in Herbert Barry and Alice Schlegel, (eds.), *Cross-cultural Samples and Codes.* Pittsburgh: University of Pittsburgh Press, 1980.

NAROLL, RAOUL, *The Moral Order: An Introduction to the Human Situation.* Beverly Hills, Calif.: Sage Publications, 1983.

NASS, GILBERT, ROGER LIBBY, and MARY PAT FISHER, *Sexual Choices.* Monterey, Calif.: Wadsworth Health Sciences Division, 1984.

NELSON, JOEL I., *Economic Inequality: Conflict Without Change.* New York: Columbia University Press, 1982.

NEW DIRECTIONS FOR WOMEN, January-February 1985.

NEWCOMER, SUSAN, F., and J. RICHARD UDRY, "Oral Sex in an Adolescent Population," *Archives of Sexual Behavior,* vol. 14, no. 1 (February 1985), pp. 41–46.

O'KELLY, CHARLOTTE G., *Women and Men in Society.* New York: D. Van Nostrand, 1980.

ORTNER, SHERRY B., and HARRIET WHITEHEAD (eds.), *Sexual Meanings: The Cultural Construction of Gender and Sexuality.* Cambridge: Cambridge University Press, 1981.

PAIGE, K.E., and J.M. PAIGE, *The Politics of Reproductive Ritual.* Berkeley: University of California Press, 1981.

PARISH, WILLIAM L., Jr., and MARTIN K. WHYTE, *Village and Family in Contemporary China.* Chicago: University of Chicago Press, 1978.

PAUL, WILLIAM, J.D. WEINRICH, J.C. GONSIOREK, and M.E. HOTVEDT, *Homosexuality: Social, Psychological and Biological Issues.* Beverly Hills, Calif.: Sage Publications, 1982.

PICKARD, CHRISTINE, "A Perspective on Female Responses to Sexual Material," Chapter 6 in Maurice Yaffe and Edward C. Nelson (eds.), *The Influence of Pornography on Behaviour.* London: Academic Press, 1982.

PINES, AYALA, and ELLIOT ARONSON, "Polyfidelity: An Alternative Lifestyle without Jealousy?" *Alternative Lifestyles,* vol. 4, no. 3 (August 1981), pp. 373–392.

PRESCOTT, J.W., "Body Pleasure and the Origins of Violence," *Futurist* (March-April 1975), pp. 64–80.

PRZEWORSKI, ADAM, and HENRY TEUNE, *The Logic of Comparative Social Inquiry.* New York: Wiley Interscience Books, 1970.

RADECKI, THOMAS, *Film Comment,* Vol. 20, no. 6 (November-December, 1984), pp. 43–45.

RAMEY, JAMES, *Intimate Friendships.* Englewood Cliffs, N.J.: Prentice-Hall, 1976.

RANDALL, JOHN HERMAN, JR., *The Making of the Modern Mind,* (rev. ed.). Boston: Houghton Mifflin, 1940.

REISS, IRA L., "The Double Standard in Premarital Sexual Intercourse: A Neglected Concept," *Social Forces,* vol. 34 (March 1956), pp. 224–230.

REISS, IRA L., "The Treatment of Premarital Coitus in Marriage and Family Texts," *Social Problems,* vol. 4, no. 4 (April 1957), pp. 334–338.

REISS, IRA L., "Toward a Sociology of the Heterosexual Love Relationship," *Marriage and Family Living,* vol. 22 (May 1960), pp. 139–145.

REISS, IRA L., *Premarital Sexual Standards in America.* New York: Free Press, 1960.

REISS, IRA L., "The Scaling of Premarital Sexual Permissiveness," *Journal of Marriage and the Family,* vol. 26 (May 1964), pp. 188–198.

REISS, IRA L., "The Universality of the Family: A Conceptual Analysis," *Journal of Marriage and the Family,* vol. 27 (November 1965), pp. 443–453.

REISS, IRA L., *The Social Context of Premarital Sexual Permissiveness*. New York: Holt, Rinehart & Winston, 1967.

REISS, IRA L., A. BANWART, and H. FOREMAN, "Premarital Contraceptive Usage: A Study and Some Theoretical Explanations," *Journal of Marriage and the Family,* vol. 37 (August 1975), pp. 619–630.

REISS, IRA L., and BRENT C. MILLER, "Heterosexual Permissiveness: A Theoretical Analysis," Chapter 4 in W. Burr, R. Hill, I. Nye, and I. Reiss (eds.), *Contemporary Theories about The Family,* (vol. 1). New York: Free Press, 1979.

REISS, IRA L., "Value Judgments and Science," Appendix 1 in Ira L. Reiss, *Family Systems in America,* (3rd ed.). New York: Holt, Rinehart & Winston, 1980.

REISS, IRA L., RONALD E. ANDERSON, and G.C. SPONAUGLE, "A Multivariate Model of the Determinants of Extramarital Sexual Permissiveness," *Journal of Marriage and the Family,* vol. 42 (May 1980), pp. 395–411.

REISS, IRA L., "Sexual Customs and Gender Roles in Sweden and America: An Analysis and Interpretation," pp. 191-220 in Helena Lopata (ed.), *Research on the Interweave of Social Roles: Women and Men.* Greenwich, Conn.: JAI Press, 1980.

REISS, IRA L., "Some Observations on Ideology and Sexuality in America," *Journal of Marriage and the Family,* vol. 43, no. 2 (May 1981), pp. 271-283.

REISS, IRA L., "Trouble in Paradise: The Current Status of Sexual Science," *Journal of Sex Research,* vol. 18 (May 1982), pp. 97-113.

REISS, IRA L., "Sexuality: A Research and Theory Perspective," pp. 141-147 in Peggy Houston (ed.), *Sexuality and the Family Life Span.* Iowa City: University of Iowa Press, 1983.

REISS, IRA L., "Human Sexuality in Sociological Perspective," Chapter 4 in K.K. Holmes, Per- anders Mardh, P. Frederick Sparling, and Paul Wiesner *(eds.), Sexuality Transmitted Diseases.* New York: McGraw-Hill, 1984.

REISS, IRA L., and GARY LEE, *Family Systems in America,* (4th ed.). New York: Holt, Rinehart & Winston, (in press).

REPORT OF THE COMMISSION ON OBSCENTITY AND PORNOGRAPHY. Washington, D.C.: GPO, 1971.

REYNOLDS, PAUL DAVIDSON, *A Primer in Theory Construction.* Indianapolis: Bobbs-Merrill, 1971.

RIMMER, ROBERT H., *The X-Rated Videotape Guide.* New York: Arlington House, 1984.

RITCHIE, JAN, and JAMES RITCHIE, "Polynesian Child Rearing: An Alternative Model," *Alternative Lifestyles,* vol. 5, no. 3 (Spring 1983), pp. 126-141.

ROOS, PATRICIA A., *Gender and Work: A Comparative Analysis of Industrial Societies.* Albany: SUNY Press, 1985.

ROSS, MARC HOWARD, "Political Decision Making and Conflict: Additional Cross-cultural Codes and Scales," *Ethnology,* vol. 22 (April 1983), pp. 169–192.

ROSSI, ALICE, "A Biosocial Perspective on Parenting," *Daedalus,* vol. 105 (Spring 1977), pp. 1–31.

ROSSI, ALICE, "Gender and Parenthood," *American Sociological Review,* vol. 49 (February 1984), pp. 1-19.

RUSSELL, DIANA E.H., *Rape in Marriage.* New York: Collier Books, 1982.

SAGHIR, MARCEL T., and E. ROBBINS, *Male and Female Homosexuality.* Baltimore: Willaims & Wilkins, 1973.

SANDAY, PEGGY REEVES, "The Socio-cultural Context of Rape: A Cross-cultural Study," *Journal of Social Issues,* vol. 37, no. 4 (October 1981), pp. 5-27.

SANDAY, PEGGY REEVES, *Female Power and Male Dominance On the Origins of Sexual Inequality.* New York: Cambridge University Press, 1981.

SANDERS, IRWIN T. (ed.), *Societies Around the World,* New York: Dryden Press, 1956.

SANDLER, JACK, MARILYN MEYERSON, and BILL N. KINDER, *Human Sexuality: Current Perspectives.* Tampa, Fla.: Mariner, 1980.

SARGENT, LYDIA (ed.), *Women and Revolution: A Discussion of the Unhappy Marriage of Marxism and Feminism.* Boston: South End Press, 1981.

SARTRE, JEAN-PAUL, *Being and Nothingness,* (trans. Hazel Barnes). New York: Philosophical Library, 1956.

SCHAPERA, I., *Married Life in an African Tribe.* New York: Sheridan House, 1941.

SCHLEGEL, ALICE, *Male Dominance and Female Autonomy.* New Haven, Conn.: HRAF Press, 1972.

267

SCHLEGEL, ALICE, "Toward a Theory of Sexual Stratification," Chapter in Alice Schlegel (ed.), *Sexual Stratification: A Cross Cultural View*. New York: Columbia University Press, 1977.

SCHLEGEL, ALICE, "Sexual Antagonism among the Sexually Egalitarian Hopi," *Ethos*, vol. 7, no. 2 (Summer 1979), pp. 124-141.

RODMAN, HYMAN, SUSAN H. LEWIS, and SARALYN B. GRIFFITH, *The Sexual Rights of Adolescents: Competence, Vulnerability, and Parental Control*. New York: Columbia University Press, 1984.

SCHMIDT, GUNTER, "Male-Female Differences in Sexual Arousal and Behavior during and after Exposure to Sexually Explicit Stimuli," *Archives of Sexual Behavior*, vol. 4 (July 1975), pp. 353-365.

SCHNEIDER, DAVID M., and KATHLEEEN GOUGH (eds.), *Matrilineal Kinship*. Berkeley: University of California Press, 1961.

SCHNEIDER, HAROLD K., "Romantic Love among the Turu," Chapter 3 in Donald S. Marshall and Robert C. Suggs (eds.), *Human Sexual Behavior: Variation in the Ethnographic Spectrum*. New York: Basic Books, 1971.

SCHOFIELD, MICHAEL, *Sociological Aspects of Homosexuality: A Comparative Study of Three Types of Homosexuals*. Boston: Little, Brown, 1965.

SCHOFIELD, MICHAEL, *Promiscuity*. London: Victor Gollancz, 1976.

SCHWENDINGER JULIA R., and HERMAN SCHWENDINGER, *Rape and Inequality*. Beverly Hills, Calif.: Sage Publications, 1983.

SIECUS REPORT, vol. 8, no. 3 (January 1980) New York: Human Sciences Press.

SIMMEL, GEORG, *Georg Simmel: On Women, Sexuality and Love*, (trans. Guy Oakes). New Haven, Conn.: Yale University Press, 1984.

SIMON, WILLIAM, and JOHN H. GAGNON, "Sexual Scripts: Permanence and Change," *Society*, vol. 22, no. 1 (November/December 1984), pp. 53-60.

SINGER, BARRY, "A Comparison of Evolutionary and Environmental Theories of Erotic Response: Part One: Structural Features," *Journal of Sex Research*, vol. 21, no. 3, (August 1985), pp. 229-257.

SKARD TORILD, and ELINA HAAVIO-MANNILA, "Equality between the Sexes—Myth or Reality in Norden," *Daedalus*, vol. 113, no. 1 (Winter 1984), pp. 141-167.

SPIRO, MEL, *Kibbutz: Venture in Utopia*. Cambridge, Mass.: Harvard University Press, 1956.

SPIRO, MEL, *Children of the Kibbutz*. Cambridge, Mass.: Harvard University Press, 1958.

STACEY, JUDITH, *Patriarchy and Socialist Revolution in China*. Berkeley: University of California Press, 1983.

STEPHENS, WILLIAM N., "A Cross Cultural Study of Modesty," *Behavior Sciences Notes*, vol. 1 (1972), pp. 1-28.

STOLLER, ROBERT J., *Sexual Excitement: Dynamics of Erotic Life*. New York: Simon & Schuster, 1979.

STORMS, M.D., "Theories of Sexual Orientation," *Journal of Personality and Social Psychology*, vol. 38 (1980), pp. 783-792.

SUGGS, ROBERT C., *Marquesan Sexual Behavior*. New York: Harcourt Brace Jovanovich, 1966.

SYMONS, DONALD, *The Evolution of Human Sexuality*. New York: Oxford University Press, 1979.

SZASZ, THOMAS, *The Myth of Mental Illness*. New York: Hoeber-Harper & Row, 1964.

TAVEL, R., *Street of Stairs*. New York: Olympia Press, 1968.

TAVRIS, CAROL and SUSAN SADD, *The Redbook Report on Female Sexuality*. New York: Delacorte, 1977.

THEODORSON, GEORGE, and ACHILLES THEODORSON, *A Modern Dictionary of Sociology*. New York: Harper & Row, Pub., 1969.

TOURNEY, GARFIELD, "Hormones and Homosexuality," Chapter 2 in Judd Marmor (ed.), *Homosexual Behavior: A Modern Reappraisal*. New York: Basic Books, 1980.

TROST, JAN, *Unmarried Cohabitation*. Vasteras, Sweden: International Library, 1979.

ULLERSTAM, LARS, *The Erotic Minorities*. New York: Grove, 1966.

U.S. DEPARTMENT OF COMMERCE, BUREAU OF THE CENSUS. *Statistical Abstract of the United States: 1984*. Washington, D.C., 1984.

U.S. DEPARTMENT OF HEALTH AND HUMAN SERVICES, NATIONAL CENTER FOR HEALTH STATISTICS, C.A. Bachrach and M.C. Horn, "Marriage and First Intercourse, Marital Dissolution, and Remarriage: U.S., 1982," no. 107. Hyattsville, Md.: Public Health Service, April 1985.

268

U.S. DEPARTMENT OF JUSTICE. *Uniform Crime Reports for the United States, 1984.* Washington, D.C., 1984.

U.S. DEPARTMENT OF JUSTICE, BUREAU OF JUSTICE STATISTICS. *Criminal Victimization in the U.S., 1981: A National Crime Survey Report,* NCJ-90208. Washington, D.C., November 1983.

U.S. DEPARTMENT OF JUSTICE, BUREAU OF JUSTICE STATISTICS. *Report to the Nation on Crime and Justice: The Data,* NCJ-87068. Washington, D.C., October 1983.

VANNOY, RUSSELL, *Sex without Love.* Buffalo: Prometheus Books, 1980.

VOLTAIRE, *Candide and Other Writings.* New York: Random House, 1956.

WALFISH, S., and M. MYERSON, "Sex Role Identity and Attitudes toward Sexuality," *Archives of Sexual Behavior,* vol. 9 (June 1980), pp. 199-205.

WALLACE, WALTER L., *Principles of Scientific Sociology.* New York: Aldine, 1983.

WEINBERG, THOMAS, and G.W. LEVI KAMEL (eds.), *S and M: Studies in Sadomasochism.* Buffalo: Prometheus Books, 19? 1.

WEINER, ANNETTE, *Women of Value: Men of Renown.* Austin: University of Texas Press, 1976.

WEITZMAN, LENORE J., *The Marriage Contract.* Englewood Cliffs, N.J.: Prentice-Hall, 1978.

WEITZMAN, LENORE J., *The Divorce Revolution.* New York: The Free Press, 1985.

WEST, D.J., *Homosexuality Re-examined.* Minneapolis: University of Minnesota Press, 1977.

WESTOFF, CHARLES F., "Coital Frequency and Contraception," *Family Planning Perspectives,* vol. 6 (Summer 1974), pp. 136-141.

WHITMAN, FREDERICK L., "Culturally Invariable Properties of Male Homosexuality: Tentative Conclusions from Cross-cultural Research," *Archives of Sexual Behavior,* vol. 12, no.3 (June 1983), pp. 207-226.

WHITMAN, FREDERICK L., and MICHAEL ZENT, "A Cross Cultural Assessment of Early Cross-gender Behavior and Familial Factors in Male Homosexuality," *Archives of Sexual Behavior,* vol. 13, no. 5 (October 1984), pp. 427-440.

WHITEHEAD, HARRIET, "The Bow and the Burden Strap: A New Look at Institutionalized Homosexuality in Native North America," Chapter 2 in Sherry B. Ortner and Harriet Whitehead (eds.), *Sexual Meanings: The Cultural Construction of Genders and Sexuality.* Cambridge: Cambridge University Press, 1981.

WHYTE, MARTIN K., "Cross-cultural Codes Dealing with the Relative Status of Women," *Ethnology,* vol. 17, no. 2 (April 1978), pp. 211-237.

WHYTE, MARTIN K., *The Status of Women in Preindustrial Societies.* Princeton, N.J.: Princeton University Press, 1978.

WILSON, EDWARD O., *Sociobiology: The New Synthesis.* Cambridge, Mass.: Harvard University Press, 1975.

WINICK, CHARLES, "A Content Analysis of Sexually Explicit Magazines Sold in an Adult Bookstore," *Journal of Sex Research,* vol. 21, no. 2 (Mary 1985), pp. 206-210.

WOLF, DEBORAH GOLEMAN, *The Lesbian Community.* Berkeley: University of California Press, 1980.

WOLFE, LINDA, *Women and Sex in the 80's: The Cosmo Report.* Toronto: Bantam Books, 1981.

WOODBRIDGE, FREDERICK J.E., *The Realm of Mind: An Essay in Metaphysics.* New York: Columbia University Press, 1926.

YLLO, KERSTI, and M. STRAUS, "The Impact of Structural Inequality and Sexist Family Norms on Rates of Wife-beating," *International of Journal Comparative Social Welfare,* vol. 1, no. 1 (Fall 1984), pp. 16-29.

ZELNIK, M., and J.F. KANTNER, "Sexual Activity, Contraceptive Use and Pregnancy among Metropolitan-area Teenagers: 1971-1979," *Family Planning Perspectives,* vol. 12, no. 5 (September-October 1980), pp. 230-237.

ZETTERBERG, HANS L., *On Theory and Verification in Sociology.* New York: Tressler Press, 1954.

ZILLMAN, DOLF, *Connections between Sex and Aggression.* Hillsdale, N.J.: Erlbaum, 1984.

ZISKIN, J., and M. ZISKIN, *The Extramarital Sex Contract.* Los Angeles: Nash Publications, 1973.

NAME INDEX

SUBJECT INDEX*

*For definitions and explanations not found here please also consult the Glossary.